Connections II

Connections II

A Cognitive Approach to Intermediate Chinese

Jennifer Li-chia Liu

劉力嘉

Illustrations by Chee Keong Kung

This book is a publication of

Indiana University Press
601 North Morton Street
Bloomington, IN 47404-3797 USA

http://iupress.indiana.edu

Telephone orders 800-842-6796
Fax orders 812-855-7931
Orders by e-mail iuporder@indiana.edu

The paper used in this publication meets the minimum requirements of
American National Standard for Information Sciences—Permanence of
Paper for Printed Library Materials, ANSI Z39.48-1984.

Manufactured in the United States of America

Cataloging information is available from the Library of Congress

By Jennifer Li-chia Liu
ISBN 0-253-21663-X paperback (Connections I)
ISBN 0-253-21664-8 paperback (Connections I: Workbook)
ISBN 0-253-34385-2 CD-ROM (Connections)

ISBN 978-0-253-21663-2 paperback (Connections I)
ISBN 978-0-253-21664-9 paperback (Connections I: Workbook)
ISBN 978-0-253-34385-7 CD-ROM (Connections)

By Jennifer Li-chia Liu
ISBN 0-253-21665-6 paperback (Connections II)
ISBN 0-253-21666-4 paperback (Connections II: Workbook)

ISBN 978-0-253-21665-6 paperback (Connections II)
ISBN 978-0-253-21666-3 paperback (Connections II: Workbook)

3 4 5 6   16 15 14 13

Contents

目錄

Preface

Connections I and ***II*** is a complete course designed for students who have finished the equivalent of one year of Chinese in a typical college setting in the U.S. or abroad. This intermediate series is closely coordinated, in terms of vocabulary, characters, grammatical structures, and approach, with its predecessor, ***Interactions I and II***. It is intended for learners with diverse interests and backgrounds and varying degrees of exposure to Chinese language and culture. No matter whether one's skills are well developed in some respects but lacking in others or whether one has no other training in the language beyond a first-year course, one will find these two learner-centered textbooks accommodating, motivating, and thought-provoking. In these textbooks one's individual needs and learning styles are facilitated by a balanced and multimodal treatment of the four language skills. Essential information is supplemented with explanatory notes, diagrams, tables, and graphics.

I. Rationale and Instructional Design

A number of convictions underlie the writing of this intermediate Chinese textbook. First, the method of instruction is a cognitive approach. The idea behind this approach is that effective teaching of Chinese must go beyond rote practice and linguistic information, by focusing on students' thought processes in order to promote more active and meaningful learning. Therefore, this book is designed to enable one not only to constructively *interact* with the language, but also to make *connections* with the language by means of mnemonic and allusive aids. For example, whenever possible, vocabulary terms are reintroduced from chapter to chapter. Grammar is explicated not only with linguistic rules but also by naming the semantic purpose of a given sentence pattern. Characters in the vocabulary lists are often listed with those having similar elements or pronunciation, so that appropriate links between characters are made. Furthermore, a variety of texts such as narratives, dialogues, stories, journal entries, riddles, jokes, news headlines, and ads are all included to enrich one's learning of the language.

Second, language acquisition is enhanced with texts written from a learner's perspective rather than that of the teacher. In these textbooks, the lesson topics revolve around events relevant to students' lives, such as studying abroad, weekend activities, and so on. The relationships between the four personae created in ***Interactions***—a Chinese from mainland China, another from Taiwan, a non-Chinese American, and a Chinese American—are further developed in ***Connections***, introducing respective family members and a new series of concerns and situations.

Third, so that one acquires natural, appropriate, and contextualized language rather than contrived textbook idioms, students are exposed not only to language structures but also to the dynamic use of language in varied socio-cultural contexts. "Appropriateness" is valued over what might be considered "standard." Thus, the different forms of Chinese characters (traditional vs. simplified) and usage (mainland China vs. Taiwan) are presented. As to the criteria for the texts, naturalness and frequency of use take precedence over considerations of difficulty. Texts are communication-oriented rather than grammar-centered. Nonetheless, due attention was paid to most of the common linguistic structures identified in *The Standard Outline of Grammatical Levels for Chinese* 漢語水平等級標準 與語法等級大綱 (1996) as appropriate for intermediate learners of Chinese. In addition, as a departure from traditional explications of grammar points, patterns and usage are presented from a functional perspective so that their "semantic value" will be easily registered in the learner's mind. Efforts were made to derive descriptions of the structures that will be comprehensible to students. Because it is a semantic approach, it is bound to be subjective and might seem inexact at certain points. Still, while it might not be as plausible to come up with a typology for the semantic aspect of a structure as it is for the syntactic aspect, I believe that it can be very beneficial to learners if the descriptions are precise and consistent.

Fourth, knowledge of culture, both past and present, is inseparable from target language instruction. Therefore, included in each lesson is important cultural information that can help one develop a better understanding of Chinese people and society.

Fifth, timeliness is an important factor in the organization of the lessons. Therefore, the first chapter of **Connections II** touches upon Chinese New Year and is intended to coincide with the actual event. The same goes for chapters dealing with the Mid-Autumn and Tomb Sweeping festivals.

Sixth, optimal learning results are achieved not merely by studying hard, but by studying effectively and cleverly. To help in this regard, these textbooks provide numerous learning cues to help students focus on key information. There are cues to lesson vocabulary listings and indexes facilitating review and preview of vocabulary and grammar. There are also helpful graphics and illustrations to maintain learning interest and provoke class discussions.

II. Organization of the Text

These books consist of twenty lessons: 1 through 10 in **Connections I,** and 11 through 20 in **Connections II**. These chapter topics progress from everyday situations to more abstract concerns. In addition, each lesson focuses on a particular theme, discussing current issues as well as important cultural concepts and practices.

Lesson Topics

Lesson 1 introduces usage related to greeting and terms of address through the narration of an American going abroad to study and his first encounter in China. Lesson 2, with a description of the school facilities and the American's peculiar roommate, explains the Chinese way of showing concern. Lesson 3 covers the Mid-Autumn Festival, an important Chinese holiday, and protocol for host and guest. Lesson 4 narrates the American student's weekend activities, focusing on interesting phenomena of Chinese daily life, such as morning exercises and bargaining with street peddlers. Lesson 5 deals with American and Chinese cuisine, introducing many expressions related to food and food preparation. Lesson 6, with its topic of fashion and leisure, describes the confession of a Chinese female who falls in love with her internet friend and her plans to meet him in person. While introducing phrases concerning personality and appearance, Lesson 7 tells the story of their date. Lesson 8 highlights critical issues such as racial discrimination and parent-child relationships by way of an argument between a mother and daughter over their views on love and marriage. Lesson 9 discusses gender roles and family matters as understood by a Chinese man and woman. With a portrait of two Chinese students' career choices, Lesson 10 contrasts the typical Chinese and American views on learning and education.

With the start of the spring semester, Lesson 11 discusses the American student's travel plans for Chinese New Year as he is about to leave mainland China. Lesson 12 underlines the problem of traffic and environmental pollution through the narration of the events encountered by the student on his trip around China and his arrival in Taiwan. Lesson 13, with its theme of animals and pets, describes how the student settles down in Taipei and introduces expressions for various delicacies, folk beliefs about food, and the impetus toward conservation. Lesson 14 describes the experience of the student's job search in Taipei and portrays various aspects of the Chinese fascination with the West. Lesson 15 highlights the concept of face, together with the Chinese way of making friends and doing business over meals. Lesson 16 examines social trends and problems in both mainland China and Taiwan and brings in the Chinese concept of utopia. Lesson 17, centering on philosophy and religion, touches upon Taoism, Confucianism, and other folk beliefs such as *feng shui* and lucky numbers. Lesson 18 talks about various language issues and problems encountered by students of Chinese such as retroflex pronunciation, accents, different scripts, and so on. Lesson 19 has its scene set in a dreamscape "adventure" taken by the American student in a museum, where prominent literary figures and works are introduced. Economics and politics are the focus of Lesson 20 and, as the American student is finishing his studies abroad, he comments on the progress made on both sides of the Taiwan Straits and offers his hopes for the future.

Lesson Structure

Throughout the textbooks, each lesson contains seven sections: (1) Vocabulary, (2) Text, (3) Mini-Dialogues, (4) Stories, (5) Characters, (6) Grammar, (7) Culture Notes, and (8) Songs. After a humorous cover illustration, meant to intrigue learners about the chapter contents, the vocabulary section, with three ways of grouping new words, facilitates preview and review. The text section is composed of one or two e-mail exchanges among the four personae relating details of their lives abroad or expressing their views and observations. It presents provocative issues from different perspectives while exposing students to a longer narrative text. The mini-dialogues provide comprehensible input and the natural use of language in a conversational setting. This section not only captures the essential communicative functions in the text, but also enriches the text by providing an outlet for further comment. It can be used for memorization or as a model for writing one's own skit or performance. The story section provides the source of a certain idiom in ancient texts and encourages one to guess at the idiom's meaning in the context of the lesson. The character section gives stroke-by-stroke analysis and sample use of twenty characters in focus. Students are, nonetheless, encouraged to read and write all of the chapter vocabulary. The grammar section covers the six major sentence patterns in each lesson and explains target language usage and structure with diagrams, examples, and notes. The section on cultural notes aims to provide students with concise tips on important concepts that will enhance their understanding of the chapter text and enable them to interact with Chinese appropriately. The songs section is intended to refresh students with fun tunes and lyrics that reintroduce lesson vocabulary and patterns.

Appendixes

Two appendixes are included in each book. The first one sketches the differences between traditional and simplified characters. The second appendix supplies a bibliography of sources used in the textbooks and refers one to other important resources.

Indexes

Each book concludes with four useful indexes: (1) lesson vocabulary, (2) lesson characters, (3) sentence patterns, and (4) idioms.

This set of textbooks stems from an ongoing attempt to tackle some of the teaching and learning issues from a fresh perspective and to share the experiences and insights that have come along over the years. I hope these textbooks will motivate more students to take the path of Chinese language studies and inspire more teachers to pioneer the frontier of Chinese language instruction with pedagogical innovations and imagination.

Jennifer Liu
Bloomington, July 2003

Acknowledgments

This textbook series is the result of many years of work and study in the field of Chinese language education. Though the conceptualization and outline of this project came long before, the research on the language data was completed during 1998–1999. This research provided a basis for selecting the core vocabulary and sentence structures appropriate for intermediate level Chinese learners and incorporating the material into these textbooks.

A project of this scope cannot succeed without institutional support and the help of many people. I would like to thank the Department of East Asian Languages and Cultures of Indiana University for funding the cartoon illustrations and the recordings that go with the books. Thanks must also be extended to the students and teachers at IU as well as at Smith College for their willingness to work with the drafts of these books and for their feedback and suggestions.

Special gratitude goes to Brian Baumann for his editorial help and for plowing through the many grammar examples with me to come up with appropriate descriptions for the function of each sentence structure. I appreciate Dawn Ollila's editorial assistance on the English text. Dr. Zhijie Wang and Zhen Chen's feedback on the grammar section is greatly appreciated. I would also like to thank Dr. Rongming Zhang, Dr. Deming An, Dr. Lihui Yang, Yan Li, Denise Gigliot, Hui-Ya Xu, and Tiaoguan Huang for their editorial help on the Chinese text. My heartfelt gratitude also goes to Chee Keong Kung for his excellent artwork and illustrations that have greatly enriched the books. I am also grateful to Ting-yi Ma, Ya-shih Liu and Yu-chen Lee for their original music and lyrics, a wonderful contribution to this project. Thanks to Mei-yun Tyan for her generous technical help, and to Janet Donley for helping me find the necessary equipment and seeing to all the paperwork.

Last but not least, I am grateful to Dr. James Chan for his inspiration during the development of this project, his excellent technical advice, and his valuable comments on book layout and design. I also thank him for the wonderful electronic resources he provided, which made the creation of visuals and modification of clipart images possible. The clip art used is from Corel Gallery by Corel Corporation (1994), ClipArt Library by Softkey International Corporation (1994), and Art Explosion 125,000 by Nova Development Corporation (1996).

Connections I-II is dedicated to my family, James, Eric, and Emily, who have put up with the numerous demands on my time and energy and support me with their characteristic good cheer and understanding. If there are any errors or inadequacies in the books, the author alone is responsible for them.

A Note to Students

Connections I and *II* will provide you with many useful resources and tools. However, you cannot benefit from them unless you actively engage in the learning process. As the subtitle of the books suggests, the cognitive aspect of language learning is being emphasized. The essence of this approach lies in the attempt of student and teacher both to take Chinese class beyond passive reception and rote memorization of presented information and rules. To this end you, as a student, need to actively try to organize, connect, sort, construct, or de-construct knowledge for yourself. You need to be creative with your own study, prioritize learning tasks, and tackle challenges from many different angles and perspectives.

At the intermediate stage, you may feel overwhelmed at times by the numerous new words or characters you will have to study. You may feel frustrated when you can't express yourself fully, despite many hours spent practicing. However, as long as you are willing to continue to venture to explore this language and culture and use it whenever you can (e.g., greeting your classmates, writing a note to your teacher in Chinese, etc.), you will find yourself picking up the language in short order. As long as you are not afraid of making mistakes and are willing to take the initiative to test your own hypotheses, again and again, you will continue to make progress in your study. A lighthearted attitude and a sense of humor will ease many of the frustrations that are part of your everyday life when you study Chinese. Certainly, the language is difficult, but you do not have to make it harder than it needs to be. If you can make things fun and relevant to you, you will surely be able to handle and even enjoy the many challenges that come with your ongoing study of Chinese.

The following are a few tips on how to make the most of these textbooks. The tips follow the different sections appearing in the textbooks and workbooks.

1. **Vocabulary**
    The chapter vocabulary is organized into three lists: order of appearance, grammatical category, and pinyin. Obviously, the first one is good for first-time study and the latter two for the purpose of review and quick reference. New lexical items appearing in the mini-dialogues are noted with asterisks and the useful ones included in the pinyin list. There are about 40 new words in each lesson. Break them down and study an acceptable segment, say 8 or 10 words each day. Pay attention not only to the new compound itself but also try to recall other terms studied previously that share similar components or characters. This practice will help you build a web of vocabulary in your mind that facilitates memorization and recall. Also, you are encouraged to guess at the meaning of

words based on their constituent characters. To this end, the definitions of some words in each chapter are intentionally omitted. If you learn to see the logic of compound formation, you will not be afraid of new terms and will develop skill at guessing the meaning of new words that native speakers have. In addition, study the example sentences provided and see how the new terms are used in context. To create opportunities for you to interact, the example sentences are usually in the form of questions. See if you can understand and answer the questions by yourself.

2. Characters

While you are encouraged to learn to read and write all the characters associated with the new words, twenty characters are selected from each chapter for additional practice or supplemental study. Although the traditional way to practice characters in China is to copy them as many times as possible, you shouldn't fall into the trap of thinking repetition alone will work magic. In fact, it will be much more effective if you can be creative with your learning methods. Break a character down into parts which you understand. Think of other characters that either look like or sound like the one you are focusing on. Compare and contrast the characters you have studied and organize them into meaningful groups. Invent your own stories or mnemonics to go with the characters you have trouble remembering. To help you in this regard, a brief etymology is provided for each character, and so is the use of the character in a sample phrase. Hopefully these will help register or anchor the image of the character in your mind. After one year of study, you may have noticed that studying characters has a snowballing effect. The more characters you acquire, the easier it is to remember them.

As with studying vocabulary, you need to adopt a disciplined approach to learning to write characters. If you want to learn twenty characters over five days, you have to study four per day; better still, you need to build a system of review for yourself. In addition, you need to be flexible in arranging your study schedule. Instead of spending three straight hours writing characters or memorizing words, it may be more effective to practice the language for shorter periods two or three times per day, making use of the odd hours when you wait for a bus or a class, when you take an afternoon break, when you retire in the evening, etc.

3. Text and Story

The text is typically a longer narrative. After studying half of the vocabulary, you should try to start reading the text and figure out its overall meaning. You can skip or circle unknown words or characters and guess at the main idea of the passage on the basis of context. Also, try to understand what you have read without translating it word-for-word into your native language. Use titles and illustrations to make inferences, and use dictionaries as a last resort. When you are done skimming the passage, you can read it again more carefully. Paraphrase what you have read and summarize paragraphs in the margin. Underline the phrases you don't understand and bring questions to your teachers. Since the text is mostly composed of e-mail exchanges, anticipate the responses and make predictions about what will come next in the text. It is important to remember that one reads not only for information, but also for fun. To this end, a story is included in each chapter and it tells the source of an ancient Chinese idiom. Learn to read the story and the example sentence first, then guess at the meaning of the idiom by yourself.

4. **Mini-Dialogues**

While the text and story will build your reading skill, mini-dialogues will enhance your abililty to interact with people in Chinese. When studying the dialogue for comprehension, try to cover up the English translation, and figure out the meaning first by yourself. English is included for you to confirm your understanding of the Chinese text or as a crutch when you have trouble. Another way to study the dialogue is to focus on one line at a time, cover up the rest, and see if you can come up with an appropriate response youself. Then uncover the next line to compare your "creation" with a typical response from a native Chinese. This practice helps you carry on a conversation with yourself. Eventually, you may want to memorize one dialogue or use it as a model, since likely you'll be asked to write your own skits and perform them in class with your classmates from time to time. If you have Chinese friends, you can even try to speak with them as you see fit. When you initiate conversations in Chinese, monitor your own utterances. If you notice errors, correct your own mistakes. Also, ask other people for confirmation that you have spoken correctly or to correct your tones, pronunciation, intonation, usage of words or grammar. Find a different way to express your idea when you can't think of the correct expression, or ask a native speaker to tell you the right word. Speaking Chinese can be a humbling experience, so be lighthearted about any embarrassment you may bring upon yourself.

5. **Grammar**

There are six grammar points in each chapter. When you study them, remember to adopt an inductive approach. That is, read the example dialogues first and then figure out what the sentence structure is doing, what function they accomplish. Then, check your own understanding with the boxed linguistic rule and English translation. After you have done these, you will find the "grammar drills" in class much more productive. You are encouraged to work on the grammar exercises in the Workbook right after you are exposed to grammar lectures and drills. Timely exercise will help reinforce and consolidate your skills and understanding. Don't put off the exercises till the night before the homework is due. Remember that you study grammar not for its own sake, but for the purpose of communication. So, when you have trouble analyzing the way a pattern works, be tolerant of its ambiguities. The more you study Chinese grammatical structure, the better you will understand the significance of contextual cues, which play an important role in the use of this language.

6. Culture Notes

As you may have already discovered, to be able to study Chinese well, you need to be tolerant of and receptive to differences, be they linguistic or cultural. You may feel disoriented or confused at times, given the differences between your native language and Chinese, and it is more than natural that you resort to your own culture and use it as a frame of reference to understand and interpret Chinese ways. Eventually, however, you will want to see things from a Chinese point of view and obtain an insider's perspective. Therefore, cultural notes are offered to help you gain some background knowledge. Read them at your own leisure and add more notes of your own as you make contact with Chinese people and culture.

7. Listening Comprehension

The listening comprehension section appears only in the Workbook. Yet, it is important enough to be singled out for discussion. When you listen to tapes or to native speakers, try to focus on the overall meaning or theme without worrying about the details or translating what you have heard word-by-word into your native language. If you are concerned with every single detail, your general comprehension will suffer. When you don't understand what you hear, use any clues you can to guess the general meaning and make associations between what you hear and what you already know about the topic. Of course, if you are listening to tapes, you can rewind the recording and listen again to confirm the main points or change your understanding. If you have trouble understanding when you are listening to a native speaker, you can ask him or her to slow down or clarify what was said. The rule of thumb is this: it will prove to be far more productive if you learn to take in chunks of information rather than isolated details.

8. Writing

At the intermediate stage, you should not be concerned only with writing individual characters. Instead, you should attempt to write coherent paragraphs and short essays. As adult learners, you may understand and learn various grammatical structures quickly. Yet, when it comes to applying all the things you have studied in writing, it might be very difficult and time-consuming. Although your writing competence probably won't progress at the same rate as your aural-oral skills, you should not avoid or delay the task of writing. Skills reinforce each other. Therefore, an integrated approach of four language skills is advocated in these textbooks. In fact, you will be encouraged to write an essay from time to time, even if it will be painfully slow at the beginning. Be patient and set a realistic goal for yourself. Plan ahead what you intend to write. If you have trouble writing, just take notes on whatever comes to your mind, without worrying about form or structure. Re-read what you have written before continuing, and make sure that your ideas are linked clearly. When you can't think of the correct expression to write, find a different way to express yourself. Stay on track as you write and revise. Always keep in mind your goals and your audience.

Most likely you will find other strategies as well, as you hone a study method of your own.

Abbreviations

Adj	Adjective	形容詞	xíngróngcí
Adv	Adverb	副詞	fùcí
AuxV	Auxiliary Verb	助動詞	zhùdòngcí
Conj	Conjunction	連詞	liáncí
CV	Co-verb	輔動詞	fŭdòngcí
Inter	Interjection	嘆詞	tàncí
IE	Idiomatic Expression	成語/習慣用語	chéngyǔ/xíguàn yòngyǔ
M	Measure Word	量詞	liàngcí
MA	Movable Adverb	可移副詞	kěyí fùcí
MTA	Movable Time Adverb	可移時間副詞	kěyí shíjiān fùcí
N	Noun	名詞	míngcí
Neg	Negative	否定詞	fŏudìngcí
No	Number	數詞	shùcí
NP	Noun Phrase	名詞詞組	míngcí cízǔ
O	Object	受詞	shòucí
Part	Particle	語助詞	yǔzhùcí
Place	Place Word	地方詞	dìfāngcí
PP	Prepositional Phrase	介詞詞組	jiècícízǔ
Pref	Prefix	詞頭	cítóu
P(rep)	Preposition	介詞	jiècí
Pron	Pronoun	代名詞	dàimíngcí
QW	Question Word	疑問詞	yíwèncí
RE	Resultative Verb Ending	結果動詞補語	jiéguǒ dòngcí bǔyǔ
RV	Resultative Verb	結果動詞	jiéguǒ dòngcí
S	Subject	主詞	zhǔcí
Suf	Suffix	詞尾	cíwěi
SV	Stative Verb	靜態動詞	jìngtài dòngcí
V	Verb	動詞	dòngcí
VO	Verb-Object Compound	動賓複詞	dòngbīn fùcí

<TW> Terms used in Taiwan
<PRC> Terms used in the People's Republic of China
<loan> Loan word (transliterated word of foreign origin)

Conventions

◎ This icon marks three subsections of Vocabulary in each lesson
—the first one groups new words by their order of appearance in
the main text (in both traditional and simplified characters), the
second by their grammatical categories (in traditional characters),
and the third by pinyin (in simplified characters).

* This symbol, at the end of entries in the Vocabulary and
Characters sections, calls the learner's attention to supplementary
lexical items of possible interest for further study.

  This icon, indicating the various mini-dialogues, highlights the
major communication functions in each lesson.

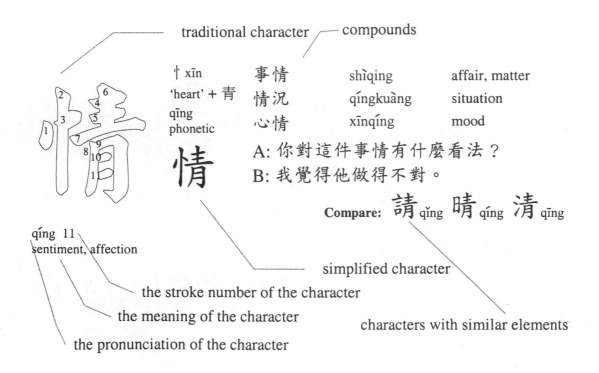

Cast of Characters
人物表Rénwùbiǎo

高德中	Gāo Dézhōng	David Gore
美國人	Měiguórén	American
研究生	Yánjiūshēng	Graduate student
專業：比較文學	Zhuānyè: bǐjiǎo wénxué	Major: Comparative Literature
年紀：二十八歲	Niánjì: èrshíbā suì	Age: 28
性別：男	Xìngbié: nán	Sex: male
個性：穩重、老實	Gèxìng: wěnzhòng, lǎoshí	Personality: practical, sincere
愛好：讀書、看電影	Aìhào: dúshū, kàn diànyǐng	Hobbies: studying, watching movies
父親：高麥克	Fùqīn: Gāo Màikè	Father: Michael Gore
職業：醫生	Zhíyè: yīshēng	Job: doctor
母親：鄧麗莎	Mǔqīn: Dèng Lìshā	Mother: Lisa Downing
職業：報社記者	Zhíyè: bàoshè jìzhě	Job: journalist
大弟：高杰森	Dàdì: Gāo Jiésēn	Elder younger brother: Jason Gore
小弟：高亞倫	Xiǎodì: Gāo Yàlún	Younger brother: Allen Gore

李明	Lǐ Mǐng	
中國人（大陸）	Zhōngguórén (dàlù)	Chinese (from the mainland)
大學生（大四）	Dàxuéshēng (dà sì)	Undergraduate (senior)
專業：商學	Zhuānyè: shāngxué	Major: Business
年紀：二十三歲	Niánjì: èrshísān suì	Age: 23
性別：男	Xìngbié: nán	Sex: male
個性：外向、好動	Gèxìng: wàixiàng, hàodòng	Personality: outgoing, active
愛好：旅行、拍照、美食	Aìhào: lǚxíng, pāizhào, měishí	Hobbies: travel, photography, fine food
父親：李鐵	Fùqīn: Lǐ Tiě	Father: Tie Li
職業：退休教授	Zhíyè: tuìxiū jiàoshòu	Job: retired professor
母親：周紅	Mǔqīn: Zhōu Hóng	Mother: Hong Zhou
職業：小學教員	Zhíyè: xiǎoxué jiàoyuán	Job: elementary school teacher

林美英	Lín Měiyīng	
華裔美國人	Huáyì Měiguórén	Chinese American
大學生（大三）	Dàxuéshēng (dà sān)	Undergraduate (junior)
專業：音樂	Zhuānyè: yīnyuè	Major: Music
年紀：二十一歲	Niánjì: èrshíyī suì	Age: 21
性別：女	Xìngbié: nǚ	Sex: female
個性：外向、活潑	Gèxìng: wàixiàng, huópō	Personality: outgoing, energetic
愛好：唱歌、跳舞、運動	Aìhào: chànggē, tiàowǔ, yùndòng	Hobbies: singing, dancing, exercising
父親：林偉平	Fùqīn: Lín Wěipíng	Father: Weiping Lin
職業：電腦工程師	Zhíyè: diànnǎo gōngchéngshī	Job: computer engineer
母親：黃樂庭	Mǔqīn: Huáng Lètíng	Mother: Leting Huang
職業：家庭主婦	Zhíyè: jiātíng zhǔfù	Job: housewife
妹妹：林美芳	Mèimei: Lín Měifāng	Younger sister: Meifang Lin

王華	Wáng Huá	
中國人（台灣）	Zhōngguórén (Táiwān)	Chinese (from Taiwan)
大學生（大二）	Dàxuéshēng (dà'èr)	Undergraduate (sophomore)
專業：電腦	Zhuānyè: diànnǎo	Major: Computer Science
年紀：二十歲	Niánjì: èrshí suì	Age: 20
性別：女	Xìngbié: nǔ	Sex: female
個性：內向、文靜	Gèxìng: nèixiàng, wénjìng	Personality: reserved, introspective
愛好：看電視、球賽	Aìhào: kàn diànshì, qiúsài	Hobbies: watching sports on TV
父親：王志強	Fùqīn: Wáng Zhìqiáng	Father: Zhiqiang Wang
職業：進出口公司經理	Zhíyè: jìnchūkǒu gōngsī jīnglǐ	Job: manager of an export-import company
母親：張如蘭	Mǔqīn: Zhāng Rúlán	Mother: Rulan Zhang
職業：旅行社職員	Zhíyè: lǔxíngshè zhíyuán	Job: travel agent
哥哥：王清	Gēge: Wáng Qīng	Elder brother: Qing Wang

第十一課

Theme Holiday and Travel

Communicative Objectives
- Talking with a taxi driver
- Climbing the Great Wall
- Talking with a travel agent
- Buying a train ticket

Focus on Characters
- 計劃參與、政治社團、建通拾束、首勝力古、春遊特安

Grammar Focus
- 再過…就要/就是…了
- 可V
- 在(沒有)V_1以前，SV_2
- 由 person V
- 與其V_1O_1不如 V_2O_2
- V QW 就 V QW

春節上哪兒玩好呢？

土不 huài = bad

生詞 Vocabulary

Study the following words for their pronunciation and meaning. When an area is shaded, guess at the meaning of the word based on its constituent characters and then fill in the blank. Read the usage of words and related terms (antonyms, synonyms, compounds sharing the constituent characters, etc.) and try to answer the sample questions in Chinese. Note that proper nouns and incidental terms are not numbered.

◎**By Order of Appearance**   *过 = celebrate*

1. 春節
   春节
   chūnjié   N   Lunar New Year   [spring-holiday]
   今年的春節是什麼時候？
   今年的春节是什么时候？

2. 結束
   结束
   jiéshù   V   to end, to conclude   [conclude-bundle]

   台北   Táiběi   N   capital of Republic of China   [platform-north]
                             (Taiwan)

3. 捨不得
   舍不得
   shěbude   RV   to hate to part with or use   [abandon-not-get]
   為什麼你捨不得穿那件衣服？
   为什么你舍不得穿那件衣服？

4. 離開
   离开
   líkāi   RV   to leave, to depart from   [separate-come loose]
   離開地方/人   vs.離不開
   你打算什麼時候離開這兒？
   你打算什么时候离开这儿？

   V+得 + 惯 = used to V

5. 習慣
   好/土不 习慣   xíguàn   V/   to be accustomed to, habit   [habit-be used to]
                                  N   生活/語言習慣；V得慣/V不慣
                                       你習慣吃漢堡包嗎？
                                       你习惯吃汉堡包吗？

6. 開水
   开水   kāishuǐ   N   boiling/boiled water   [boil-water]
                             喝/燒開水；vs. 自來水 zìláishuǐ
                             你平常喝開水還是自來水？
                             你平常喝开水还是自来水？

7. 豆漿
   豆浆   dòujiāng   N   soybean milk   [bean-thick liquid]

8. 燒餅
   烧饼   shāobǐng   N   baked sesame seed flatbread [burn-round flat cake]

可笑 = kexiao = ridiculous   可怕 = kepà = scared/scary

Where Is a Good Place to Go for Chinese New Year?   Lesson 11—3

| 9. | 油條
油条 | yóutiáo | N | deep-fried twisted dough sticks | [oil-strip] |

| 10. | 打的 | dǎdī | VO | to hire a taxi | [hit-taxi] |

在北京現在打的要多少錢？
在北京现在打的要多少钱？

| 11. | 溝通
沟通 | gōutōng | V | to communicate | [ditch-through] |

你能用中文跟人溝通嗎？
你能用中文跟人沟通吗？

| 12. | 吃力 | chīlì | SV | very difficult | [exhaust-strength] |

你做什麼事覺得很吃力？
你做什么事觉得很吃力？

| 13. | 收拾 | shōushi | V | to pack, to put in order | [gather-pick up] |

收拾東西/行李/房間
你的行李收拾好了嗎？
你的行李收拾好了吗？

14.	首都	shǒudū	N	capital (of country)	[head-metropolis]
15.	政治	zhèngzhì	N	politics	[government-to manage]
16.	中心	zhōngxīn	N		[center-heart]

經濟/文化/政治/市中心
哪兒是美國的經濟中心？
哪儿是美国的经济中心？

| 17. | 博物館
博物馆 | bówùguǎn | N | museum | [plentiful-thing-building] |

你去過哪些博物館？
你去过哪些博物馆？

| 18. | 到處
到处 | dàochù | N/Adv | everywhere | [to-place] |

Place + 到处 + 都是

| 19. | 名勝古蹟
名胜古迹 | míngshèng-gǔjī | NP | places of historic interest and scenic beauty | [famous-scenic view-ancient-trace] |

Characters with Many Strokes

離　慣　漿　燒　餅　溝　博　處　勝　蹟

20.	參觀 参观	cānguān	V	to visit, to tour	[join-veiw]

参觀名勝古蹟/博物館；參加活動

看朋友/家人；訪問 fǎngwèn 國家

我應該去參觀美國哪些名勝古蹟？

我应该去参观美国哪些名胜古迹？

	故宮	Gùgōng	N	former Imperial Palace	[old-palace]
	頤和園 颐和园	Yíhéyuán	N	Summer Palace (in Beijing)	[hexagram-harmony-garden]
	香山	Xiāngshān	N	a hiking place in Beijing	[fragrant-mountain]
	北海	Běihǎi	N	a park in Beijing	[north-sea]
	長城 长城	Cháng chéng	N	Great Wall	[long-wall]
21.	城市	chéngshì	N	town, city	[wall-city]

你覺得美國哪個城市最有特色？

你觉得美国哪个城市最有特色？

22.	台灣 台湾	Táiwān	N	Taiwan	[platform-bay]
23.	難得 难得 +的+ N	nándé	Adj	difficult to get	[hard-to get]

難得見面；難得的機會/假期/朋友

你難得來一次，今天我請客。

你难得来一次，今天我请客。

24.	大陸 大陆	dàlù	N	mainland (or mainland China)	[big-continent]
25.	旅遊團 旅游团	lǚyóutuán	N	tour group = 旅行團	[travel-rove-group]
26.	訂 订	dìng	V	to book, to subscribe to	

訂房間/位子/機票/書/報

你下個月要回家，機票訂了沒有？

你下个月要回家，机票订了没有？

27.	房間 房间	fángjiān	N	room	[house-between]
28.	由	yóu	Prep	by, through, from	

由……決定/安排/辦

你家的事常常由誰決定？

你家的事常常由谁决定？

29.	旅行社	lǚxíngshè	N	travel agent	[travel-go-agency]
30.	安排	ānpái	V/	to arrange, to plan	[fix-put in order]

安排時間/學習/生活；做好安排

你春假要去哪兒玩，安排好了嗎？

你春假要去哪儿玩，安排好了吗？

	西安	Xī'ān	N	Xi'an (capital of Shanxi)	[west-safe]
	上海	Shànghǎi	N	Shanghai	[up-sea]
	蘇州	Sūzhōu	N	Suzhou (in Jiangsu province)	[Su-prefecture]
	苏州				
	杭州	Hángzhōu	N	Hangzhou (capital of Zhejiang)	[boat-prefecture]
31.	值得	zhíde	V/	to deserve, to merit	[be worth-particle]

值得學習/注意/研究/一V

你覺得最近哪部電影值得一看？

你觉得最近哪部电影值得一看？

32.	建議	jiànyì	N/	suggestion, to suggest	[propose-view]
	建议		V		

給人建議；建議很好

我建議你少喝咖啡。

我建议你少喝咖啡。

33.	特色	tèsè	N		[special-look]
34.	計劃	jìhuà	N/	plan, program	[count-mark]
	计划		V		

做/有計劃；計劃出國

你今年夏天xiàtiān有什麼計劃？

你今年夏天有什么计划？

35.	與其	yǔqí	Conj	rather than	[with-that]
	与其				

去紐約Niǔyuē與其坐火車不如搭飛機。

去纽约与其坐火车不如搭飞机。

Characters with Many Strokes

參　觀　灣　團　值　建　議　特　劃　與

| 36. | 火車
火车 | huǒchē | N | | [fire-car] |

坐/搭火車　　→火車站、火車票

請問，火車站離這兒還有多遠？

请问，火车站离这儿还有多远？

| 37. | 過年
过年 | guònián | VO | to celebrate/spend New Year | [pass-year] |

| 38. | 一路 | yílù | N | whole journey | [one-path] |

vs.路上、街上

| 39. | 緊張
紧张 | jǐnzhāng | Adj | ~~<PRC> scarce, in short supply~~ | [tight-stretch] |

東西/票/房子緊張

最近什麼東西很緊張？

最近什么东西很紧张？

| 40. | 最好 | zuìhǎo | Adv | had better, it would be best | [most-good] |

最好V　　↔千萬不要

你不去，最好給他打個電話。

你不去，最好给他打个电话。

| 41. | 提前 | tíqián | Adv/
V | in advance, to advance date | [lift-front] |

提前準備/考試/告訴……　　　=提早

為什麼你要提前考試？

为什么你要提前考试？

42.	明信片	míngxìnpiàn	N		[open-letter-card]
43.	祝	zhù	V	to express good wishes	
44.	平安	píng'ān	Adj	safe and sound, quiet and stable	[peaceful-quiet]

Characters with Many Strokes

緊　張　提

◎By Grammatical Categories

Nouns/Pronouns

建議	jiànyì	suggestion
計劃	jìhuà	plan
春節	chūnjié	Spring Festival
首都	shǒudū	capital
政治	zhèngzhì	politics
中心	zhōngxīn	center
博物館	bówùguǎn	museum
城市	chéngshì	town, city
房間	fángjiān	room
台灣	Táiwān	Taiwan
大陸	dàlù	mainland (or mainland China)
旅行社	lǚxíngshè	travel agent
旅遊團	lǚyóutuán	tour group

名勝古蹟	míngshèng-gǔjī	places of historic interest and scenic beauty
特色	tèsè	distinguishing feature/quality
明信片	míngxìnpiàn	postcard
火車	huǒchē	train
一路	yílù	whole journey
到處	dàochù	everywhere
開水	kāishuǐ	boiling/boiled water
豆漿	dòujiāng	soybean milk
燒餅	shāobǐng	baked sesame seed flatbread
油條	yóutiáo	deep-fried twisted dough sticks

Verbs/Stative Verbs/Adjectives

訂	dìng	to book, to subscribe to
祝	zhù	to express good wishes
收拾	shōushi	to pack, to put in order
安排	ānpái	to arrange, to plan
溝通	gōutōng	to communicate
參觀	cānguān	to visit, to tour
值得	zhíde	to deserve, to merit
習慣	xíguàn	to be accustomed to, habit
打的	dǎdī	to hire a taxi

過年	guònián	to celebrate/spend New Year
捨不得	shěbude	to hate to part with or use
離開	líkāi	to leave, to depart from
結束	jiéshù	to end
難得	nándé	rare
緊張	jǐnzhāng	scarce, in short supply
平安	píng'ān	safe and sound, quiet and stable
吃力	chīlì	strenuous

Adverbs and Others

由	yóu	by, through, from
提前	tíqián	in advance, advance date
最好	zuìhǎo	had better, it would be best

與其	yǔqí	rather than

◎ By Pinyin

Entries with * indicate lexical items used in Mini-Dialogues and of possible interest for supplemental study.

ānpái	安排	to arrange, to plan	míngshèng-gǔjī	名胜古迹	places of historic interest and scenic beauty
bówùguǎn	博物馆	museum	míngxìnpiàn	明信片	postcard
cānguān	参观	to visit, to tour	nándé	难得	rare
chéngshì	城市	town, city	pá*	爬	to climb, to crawl
chīlì	吃力	strenuous	píng'ān	平安	safe and sound
chūnjié	春节	Spring Festival	Rénmínbì*	人民币	RMB
dǎdī	打的	to hire a taxi	shāobǐng	烧饼	baked sesame seed flatbread
dàlù	大陆	mainland (or mainland China)	shěbude	舍不得	to hate to part with or use
dàochù	到处	everywhere	shǒudū	首都	capital
dìng	订	to book, to subscribe to	shōushi	收拾	to pack, to put in order
dòujiāng	豆浆	soybean milk	Táiwān	台湾	Taiwan
fángjiān	房间	room	tèsè	特色	distinguishing feature/quality
gōutōng	沟通	to communicate	tíqián	提前	in advance
guònián	过年	to celebrate New Year	xíguàn	习惯	to be accustomed to, habit
huǒchē	火车	train	yílù	一路	whole journey
jiànyì	建议	suggestion	yóu	由	by, through, from
jiāyóu*	加油	Cheers! Go!	yóutiáo	油条	deep-fried twisted dough sticks
jiéshù	结束	to end	yǔqí	与其	rather than
jìhuà	计划	plan, project	zhèngzhì	政治	politics
jǐnzhāng	紧张	in short supply	zhíde	值得	to deserve, to merit
kāishuǐ	开水	boiling/boiled water	zhōngxīn	中心	center, heart
líkāi	离开	to leave, to depart from	zhù	祝	to express good wishes
lǚxíngshè	旅行社	travel agent	zuìhǎo	最好	had better, it would be best
lǚyóutuán	旅游团	tour group			

課文 Text

Use the following questions to guide your reading of the text.

1. 小高為什麼不想離開北京？

2. 小高要小李給他什麼建議？

3. 小李覺得小高應該去哪兒玩比較好？應該怎麼玩？

 小李：

　　[1]再過一個星期，我在北京的課就要結束了，下個學期我得到台北去繼續學中文。雖然我很想去看看另一個中國人的社會，可我真捨不得離開這個地方。我在這兒才待六個月，就已經很習慣北京的生活了：我不但喜歡喝開水、豆漿，吃燒餅、油條，而且喜歡打的、跟司機聊天。可惜的是，我剛覺得跟人溝通沒那麼吃力、覺得對這個地方比較熟悉時，就得收拾行李走了。

　　我不想離開的另外一個原因是，這兒[2]可看的東西還很多呢！你知道北京不但是中國的首都，而且是全國的政治、文化中心，住在這兒就像住在一個博物館一樣，到處都有名勝古蹟可以參觀。我去過故宮、頤和園，也去過香山、北海和長城。除了北京以外，我還想去別的城市看看呢！可能[3]在沒有去台灣以前，我應該利用春節這個難得的假期，到大陸各地玩玩。我打算參

加旅遊團，買機票、訂房間，一切 [4]由旅行社安排，可以少很多麻煩，你覺得怎麼樣？我應該去西安、上海、蘇州還是杭州？什麼地方值得一遊呢？你給我個建議吧！

德中上

小高：

你問我春節上哪兒玩好，我想中國每個城市都有它的特色。去哪兒玩都沒關係，只要你先做好計劃就行了。但是我覺得 [5]與其參加旅遊團，不如自己坐火車去旅行，這樣不但比較經濟，而且自由多了，你想去 [6]哪兒就去哪兒，什麼時候都可以下車來玩，再說，一路上還可以吃到各地特別的點心。不過，過年的時候，火車票可能會很緊張，你最好提前買票。別忘了多拍幾張照片，有機會寄張明信片來！

　祝
一路平安

李明上

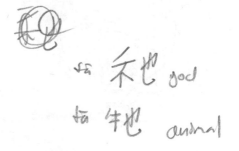

课文 Text

Use the following questions to guide your reading of the text.

1. 小高为什么不想离开北京？

2. 小高要小李给他什么建议？

3. 小李觉得小高应该去哪儿玩比较好？应该怎么玩？

小李：

　　[1]再过一个星期，我在北京的课就要结束了，下个学期我得到台北去继续学中文。虽然我很想去看看另一个中国人的社会，可我真舍不得离开这个地方。我在这儿才待了六个月，就已经很习惯北京的生活了：我不但喜欢喝开水、豆浆，吃烧饼、油条，而且喜欢打的、跟司机聊天。可惜的是，我刚觉得跟人沟通没那么吃力、觉得对这个地方比较熟悉时，就得收拾行李走了。

　　我不想离开的另外一个原因是，这儿[2]可看的东西还很多呢！你知道北京不但是中国的首都，而且是全国的政治、文化中心，住在这

儿就象住在一个博物馆一样，到处都有名胜古迹可以参观。我去过故宫、颐和园，也去过香山、北海和长城。除了北京以外，我还想去别的城市看看呢！可能[3]在

没有去台湾**以前**，我应该利用春节这个难得的假期，到大陆各地玩玩。我打算参加旅游团，买机票、订房间，一切 [4]**由**旅行社安排，可以少很多**麻烦**，你觉得怎么样？我应该去西安、上海、苏州还是杭州？什么地方值得一游呢？你给我个建议吧！

德中上

 小高：

　　你问我春节上哪儿玩好，我想中国每个城市都有它的特色。去哪儿玩都没关系，只要你先做好计划就行了。但是我觉得 [5]**与其**参加旅游团，**不如**自己坐火车去旅行，这样不但比较经济，而且自由多了，你想去 [6]**哪儿就去哪儿**，什么时候都可以下车来玩，再说，一路上还可以吃到各地特别的点心。不过，过年的时候，火车票可能会很紧张，你最好提前买票。别忘了多拍几张照片，有机会寄张明信片来！

　　祝
一路平安

李明上

小對話 Mini-Dialogues

Read the supplementary dialogues for a better understanding of the text. See if you can memorize one and perform it in class.

(1) Talking with a taxi driver

A:	你剛來北京嗎？
Gao:	不，我在這兒已經住了六個月了。
A:	怪不得你中文說得不錯。還適應這兒的生活嗎？
Gao:	很習慣了，不過我下個月就得離開了，真捨不得。

A:	你刚来北京吗？
Gao:	不，我在这儿已经住了六个月了。
A:	怪不得你中文说得不错。还适应这儿的生活吗？
Gao:	很习惯了，不过我下个月就得离开了，真舍不得。

A: Did you just come to Beijing?

Gao: No. I've lived here for six months.

A: No wonder your Chinese is pretty good. Are you used to life here?

Gao: Yes, very much so. But, I'll have to leave next month. I really hate to do so.

(2) Climbing the Great Wall

A:	高德中，加油jiāyóu！要不要我幫你一下？
Gao:	不要，不要！那我就不是「好漢hǎohàn」了。
A:	終於爬pá上了長城！
Gao:	真偉大！長城有多長啊？
A:	有一萬兩千多里，所以叫萬里長城。

A:	高德中，加油！要不要我帮你一下？
Gao:	不要，不要！那我就不是"好汉"了。
A:	终于爬上了长城！
Gao:	真伟大！长城有多长啊？
A:	有一方两千多里，所以叫万里长城。

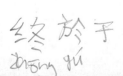
終於 于
zhōngyú

A: Gao Dezhong, cheers!
Do you want me to give
you a hand?

Gao: No, no. If you help me, I
won't be a "real man."

A: We finally climbed the
Great Wall.

Gao: It's so magnificent! How
long is the Great Wall?

A: It is more than twelve thousand *li,* so it is called the Ten-Thousand-Mile (*li*) Long Wall.

(3) Talking with a travel agent

Gao: 請問，你們這兒有沒有旅行團
到西安、上海、或者蘇杭？

A: 有，你想參加多少天的旅行
團？

Gao: 兩個星期的要多少錢？

A: 五千塊人民幣Rénmínbì。

Gao: 那麼貴。

A: 我們住的都是五星級的酒店，
而且買機票、訂房間，一切都
由我們幫你安排。

Gao: 请问，你们这儿有没有旅行团
到西安、上海、或者苏杭？

A: 有，你想参加多少天的旅行
团？

Gao: 两个星期的要多少钱？

A: 五千块人民币。

Gao: 那么贵。

A: 我们住的都是五星级的酒店，
而且买机票、订房间，一切都
由我们帮你安排。

Gao: Excuse me, do you have a tour group to Xi'an,
Shanghai, or Suzhou and Hangzhou?

A: Yes, we do. For how many days would you like
to participate in a tour?

Gao: How much does it cost for two weeks?

A: Five thousand RMB.

Gao: So expensive…

A: We'll stay only in five-star hotels. Besides, things like buying tickets and booking
      rooms are all arranged for you.

(4) Buying a train ticket

车欠
ruǎn
soft

走尚
tàng
mw trip

Gao: 請問，去西安現在有車嗎？   请问，去西安现在有车吗？

A: 半小時後有。   半小时后有。

Gao: 太好了，是快車嗎？   太好了，是快车吗？

A: 是。   是。

Gao: 多少次？   多少次？

A: 三一七次。   三一七次。

Gao: 還有軟座ruǎnzuò票嗎？   还有软座票吗？
                                              ✓

A: 有。   有。

Gao: 好，買一張。這趟tàng車從北京   好，买一张。这趟车从北京几
        幾點開？   点开？

A: 八點半。這是你的票。   八点半。这是你的票。

Gao: 謝謝。   谢谢。

Gao: Excuse me, is there a train to Xi'an now?
A: There is one in half an hour.
Gao: That's great. Is it an express?
A: Yes.
Gao: What number is it?
A: Number 317.
Gao: Is there a soft-seat ticket?
A: Yes.
Gao: Good, I'll take one. When will this train
        leave Beijing?
A: Eight-thirty. Here is your ticket.
Gao: Thanks.

小故事 Stories

Read the following tale for your own enjoyment and for your understanding of the highlighted expression that is relevant to the theme of the chapter.

 走馬觀花/走馬看花　zǒumǎ guān/kàn huā

❀　我這次旅遊只是走馬觀花，沒有時間好好參觀每個博物館。

傳說從前有一個小伙子，他的腳有毛病，走路很困難。他想找一個漂亮的妻子，就要他的朋友華漢幫他介紹一個姑娘。剛好有個女孩兒也要華漢幫她介紹對象，那個女孩兒長得很漂亮，可是鼻子有點兒問題。華漢想：「讓這兩個人結婚，不是很好嗎？」

華漢	Huàhàn	name of a person
鼻子	bízi	nose
於是	yúshì	therefore
門口	ménkǒu	entrance, doorway
朵	duǒ	measure word for flowers
聞	wén	to smell
說起	shuōqǐ	to mention
情形	qíngxíng	situation

於是有一天，華漢讓那個小伙子騎著馬從那個女孩兒家門口走過，又叫那個女孩兒手上拿一朵花，看起來好像在聞花的樣子。結果，那個小伙子愛上了那個聞花的姑娘，那個女孩兒也看上了這個騎著馬的小伙子。

結婚那天，兩個人說起「走馬觀花」的情形，彼此才明白到底發生了什麼事。

✐走馬觀花的意思是＿＿＿＿＿＿＿＿＿＿＿＿＿＿＿＿

走马观花/走马看花 zǒumǎ guān/kàn huā

❀　我这次旅游只是走马观花，没有时间好好参观每个博物馆。

传说从前有一个小伙子，他的脚有毛病，走路很困难。他想找一个漂亮的妻子，就要他的朋友华汉帮他介绍一个姑娘。刚好有个女孩儿也要华汉帮她介绍对象，那个女孩儿长得很漂亮，可是鼻子有点儿问题。华汉想："让这两个人结婚，不是很好吗？"

华汉	Huàhàn	name of a person
鼻子	bízi	nose
于是	yúshì	therefore
门口	ménkǒu	entrance, doorway
朵	duǒ	measure word for flowers
闻	wén	to smell
说起	shuōqǐ	to mention
情形	qíngxíng	situation

于是有一天，华汉让那个小伙子骑着马从那个女孩儿家门口走过，又叫那个女孩儿手上拿一朵花，看起来好象在闻花的样子。结果，那个小伙子爱上了那个闻花的姑娘，那个女孩儿也看上了这个骑着马的小伙子。

结婚那天，两个人说起"走马观花"的情形，彼此才明白到底发生了什么事。

漢字 Characters

Study the following selected characters for further enrichment of your writing and vocabulary.

言 yán 'words' + 十 shí 'ten'—ten words used for counting: one, two, three, etc.

計

jì 9
to count, to plan

計算	jìsuàn	to count, to compute
設計	shèjì*	design, plan
計程車	jìchéngchē	<TW> (metered) taxi

A: 你看設計這個東西得花多長時間？
B: 可長可短，就看你怎麼計算了。

Compare: 記jì 紀jì

刂 dāo 'knife' + 畫 huà 'draw' phonetic

划

huà 14
to draw, stroke

| 計劃 | jìhuà | plan, project, program |

A: 你計劃怎麼上那兒去？
B: 我坐火車去。

Compare: 畫huà 書shū

厽 'the three stars of Orion' + function of 参 uncertain—come together, mix, consult with

參

cān, shēn 11
to join, to refer

參觀	cānguān	to visit, to tour
參加	cānjiā	to join, to take part in
人參	rénshēn*	ginseng

A: 你昨天怎麼沒來參加我們的活動？
B: 我去參觀博物館了。

Compare: 慘cǎn

一 yī 'one' + 勺 sháo 'spoon' + 舁 yú 'two pairs of hands—the giver and the receiver' phonetic

与

yǔ, yù 13
to give, with, and

| 與其 | yǔqí | rather than |
| 參與 | cānyù* | to participate in |

A: 我看與其找小李不如找小高來開會。
B: 對！小李從來不參與我們的討論。

Compare: 舉jǔ 興xìng

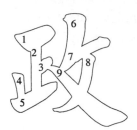

攵 pū 'strike, beat' + 正 zhèng 'correct'

政

政府	zhèngfǔ	government
政策	zhèngcè*	policy
內政	nèizhèng*	internal affairs

A: 你覺得政府最近的政策怎麼樣？

B: 內政還行，外交 wàijiāo 'foreignaffairs' 就不行了。

zhèng 9
government, politics

氵 shuǐ 'water' + 台 tái phonetic

治

政治	zhèngzhì	politics
政治家	zhèngzhìjiā*	statesman
三明治	sānmíngzhì	\<loan\> sandwich

A: 美國最偉大的政治家是誰？

B: 我不知道，我對政治沒興趣。

zhì 8
to rule, to cure, to control

礻 shì 'altar' + 土 tǔ 'earth'—altar to the spirits of the land, village, society

社

旅行社	lǚxíngshè	travel service/agent
社會	shèhuì	society
社會學	shèhuìxué*	sociology
社區	shèqū*	community

A: 我想多了解這裏的社會。

B: 那你得到各個社區走走。

shè 7
agency, society, club

囗 wéi 'circle' + 專 zhuān phonetic

团

| 旅遊團 | lǚyóutuán | tour group |
| 旅行團 | lǚxíngtuán | tour group |

A: 我想參加旅遊團到加州玩。

B: 你可以去那個旅行社問問。

Compare: 專 zhuān

tuán 14
to unite, lump, group

聿 yù 'a hand holding a pen, writing on paper' + 攵 yǐn phonetic

建議	jiànyì	to propose, to suggest
建築	jiànzhù/zhú	to build, architecture

A: 我想去芝加哥玩，你有什麼建議？

B: 好極了，那兒的建築很有特色。

Compare: 健 jiàn

jiàn 8
to build, to set up, to propose

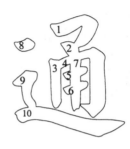

辶 chuò 'go' + 甬 yǒng phonetic— penetrate, wholly, completely know, communicate

溝通	gōutōng	to communicate
交通	jiāotōng	traffic
通信	tōngxìn*	to correspond

A: 你能用中文和他溝通嗎？

B: 可以，我和他通過兩次信。

tong 10
to communicate, to master, open, through

扌 shǒu 'hand' + 合 hé 'put together'

收拾	shōushi	to put in order, to pack

A: 你的行李收拾好了嗎？

B: 早就收拾好了。

Compare: 合 hé

shí 9
to pick up, ten (on checks)

木 mù plants (or wood) 口 tied up in a bundle

結束	jiéshù	to end, to conclude

A: 這個學期什麼時候結束？

B: 四月底。

Compare: 整 zhěng 速 sù

shù 7
to bind, bundle

Picture of a head 百, with the ㇒㇒ hair at the top

首

shǒu 9
head, leader, first

| 首都 | shǒudū | capital (of country) |
| 首先 | shǒuxiān* | first, in the first place |

A: 美國的首都在哪兒？
B: 在華盛頓特區 Huáshèngdùn tèqū。

Compare: 道 dào

力 lì 'strength' + 朕 zhèn phonetic

胜

shèng 12
to win, to excel, victory, superb

| 名勝古蹟 | míngshèng- gǔjī | scenic spots and historic sites |

A: 你喜歡這兒的名勝古蹟嗎？
B: 參觀的人太多了，不太喜歡。

Picture of a strongly muscled arm

力

lì 2
power, strength, vigorously

吃力	chīlì	to be a strain
努力	nǔlì	to try hard
能力	nénglì	ability, capacity

A: 學習中文對你來說很吃力嗎？
B: 對，我雖然努力，可是還是學不好。

Compare: 加 jiā 男 nán 動 dòng 辦 bàn

十 shí 'ten' + 口 kǒu 'mouth'—that which has passed through ten mouths, i.e., a tradition dating back a long time

gǔ 5
ancient, age-old

古

| 古代 | gǔdài | antiquity |
| 古老 | gǔlǎo* | ancient, old |

A: 你想去參觀歷史博物館嗎？
B: 我對古老的東西沒有興趣。

Compare: 個 gè 做 zuò 苦 kǔ 故 gù

The upper part may be a tree or bush, under the influence of 日 the sun

春

春節	chūnjié	Spring Festival
春假	chūnjià	spring break
春天	chūntiān*	spring(time)

A: 春節和春假有什麼不同？
B: 春節是在冬天，春假是在春天。

chūn 9
spring (season), life

扩 'waving motions of a 子 swimmer' + 辶 chuò 'go'

游

旅遊團	lǚyóutuán	tour group
旅遊	lǚyóu	tour, tourism
遊客	yóukè	tourist, sightseer
遊行	yóuxíng	to parade, to march

A: 你想去哪兒旅遊？
B: 去遊客少的地方。

Compare: 游 yóu

yóu 12
to travel, to rove

牛 niú 'bull' + 寺 sì 'temple'—a bull used in halls: for sacrifice

特

特色	tèsè	distinguishing feature
特別	tèbié	special, particular
特地	tèdì*	on purpose, specially

A: 那個地方有什麼特別，值得你特地去玩三天？
B: 那兒的名勝古蹟很有特色。

tè 10
special, secret agent

宀 mián 'roof' + 女 nǔ 'woman' —a woman relaxing indoors where it's quiet and peaceful

安

安排	ānpái	to arrange, to plan
平安	píng'ān	safe and sound
不安	bù'ān*	uneasy, unstable
安全	ānquán	safe, safety

A: 你這麼安排我心裏很不安。
B: 只要安全就好了。

Compare: 按 àn

ān 6
still, safe, to rest content

語法和用法 Grammar and Usage

Pay attention to the function of the structure and then study the example sentences.

1. Expressing the sooner-than-expected occurrence of an event

(S)再過time span, (S)就要V了	zài guò… jiùyào…le	After a certain period of time, S will do sth.
再過time span 就是N了	zài guò… jiùshì… le	After a certain period of time, it will be N

再過一個星期，我在北京的課**就要**結束**了**……

1. 我們什麼時候放春假？

   我们什么时候放春假？

   When do we go on Spring Break?

   再過一個月就要放春假了。

   再过一个月就要放春假了。

   We will go on Spring Break in another month.

2. 再過五分鐘，電影就要開始了。

   再过五分钟，电影就要开始了。

   The movie will start in another five minutes.

   沒關係，我去一下廁所，馬上就回來。

   没关系，我去一下厕所，马上就回来。

   No problem. I will go to the restroom and be right back.

3. 中文課的考試真多。

   中文课的考试真多。

   There really are a lot of quizzes in Chinese classes.

   是啊！我們再過五天就又要考試了。

   是啊！我们再过五天就又要考试了。

   That's right. We will have a test again in another five days.

This pattern indicates something will occur sooner than the speaker expects. The duration of time can precede or follow the subject, if it is given. The action is typically preceded by 要 (examples 1–3) or 是, e.g., 再過四天就是我的生日了. There is often a verb 過 after 再. If one wants to express something that takes longer than expected, the pattern "(S) 還要 time span, (S) 才 V" should be used.

2. Expressing possibility

可 v	kě V	can be V-ed; V-ful/able
可笑/可愛/可怕	kěxiào/ kě'ài/ kěpà	ridiculous/lovable/fearful
可玩/可說/可做	kěwán/ kěshuō/ kězuò	worth visiting/mentioning/doing
可行/可見	kěxíng/ kějiàn	feasible/it is this clear

這兒**可看**的東西還很多呢！

1. 你去了中國半年，
   一定有很多有意思
   的事，快告訴我！

   你去了中国半年，
   一定有很多有意思
   的事，快告诉我！

   You went to China for half a year and surely have a lot of interesting things to say. Tell me about them now!

   可說的事情太多
   了，你要我從哪兒
   說起。

   可说的事情太多
   了，你要我从哪儿
   说起。

   There are so many things worth mentioning. Where do you want me to start?

2. 我覺得那個女孩很
   可愛。

   我觉得那个女孩很
   可爱。

   I think that girl is lovely.

   她是我的女兒。

   她是我的女儿。

   She is my daughter.

3. 你喝過可口可樂
   嗎？

   你喝过可口可乐
   吗？

   Have you drunk Coca-Cola?

   就是那種「好喝又
   讓你快樂」的汽水
   嗎？

   就是那种"好喝又
   让你快乐"的汽水
   吗？

   Is that the soda which is "tasty and makes one happy"?

可, followed by a verb or an adjective, can form compounds in which 可 functions as the English suffixes, "-(l)y, -able, -ible, -ful, or worth doing something." This usage of 可 illustrates how new lexical items were generated. Your word power will be greatly enhanced if you learn to create networks of such compounds. See the differences between 可玩 and 好玩 in the sentence: 北京可玩的地方很多，比方說北海公園就很好玩. Also note that although both 看 and 見 means "to see," distinguish the difference between 可看 'things/places that are worth viewing/visiting' and 可見 'visible or obviously.' Study the use of 可見 in the sentence, 他有三輛跑車，可見他很有錢。

3. Expressing a previous condition

在(沒有)V₁以前, S V₂	zài (méiyǒu) …yǐqián, …	S V₂ before V₁

也許**在**沒有去台灣**以前**，我應該趁著春節這個難得的假期，到大陸各地玩玩。

1. 在 沒 有 學 中 文 以 前，你 認 為 中 文 怎 麼 樣 ？

   在 没 有 学 中 文 以 前，你 认 为 中 文 怎 么 样 ？ rèn

   Before studying, what did you think of the Chinese language?

   我 以 為 中 文 很 容 易 。

   我 以 为 中 文 很 容 易 。

   I thought Chinese would be very easy.

2. 在 下 次 開 會 以 前，請 你 把 報 告 準 備 好 。

   在 下 次 开 会 以 前，请 你 把 报 告 准 备 好 。 bào

   Before we hold the next meeting, please have your report well prepared.

   沒 問 題，經 理 jīnglǐ 'manager' 。

   没 问 题，经 理 。

   No problem, sir.

3. 在 沒 有 發 明 電 視 以 前，人 們 吃 完 飯 後 常 做 什 麼 ？

   在 没 有 发 明 电 视 以 前，人 们 吃 完 饭 后 常 做 什 么 ？

   Before TV was invented, what did people usually do around dinnertime?

   我 想 他 們 看 看 書 或 者 聊 聊 天 liáotiān 'to chat' 。

   我 想 他 们 看 看 书 或 者 聊 聊 天 。

   I think that they either read books or had conversation.

It's interesting to note that this pattern expresses the same meaning in Chinese, with or without the negative marker 沒有. Therefore, these two sentences mean the same thing in Chinese: (1) 在沒有學中文以前，我覺得中文很容易。 (2)在學中文以前，我覺得中文很容易。

4. Expressing the agent of an action

由 person V	yóu …	be V-ed by person/agent

我打算參加旅遊團，買機票、訂房間，一切**由**旅行社安排……

1. | 這件事還得由他做最後的決定。 | 这件事还得由他做最后的决定。 | The final decision on this matter has to come from him. |
|---|---|---|
| 好，就這麼辦吧！ | 好，就这么办吧！ | All right, let's do it this way. |

2. | 這次的晚會由誰安排？ | 这次的晚会由谁安排？ | Who will plan the party this time? |
|---|---|---|
| 由我們安排。 | 由我们安排。 | We'll arrange it. |

3. | 今天由誰洗碗？ | 今天由谁洗碗？ | Whose turn is it to do the dishes today? |
|---|---|---|
| 今天由我燒飯，由弟弟洗碗。 | 今天由我烧饭，由弟弟洗碗。 | Today, it's my turn to cook and my little brother's turn to do the dishes. |

由 indicates an agent with an official capacity to carry out an action. Therefore, it is often used with verbs like 決定 'to decide,' 安排 'to arrange,' 分配 'to assign,' 主持 'to preside over,' 處理 'to deal with,' 帶領 'to lead.' Though 由 is translated into English as "by," it's not a passive sentence in Chinese, which is often marked by 被.

5. Expressing an alternative preference

與其 V_1O_1, 不如 V_2O_2 與其 A V, 不如 B V	yŭqí …bùrú …	rather $V_2 O_2$ than $V_1 O_1$ Letting A do it is not as good as letting B do it.

我覺得**與其**參加旅遊團，**不如**自己坐火車去旅行……

1. | 沒事做，看電視怎麼樣？ | 没事做，看电视怎么样？ | We have nothing to do. How about watching TV? |
|---|---|---|
| 與其看電視，不如看本書。 | 与其看电视，不如看本书。 | I would rather read a book than watch TV. |

2. | 與其出去吃飯，不如自己在家做點兒什麼。 | 与其出去吃饭，不如自己在家做点儿什么。 | Instead of dining out, I would rather stay home and make something for myself. |
|---|---|---|

是啊！去飯館吃又貴又不健康。	是啊！去饭馆吃又贵又不健康。	That's right. Going to a restaurant is both expensive and unhealthy.
3. 我想去日本旅行。	我想去日本旅行。	I want to travel in Japan.
與其去日本那麼貴的地方，不如先在美國各地玩一玩。	与其去日本那么贵的地方，不如先在美国各地玩一玩。	Instead of going to a place as expensive as Japan, it would be better first to have some fun in different parts of the U.S.

This pattern expresses an alternative preference to a suggestion in a conversation. Therefore, the subject 你 (examples 1 and 3) or 我 (example 2), understood within the context, is often dropped. Remember that there should be verb phrases after 與其 and 不如, e.g., 與其喝咖啡不如喝茶. It's wrong to say 與其咖啡不如茶 or 與其咖啡不好，不如喝茶. Note: The preferred action follows 不如, and the non-prefered action follows 與其.

6. Expressing resignation

	… jiù…	
誰(想)V，誰就V		whoever
(想)什麼時候V，就什麼時候V		whenever
(想)怎麼V，就怎麼V		however
(想)V什麼，就V什麼		whatever
(想)V哪兒，就V哪兒		wherever
(想)V誰，就V誰		whomever

你想去**哪兒就**去**哪兒**，什麼時候都可以下車來玩……

1. 有句話，我不知道該不該說。	有句话，我不知道该不该说。	There is something … I don't know if I should say it or not.
你想說什麼，就說什麼，不用不好意思。	你想说什么，就说什么，不用不好意思。	If you want to say something, then go ahead and say it. Don't feel embarrassed.
2. 這個問題，誰知道答案 dá'àn 'answer'，誰	这个问题，谁知道答案，谁就回答。	Whoever knows the answer to the question should answer it.

就回答 huídá 'to answer.'

老師，我知道。	老师，我知道。	I know it, teacher.

3. 我們什麼時候去看
電影？

我们什么时候去看
电影？

When should we go see a movie?

你想什麼時候去，
就什麼時候去。

你想什么时候去，
就什么时候去。

We can go whenver you feel like going.

The first clause of this pattern indicates an open-ended possibility (whoever..., whatever..., however..., however much..., etc.), and the second clause indicates the resolution. The question word used in the first clause is usually repeated in the second clause and 就 often occurs (after the subject) in the second clause. Note that the position of the question word varies; it can stand in place of the subject and precede the verb, 誰想吃，誰就吃, or stand in place of the object and follow the verb, 你想吃什麼，就吃什麼, or in place of the adverb, 你想怎麼吃，就怎麼吃.

文化點滴 Culture Notes

1. **Spring Festival**: In the old days, Chinese New Year was an occasion for people to have a great feast after a year of hard work and to indulge themselves in buying and revelry. Since modern Chinese can afford many luxuries, the glory of Lunar New Year seems to have diminished. But the Spring Festival is still a time for all family members to get together. Most people try to come home before or on New Year's Eve. Therefore, the week before the Chinese New Year is the busiest time for traveling in China. It can be very difficult to get train tickets.

2. **Great Wall**: Changcheng 長城 was built 2,500 years ago and stretches more than 6,000 km. Most visitors flock to the wall at Badaling, a section that was constructed during the Ming dynasty (1368–1644 A.D.) and which is about 70 km northwest of Beijing. Here they walk up steep steps to the ramparts, and climb inside watchtowers. There is a Chinese saying: If you don't go to the Great Wall, you aren't a good Chinese. 不到長城非好漢 búdào Chángchéng fēi hǎohàn.

3. **The Palace Museum**: The Palace Museum 故宫 Gùgōng, also known as the Forbidden City 紫禁城 Zǐjìnchéng, is at the centre of Beijing. Built between 1406 and 1420, it served as Imperial Palace for the Ming and Qing dynasties. With approximately 9,000 halls and rooms, it's the largest palace in the world. The front gateway to the Palace Museum is Tian'anmen 天安門 (the Gate of Heavenly Peace).

4. **Imperial Gardens**: The Summer Palace 頤和園 Yíhéyuán was a royal garden of the Qing Dynasty. Another imperial garden of the Liao, Jin, Yuan, Ming and Qing dynasties was Beihai Park 北海公園 Běihǎi gōngyuán, one of the oldest Chinese gardens.

歌兒 Songs

一個人旅行
Traveling Alone

Adagietto

詞：劉雅詩　　曲：馬定一

1. 關上　門，提著我　收拾　好　的　大　行　李。捨不
   Guānshàng　mén, tízhe wǒ　shōushí　hǎo　de　dà　xínglǐ. Shěbù
   I close the door, and take up the much too heavy bag I packed.　　　　　Unwillingly,

2. 坐火　車，帶著我　到處　玩　名勝　古　蹟。一路
   Zuò huǒ　chē,　dàizhe wǒ dàochù wán　míngshènggǔ jī. Yílù
   By train, I am taken to places of historic interest and scenic beauty.　　On the way,

1. 得，　還是　離開　你。　說好了，這次我　一個　人　旅　行。
   dé,　háishì líkāi　nǐ.　Shuōhǎole, zhècì wǒ yí ge rén　lǚxíng.
   I finally leave you.　　　　We agreed that this time I will travel alone.

2. 上，　風景 多美　麗。　卻發現，身邊還　是　習慣 有你。
   shàng, fēngjǐng duō měi　lì.　Què fā xiàn, shēnbiān hái shì　xíguàn yǒu nǐ.
   the landscape is so beautiful.　　Yet I notice I'm still used to having you around.

1. 結束了，以後 不再 相 守　相　依。　從今後，許 多快樂 成為
   Jiéshùle,　yǐhòu búzài xiāng shǒu xiāng　yī.　Cóng jīnhòu, xǔ duō kuàilè chéngwéi
   It's over; we won't cling to each other any more.　From now on, the many happinesses become

2. 忍不住，想要 買張明 信 片　寄。　報平安，我 卻 寫得 十分
   Rěnbúzhù, xiǎng yào mǎi zhāng míngxìnpiàn jì.　Bào píng ān, wǒ què xiěde　shífēn
   Relentlessly, I get the urge to buy a postcard to send you.　I want to tell you that I'm safe and sound;

1. 回　憶。不說 再見，把悲　傷 放 在 心　裏。
   huí　yì. Bùshuō zàijiàn,　bǎ bēi　shāng fàng zài xīn　lǐ.
   memories.　Without bidding you farewell, I leave my sadness in my heart.

2. 吃　力。這才 知道，你原　來 在我 心　裏。
   chī　lì. Zhè cái zhīdào,　nǐ yuán lái zài wǒ xīn　lǐ.
   yet it's so hard for me to write.　Then I know you're still in my heart.

第十二課

Theme Environment and Traffic

Communicative Objectives
- Shopping for a souvenir
- Talking with a passenger on the train
- Complaining about pollution
- Chatting with children

Focus on Characters
- 髒擠亂嚴、複雜紙圖、農戶租金、確吸煙汽、驚答品部

Grammar Focus
- 由/從 A 經 B 到 C
- S 還是 V（的）好；S 最好 V
- 讓 person VP；害（得）person VP
- V 了 (person) 一 O
- 拿 A 跟 B 比較；和 B 比（起來），A
- S 得…才行

什麼時候能向污染說再見？

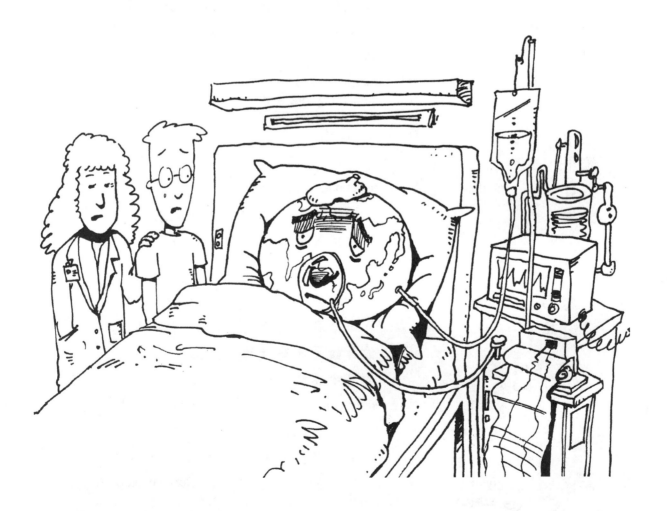

生詞 Vocabulary

Study the following words for their pronunciation and meaning. When an area is shaded, guess at the meaning of the word based on its constituent characters and then fill in the blank. Read the usage of words and related terms (antonyms, synonyms, compounds sharing the constituent characters, etc.) and try to answer the sample questions in Chinese. Note that proper nouns and incidental terms are not numbered.

◎ By Order of Appearance

1. 向　　　xiàng　　Prep　towards (direction)

   向人問好/說再見/學習

   你覺得自己應該向誰學習？

   你觉得自己应该向谁学习？

2. 污染　　wūrǎn　　N/V　pollution, to contaminate　[smear-soil]

   感染 to catch (a disease)

   土地污染 land pollution

   環境/空氣kōngqì/水污染； 污染嚴重

   這兒的空氣污染嚴重嗎？

   这儿的空气污染严重吗？

3. 條　　　tiáo　　M/N　measure word for something long and narrow, stripe

   条

   一条建议

4. 絲巾　　sījīn　　N　silk scarf　[silk-piece of cloth]

   丝巾

   一匹丝 喜欢 紧张 trace of like / of nervous

5. 出發　　chūfā　　V　to set out, to start from　[out-start]

   出发

   你決定什麼時候出發去中國旅行？

   你决定什么时候出发去中国旅行？

   秀水街　Xiùshuǐjiē　N　name of a street in Beijing

6. 紀念品　jìniànpǐn　N　souvenir　[record-think of-product]

   紀念品

   買紀念品；值得紀念；留/作個紀念

   你喜歡買什麼樣的紀念品？

   你喜欢买什么样的纪念品？

   初 = beginning
   中 = middle

7. 月底　　yuèdǐ　　N　end of month　[month-bottom]

   這個月底你回家嗎？

   这个月底你回家吗？

8. 古代　　gǔdài　　N　ancient times　[ancient-generation]

   现代 = modern ten/dur

   死 阵亡 shoot in battle | 战士 soldier | 纪念日 anniversary

   口口 到处扔垃圾

ōu zhōu Europe
欧州

chāi : to demolition
拆

9.	建築 建筑	Jiànzhù/zhú	N/V	architecture, building, to build	[set up-construct]

中國式的建築有什麼特色？
中国式的建筑有什么特色？

10.	文物	wénwù	N	cultural/historical relics	[culture-thing]
11.	吸引	xīyǐn	V	to attract, to draw	[absorb-draw]

A 很 xīyǐn 我

哪個演員很有吸引力？
哪个演员很有吸引力？

⊠ 吸入 inhale
呼气 to exhale
hū qì

12.	種 种	zhǒng	M/N	kind, sort, type, race, seed	

種種子 zhǒng zhǒng zi

13.	農民 农民	nóngmín	N	peasant/farmer	[agriculture-people]
14.	工人	gōngrén	N	worker	[labor-person]
15.	個體戶 个体户	gètǐhù	N	individual entrepreneur	[individual-body-person of certain status]

not in national system

16.	部分	bùfen	N	part, section	[unit-component]

這兒大部分的學生都從哪兒來？
这儿大部分的学生都从哪儿来？

17.	感謝 感谢	gǎnxiè	V	to thank, to be grateful	[feel-thank]

感謝……的幫助/關心/理解
你覺得自己成功應該感謝誰？
你觉得自己成功应该感谢谁？

18.	害	hài	V	to do harm to, to cause trouble to	

害人遲到/沒法做功課；讓人難過/快樂
你的同屋常常害得你怎麼樣？
你的同屋常常害得你怎么样？

19.	二手煙 二手烟	èrshǒuyān	N		[second-hand-smoke]

吸太多的二手煙會有什麼問題？
吸太多的二手烟会有什么问题？

Characters with Many Strokes

二手衣服

染 發 建 築 種 農 體 感 謝 煙

order of respect
士 農 工 商

(handwritten top: 卫生间 toilet (polite))

20.	衛生紙	wèishēng	N	toilet paper	[sanitary-paper]
	卫生纸	zhǐ		=手紙	

(handwritten: sanitary)

21.	的確	díquè	Adv	certainly, surely	[target-truly]
	的确				

的確不知道/很好/有問題
你的確不知道今天有考試嗎？
你的确不知道今天有考试吗？

22.	遊客	yóukè	N	tourist	[travel-visitor]
	游客				

23.	垃圾	lājī <PRC>	N	garbage	
		lèsè <TW>			

(handwritten: dump/drop/dissal 倒 dào empty over a bucket)

倒/丟垃圾　→垃圾箱xiāng、垃圾回收huíshōu
你家的垃圾都是誰倒？
你家的垃圾都是谁倒？

24.	髒	zāng	Adj	dirty	
	脏				

把……搞髒了；髒衣服/話　　↔乾淨
誰把我的車子搞髒了？
谁把我的车子搞脏了？

(handwritten: 脏脏 a little off; gānjìng (clean))

25.	擠	jǐ	Adj/	crowded, to squeeze, to push	
	挤		V		

擠滿了人；人擠人；擠不進去
這兒什麼地方常常擠滿了人？
这儿什么地方常常挤满了人？

(handwritten: 挤来挤去 to squeeze this way & that way; squeeze into (a car))

26.	環境	huánjìng	N	environment	[surround-area]
	环境				

環境污染/保護；在……的家庭環境中長大
他的家庭環境怎麼樣？
他的家庭环境怎么样？

27.	保護	bǎohù	N/V	protection, to protect	[protect-guard]
	保护				

保護環境/自己/動物dòngwù　　→愛護 àihù
你覺得我們應該怎樣保護環境？
你觉得我们应该怎样保护环境？

	西湖	Xīhú	N	West Lake (in Hangzhou)	[west-lake]

28.	死	sǐ	Adj/	dead, to die	
			V		

嚇/累/餓/渴/笑/高興死了　　↔活
昨天做什麼事情把你累死了？
昨天做什么事情把你累死了？

(handwritten bottom left: 冷死了 / 饿死了 / 开心死了)

面式
interview

兴奋 xīn fèn excited 吃了一惊

When Can We Bid Farewell to Pollution?   Lesson 12—35

29.	外星人	wàixīngrén	N	E.T., Alien	[other-star-person]
30.	金	jīn	N	gold, blonde (hair)	
31.	怪物	guàiwu	N	monster, freak	[strange-thing]
32.	其他	qítā	Adj/	other, the rest	[that-other]

另外的
the other

| | | | Pron | 其他人/東西/事情 | |

vs.別人、另外 lìngwài兩個人

你今天還有什麼其他的考試嗎？

你今天还有什么其他的考试吗？

| 33. | 回答 | huídá | V/N | to reply, answer | [return-answer] |

回答人問題；很好的回答

誰可以回答我的問題？

谁可以回答我的问题？

| 34. | 吃驚
吃惊 | chījīng | VO | to be shocked | [soak up-alarm] |

感到吃惊
or
让...吃惊

大吃一驚；讓……很吃驚

來美國後，什麼事情讓你很吃驚？

来美国后，什么事情让你很吃惊？

| 35. | 對話
对话 | duìhuà | VO/
N | to carry on dialogue | [mutual-talk] |
| 36. | 交通 | jiāotōng | N | traffic | [join-go through] |

交通很糟糕/亂

什麼地方的交通很糟糕？

什么地方的交通很糟糕？

职业
professional

| 37. | 亂
乱 | luàn | Adj | chaotic, messy | |

乱扱
乱花钱
乱说

亂吃/花錢/說話/交朋友

→亂七八糟   ↔整齊

亂吃東西容易有什麼問題？

乱吃东西容易有什么问题？

| 38. | 機車
机车 | jīchē | N | \<TW\> motorcycle
\<PRC\> 摩托車mótuōchē | [machine-car] |

红 灯 坏了

Characters with Many Strokes

髒 擠 環 護 驚 對 亂 機

Grant Nohleder

39.	計程車 计程车	jìchéngchē	N	<TW> (metered) taxi	[count-distance-car]
40.	出租汽車 出租汽车	chūzū qìchē	N	<PRC> taxi	[go out-rent-car]
41.	嚇 吓	xià	V	to scare	
				把人嚇了一跳；嚇死人；嚇壞了 什麼樣的電影特別嚇人？ 什么样的电影特别吓人？	
	捷運 捷运	jiéyùn	N	<TW> rapid transportation system <PRC> 地鐵 dìtiě 'subway'	
42.	塞車 塞车	sāichē	N/ VO	traffic jam <PRC> 堵車 dǔchē	[stuff in-car]
43.	嚴重 严重	yánzhòng	Adj	serious, grave	[tight-heavy]
				塞車/問題/事情嚴重 最近誰病得很嚴重？ 最近谁病得很严重？	
44.	複雜 复杂	fùzá	Adj	complicated, complex	[compound-mixed]
				事情/問題/心情複雜　　↔簡單 現在什麼問題很複雜？ 现在什么问题很复杂？	
45.	地圖 地图	dìtú	N	map	[land-chart]

Characters with Many Strokes

程　租　嚇　捷　塞　嚴　複　雜　圖

◎ By Grammatical Categories

Nouns/Pronouns

其他	qítā	others, other
部分	bùfen	part, section
月底	yuèdǐ	end of month
古代	gǔdài	ancient times
建築	jiànzhù	architecture, building
文物	wénwù	cultural/historical relics
絲巾	sījīn	silk scarf
紀念品	jìnìanpǐn	souvenir
遊客	yóukè	tourist
農民	nóngmín	peasant
工人	gōngrén	worker
個體戶	gètǐhù	individual entrepreneur
外星人	wàixīngrén	an extra-terrestrial
怪物	guàiwu	monster, freak

金	jīn	gold, blonde
二手煙	èrshǒuyān	secondhand smoke
衛生紙	wèishēngzhǐ	toilet paper
垃圾	lājī, lèsè	garbage
環境	huánjìng	environment
交通	jiāotōng	traffic
塞車	sāichē	traffic jam
機車	jīchē	<TW> motorcycle
計程車	jìchéngchē	<TW> (metered) taxi
出租汽車	chūzū qìchē	<PRC> taxi
地圖	dìtú	map
條	tiáo	measure word for sth. long and narrow
種	zhǒng	kind, sort, type

Verbs/Stative Verbs/Adjectives

嚇	xià	to scare
害	hài	to do harm to, to cause trouble to
出發	chūfā	to set out, to start from
吸引	xīyǐn	to attract, to draw
污染	wūrǎn	pollution, to contaminate
感謝	gǎnxiè	to thank, to be grateful
保護	bǎohù	protection, to protect
回答	huídá	to reply, answer

對話	duìhuà	to carry on dialogue
吃驚	chījīng	to be shocked
髒	zāng	dirty
亂	luàn	chaotic, messy
擠	jǐ	crowded, to squeeze, to push
死	sǐ	dead, to die
嚴重	yánzhòng	serious, grave
複雜	fùzá	complicated, complex

Adverbs and Others

的確	díquè	certainly, surely
向	xiàng	towards (direction)

◎ By Pinyin

Entries with * indicate lexical items used in Mini-Dialogues and of possible interest for supplemental study.

bǎohù	保护	protection, to protect	jǐ	挤	crowded, to squeeze
bùfen	部分	part, section	jìniànpǐn	纪念品	souvenir
chījīng	吃惊	to be shocked	lājī, lèsè	垃圾	garbage
chūfā	出发	to set out	láojià*	劳驾	excuse me
chūzū qìchē	出租汽车	<PRC> taxi	luàn	乱	chaotic, messy
dānwèi*	单位	(work) unit	nóngmín	农民	peasant
díquè	的确	certainly, surely	qítā	其他	other, the rest
dìtú	地图	map	sāichē	塞车	traffic jam
duìhuà	对话	to carry on dialogue	sījīn	丝巾	silk scarf
èrshǒuyān	二手烟	secondhand smoke	sǐ	死	dead, to die
fāngbiàn*	方便	to go to the restroom, convenient	suànle*	算了	forget it, let it be, let it pass
fùzá	复杂	complicated	tiáo	条	measure word for sth. long and narrow
gǎnxiè	感谢	to thank, to be grateful	wàixīngrén	外星人	an extra-terrestrial
gètǐhù	个体户	individual entrepreneur	wèishēngzhǐ	卫生纸	toilet paper
gōngrén	工人	worker	wénwù	文物	cultural/historical relics
guàiwu	怪物	monster, freak	wūrǎn	污染	pollution, to contaminate
gǔdài	古代	ancient times	xià	吓	to scare
hài	害	to do harm to, to cause trouble to	xiàng	向	towards (direction)
huánjìng	环境	environment	xīyǐn	吸引	to attract, to draw
huídá	回答	to reply, answer	yánzhòng	严重	serious, grave
jiànzhù	建筑	architecture, to build	yóukè	游客	tourist
jiāotōng	交通	traffic	yuèdǐ	月底	end of month
jīchē	机车	<TW> motor-cycle	zāng	脏	dirty
jìchéngchē	计程车	<TW> taxi	zhǒng	种	kind, sort, type
jīn	金	gold, blonde			

課文 Text

Use the following questions to guide your reading of the text.

1. 小高喜歡坐火車旅行嗎？坐火車旅行有什麼好處、壞處？

2. 小高喜歡去看名勝古蹟嗎？為什麼？他遇到什麼有趣的事？

3. 小高對台北有什麼印象？

小高：

　　我收到你寄來的包裹了，那條絲巾很漂亮，謝謝！聽小李說你去台灣以前在大陸各地旅行，你是哪一天出發的？去了哪些地方？現在到台北了沒有？希望早點兒聽到你的消息。

　　祝
一切順利！

美英上

美英：

　　送你的一點兒小禮物，希望你喜歡，那條絲巾是我在秀水街買的，算是我在北京最後的紀念品吧！我是月底出發的，我先去了西安，然後再[1]由北京經上海到蘇杭。看了許多古代的建築和文物。但最吸引我的還不是那些，而是有機會在火車上和各種不同的人聊天，我和農民、工人、個體戶都談過話，大部分的人都很親切。這都得感

謝小李，他說得對，²還是自己坐火車去玩的好。當然火車上也有一些問題。最麻煩的是吸煙的人太多，³害得我吸了不少二手煙，另外，廁所不太乾淨，也沒有衛生紙。

中國的名勝古蹟的確很值得一看，可惜的是遊客多的地方小販也多，垃圾也多，到處又髒又擠，讓人難過，環境保護做得不夠好。你知道嗎？我居然在有名的西湖裏看到一條很大的死魚！我們什麼時候能向污染說再見呢？在蘇州我遇到了一件有趣的事：有一天很多孩子一直看著我，好像我是個「外星人」──一個金髮藍眼的怪物。有個孩子⁴看了我一眼就問其他人：「你覺得他看得見嗎？」我用中文回答：「當然看得見！」他們大吃一驚。孩子以為我這個老外聽不懂中文，哪知道我不但聽得懂，而且還能跟他們對話。

我到台北已經三天了。⁵拿台北和北京比較，這兒的交通和北京的一樣亂，只是機車比自行車多多了。我到台北的時候，搭了一輛「計程車」，就是北京的出租汽車，那個司機在路上左轉右轉，把我嚇死了！他還說自從有了捷運以後，台北的交通已經好多了，上下班時間塞車沒有那麼嚴重了。這兒的路很複雜，找房子不容易，我⁶得馬上去買張地圖才行。下次再聊吧！

德中上

严肃
xián sù　grave (person)

木各 strict

搭 dā

口下 坏 找了
huài

认真　earnest,

课文 Text

Use the following questions to guide your reading of the text.

1. 小高喜欢坐火车旅行吗？坐火车旅行有什么好处、坏处？

2. 小高喜欢去看名胜古迹吗？为什么？他遇到什么有趣的事？

3. 小高对台北有什么印象？

 小高：

　　我收到你寄来的包裹了，那条丝巾很漂亮，谢谢！听小李说你去台湾以前在大陆各地旅行，你是哪一天出发的？去了哪些地方？现在到台北了没有？希望早点儿听到你的消息。

　　祝

一切顺利！

美英上

 美英：

　　送你的一点儿小礼物，希望你喜欢，那条丝巾是我在秀水街买的，算是我在北京最后的纪念品吧！我是月底出发的，我先去了西安，然后再[1]由北京经上海到苏杭。看了许多古代的建筑和文物。但最吸引我的还不是那些，而是有机会在火车上和各种不同的人聊天，我和农民、工人、个体户都谈过话，大部分的人都很亲切。这都得感谢小李，他说得对，[2]**还是**自己坐火车去玩**的好**。当然火车上也有一

些问题。最麻烦的是吸烟的人太多，³**害得**我吸了不少二手烟，另外，厕所不太干净，也没有卫生纸。

中国的名胜古迹的确很值得一看，可惜的是游客多的地方小贩也多，垃圾也多，到处又脏又挤，让人难过，环境保护做得不够好。你知道吗？我居然在有名的西湖里看到一条很大的死鱼！我们什么时候能向污染说再见呢？在苏州我遇到了一件有趣的事：有一天很多孩子一直看着我，好象我是个外星人——一个金发蓝眼的怪物。有个孩子⁴**看了我一眼**就问其他人："你觉得他看得见吗？"我用中文回答："当然看得见！"他们大吃一惊。孩子以为我这个老外听不懂中文，哪知道我不但听得懂，而且还能跟他们对话。

我到台北已经三天了。⁵**拿**台北**和**北京**比较**，这儿的交通和北京的一样乱，只是机车比自行车多多了。我到台北的时候，搭了一辆"计程车"，就是北京的出租汽车，那个司机在路上左转右转，把我吓死了！他还说自从有了捷运以后，台北的交通已经好多了，上下班时间塞车没有那么严重了。这儿的路很复杂，找房子不容易，我⁶**得**马上去买张地图**才行**。下次再聊吧！

德中上

小對話 Mini-Dialogues

Read the supplementary dialogues for a better understanding of the text. See if you can memorize one and perform it in class.

(1) Shopping for a souvenir

Gao: 這條絲巾多少錢？

A: 一百塊！一百八買兩條。

Gao: 太貴了，能不能打八折？我買來送人的。

A: 這條的顏色好，樣子也大方，送人最好了。這樣吧，打九折，要買就買，不買就算了 suànle 'let it be'。

Gao: 好吧！好吧！這可是我在北京最後的紀念品了。

这条丝巾多少钱？

一百块！一百八买两条。

太贵了，能不能打八折？我买来送人的。

这条的颜色好，样子也大方，送人最好了。这样吧，打九折，要买就买，不买就算了。

好吧！好吧！这可是我在北京最后的纪念品了。

Gao: How much is this scarf?

A: One hundred dollars! One hundred-eighty dollars if you get two.

Gao: It's too expensive. Can you give me a 20 percent discount? I'm buying this as a gift.

A: This one's a nice color and the look is great. It's best for giving someone as a gift. How about this one? I'll give you a ten percent discount. If you want it, get it. If not, that's that.

Gao: O.K.! O.K.! This is certainly the last souvenir that I buy in Beijing.

👥 (2) Talking with a passenger on the train

A: 您上哪兒去？   您上哪儿去？

Gao: 我去上海。您是哪個單位 dānwèi   我去上海。您是哪个单位的？
        的？

A: 本來在中學教書，現在「下   本来在中学教书，现在" 下
        海」了。   海"了。

Gao: 怎麼？老師不做，跑去當漁民   怎么？老师不做，跑去当渔
          yúmín。   民。

A: 不、不、不。我現在是個體戶   不、不、不。我现在是个体户
        了。   了。

Gao: 噢！個體戶的收入比老師的好   噢！个体户的收入比老师的好
        多了吧？   多了吧？

A: 還行（一直吸煙）。   还行（一直吸烟）。

Gao: 對不起，我得去「方便」 fāngbiàn   对不起，我得去"方便"一
        一下，勞駕 láojià。   下，劳驾。

A: Where are you going?

Gao: I am going to Shanghai. Where do you
        work?

A: Originally I taught at a middle school.
        Now I'm "headed out to sea."

Gao: What? You don't want to be a teacher,
        and now you work as a fisherman.

A: No, no, no. I am an individual
        entrepreneur.

Gao: Oh! Now you earn a lot more than
        working as a teacher, I guess?

A: It's fine (keeps on smoking).

Gao: Sorry, I have to go to the restroom. Excuse me.

(3) Complaining about pollution

A: 聽說你今年坐火車去杭州旅行。怎麼樣？

Gao: 很糟，火車非常擠、吸煙的人又多，而且廁所很髒。

A: 到了杭州，看到西湖，那兒應該很美吧？

Gao: 我原來也以為那兒很美，沒想到到處都是垃圾。

A: 怎麼會這樣呢？

Gao: 因為那兒遊客太多，環境保護做得不夠好。

A: 听说你今年坐火车去杭州旅行。怎么样？

很糟，火车非常挤、吸烟的人又多，而且厕所很脏。

到了杭州，看到西湖，那儿应该很美吧？

我原来也以为那儿很美，没想到到处都是垃圾。

怎么会这样呢？

因为那儿游客太多，环境保护做得不够好。

A: I heard that you traveled to Hangzhou this year by train. How was your trip?

Gao: Very bad. The train was extremely crowded and many people smoked. Besides, the restroom was filthy.

A: When you arrived at Hangzhou and saw the West Lake, it was very beautiful, I suppose?

Gao: I originally thought it would be beautiful also. Who knew there would be garbage everywhere!

A: How has it come to be this way?

Gao: Because there are too many tourists there and enough is not done in the way of environmental protection.

(4) Chatting with children

A: 你們看，那兒有個老外！

B: 你看他的頭髮是金色的，眼睛

你们看，那儿有个老外！

你看他的头发是金色的，眼睛

是藍的，像不像個怪物？　　　　　　　是蓝的，象不象个怪物？

C:　我看像外星人！　　　　　　　　　　我看象外星人！

D:　他的藍眼睛看起來像玻璃球兒 bōli qiúr 一樣，你覺得他看得見嗎？

他的蓝眼睛看起来象玻璃球儿一样，你觉得他看得见吗？

Gao:　當然看得見！　　　　　　　　　　当然看得见！

B:　噢！原來你聽得懂中文。　　　　　　噢！原来你听得懂中文。

A:　You see, there is a foreigner.

B:　See, his hair is blonde and eyes are blue. Doesn't he look like a monster?

C:　I think he looks like an extra-terrestrial!

D:　His blue eyes look like marbles. Do you think he can see things?

Gao: Of course I can.

B:　Oh! You understand Chinese.

小故事 Stories

Read the following tale for your own enjoyment and for your understanding of the highlighted expression that is relevant to the theme of the chapter.

 爭先恐後 zhēngxiān-kǒnghòu

❀ 這兒的人開車都爭先恐後，難怪交通問題很嚴重。

爭	zhēng	to strive, to fight for
恐	kǒng	to fear
王良	Wáng Liáng	name of a person
趕車	gǎn chē	to drive a carriage
趙王	Zhào wáng	King Zhao
認真	rènzhēn	earnest, serious
輸	shū	to lose
注意力	zhùyìlì	attention
趕不上	gǎnbu shàng	can't catch up with

　　從前有一個人叫王良，他很會趕車，所以趙王就請他教自己趕車。王良很認真地教，趙王也很努力地學，學會以後，他就和王良比賽。可是比了三次，趙王都輸了。

　　趙王很不高興地對王良說：「你教得不夠好。」王良說：「是你沒有把我教你的東西好好地用上。趕車的時候，應該把注意力放在自己的馬上，這樣才能跑得快。可是你在我後邊的時候，只怕趕不上我；在我前邊的時候，又怕被我趕上。你只注意我，卻沒有注意自己的馬，這就是你輸的原因。」

✎ 爭先恐後的意思是＿＿＿＿＿＿＿＿＿＿＿＿＿＿＿＿＿＿＿＿＿

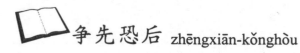

争先恐后 zhēngxiān-kǒnghòu

❀ 这儿的人开车都争先恐后，难怪交通问题很严重。

从前有一个人叫王良，他很会赶车，所以赵王就请他教自己赶车。王良很认真地教，赵王也很努力地学，学会以后，他就和王良比赛。可是比了三次，赵王都输了。

赵王很不高兴地对王良说："你教得不够好。"王良说："是你没有把我教你的东西好好地用上。赶车的时候，应该把注意力放在自己的马上，这样才能跑得快。可是你在我后边的时候，只怕赶不上我；在我前边的时候，又怕被我赶上。你只注意我，却没有注意自己的马，这就是你输的原因。"

争	zhēng	to strive, to fight for
恐	kǒng	to fear
王良	Wáng Liáng	name of a person
赶车	gǎn chē	to drive a carriage
赵王	Zhào wáng	King Zhao
认真	rènzhēn	earnest, serious
输	shū	to lose
注意力	zhùyìlì	attention
赶不上	gǎnbu shàng	can't catch up with

漢字 Characters

Study the following selected characters for further enrichment of your writing and vocabulary.

骨 gǔ 'bone' +
葬 zàng 'bury'
phonetic

脏

zāng 21
dirty, filthy

| 髒衣服 | zāng yīfu* | dirty clothes |
| 髒亂 | zāngluàn* | dirty and messy |

A: 你的髒衣服不要到處亂放。

B: 我的屋子還沒有你的那麼髒亂呢！

扌 shǒu 'hand'
+ 齊 qí
phonetic

挤

jǐ 17
to squeeze, crowd

| 擠來擠去 | jǐlái-jǐqù* | to mill about |
| 擠滿 | jǐmǎn | filled to overflowing |

A: 中國的公共汽車總是擠滿了人。

B: 對啊！上次我擠來擠去都擠不上。

Compare: 齊 qí

爪又 two hands
working with 幺
silk threads hung
up on 冂 a stand
乚 was added to
represent one of
the threads

乱

luàn 13
messy, random, chaos

| 亂七八糟 | luànqībāzāo* | in a mess, in a muddle |
| 亂說 | luànshuō* | to speak carelessly/ irresponsibly |

A: 你的房間亂七八糟，誰敢來看你？

B: 別亂說，我現在不是在收拾嗎？

two 口 kǒu
'mouths' + 厂
'a cliff or a
cave' + 敢 gǎn
phonetic

严

yán 19
tight, strict, severe

| 嚴重 | yánzhòng | serious (matters) |
| 嚴肅 | yánsù* | solemn (attitude) |

A: 這件事情有多嚴重？

B: 你看看他那嚴肅的樣子就知道了。

Compare: 敢 gǎn

衤 yī 'clothing' + 复 fù phonetic—lined garment, double

複習	fùxí	to review
重複	chóngfù*	to repeat, repetition
複印	fùyìn*	to copy, to duplicate

A: 這一課的生詞你複習了嗎？

B: 複習了，我把所有的字重寫了十次。

Compare: 復 fù

复

fù 14
to duplicate

Originally 衣 yī 'clothing' + 集 jí 'collect' 木 moved over beneath 衣—garments made with variegated pieces stitched together

| 複雜 | fùzá | complicated, complex |
| 雜誌 | zázhì* | magazine, journal |

A: 你為什麼不看那本雜誌呢？

B: 它討論的問題太複雜了！

杂

zá 18
mixed, to mix

糸 sī 'silk' + 氏 shì phonetic—in ancient times, silk cloth was used for writing on

衛生紙	wèishēngzhǐ	toilet paper
報紙	bàozhǐ*	newspaper
信紙	xìnzhǐ*	letter/writing paper

A: 我想寫點兒東西，你有沒有信紙？

B: 沒有，我只有幾張衛生紙。

纸

Compare: 低 dī

zhǐ 10
paper, (for piece/sheet)

囗 a wall around 啚 bǐ, which represents more walls, like a floor plan

地圖	dìtú	map
圖書	túshū*	books
圖書館	túshūguǎn	library

A: 那個圖書館有什麼特色？

B: 除了圖書以外，還有很多地圖。

图

tú 14
picture, chart, to seek

囟 'a head' + 臼 'two hands' + 晨 chén 'the break of day' contracted—the man who works from early dawn

農

nóng 13
agriculture, peasant

| 農民 | nóngmín | peasant, peasantry |
| 農村 | nóngcūn* | rural area, village |

A: 你參觀過中國的農村嗎？

B: 參觀過，還跟很多農民談過話呢！

Compare: 濃 nóng

戶

hù 4
door, household, account

Picture of a door, one side of 門 mén

戶

個體戶	gètǐhù	individual entrepreneur
窗戶	chuānghù*	window
戶頭	hùtóu*	bank account

A: 那個個體戶在銀行裏有很多戶頭。

B: 他一定賺zhuàn 'earn' 了很多錢。

Compare: 所 suǒ 房 fáng 偏 piān

禾 hé 'grain' + 且 qiě phonetic —presumably feudal lords were sometimes paid in grain rather than money

租

zū 10
to rent, lease, tax

| 出租汽車 | chūzū qìchē | <PRC> taxi |
| 房租 | fángzū* | rent (for house/flat/etc.) |

A: 這兒住的很貴，一個月房租要一千。

B: 出租汽車也很貴，一上車就要一百。

Compare: 組 zǔ 祖 zǔ

金

jīn 8
metals, gold, money

Picture of gold nuggets (dots) covered up in the ground 土 tǔ 'earth'

金

金髮	jīnfà	blonde hair
金色	jīnsè*	gold color, golden
金魚	jīnyú*	goldfish
現金	xiànjīn	ready money, cash

A: 那個人長什麼樣子？

B: 除了金髮以外，還有一對金魚眼。

Compare: 錢 qián 錯 cuò 銀 yín 鐘 zhōng

石 shí
'stone'—solid,
firm, certain +
隹 hè phonetic

确

的確	díquè	certainly, surely
確定	quèdìng*	to define, fix, definitely

A: 你確定他明天的確不會來嗎？

B: 沒錯，我剛才跟他談過。

Compare: 難 nán

què 15
true, indeed

口 kǒu 'mouth'
+ 及 jí phonetic

吸

吸引	xīyǐn	to attract, to draw
呼吸	hūxī*	to breathe

A: 這個地方每年吸引了很多遊客。

B: 所以空氣kōngqì 'air'髒得讓人沒法呼吸。

Compare: 及 jí

xī 6
to inhale, to absorb, to
attract

火 huǒ 'fire' +
因/ 垔 yīn
phonetic

烟

二手煙	èrshǒuyān	secondhand smoke
香煙	xiāngyān*	cigarette
抽煙	chōuyān	to smoke (cigarette/pipe)

A: 我能在這兒抽煙嗎？

B: 不能，沒有人想吸你的二手煙。

yān 13
smoke, mist, tobacco

气 qì 'air,
vapor, vital
energy,'
enlarged by shuǐ
'water'

汽

汽車	qìchē	motor vehicle, auto
汽油	qìyóu*	gasoline
汽水	qìshuǐ	soft drink, soda water

A: 你的汽車出了什麼問題？

B: 沒有問題，只是汽油沒了。

Compare: 氣 qì

qì 7
vapor, steam

馬 mǎ 'horse'
+ 敬 jìng
'respect'
phonetic

惊

吃驚	chījīng	to be shocked
驚人	jīngrén*	amazing, alarming
驚奇	jīngqí*	to wonder, to be amazed

A: 你為什麼這麼驚奇的樣子？

B: 他一天就學會五十個漢字，真驚人！

jīng 22
to startle, to surprise

zhú 'bamboo' +
合 hé 'together'
—to connect,
answer, pay
back

答

回答	huídá	to answer, to reply
答案	dá'àn*	solution, answer, key
答錯	dácuò*	to anwer incorrectly
問答	wèndá*	questions and answers

A: 請你做這道問答題，答錯也沒關係。

B: 我不知道怎麼回答，答案應該是什麼。

dá, dā 12
to answer, to reply

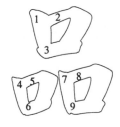

Symbol for
objects piled
up, arranged in
groups,
classified

品

紀念品	jìniànpǐn	souvenir
作品	zuòpǐn	works (of literature/art)
食品	shípǐn	foodstuff, food

A: 你希望我買什麼紀念品回來？

B: 買一點食品就好了。

Compare: 區 qū 澡 zǎo 操 cāo

pǐn 9
article, goods, rate, to
taste

阝 yì 'city' +
音 pǒu phonetic

部

部分	bùfēn	part, section
大部分	dàbùfēn*	most part, majority
全部	quánbù*	whole, complete, total
西部	xībù	the west, western part

A: 這兒大部分的人都去過西部嗎？

B: 對，只有一小部分的人沒去過。

bù 10
part, unit, headquarters

語法和用法 Grammar and Usage

Pay attention to the function of the structure and then study the example sentences.

1. Expressing a route

車专机 *transfer flight*

由/從A經B到C	yóu/cóng…jīng…dào…	from A via B to C

我先去了西安，然後再**由**北京**經**上海**到**蘇杭。

1.	你怎麼去加拿大 Jiānádà 的？	你怎么去加拿大 的？	What route did you take to Canada?
	我由印地經芝加哥 轉機，再到溫哥華 Wēngēhuá。	我由印地经芝加哥 转机，再到温哥华 。	I flew from Indianapolis, changed planes in Chicago, and then arrived in Vancouver.
2.	從這兒到義大利 Yìdàlì 坐飛機要多 久？	从这儿到义大利坐 飞机要多久？	How long does it take to fly from here to Italy?
	通常從印地經倫敦 Lúndūn 到羅馬 Luómǎ 要十幾個小時。	通常从印地经伦敦 到罗马要十几个小 时。	It usually takes more than ten hours to get from Indianapolis, via London, to Rome.
3.	從美國經日本到台 灣比較快，還是經 香港到台灣比較 快？	从美国经日本到台 湾比较快，还是经 香港到台湾比较 快？	Is it faster to go from the U.S. to Taiwan by way of Japan or by way of Hong Kong?
	我想都差不多。	我想都差不多。	I think it's about the same.

This pattern typically expresses a route taken on a trip. One can use 由 or 從 for the place of departure, and 經 stands for 經過. Compare this with the pattern to express sequence of events, 先⋯等/然後⋯再V (L9, G4).

2. Expressing an alternative preference

(S)還是V(的)好	háishì…(de) hǎo	it's better (for S) to V
S最好V	zuìhǎo…	it would be best for S to V

他說的對,**還是**自己坐火車去玩**的好**。

1.	餐館的飯吃來吃去都沒有自己在家做的好。	餐馆的饭吃来吃去都没有自己在家做的好。	No matter [where] you eat, it's never as good as what you make at home, yourself.
	對,飯還是自己做好,便宜又健康。	对,饭还是自己做好,便宜又健康。	That's right. Homemade dishes are the best. They're both inexpensive and healthy.
2.	等我大學畢業再學中文吧!	等我大学毕业再学中文吧!	Let me wait until I graduate from college and then I will study Chinese.
	中文還是早點兒學的好。	中文还是早点儿学的好。	The earlier you begin to study Chinese, the better.
3.	這件事由我決定就可以了。	这件事由我决定就可以了。	I can decide this matter by myself.
	你還是跟他商量一下的好。	你还是跟他商量一下的好。	It's better for you to discuss this with him.

Literally, 還是 means "still, after all." It is used to convey a preference after the pros and cons of an issue have been considered; usually (的)好 or 吧 comes at the end of the sentence. Compare this with 與其…不如… (L11, G5).

3. Expressing the cause of an (unfavorable) result

…(不)讓person VP	(bú) ràng…	(not) to cause/make person VP
…害(得) person VP	hài(de)…	to cause trouble for person

最麻煩的是吸煙的人太多,**害**我吸了不少二手煙……

1.	你怎麼遲到了?	你怎麼迟到了?	Why were you late?

我同屋洗澡洗了半個小時，害得我沒趕上_{gǎnshàng}公車。	我同屋洗澡洗了半个小时，<u>害得</u>我没赶上公车。	My roommate took a bath for half an hour, and made me miss my bus.

迟到
to be late

2.

你為什麼生我的氣？	你为什么生我的气？	Why were you angry with me?
你把我的話都說完了，害得我不知道說什麼才好。	你把我的话都说完了，<u>害得</u>我不知道说什么才好。	You've left me speechless—I don't know what else to say.

3.

你的表現 _{biǎoxiàn} 讓我很不滿意。	你的表现让我很不满意。	Your performance has left me very unsatisfied.
對不起，讓您失望_{shīwàng}了。	對不起，让您失望了。	I'm sorry I let you down.

Both 讓/害 share the meaning of "to make (someone to do something)," but 害 'to harm' always indicates an unfavorable consequence, whereas 讓 could have a neutral or even favorable result. So, one will not say "他害得我很高興."

4. Expressing a momentary action

V 了 (person) 一O	…le…yī…	to do sth. quickly
		說了一聲、嚇了一跳
		打了一拳、踢了一腳
		看了一眼、吃/喝了一口

其中一個孩子**看了**我**一眼**就問其他人：「你想他看得見嗎？」

1.

他喜歡這道菜嗎？	他喜欢这道菜吗？	Does he like this dish?
他才吃了一口就一直喝水，一定是嫌太鹹了。	他才吃了一口就一直喝水，一定是嫌太咸了。	He had just one bite and then kept drinking water. He certainly must think this dish is too salty.

2.

你為什麼踢 _{tī} 了他一腳 _{jiǎo}？	你为什么踢了他一脚？	Why did you kick him?

我是要讓他知道，上課的時候不要睡覺。	我是要让他知道，上课的时候不要睡觉。	I just wanted to let him know that he shouldn't doze off in class.

3.

他剛學會走路。	他刚学会走路。	He just learned to walk.
怪不得才走了一步就跌倒diēdǎo了。	怪不得才走了一步就跌倒了。	No wonder he stumbled after just one step.

This pattern expresses a momentary action. The list of Chinese verbs and cognate objects is limited. Remember that the recipient of the action, if present, occurs between verbs and objects, e.g., 我看了他一眼，就知道他不是好人.

5. Expressing a comparison

拿A跟B比較, A/B...	Ná...gēn...bǐjiào, ...	Taking A to compare with B, A/B...
和B比(起來), A...	Hé...bǐ(qǐlái), ...	Comparing to B, A...

我到台北已經三天了。**拿**台北**和**北京**比較**……

1.

中國父母很重視成績。	中国父母很重视成绩。	Chinese parents take grades very seriously.
是啊！我父母總是拿我的成績跟我同學的比較。	是啊！我父母总是拿我的成绩跟我同学的比较。	That's right. My parents always compare my grades with those of my classmates.

2.

和紐約 Niǔyuē 比，台北的交通怎麼樣？	和纽约比，台北的交通怎么样？	Compared to New York, how is Taipei's traffic?
台北的交通問題更嚴重。	台北的交通问题更严重。	The traffic problem in Taipei is more serious.

3.

中國文化和美國文化有什麼不同？	中国文化和美国文化有什么不同？	What are the differences between Chinese and American culture?
拿中國文化和美國	拿中国文化和美国	Comparing Chinese and American culture, Chinese

文化比較，中國人重視家族 jiāzú 'clan, family'，美國人更重視個人 gèrén 。	文化比较，中国人重视家族，美国人更重视个人。	value families and Americans place more emphasis on the individual.

This pattern expresses a comparison, which often contains 更 or Adj 多了 in its statement illustrating the difference. Compare this with 拿⋯來說 (L15, G3).

6. Expressing a mandated alternative

S 得⋯才行	děi…cáixíng	S will have to do sth., then it will be O.K.

這兒的路很複雜，找房子不容易，我**得**馬上去買張地圖**才行**。

1.	下星期一就要考試了。	下星期一就要考试了。	We are going to have a test next Monday.
	你得提前準備才行。	你得提前准备才行。	You'll have to prepare for it ahead of time.
2.	買電腦真貴。	买电脑真贵。	Buying a computer costs a lot.
	你得每天打工賺錢才行。	你得每天打工赚钱才行。	Every day you have to work part-time and earn the money.
3.	怎樣才能把中文學好？	怎样才能把中文学好？	What's the key to learning Chinese well?
	你得多聽、多讀、多說、多寫才行。	你得多听、多读、多说、多写才行。	You have to do a lot of listening, reading, speaking and writing.

得⋯才行 literally means "only then will it be all right." 才行 always comes at the end of a sentence. Compare this with 非⋯不可 (L8, G2).

文化點滴 Culture Notes

1. **Transportation system**: Although more and more people in China and Taiwan desire cars as a symbol of wealth and status, there is very little space to park them or even to drive around. Thus, public transportation such as trains, subways, and buses are still the choice of most people. In mainland China, bicycles are also very popular. Hundreds of them lining an intersection during rush hour can be a real spectacle for first-time visitors. In Taiwan, instead of bicycles, motorcycles are filling the streets. Foreigners are often amazed at the heavy traffic in Taipei. Yet, Chinese drivers and pedestrians seem to have little trouble finding their way through the chaos.

2. **Trains**: In general, it is quite convenient to take trains in China. But one needs to be sure that one buys the tickets ahead of time. There are four kinds of tickets: hard seat 硬座 yìngzuò, soft seat 軟座 ruǎnzuò, hard sleep 硬臥 yìngwò, and soft sleep 軟臥 ruǎnwò.

3. **Hangzhou**: Hangzhou 杭州, the capital of Zhejiang Province 浙江省, is located along the banks of the Qiantang River 錢塘江 and at the southern end of the Beijing-Hangzhou Grand Canal 大運河 Dàyùnhé. One of the seven capitals of ancient China, Hangzhou was praised by Marco Polo in the 13th century as the most beautiful city in the world. A Chinese saying goes like this: "Above there is heaven, below there is Suzhou and Hangzhou" 上有天堂、下有蘇杭 Shàng yǒu tiāntáng, xià yǒu sūháng. Although there are many places to visit in Hangzhou, the place most famous for its beautiful scenery is the West Lake 西湖 Xīhú, which covers an area of about 60 square kilometers, and has ten scenic spots (e.g., the Su Causeway 蘇堤 Sūtí, Bai Causeway 白堤 Báití, Temple of the Soul's Retreat 靈隱寺 Língyǐnsì).

歌兒 Songs

看野鴨
Seeing the Wild Ducks

Moderato

詞：劉雅詩　　曲：馬定一

1. 剛 開 學，才 過 了　　寒 假，朋 友 找 我　一塊 看 野 鴨。
   Gāng kāixué, cái guòle　hánjià,　péngyǒu zhǎo wǒ　yíkuài kàn yěyā.
   School had just started, right after winter break.　My friend asked me to go see wild ducks with him.

2. 到 湖 邊，卻 不 見　　野 鴨，只 有垃圾　還有烤 肉 架。
   Dào húbiān, què bújiàn　yě yā,　zhǐyǒu lājī　háiyǒu kǎoròu jià.
   We arrived at the lakeside and saw no wild ducks.　There were only trash and barbecue racks.

1. 坐上車子我 們馬上　出　發。　　忘 記帶地 圖，方向感又很差。路 上
   Zuòshàng chēzi wǒmen mǎshàng chū fā.　Wàngjì dài dìtú,　fāngxiànggǎn yòu hěn chā. Lùshàng
   Getting into the car, we set off right away.　We forgot to bring a map, and had poor sense of direction.

2. 環境髒亂 害 我好想　回　家。　　朋 友很吃 驚，他把外套脫下。我 們
   Huánjìng zāngluàn hài wǒ hǎo xiǎng huíjiā.　Péngyǒu hěn chījīng,　tā bǎ wàitào tuōxià.　Wǒmen
   The environment was so dirty and messy I wanted to go home. My friend was so surprised; he took off his coat.

1. 交通亂開 著 車好可 怕，　到 了山裏 條 條 道 路 很 複 雜。
   jiāotōng luàn, kāizhe chē hǎo kěpà,　dàole shānlǐ, tiáotiáo dàolù hěn fù zá.
   The traffic on the road was chaotic and scary.　On the mountain, the trails were complicated.

2. 一塊兒 把　垃圾帶回家，　保 護 環 境 的 確 需 要 靠 大 家。
   yíkuàir bǎ　lājī dài huíjiā,　bǎohù huánjìng díquè xūyào kào dā jiā.
   Together we brought back the trash.　Protecting the environment indeed takes everyone's support.

Theme Animals and Pets

Communicative Objectives
- Looking for an apartment
- Dining at a night market
- Talking about food
- Going to the zoo

Grammar Focus
- （S）只有…，（S）才…
- 到…為止；一直V到…（為止）
- 把A V成/做B
- A也好，B也好，（O）S都V
- 所有（…）的O S都V
- N₁佔N₂的A分之B

Focus on Characters
- 態度佔責、綠貓豬腳、省源燈具、洲界冬止、決概絕種

誰來保護我？

生詞 Vocabulary

Study the following words for their pronunciation and meaning. When an area is shaded, guess at the meaning of the word based on its constituent characters and then fill in the blank. Read the usage of words and related terms (antonyms, synonyms, compounds sharing the constituent characters, etc.) and try to answer the sample questions in Chinese. Note that proper nouns and incidental terms are not numbered.

◎By Order of Appearance

1.	家具	jiājù	N	Furniture [home-tool]

買/賣/帶家具；一套家具　　=傢具

你家裏有哪些家具？

你家里有哪些家具？

2.	日用品	rìyòngpǐn	N	articles for daily use [daily-use-product]
3.	省	shěng	N/V	province, to save/economize

事
電，事，時间，力，錢钱

省油/電/水/錢/事/力/時間

你覺得什麼車最省油？

你觉得什么车最省油？

4.	快餐	kuàicān	N	fast food [fast-food]

哪些快餐店最受孩子的歡迎？

哪些快餐店最受孩子的欢迎？

5.	歐洲 欧洲	Ōuzhōu	N	Europe [Europe-continent]

→　亞洲、非洲、美洲、澳洲

6.	夜市	yèshì	N	night market [night-market]
7.	擠滿 挤满	jǐmǎn	RV	to be filled to overflowing [squeeze-full]

擠/坐/站滿了人

什麼時候商場裏會擠滿了人？

什么时候商场里会挤满了人？

8.	大概	dàgài	Adv/ Adj	probably, approximate [big-roughly]

你計劃大概什麼時候回家？

你计划大概什么时候回家？

9.	只有	zhǐyǒu	Conj/ Adv	only, alone [only-have]
	紐約 纽约	Niǔyuē	N	New York [pivot-pact]

| 10. | 為止
为止 | wéizhǐ | IE | up to, till
到……為止 | [become-stop] |
| 11. | 宵夜 | xiāoyè | N | midnight snack | [take-night] |

你平常吃宵夜嗎？幾點吃？

你平常吃宵夜吗？几点吃？

| 12. | 散步 | sànbù | VO | to take a walk | [break up-step] |

現在公園裏散步的人多嗎？

现在公园里散步的人多吗？

| 13. | 綠豆湯
绿豆汤 | lǜdòutāng | N | mung bean soup | [green-bean-soup] |
| 14. | 上火 | shànghuǒ | VO | to suffer excessive internal heat | [up-fire] |

中國人說吃什麼東西容易上火？

中国人说吃什么东西容易上火？

| 15. | 例如 | lìrú | Conj | for instance, such as | [example-like] |

上火的人有很多問題，例如什麼？

上火的人有很多问题，例如什么？

	雞爪 鸡爪	jīzhuǎ	N	chicken claw	[chicken-claw]
16.	豬腳 猪脚	zhūjiǎo	N	pig's feet <PRC>豬手、豬蹄兒	[pig-foot]
	牛筋	niújīn	N	beef tendons	[beef-sinew]
17.	冬天	dōngtiān	N	winter	[winter-season]

冬天到/來了　　→春天、夏天、秋天qiūtiān

這個地方冬天常下雪嗎？

这个地方冬天常下雪吗？

| 18. | 人們
人们 | rénmen | N | People, the public | [person-plural] |

現在人們喜歡開什麼樣的車？

现在人们喜欢开什么样的车？

Characters with Many Strokes

餐 歐 擠 滿 概 宵 散 綠 豬

| 19. | 補品
补品 | bǔpǐn | N | tonic | [nourish-product] |

吃補品　　→日用品、商品 shāngpǐn

中國人覺得什麼東西很補？

中国人觉得什么东西很补？

| 20. | 殺
杀 | shā | V | to kill | |

e.g. 吃光了
ate all the food

非洲什麼動物快被人殺光了？

非洲什么动物快被人杀光了？

| 21. | 動物
动物 | dòngwù | N | animal | [move-thing] |

→動物園 dòngwùyuán 'zoo'

| 22. | 可憐
可怜 | kělián | Adj | pitiable, poor | [able-poor] |

azioawmzo

可憐的樣子；可憐他；東西少得可憐

你覺得什麼人很可憐？

你觉得什么人很可怜？

| 23. | 絕種
绝种 | juézhǒng | V | to become extinct | [cut off-species] |

什麼動物快要絕種了？

什么动物快要绝种了？

| 24. | 大熊貓
大熊猫 | dàxióng
māo | N | giant panda | [big-bear-cat] |

| 25. | 寵物
宠物 | chǒngwù | N | pet | [love-thing] |

to dote, love

你養過什麼寵物？

你养过什么宠物？

| 26. | 態度
态度 | tàidu | N | attitude, manner | [demeanor-extent] |

學習／工作／做事態度；態度好／差

我們班誰的學習態度很好？

我们班谁的学习态度很好？

| 27. | 過分
过分 | guòfèn | Adj/
Adv | excessive, over- | [exceed-one's rights] |

做法／想法／要求太過分；過分嚴格／重視

學校對外語的要求過分嗎？

学校对外语的要求过分吗？

| 28. | 兒女
儿女 | ér-nǚ | N | | [son-daughter] |

兒子、女兒、孩子

他們的兒女都長大了嗎？

他们的儿女都长大了吗？

29.	非洲	Fēizhōu	N	Africa	[Africa-continent]

30. 浪費 | làngfèi | V/ | to waste, extravagant | [unrestrained-expense]
浪费 | | Adj | 浪費水／能源／時間／錢

你覺得做什麼事很浪費時間？

你觉得做什么事很浪费时间？

31. 可怕 | kěpà | Adj | fearful, terrible | [able-fear]

事情／動物／樣子可怕

你覺得什麼很可怕？

你觉得什么很可怕？

32. 做法 | zuòfǎ | N | | [do-method]

這種好的做法　　→想法、看法、教法

你認為他對這件事的做法對嗎？

你认为他对这件事的做法对吗？

33. 所有 | suǒyǒu | Adj | all | [so-have]

所有的學生都喜歡誰？

所有的学生都喜欢谁？

34. 燈 | dēng | N | lamp
灯

開／關燈；把燈關上

出門的時候，請把燈關上。

出门的时候，请把灯关上。

35. 佔 | zhàn | V | to occupy
占

36. 世界 | shìjiè | N | world | [world-boundary]

世界上；全世界

你覺得世界上最好的地方在哪兒？

你觉得世界上最好的地方在哪儿？

37. 人口 | rénkǒu | N | population | [person-mouth]

現在哪個國家的人口最多？

现在哪个国家的人口最多？

Characters with Many Strokes

補　殺　憐　絕　種　熊　寵　態　費　燈

38.	分	fēn	N/ M/ V	fraction, one-tenth, percent, (of length/area/weight/ money/time/etc.), to divide	

分組zǔ討論；分三天看完

這個蛋糕可以分成幾份？

这个蛋糕可以分成几份？

39.	能源	néngyuán	N	energy	[energy-source]

浪費/節省能源

40.	合作	hézuò	V/N	to cooperate, cooperation	[join-do]

一塊/共同/互相合作

這個對話是你們合作寫的嗎？

这个对话是你们合作写的吗？

41.	解決 解决	jiějué	V	to solve, to settle	[untie-decide]

解決問題/困難

中國怎麼解決人口問題？

中国怎么解决人口问题？

42.	責任 责任	zérèn	N	duty, responsibility	[duty-appoint]

負……的責任；負責V

在你家誰負責洗碗？

在你家谁负责洗碗？

43.	倒	dào	V	to dump (rubbish), to pour (water, tea)	

Characters with Many Strokes

源 解 責

◎By Grammatical Categories

Nouns/Pronouns

冬天	dōngtiān	winter	人們	rénmen	people, the public
夜市	yèshì	night market	兒女	ér-nǚ	children
宵夜	xiāoyè	midnight snack	做法	zuòfǎ	way of doing/making sth.
家具	jiājù	furniture	態度	tàidu	attitude, manner
日用品	rìyòngpǐn	articles for daily use	責任	zérèn	duty, responsibility
補品	bǔpǐn	tonic	能源	néngyuán	energy
快餐	kuàicān	fast food	燈	dēng	lamp
豬腳	zhūjiǎo	pig's feet	世界	shìjiè	world
綠豆湯	lǜdòutāng	mung bean soup	歐洲	Ōuzhōu	Europe
動物	dòngwù	animal	非洲	Fēizhōu	Africa
寵物	chǒngwù	pet	省	shěng	province, to save
大熊貓	dàxióngmāo	giant panda	分	fēn	fraction, one-tenth, percent
人口	rénkǒu	population			

Verbs/Stative Verbs/Adjectives

佔	zhàn	to occupy	散步	sànbù	to take a walk
殺	shā	to kill	上火	shànghuǒ	to suffer excessive internal heat
倒	dào	to dump (rubbish), to pour (water, tea)	擠滿	jǐmǎn	to be filled to overflowing
解決	jiějué	to solve, to settle	可憐	kělián	pitiable, poor
合作	hézuò	to cooperate, cooperation	可怕	kěpà	fearful, terrible
絕種	juézhǒng	to become extinct	所有	suǒyǒu	all
浪費	làngfèi	to waste, extravagant	過分	guòfèn	excessive, over-

Adverbs and Others

| 大概 | dàgài | probably, approximate | 為止 | wéizhǐ | up to, till |
| 例如 | lìrú | for instance, such as | 只有 | zhǐyǒu | only, alone |

◎By Pinyin

Entries with * indicate lexical items used in Mini-Dialogues and of possible interest for supplemental study.

bīng*	冰	to ice, ice	làngfèi	浪费	to waste, extravagant
bǔpǐn	补品	tonic	lǎohǔ*	老虎	tiger
chángjǐnglù*	长颈鹿	giraffe	lìrú	例如	for instance, such as
chǒngwù	宠物	pet	lǜdòutāng	绿豆汤	mung bean soup
chòu*	臭	smelly, foul	ménpiào*	门票	admission ticket
dàgài	大概	probably, approximate	néngyuán	能源	energy
dào	倒	to dump (rubbish), to pour (water, tea)	Ōuzhōu	欧洲	Europe
dàrén*	大人	adults	rénkǒu	人口	population
dàxiàng*	大象	elephant	rénmen	人们	people, the public
dàxióngmāo	大熊猫	giant panda	rénshān-rénhǎi*	人山人海	huge crowds of people, a sea of people
dēng	灯	lamp	rìyòngpǐn	日用品	articles for daily use
dōngtiān	冬天	winter	sànbù	散步	to take a walk
dòngwù	动物	animal	shā	杀	to kill
dòngwùyuán*	动物园	zoo	shànghuǒ	上火	to suffer excessive internal heat
ér-nǚ	儿女	children	shěng	省	province, to save
fángzū*	房租	rent	shìjiè	世界	world
Fēizhōu	非洲	Africa	shīzi*	狮子	lion
fēn	分	fraction, one-tenth, percent	suǒyǒu	所有	all
fēnglí*	凤梨	pineapple	tàidu	态度	attitude, manner
guòfèn	过分	excessive, over-	wéizhǐ	为止	up to, till
hézuò	合作	to cooperate, cooperation	xiāoyè	宵夜	midnight snack
jiājù	家具	furniture	yèshì	夜市	night market
jiějué	解决	to solve, to settle	zérèn	责任	duty, responsibility
jǐmǎn	挤满	to be filled to overflowing	zhàn	占	to occupy
juézhǒng	绝种	to become extinct	zhǐyǒu	只有	only, alone
kělián	可怜	pitiable, poor	zhūjiǎo	猪脚	pig's feet
kěpà	可怕	fearful, terrible	zuòfǎ	做法	way of doing/ making sth.
kuàicān	快餐	fast food			

課文 Text

Use the following questions to guide your reading of the text.

1. 小高對自己在台北住的條件滿意嗎？

2. 小高受不了中國人的什麼習慣？為什麼？

3. 在小李看來，美國人對食物、能源的用法有什麼問題？

 小李：

我在學校附近找到了一間
公寓，雖然不住宿舍，但是很
方便，出門沒多遠就可以買到
家具、日用品什麼的。要是不
想做飯也沒關係，街上到處都
有飯館。不管是大陸各省的菜
還是美國快餐、歐洲點心，都
吃得到。附近還有一個有名的
夜市，整條街每天晚上都擠滿了人，吃的吃、喝的喝，熱鬧極了。美
國大概[1]**只有**紐約的人**才**有機會過這種「夜生活」吧！

　　[2]**到目前為止**，我只當了兩週的「台北人」，但也慢慢地習慣吃
宵夜了，我特別喜歡出去散步，到夜市喝綠豆湯，聽說那對上火的人
特別好。不過有一些中國人吃的東西，我實在受不了，例如雞爪、豬
腳、牛筋、魚頭湯等。聽說狗肉到了冬天的時候，也可能變成人們的
補品，你不覺得那些被殺的動物很可憐嗎？沒有人聽到那些動物說：
「誰來保護我」嗎？

　　　　　　　　　　　　　　　　　　　　　　　　　　　德中

小高：

當然我不反對我們應該保護那些快要絕種的動物，像大熊貓等。不過很多美國人對寵物的態度有時候也有點兒過分，他們幾乎[3]**把**貓、狗**當成**自己的兒女一樣。美國的貓、狗吃的可能比非洲的很多孩子還好、還多，你覺得有道理嗎？傳統的中國人總是覺得，能吃的東西就不要浪費，所以魚頭[4]**也好**、豬腳**也好**，什麼部分**都**能利用。聽起來雖然可怕，卻是很經濟的做法。我覺得美國人不但浪費食物，而且也不會省電、省水，例如很多商店、學校，

晚上就算一個人都沒有的時候，也**把**[5]**所有的**燈**都**開著。美國人雖然只[6]**佔**世界人口的二十五**分之**一，可是他們用了全世界七分之一的能源呢！在我看來，世界各國應該共同合作解決各種問題，環保應該是我們每個人的責任。我現在就得去

「環保」：整理房間、洗碗、倒垃圾了，再見！

李明

课文 Text

Use the following questions to guide your reading of the text.

1. 小高对自己在台北住的条件满意吗？

2. 小高受不了中国人的什么习惯？为什么？

3. 在小李看来，美国人对食物、能源的用法有什么问题？

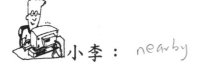 小李：

　　我在学校附近找到了一间公寓，虽然不住宿舍，但是很方便，出门没多远就可以买到家具、日用品什么的。要是不想做饭也没关系，街上到处都有饭馆。不管是大陆各省的菜还是美国快餐、欧洲点心，都吃得到。附近还有一个有名的夜市，整条街每天晚上都挤满了人，吃的吃、喝的喝，热闹极了。美国大概[1]只有纽约的人才有机会过这种"夜生活"吧！

　　[2]到目前为止，我只当了两周的"台北人"，但也慢慢地习惯吃宵夜了，我特别喜欢出去散步，到夜市喝绿豆汤，听说那对上火的人特别好。不过有一些中国人吃的东西，我实在受不了，例如鸡爪、猪脚、

牛筋、鱼头汤等。听说狗肉到了冬天的时候，也可能变成人们的补品，你不觉得那些被杀的动物很可怜吗？没有人听到那些动物说："谁来保护我"吗？

德中

小高：

当然我不反对我们应该保护那些快要绝种的动物，象大熊猫等。不过很多美国人对宠物的态度有时候也有点儿过分，他们几乎[3]**把**猫、狗**当成**自己的儿女一样。美国的猫、狗吃的可能比非洲的很多孩子还好、还多，你觉得有道理吗？传统的中国人总是觉得，能吃的东西就不要浪费，所以鱼头[4]**也好**、猪脚**也好**，什么部分**都**能利用。听起来虽然可怕，却是很经济的做法。我觉得美国人不但浪费食物，而且也不会省电、省水，例如很多商店、学校，晚上就算一个人都没有的时候，也把[5]**所有的**灯都开着。美国人虽然只[6]**占**世界人口的二十五分之一，可是他们用了全世界七分之一的能源呢！在我看来，世界各国应该共同合作解决各种

问题，环保应该是我们每个人的责任。我现在就得去"环保"：整理房间、洗碗、倒垃圾了，再见！

李明

小對話 Mini-Dialogues

Read the supplementary dialogues for a better understanding of the text. See if you can memorize one and perform it in class.

(1) Looking for an apartment

Gao:　請問，你們這兒還有沒有空房？

A:　現在沒有，不過下個星期有個房客會搬走。

Gao:　太好了！這兒一個月房租 fángzū 多少？

A:　六千五，包水電，電話費自己付。

Gao:　有沒有家具啊？

A:　床、桌、椅都有，需要別的東西得自己買。前面就有個家具行 jiājùháng。

Gao:　我能不能先付押金 yājīn？

A:　好，一千塊。

Gao:　請问，你们这儿还有没有空房？

A:　现在没有，不过下个星期有个房客会搬走。

Gao:　太好了！这儿一个月房租多少？

A:　六千五，包水电，电话费自己付。

Gao:　有没有家具啊？

A:　床、桌、椅都有，需要别的东西得自己买。前面就有个家具行。

Gao:　我能不能先付押金？

A:　好，一千块。

Gao:　Excuse me, do you still have a room available?

A:　Not now. But there will be a tenant moving out next week.

Gao:　That's great! How much is the rent here per month?

A:　Six thousand five hundred *kuai,* including water and electricity. You have to pay the phone bill yourself.

Gao:　Is the room furnished?

A:　There is a bed, desk and chair. If you need anything else, you'll have to buy it yourself. There is a furniture store a few steps away.

Gao:　Can I pay you to hold the room for me?

A:　Fine, one thousand *kuai.*

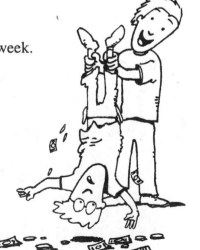

(2) Dining at a night market

Gao: 這兒擠得人山人海 rénshān-rénhǎi，大家在做什麼？

　　　这儿挤得人山人海，大家在做什么？

A: 吃、喝、玩、樂啊！你想試試牛筋麵嗎？

　　　吃、喝、玩、乐啊！你想试试牛筋面吗？

Gao: 不要，謝謝！

　　　不要，谢谢！

A: 雞爪怎麼樣？鴨舌 yāshé 也不錯，還是來碗「豬腳麵線」miànxiàn？

　　　鸡爪怎么样？鸭舌也不错，还是来碗"猪脚面线"？

Gao: 這些東西好吃嗎？看起來真可怕！我吃素 sù 的好了。

　　　这些东西好吃吗？看起来真可怕！我吃素的好了。

A: 那就來個「臭 chòu 豆腐」吧！

　　　那就来个"臭豆腐"吧！

Gao: 臭死了！這是什麼東西啊？

　　　臭死了！这是什么东西啊？

Gao: It's so crowded here. What is everyone doing?

A: They eat, drink, and are merry. Do you want to try beef tendon noodles?

Gao: No, thanks.

A: How about a chicken claw? The tongue of duck is also great. Or do you want a bowl of "fine noodles with pig's feet"?

Gao: Do these taste good? They look awful. Let me have vegetarian dishes.

A: Then have a "stinky beancurd."

Gao: This smells awful. What is it?

(3) Talking about food

A: 你看你臉上長了痘子 dòuzi，八成是上火了。

　　　你看你脸上长了痘子，八成是上火了。

Gao: 這幾天我睡得不太好，早上起來還流鼻血 liúbíxiě 呢！

　　　这几天我睡得不太好，早上起来还流鼻血 呢！

A:　　吃點兒涼的東西就好了，像西　　　　吃点儿凉的东西就好了，象西
　　　瓜、綠豆湯什麼的。　　　　　　　　瓜、绿豆汤什么的。

Gao:　我喜歡吃這兒的鳳梨 fēnglí，又甜　　我喜欢吃这儿的凤梨，又甜又
　　　又香。　　　　　　　　　　　　　　香。

A:　　鳳梨太熱，吃多了容易上火。　　　　凤梨太热，吃多了容易上火。

Gao:　真奇怪，我吃的鳳梨是冰 bīng 過　　真奇怪，我吃的凤梨是冰过
　　　的，怎麼會「熱」呢？　　　　　　　的，怎么会"热"呢？

A:　　聽我的，沒錯。　　　　　　　　　　听我的，没错。

A:　　See, you have pimples on your face. You're probably suffering from excessive internal
　　　heat.

Gao: I haven't slept very well these past few days, and my nose bleeds in the morning.

A:　　You will get better if you have something cool, like watermelon or mung bean soup.

Gao: I like the pineapples here. They taste sweet and smell good.

A:　　Pineapples are too hot. If you have too many of them, you will have more internal heat.

Gao: How strange—the pineapples that I had were all iced. How could they be "hot"?

A:　　Just listen to me.

(4) Going to the zoo

Gao:　今天動物園 dòngwùyuán 開嗎？　　　今天动物园开吗？

A:　　開啊！　　　　　　　　　　　　　　开啊！

Gao:　門票 ménpiào 一張多少錢？　　　　　门票一张多少钱？

A:　　大人 dàrén 五十，小孩三十。　　　　大人五十，小孩三十。

Gao:　買兩張大人的票。(進去)看！　　　　买两张大人的票。(进去)看！
　　　這兒有老虎 lǎohǔ、獅子 shīzi、大　　　这儿有老虎、狮子、大象、长
　　　象 dàxiàng、長頸鹿 chángjǐnglù。什　　　颈鹿。什么都有，就是没有大
　　　麼都有，就是沒有大熊貓。　　　　　熊猫。

B: 你是來這兒看動物的，還是讓 你是来这儿看动物的，还是让
    動物看你啊？快走吧！ 动物看你啊？快走吧！

Gao: Is the zoo open today?

A: Yes.

Gao: How much is a ticket?

A: Fifty Taiwanese dollars for
    adults and thirty for children.

Gao: I want to buy a ticket for two
      adults. (They go in) Look,
      there are tigers, lions,
      elephants, and giraffes. They
      have every kind of animal, except for the giant panda.

B: Are you here to see the animals or let the animals see you? Hurry up.

小故事 Stories

Read the following tale for your own enjoyment and for your understanding of the highlighted expression that is relevant to the theme of the chapter.

 畫蛇添足 huà shé tiān zú

❀ 　她穿皮衣，你說好看就行了，還告訴她她這麼做對不起那些快絕種的動物，這不是畫蛇添足嗎？

　　從前有幾個人在一起喝酒，酒只夠一個人喝，到底給誰喝呢？大家都沒辦法決定，有一個人建議：「我們每個人都在地上畫一條蛇，誰先畫完，誰就喝這壺酒。」

蛇	shé	snake
添	tiān	to add
足	zú	leg, foot
地上	dìshàng	on the floor
壺	hú	pot, kettle
加上	jiāshàng	to add
搶	qiǎng	to grab, to snatch

　　有一個人很快就畫好了，他看到別人都還沒畫完，就說：「你們畫得多慢啊！你們看我還能給蛇加上幾隻腳。」當他這麼做的時候，另外一個人已經把蛇畫完了，就把那壺酒搶了過去。他說：「蛇是沒有腳的，你現在給蛇畫了腳，就不是蛇了。所以第一個畫完的人是我，不是你啊！」

✎ 畫蛇添足的意思是＿＿＿＿＿＿＿＿＿＿＿＿＿＿＿＿＿＿＿

画蛇添足 huà shé tiān zú

✿   她穿皮衣，你说好看就行了，还告诉她她这么做对不起那些快
    绝种的动物，这不是画蛇添足吗？

从前有几个人在一起喝酒，酒只够
一个人喝，到底给谁喝呢？大家都没办法
决定，有一个人建议："我们每个人都在
地上画一条蛇，谁先画完，谁就喝这壶
酒。"

蛇	shé	snake
添	tiān	to add
足	zú	leg, foot
地上	dìshàng	on the floor
壶	hú	pot, kettle
加上	jiāshàng	to add
抢	qiǎng	to grab, to snatch

有一个人很快就画好了，他看到别人都还没画完，就说："你
们画得多慢啊！你们看我还能给蛇加上几只脚。"当他这么做的时
候，另外一个人已经把蛇画完了，就把那壶酒抢
了过去。他说："蛇
是没有脚的，你现
在给蛇画了脚，就
不是蛇了。所以第
一个画完的人是
我，不是你啊！"

漢字 Characters

Study the following selected characters for further enrichment of your writing and vocabulary.

心 xīn 'heart' +
能 néng/tái
phonetic

| 態度 | tàidù | manner, attitude |

A: 那個學生怎麼樣？

B: 很聰明，可是態度不太好。

Compare: 熊 xióng

态

tài 14
appearance, attitude

广 guǎng
'house' + 廿 niàn
'twenty' + 又
yòu 'hand'—to
have in one's
hand all the
inhabitants of the
house

長度	chángdù*	length
高度	gāodù*	altitude, height
溫度	wēndù*	temperature

A: 那張桌子用起來怎麼樣？

B: 長度正好，可是高度不夠。

Compare: 渡 dù

度

dù 9
degree, extent

亻 rén 'person' +
卜 bǔ 'cracks on
a tortoise shell' +
口 kǒu 'mouth'
—to interpret
prognostics

| 佔便宜 | zhàn piányi* | to profit at another's expense, advantageous |

A: 他個子 gèzi 'build' 高，打籃球佔便宜。

B: 高個兒打球不一定打得好。

Compare: 點 diǎn 站 zhàn 店 diàn 貼 tiē

占

zhàn 7
to occupy, to constitute

貝 bèi 'money'
+ 主 cì
phonetic

| 責任 | zérèn | duty, responsibility |
| 責任感 | zérèngǎn* | sense of responsibility |

A: 你覺得她是個有責任感的人嗎？

B: 對，她非常負 fù 責任。

Compare: 績 jī

责

zé 11
duty, to demand

糸 sī 'silk' + 录
lù phonetic

绿

lǜ
green
14

綠豆湯	lǜdòutāng	mung bean soup
綠色	lǜsè*	green color
綠茶	lǜchá*	green tea
紅綠燈	hónglǜdēng	traffic light

A: 你喝過綠豆湯嗎？

B: 沒有，我只喝過中國的綠茶。

豸 zhì 'beast' +
苗 miáo
phonetic

猫

māo 15
cat

| 大熊貓 | dàxióngmāo | giant panda |

A: 大熊貓為什麼快絕種了？

B: 他們竹子吃得多，孩子生得少嘛。

豕 shǐ 'pig' +
者 zhě phonetic

猪

zhū 15
pig, hog, swine

豬腳	zhūjiǎo	pig's feet
豬肉	zhūròu*	pork
豬排	zhūpái*	pork chop

A: 我做豬排或豬腳給你吃，怎麼樣？

B: 對不起，我不吃豬肉。

Compare: 者 zhě

月 ròu 'flesh' +
卻 què
phonetic

脚

jiǎo 13
foot, base

| 腳跟 | jiǎogēn* | heel |
| 腳底 | jiǎodǐ* | sole (of feet) |

A: 你怎麼走不動了？

B: 穿的是新鞋，腳跟、腳底都很痛。

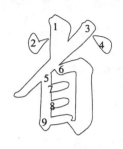

少 shǎo 'little'
+ 目 mù
'eye'—to watch
carefully, to use
little, to
economize

省油	shěngyóu*	to save gas
省錢	shěngqián*	to save money
省事	shěngshì*	to save trouble

A: 這種車很省油。

B: 對啊！每年可以省不少錢呢！

省

shěng 9
to save, to omit,
province

氵 shuǐ 'water'
+ 原 yuán
'original': a 泉
spring coming
out of a 厂
cliff.

| 能源 | néngyuán | energy sources |
| 資源 | zīyuán* | natural resources |

A: 我們現在有能源危機嗎？

B: 就算沒有，也不應該浪費自然資源。

源

yuán 13
source, origin

火 huǒ 'fire' +
登 dēng
phonetic

開燈	kāi dēng	to turn on the light
關燈	guān dēng	to turn off the light
電燈	diàndēng*	electric lamp/light
燈泡	dēngpào*	light bulb

A: 你為什麼不開燈？

B: 燈泡壞了，開了也不亮 liàng 'bright'。

灯

Compare: 登 dēng

dēng 16
lamp, lantern, light

廾 Two hands
holding 貝 bèi
'cowrie'
money—to
possess

家具	jiājù	furniture
文具	wénjù*	stationery
玩具	wánjù*	toy, plaything

A: 你們家的家具多嗎？

B: 家具不多，玩具倒不少。

具

Compare: 俱 jù

jù 8
utensil, tool, to possess

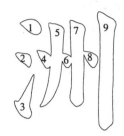

氵 shuǐ 'water' + 州 zhōu 'prefecture'

洲

zhōu 9
continent, shoal

歐洲	Ōuzhōu	Europe
非洲	Fēizhōu	Africa
亞洲	Yàzhōu*	Asia
美洲	Měizhōu*	(North and South) America
澳洲	Àozhōu*	Australia

A: 你去過世界各地嗎？
B: 對！我歐洲、亞洲、非洲都去過了。

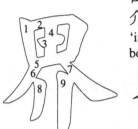

田 tián 'field' + 介 jiè 'introduce, boundary'

界

jiè 9
boundary, scope, circles

世界	shìjiè	world
國界	guójiè*	national boundaries
教育界	jiàoyùjiè*	educational circles

A: 現在的世界越變越小了。
B: 對啊！網上溝通根本沒有國界。

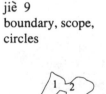

夂 a pair of legs with the heels indicated: 'walk slowly' + 冫 bīng 'ice'—walk slowly to avoid slipping on the ice

冬

dōng 5
winter

冬天	dōngtiān	winter
冬季	dōngjì*	winter
冬衣	dōngyī*	winter clothes
過冬	guòdōng*	to pass winter

A: 冬天到了，你的冬衣準備好了嗎？
B: 我可不想在這兒過冬。

Compare: 終 zhōng 疼 téng

Picture of a left footprint, the toes were at the top, the heel at the bottom

止

zhǐ 4
to stop, to stay, until, merely

為止	wéizhǐ	up to, till
止渴	zhǐkě*	to quench thirst
止痛	zhǐtòng*	to relieve pain

A: 汽水止渴嗎？
B: 越喝越渴，還不如喝開水。

Compare: 走 zǒu 足 zú 步 bù 此 cǐ

氵 shuǐ 'water' +
夬 guài 'break through'—rupture, break off, decide, certainly

解決   jiějué   to solve
決定   juédìng   to decide, decision

A: 你怎麼解決這個問題？
B: 我決定和老師談一談。

Compare: 快 kuài

決

jué 7
to decide, definitely

木 mù 'wood' +
既 jì phonetic

大概   dàgài   probably, approximate
概念   gàiniàn*   concept, notion, idea

A: 他大概沒去過中國。
B: 對，他對中國人的生活習慣一點兒
　　概念也沒有。

概

Compare: 既 jì 即 jí

gài 13
general, approximate

糸 sī 'silk' +
刀 dāo 'knife' +
巴/卩 jié phonetic —to cut a thread

絕種   juézhǒng   to become extinct
絕對   juéduì*   absolutely, definitely
絕望   juéwàng*   to give up all hope

A: 我想她今天絕對不會來了。
B: 別絕望，再給她打個電話。

绝

jué 12
to cut off, finished, most

禾 hé 'grain' +
重 zhòng phonetic

各種   gèzhǒng*   various kinds
種子   zhǒngzi*   seed

A: 那家店賣什麼東西？
B: 各種東西都賣，連白菜種子都有！

种

zhǒng, zhòng 14
species, seed, kind, to plant

語法和用法 Grammar and Usage

Pay attention to the function of the structure and then study the example sentences.

1. Expressing a requisite condition

(S) 只有···，(S) 才···	zhǐyǒu...cái...	only (in a single sentence)
只有 S₁ ···，S₂ 才···		only if (in a compound sentence)

美國大概**只有**紐約的人**才**有機會過這種「夜生活」吧！

1. 這兒只有冬天才下雪嗎？

   这儿只有冬天才下雪吗？

   Does it snow here only in the winter?

   不，有時候秋天 qiūtiān 和春天 chūntiān 也下雪。

   不，有时候秋天和春天也下雪。

   No. Sometimes it snows both in fall and spring.

2. 只有在中國才看得到大熊貓嗎？

   只有在中国才看得到大熊猫吗？

   Can one see giant pandas only in China?

   不，在美國的一些動物園也看得到。

   不，在美国的一些动物园也看得到。

   No. You can also see them in zoos in the U.S.

3. 怎樣才能把這些生詞記住？

   怎样才能把这些生词记住？

   How can I remember these words?

   只有每天練習寫漢字才能把它們記起來。

   只有每天练习写汉字才能把它们记起来。

   You can remember them only if you practice writing them every day.

The 只有 clause indicates a necessary condition for the circumstance stated in the second clause. If 只有···才 is used in a sentence with a single subject, the subject often precedes 只有. For example, one can say "我只有生病的時候，才吃補品" or "只有生病的時候，我才吃補品" but in a sentence with two subjects the subject must follow 只有. Compare this with 只要···就 (L4, G5) which indicates a sufficient condition.

(handwritten at top: hằng niên / năng báo / chào 每天)

2. Expressing a terminal degree

到…為止	dào…wéizhǐ	until, up to a point (of time)
一直 V 到…（為止）	yìzhí…dào…(wéizhǐ)	keep V-ing until…

到目前**為止**，我只當了兩週的「台北人」，但也慢慢地習慣吃宵夜了。

1. 到目前為止，你去過哪些國家？ | 到目前为止，你去过哪些国家？ | Up until now, which countries have you visited?

   我只去過加拿大。 | 我只去过加拿大。 | I have only been to Canada.

2. 到這個學期為止，你學過多久中文？ | 到这个学期为止，你学过多久中文？ | Up to this semester, how long have you been studying Chinese?

   到這個學期為止，我學過三個學期的中文，這學期是第四個學期。 | 到这个学期为止，我学过三个学期的中文，这学期是第四个学期。 | Up to this semester, I have studied Chinese for three semesters. This will be my fourth semester.

3. 我每天跑步得跑多長時間？ | 我每天跑步得跑多长时间？ *(handwritten: děi)* | How long do I need to run every day?

   你可以一直跑，跑到你累了為止。 | 你可以一直跑，跑到你累了为止。 *(handwritten: lèi)* | You can keep running until you are tired.

This pattern is used to express an action or activity up to a certain time or degree. The degree is often conveyed by verbs with extent complements, e.g., 吃不下、喝不了、走不動、拿不動.

3. Expressing a (mis)conception or transformation

把 A V 成／做 B	bǎ …V chéng/zuò…	to consider A as B to mistake A for B to make A into B

不過很多美國人**把**貓、狗**當成**家庭中的一份子，對寵物幾乎跟自己的兒女一樣。

1. 我把你當做好朋
友，才告訴你那件
事，你怎麼去告訴
了別人？

我把你当做好朋
友，才告诉你那件
事，你怎么去告诉
了别人？

I only told you that
because I thought you
were my friend. Why did
you go tell someone else?

對不起，我是不小
心說出來的！

对不起，我是不小
心说出来的！

Sorry. It just slipped out
of my mouth.

2. 我把你看成了美國
人，沒想到你是中
國人。

我把你看成了美国
人，没想到你是中
国人。

I thought you were an
American. It never
occurred to me that you
were Chinese.

我只是把頭髮染 rǎn
成了金色。

我只是把头发染成
了金色。

I just dyed my hair
blonde.

3. 你笑什麼？

你笑什么？

What are you laughing
at?

他把「中國的文字
有很長的歷史」，
說成「中國的蚊子
有很長的歷史」。

他把"中国的文字
有很长的历史"说
成"中国的蚊子有
很长的历史"。

Instead of "Chinese
language," he said
"Chinese mosquitoes have
a long history."

V 成/做, i.e. verbs with resultative complements, mean "to V into..., to V as" and thus
often indicate a (mis)conception or transformation. For example, "她喜歡那個男的，
但是他把她看成自己的妹妹." "你把我想成了什麼人，只會念書的書呆子嗎？"

4. Expressing indifference

A也好，B也好，O S都V A也好，B也好，S O都V	...yěhǎo... yěhǎo... dōu	No matter whether A or B, everything is fine with S.

能吃的東西就不要浪費，所以魚頭**也好**、豬腳**也好**，什麼部分**都**能
利用。

1. 他那麼窮，你還要
跟他結婚嗎？

他那么穷，你还要
跟他结婚吗？

He is so poor. Do you
still want to marry him?

他有錢也好，沒錢也好，我都要跟他結婚。	他有钱也好，没钱也好，我都要跟他结婚。	No matter whether or not he is rich, I will marry him.

2.

你想去哪兒旅行？	你想去哪儿旅行？	Where do you want to go on vacation?
歐洲也好、亞洲 Yàzhōu 也好，我都想去看看。	欧洲也好、亚洲也好，我都想去看看。	I would like to see either Europe or Asia.

3.

你想兒子好還是女兒好？	你想儿子好还是女儿好？	Do you think a son or a daughter is better?
兒子也好、女兒也好，只要孩子健康，我都喜歡。	儿子也好、女儿也好，只要孩子健康，我都喜欢。	It doesn't matter if it is a son or daughter; as long as they are healthy, I am happy.

This pattern indicates that the subject maintains his/her view of something despite the two aspects (A or B) highlighted. A and B the two aspects or examples of O, both either have to be nouns or verbs, e.g.,紅的也好，黑的也好，你穿什麼都好看. Also, the topic usually precedes the subject. Therefore, it is odd to say餃子也好，包子也好，我都喜歡吃中國菜. The subject and object in this pattern may sometimes be dropped.

5. Expressing total inclusiveness

所有(…)的S都VO	suǒyǒu (...) de...dōu...	All the S (pl.) do this.
所有(…)的O, (S)都V		S does all these O (pl.)

很多商店、學校晚上就算一個人都沒有的時候，也把**所有的**燈**都**開著。

1.

所有的女孩我都喜歡。	所有的女孩我都喜欢。	I like all of the girls.
可是所有的女孩都不喜歡你。	可是所有的女孩都不喜欢你。	But none of the girls like you.

2. 公園裏人真多！　公园里人真多！　What a lot of people in the park!

　　吃完飯，所有的人　吃完饭，所有的人　After dinner, they all
　　都來散步。　　　都来散步。　　　come here for a walk.

3. 你去過非洲嗎？　你去过非洲吗？　Have you been to Africa?

　　所有的非洲國家我　所有的非洲国家我　I've never been to any of
　　都沒去過。　　　都没去过。　　　the countries in Africa.

This pattern 所有…的 expresses inclusiveness so it always occurs with 都. Note that a modifier can go between 所有 and 的, e.g., 所有去過那兒的人都喜歡那個地方 and 所有那家店賣的東西我都喜歡.

6.　Expressing fractions and percentages

N₁佔 N₂的A分之B	…zhàn…de…fēnzhī…	N₁ makes up B/A of N₂

美國人雖然只**佔**世界人口的二十五**分之**一，可是他們用了全世界七分之一的能源呢！

1. 說漢語的人口是世　说汉语的人口是世　The population of
　　界第一。　　　　界第一。　　　　Mandarin speakers is the
　　　　　　　　　　　　　　　　　　largest in the world.

　　對，說漢語的人佔　对，说汉语的人占　Right. Mandarin
　　世界人口的五分之　世界人口的五分之　speakers comprise one
　　一。　　　　　　一。　　　　　　fifth of the world's
　　　　　　　　　　　　　　　　　　population.

2. 在美國，民主黨員　在美国，民主党员　In the U.S., are there more
　　Mínzhǔdǎngyuán 多還是　多还是共和党员　Democrats or
　　共和黨員 Gònghé　多？　　　　　Republicans?
　　dǎngyuán 多？

　　我想各佔二分之　我想各占二分之　I think each comprises
　　一，一樣多！　　一，一样多！　　fifty percent—it's about
　　　　　　　　　　　　　　　　　　the same.

3. 「比本來的價錢　"比本来的价钱便　How do you say "to mark
　　　　　　　　　　　　　　　　　　20% off of the original

jiàqián 'price' 便宜百分之二十」中文怎麼說?	宜百分之二十" 中文怎么说?	price" in Chinese?
中文說打八折。	中文说打八折。	In Chinese you say "dǎ bā zhé."

To express fractions in Chinese, one goes from denominator to numerator, just the opposite of English. Remember that one half is always 二分之一, never 兩分之一. When indicating hundredths (or percent), it is customary to drop 一 and just say 百分之 X.

文化點滴 Culture Notes

1. **Night market**: In Taiwan, nightfall does not conclude the day's activities. In areas of major cities such as 台北 Táiběi, 台中 Táizhōn, 台南,Táinán, 高雄 Gāoxióng, business begins at dusk. Around five or six o'clock in the evening night markets open with food stands catering to all kinds of eaters. Peddlers, lining the streets, spread their goods on the ground and yell about sales and discounts. People come for fun, for bargains, or for a taste of almost anything.

2. **Tonic food**: In addition to daily meals, many Chinese people take tonic food 補品 bǔpǐn, especially with the onset of winter or when recuperating from illness. It is believed that consuming invigorating tonic food (e.g., sea horses, sea slugs, sparrow's nests) can help treat deficiencies in the body's blood and balance the five types of vital energy, which are named after the Five Elements of metal 金 jīn, wood 木 mù, water 水 shuǐ, fire 火 huǒ and earth 土 tǔ. Thus, tonifying is a way of keeping healthy. Those who need tonic food most are the elderly, the weak, mothers, and children. Thus, it is common to see patients drinking perch soup to help recover after an operation; post-partum mothers eat sesame-oil chicken; and hard-working schoolchildren drink pig's brain soup to boost their mental powers.

3. **Hot/cold food**: In Chinese medicine, people's physical nature is classified as "hot"/yang 陽 or "cold"/yin 陰, and foods are similarly classified. For example, goat's meat is "hot," pork is "warm" and duck is "cool." Vegetables and fruit are largely determined by their color: Pale foods like turnips and Chinese cabbage are "cool," while colorful foods such as red beans, spinach, and pineapples are "hot." People who are "hot-natured" should eat "cool" foods and vice-versa, to achieve a proper balance. For example, those who have a "cold"/yin state of health, such as those who suffer anaemia should eat foods with a yang nature, such as liver, eggs and dates. Those who with yang symptons like high blood pressure should take food with a yin nature such as watermelon, duck or cucumber. If they fortify themselves further with "hot" foods such as dog or sheep meat, detrimental

results such as nosebleeds might occur. This is also why tonic foods are often taken in winter but not in summer because tonics are mostly "hot." Although for many young people today, it is hard to distinguish what's cold and what's hot, this belief in achieving harmony with one's body has long been an important part of Chinese popular culture.

4. **Animals**: There is a joke about the Chinese view of animals: When a Westerner catches a strange fish, he will try to classify it; when a Chinese does, he will try to figure out how to cook it. In the past, this was generally true. But, modern Chinese are more conservation-minded. The Chinese government has passed laws to protect most endangered species. One example of how animals have inspired the Chinese imagination are the twelve legendary animals—Rat 鼠 shǔ, ox 牛niú, tiger 虎 hǔ, rabbit 兔 tù, dragon 龍 lóng, snake 蛇 shé, horse 馬 mǎ, sheep 羊 yáng, monkey 猴 hóu, rooster 雞 jī, dog 狗 gǒu and pig 豬 zhū—of the Chinese zodiac adopted as the names of the well-known twelves year cycle. It is said that a race was held to decide the order of the animals in the yearly cycle. The ox was the fastest, but the rat hung on to its tail and reached the finish line before him. The legend also says that the cat was tricked by the rat and couldn't even break into the ranks of the first twelve. This is why cats and rats don't get along even today. In Chinese mythology, dragons, the rain spirits of China, were believed to be auspicious and most powerful. Thus, when the year of the dragon comes, the birth rate typically increases. This is because many couples try to have "children of the dragon" 龍子 lóngzǐ, 龍女 lóngnǚ.

歌兒 Songs

走，逛夜市去！
Let's Go to the Night Market!

Moderato   詞：劉雅詩　曲：馬定一

1. 來　到　了　台　灣，別忘記　到夜市　裏來。　這兒人們
   Lái dào le Táiwān bié wàngjì dào yèshì lǐ lái. Zhèr rénmen
   If you come to Taiwan, don't forget to go to the night market.　Here people

2. 宵　夜　先　吃　碗綠豆湯，讓胃口　大開。　再吃春捲
   Xiāo yè xiān chī wǎn lǜdòu tāng ràng wèikǒu dàkāi. Zài chī chūnjuǎn
   First have a bowl of mung bean soup to whet your appetite, then eat springrolls,

1. 帶　著兒女擠　得人山人海。　夜　市　裏　所　有商品
   dài zhe ér nǚ jǐ de rénshān rén hǎi. Yè shì lǐ suǒyǒu shāngpǐn
   bring their children and it's extremely crowded.　Inside the night market all the goods

2. 烤　鴨餃子還　有份燙青菜。　吃　飽　了　散　步逛街
   kǎo yā jiǎozi hái yǒu fèn tàng qīngcài. Chī bǎo le sànbù guàngjiē
   roast duck, dumplings, and boiled vegetables.　After you're full, take a walk,

1. 都　會　擺　出來，衣　服日用品　鞋子家具玩　具
   dōu huì bǎi chūlái, yī fú rìyòngpǐn xiézi jiājù wán jù
   are spread out.　Clothes, daily necessities, shoes, furniture, toys

2. 再　順　便　看看，常　常會聽見　有人　喊著「跳　樓
   zài shùn biàn kànkàn, chángcháng huì tīngjiàn yǒurén hǎnzhe "tiàolóu
   go window-shopping and then look around.　Often you'll hear people yell "Leaping from the

1. 滿　地　賣。喜　歡　這　頂　帽子　拿　起來試戴，
   mǎn dì mài. Xǐ huān zhè dǐng màozi ná qǐlái shì dài,
   are on sale.　If you like this hat, just pick it up and try it on.

2. 大　拍　賣。」他　們　不　是　跳樓　只　是　便　宜賣，
   dà pāi mài." Tā mén bú shì tiàolóu, zhǐ shì pián yí mài
   sale."　They are not jumping off of buildings, just selling things dirt cheap.

1. 看　中　手套圍巾　就　問問多　少錢可買。
   Kàn zhòng shǒutào wéijīn jiù wènwèn duō shǎo qián kě mǎi.
   If you like those gloves or scarves, just ask how much they are.

2. 看　他　那邊擠　滿　了人群大家　一　直　買。
   Kàn tā nàbiān jǐ mǎn le rénqún dàjiā yì zhí mǎi
   Look over there—he is surrounded by a throng that keeps on buying.

✎　我的問題：

✎　我的學習方法：

第十四課

Theme Interviews and Jobs

Communicative Objectives
- Having an interview
- Going to a "tutoring center"
- Tutoring a student
- Singing along with kids

Grammar Focus
- A…；至於 B 就…
- （O）S 再（怎麼）V 也 V 不…
- …於是／因此 S 就 V 了
- 既然…，（那）(S)就…吧
- A 引（不）起／不會引起 B 的 N
- S 可 Adj /VO/AuxV 了

Focus on Characters
- 翻譯閱讀、簡差畢證、推補缺碗、李司引訓、儘此乎羊

你們這兒缺人嗎？

生詞 Vocabulary

Study the following words for their pronunciation and meaning. When an area is shaded, guess at the meaning of the word based on its constituent characters and then fill in the blank. Read the usage of words and related terms (antonyms, synonyms, compounds sharing the constituent characters, etc.) and try to answer the sample questions in Chinese. Note that proper nouns and incidental terms are not numbered.

◎By Order of Appearance

1.	缺	quē	V	to be short of, to lack
				……缺人/課/水/錢
				你們這兒現在缺不缺人？
				你们这儿现在缺不缺人？
2.	公司	gōngsī	N	company [public affairs-manage]
3.	面談 面谈	miàntán	V	to discuss face to face [face-talk]
				跟……面談 vs. 面試 miànshì
				你今天要跟誰面談？
				你今天要跟谁面谈？
4.	拉關係 拉关系	lā guānxi	VO	to saddle up to [pull-connection]
5.	走後門 走后门	zǒu hòumén	VO	to secure sth. through pull or influence [walk-back-door]
6.	簡歷 简历	jiǎnlì	N	résumé, curriculum vitae [simple-experience]
7.	推薦信 推荐信	tuījiànxìn	N	recommendation letter [push-recommend-letter]
8.	證書 证书	zhèngshū	N	certificate, credentials [prove-document]
				申請這份工作要不要畢業證書？
				申请这份工作要不要毕业证书？
9.	翻譯 翻译	fānyì	N/V	translation, to translate, translator [translate-translate]
				你能不能把這個句子翻成英文？
				你能不能把这个句子翻成英文？
10.	日常	rìcháng	Adj	Day-to-Day [day-common]

補 bǔ to patch up   補衣服 patch clothes

日常對話/生活/習慣

你在這兒的日常生活有問題嗎？

你在这儿的日常生活有问题吗？

| 11. | 閱讀
阅读 | yuèdú | N | reading comprehension | [review-read] |

閱讀能力/水平

這一次的閱讀理解考得怎麼樣？

这一次的阅读理解考得怎么样？

| 12. | 能力 | nénglì | N | ability, capacity | [able-power] |

有……的能力；能力強   →聽力

你聽說讀寫哪方面的能力最強？

你听说读写哪方面的能力最强？

13.	強	qiáng	Adj	strong, powerful, better	
14.	至於 至于	zhìyú	Prep/ Adv	as for/to, (go) so far as to	[to-at]
15.	對不起 对不起	duìbuqǐ	RV	to let sb. down	[reply-not-up]

你不好好學習，對得起父母嗎？

你不好好学习，对得起父母吗？

16.	家教	jiājiào	N	home tutoring, upbringing, tutor	[family-education]
17.	家長 家长	jiāzhǎng	N	parent of schoolchildren, head of household	[family-head]
18.	薪水	xīnshui	N	salary, wages	[salary-water]

薪水高/低/多/少   =收入   →年薪、月薪

這份工作年薪多少？

这份工作年薪多少？

| 19. | 差 | chà | Adj | poor, inferior | |
| 20. | 被動
被动 | bèidòng | Adj | passive, lack of agency | [by-move] |

做……很被動   ↔主動 zhǔdòng

你做什麼事的時候很被動？

你做什么事的时候很被动？

Characters with Many Strokes

缺 關 歷 薦 證 翻 譯 讀 薪 差

21.	在乎	zàihu	V	to care about, to mind	[depend on-with]
22.	打瞌睡	dǎ kēshuì	VO	to doze off, to nod	[hit-sleepy]

你上課的時候，常打瞌睡嗎？

你上课的时候，常打瞌睡吗？

| 23. | 醒 | xǐng | V | to wake up, to sober up | |

你每天早上幾點醒來？

你每天早上几点醒来？

| 24. | 對牛彈琴
对牛弹琴 | duìniú-
tánqín | IE | to cast pearls before swine | [face-cow-play-instrument] |
| 25. | 於是
于是 | yúshì | Conj | thereupon, hence | [in-this] |

我不喜歡他，於是就和他分手了。

我不喜欢他，于是就和他分手了。

| 26. | 因此 | yīncǐ | Conj | therefore, consequently | [because-this] |
| 27. | 辭
辞 | cí | V | to quit, to decline | |

你為什麼辭了那份工作？

你为什么辞了那份工作？

| 28. | 既然 | jìrán | Conj | since, now that | [already-so] |

既然你很累，就回家休息吧！

既然你很累，就回家休息吧！

| 29. | 補習班
补习班 | bǔxíbān | N | supplemental studies program | [lessons after school-class] |

一家補習班；給……補習；補 subject

你上過補習班嗎？補什麼？

你上过补习班吗？补什么？

| 30. | 望子成龍
望子成龙 | wàngzǐ
chénglóng | IE | to hope one's children will have a bright future | [expect-child-become-dragon] |
| 31. | 白天 | báitiān | N | Daytime | [white-day] |

你白天都在家嗎？

你白天都在家吗？

| 32. | 兒童
儿童 | értóng | N | children | [child-child] |

哪個兒童文學作家很有名？

哪个儿童文学作家很有名？

33.	專門 专门	zhuānmén	Adj	special, specialized	[special-school]

受過專門訓練

這家店專門賣什麼？

这家店专门卖什么？

34.	訓練 训练	xùnliàn	N/V	training, to train	[lecture-practice]

語言/短期/長期/游泳訓練

你參加過短期的語言訓練班嗎？

你参加过短期的语言训练班吗？

	汪汪	wāngwāng	ON	sound of a dog, bowwow	
35.	羊	yáng	N	sheep	
	咩咩	miēmiē	ON	sound of a sheep, baa	
36.	信心	xìnxīn	N	confidence, faith	[believe-heart]

你對美國的將來很有信心嗎？

你对美国的将来很有信心吗？

37.	果然	guǒrán	Adv	as expected, sure enough	[surely-so]

你看，他今天果然沒來。

你看，他今天果然没来。

38.	儘管 尽管	jǐnguǎn	Conj	even though, despite	
39.	引起	yǐnqǐ	V	to give rise to, to lead to	[draw-up]

什麼能引起學生的興趣？

什么能引起学生的兴趣？

40.	金飯碗 金饭碗	jīnfànwǎn	N	*well-paying job*	[gold-rice-bowl]

找到金飯碗 →鐵飯碗 tiěfànwǎn

哪些工作算是金飯碗？

哪些工作算是金饭碗？

41.	桃李滿天下 桃李满天下	táolǐ mǎn tiānxià	IE	to have pupils (桃李) everywhere	[peach-plum-fill-world]

(students all over the world)

An old, experienced teacher

Characters with Many Strokes

瞌 醒 彈 辭 補 龍 童 專 儘 碗

◎By Grammatical Categories

Nouns/Pronouns

能力	nénglì	ability, capacity
閱讀	yuèdú	reading, comprehension
翻譯	fānyì	translation, to translate, translator
訓練	xùnliàn	training, to train
信心	xìnxīn	confidence, faith
證書	zhèngshū	certificate, credentials
簡歷	jiǎnlì	résumé, curriculum vitae
推薦信	tuījiànxìn	recommendation letter

金飯碗	jīnfànwǎn	well-paying job
薪水	xīnshui	salary, wages
公司	gōngsī	company
補習班	bǔxíbān	supplemental studies program
家教	jiājiào	home tutoring, upbringing, tutor
家長	jiāzhǎng	parent of school-children
兒童	értóng	children
白天	báitiān	daytime, day
羊	yáng	sheep

Verbs/Stative Verbs/Adjectives

缺	quē	to be short of, to lack, opening
辭	cí	to quit, to decline
醒	xǐng	to wake up, to sober up
面談	miàntán	to discuss face to face
在乎	zàihu	to care about, to mind
引起	yǐnqǐ	to give rise to, to lead to
打瞌睡	dǎ kēshuì	to doze off, to nod
拉關係	lā guānxi	to saddle up to

走後門	zǒu hòumén	to secure sth. through pull or influence
對不起	duìbuqǐ	to let sb. down
差	chà	poor, inferior
強	qiáng	strong, powerful, better
日常	rìcháng	day-to-day, everyday
專門	zhuānmén	special, specialized
被動	bèidòng	passive

Adverbs and Others

果然	guǒrán	as expected, sure enough
至於	zhìyú	as for/to, (go) so far as to
於是	yúshì	thereupon, hence, as a result
因此	yīncǐ	therefore, consequently
既然	jìrán	since, now that
儘管	jǐnguǎn	even though, despite

對牛彈琴	duìniú-tán qín	to cast pearls before swine
望子成龍	wàngzǐ chéng lóng	to hope one's children will have a bright future
桃李滿天下	táolǐ mǎn tiānxià	to have pupils everywhere

◎By Pinyin

Entries with * indicate lexical items used in Mini-Dialogues and of possible interest for supplemental study.

báitiān	白天	daytime, day
bèidòng	被动	passive
bǔxíbān	补习班	supplemental studies program
chà	差	poor, inferior
cí	辞	to quit, to decline
dǎ kēshuì	打瞌睡	to doze off, to nod
duìbuqǐ	对不起	to let sb. down
duìniú-tánqín	对牛弹琴	to cast pearls before swine
értóng	儿童	children
fānyì	翻译	translation, to translate , translator
gōngsī	公司	company
guǒrán	果然	as expected, sure enough
jiājiào	家教	home tutoring, upbringing, tutor
jiǎnlì	简历	résumé, curriculum vitae
jiāzhǎng	家长	parent of school-children
jīnfànwǎn	金饭碗	well-paying job
jīnglǐ*	经理	manager
jǐnguǎn	尽管	even though
jìrán	既然	since, now that
kǎojuàn*	考卷	test paper
lā guānxi	拉关系	to saddle up to
lǎoshǔ*	老鼠	mouse, rat
miàntán	面谈	to discuss face to face
nénglì	能力	ability, capacity
qiáng	强	strong, powerful, better

quē	缺	to be short of, to lack, opening
rìcháng	日常	day-to-day
shǒu*	首	measure word for songs, poems
táolǐ mǎn tiānxià	桃李满天下	to have pupils everywhere
tōngzhī*	通知	to notify, to notice
tuījiànxìn	推荐信	recommendation letter
wàngzǐchéng lóng	望子成龙	to hope one's children will have a bright future
xǐng	醒	to wake up
xīnshui	薪水	salary, wages
xìnxīn	信心	confidence, faith
xùnliàn	训练	training, to train
yáng	羊	sheep
yīncǐ	因此	therefore, consequently
yǐnqǐ	引起	to give rise to, to lead to
yúshì	于是	thereupon, hence
yuèdú	阅读	reading comprehension
zàihu	在乎	to care about, to mind
zhāngláng*	蟑螂	cockroach
zhèngshū	证书	certificate
zhìyú	至于	as for/to, (go) so far as to
zhuānmén	专门	special, specialized
zǒu hòumén	走后门	to secure sth. through pull or influence

課文 Text

Use the following questions to guide your reading of the text.

1. 小高為什麼不在王華爸爸的公司工作？

2. 小高為什麼辭了那份家教？

3. 小高對兒童英語補習班的工作滿意嗎？為什麼？

　小王：

　　多謝你跟你父親聯繫，上星期他請我到他的公司面談。我不知道這算不算拉關係、走後門。我是希望能靠自己找個工作，賺點兒生活費。我把簡歷、申請信、推薦信、和畢業證書都交了上去，你父親對我好像很滿意，不過他需要的是一個能搞翻譯的人。我日常對話和閱讀還可以，可是寫的能力不強，[1]**至於**翻譯就更不行了。我怕對不起你父親，只好放棄了這個難得的機會。

　　後來我去了一個「家教中心」，打算教中學生英文。那個中心給我介紹了一位家長，人很不錯，給的薪水也很高，可是他那個孩子態度很差，非常被動，根本不想學習，也不在乎成績好不好。給他上課的時候，他老打瞌睡，只有談到美國的歌星、影星的時候，才會醒過來。所謂的「對牛彈琴」，大概就是這個樣子吧！我想[2]**再怎麼**教**也**教不好，很沒有成就感，[3]**於是**就把那份工作辭了。

[4]**既然**家教不行，**那就**教補習班**吧**！你知道台灣的父母望子成龍，什麼都要「補」，所以很多學生白天上課，晚上就去補習。可是這一次我想來想去，還是去教兒童的好，我雖然沒有受過專門的訓練，帶孩子唱唱「小狗汪汪、小羊咩咩」應該不難吧？我很有信心地走進一家「兒童英語補習班」，問他們：「你們這兒

缺人嗎？」運氣不錯，他們果然要人。真沒想到我居然會教起五、六歲的孩子來，儘管孩子的水平不高，可是他們很願意學，進步得也很快，最好的是不管我做什麼，都能[5]**引起**他們**的興趣**。雖然這不是個金飯碗，但我教得很愉快。我現在「桃李滿天下」，學生[6]**可多了**！請告訴美英，等我這幾天忙完了，再和她聯繫。

德中上

课文 Text

Use the following questions to guide your reading of the text.

1. 小高为什么不在王华爸爸的公司工作？

2. 小高为什么辞了那份家教？

3. 小高对儿童英语补习班的工作满意吗？为什么？

小王：

多谢你跟你父亲联系，上星期他请我到他的公司面谈。我不知道这算不算拉关系、走后门。我是希望能靠自己找个工作，赚点儿生活费。我把简历、申请信、推荐信、和毕业证书都交了上去，你父亲对我好象很满意，不过他需要的是一个能搞翻译的人。我日常对话和阅读还可以，可是写的能力不强，[1]至于翻译就更不行了。我怕对不起你父亲，只好放弃了这个难得的机会。

后来我去了一个"家教中心"，打算教中学生英文。那个中心给我介绍了一位家长，人很不错，给的薪水也很高，可是他那个孩子态度很差，非常被动，根本不想学习，也不在乎成绩好不好。给他上课的时候，他老打瞌睡，只有谈到美国的歌星、影星的时候，才会醒过来。所谓的"对牛弹琴"，大概就是这个样子吧！我想[2]再怎么教也教不好，很没有成就感，[3]于是就把那份工作辞了。

⁴**既然**家教不行，**那就**教补习班**吧**！你知道台湾的父母望子成龙，什么都要"补"，所以很多学生白天上课，晚上就去补习。可是这一次我想来想去，还是去教儿童的好，我虽然没有受过专门的训练，带孩子唱唱"小狗汪汪、小羊咩咩"应该不难吧？我很有信心地走进一家"儿童英语补习班"，问他们："你们这儿缺人吗？"运气不错，他们果然要人。真没想到我居然会教起五、六岁的孩子来，尽管孩子的水平不高，可是他们很愿意学，进步得也很快，最好的是不管我做什么，都能⁵**引起**他们**的兴趣**。虽然这不是个金饭碗，但我教得很愉快。我现在"桃李满天下"，學生⁶**可**多**了**！请告诉美英，等我这几天忙完了，再和她联系。

德中上

小對話 Mini-Dialogues

Read the supplementary dialogues for a better understanding of the text. See if you can memorize one and perform it in class.

(1) Having an interview

A: 你是來做什麼的？

Gao: 我是來面談的。你們經理jīnglǐ讓我今天來見他。

A: 好，請等一下，我去告訴他，你來了。

Wang: 你是高德中吧？太好了，我看了你的簡歷、申請信和推薦信。你的中文很不錯吧？能不能做翻譯？

Gao: 我日常對話還可以，閱讀也沒問題，不過寫得不太好，翻譯也沒試過。

Wang: 你太客氣了！我女兒說你是個「中國通tōng」呢！

A: 你是来做什么的？

Gao: 我是来面谈的。你们经理让我今天来见他。

A: 好，请等一下，我去告诉他，你来了。

Wang: 你是高德中吧？太好了，我看了你的简历、申请信和推荐信。你的中文很不错吧？能不能做翻译？

Gao: 我日常对话还可以，阅读也没问题，不过写得不太好，翻译也没试过。

Wang: 你太客气了！我女儿说你是个"中国通"呢！

A: What are you here for?

Gao: I am here for an interview. Your manager asked me to come and see him today.

A: O.K. Wait a second. I'll go tell him you are here.

Wang: Are you Gao Dezhong? Very good. I saw your résumé, application letter, and letters of recommendation. Your Chinese is all right, I suppose? Can you do translation?

Gao: I am fine with everyday conversation. Reading is no problem, but my writing is not very good and I have never tried translation.

Wang: You are too modest! My daughter said that you are an expert on China!

(2) Going to a "tutoring center"

Gao:　你們能幫我找個家教嗎？　　　　　你们能帮我找个家教吗？

A:　　可以，你想教什麼樣的學生？　　可以，你想教什么样的学生？
　　　孩子還是大人？　　　　　　　　孩子还是大人？

Gao:　中學生吧！　　　　　　　　　　中学生吧！

A:　　留下你的姓名、地址、電話，　　留下你的姓名、地址、电话，
　　　有合適的，我們會通知 tōngzhī 'to　有合适的，我们会通知你。成
　　　notify' 你。成了的話，第一個月　了的话，第一个月的薪水得付
　　　的薪水得付我們百分之四十。　　我们百分之四十。

Gao:　好吧！　　　　　　　　　　　　好吧！

Gao: Can you help me find a home tutoring job?

A: Yes. What kind of students do you want to teach? Children or adults?

Gao: Middle-school students.

A: Leave us your name, address, and phone number. If there is someone appropriate, we will contact you. If everything works out, you'll have to pay us forty percent of your first month's salary.

Gao: Fine.

(3) Tutoring a student

Gao:　這個句子是什麼意思？　　　　　这个句子是什么意思？

A:　　我不知道。　　　　　　　　　　我不知道。

Gao:　你在學校從來沒學過嗎？　　　　你在学校从来没学过吗？

A:　　可能學過，我忘了。這是我上　　可能学过，我忘了。这是我上

次的英文考卷 kǎojuàn。

Gao: 六十五分！怎麼我們複習過的
語法你全錯了？醒醒！

A: 老師，我太累了，咱們唱首 shǒu
英文歌吧！

次的英文考卷。

六十五分！怎么我们复习过的
语法你全错了？醒醒！

老师，我太累了，咱们唱首英
文歌吧！

Gao: What does this sentence mean?

A: I don't know.

Gao: Have you ever studied this at school?

A: I probably have. I don't remember.
This is my last English test.

Gao: Sixty-five points! How come you
missed all the grammar points we just
reviewed? Wake up!

A: I'm too tired, teacher. Let's sing an English song.

(4) Singing along with kids

Gao: 小朋友，你們會不會唱A, B, C？

A: 不會，我們會唱ㄅㄆㄇㄈ。

Gao: 我教你們唱「王老先生有塊
地」，好不好？「王老先生有
塊地，伊 yī 啊伊啊哦，他在家裏
養小雞啊，伊啊伊啊哦……」

B: 老師，我家裏有狗！

C: 我家裏有貓！

D: 我家裏有老鼠 lǎoshǔ！

Gao: 好了！好了！我家還有蟑螂
zhāngláng 呢！我們繼續唱吧！

小朋友，你们会不会唱A, B, C？

不会，我们会唱ㄅㄆㄇㄈ。

我教你们唱"王老先生有块
地"，好不好？"王老先生有
块地，伊啊伊啊哦，他在家里
养小鸡啊，伊啊伊啊哦……"

老师，我家里有狗！

我家里有猫！

我家里有老鼠！

好了！好了！我家还有蟑螂
呢！我们继续唱吧！

Gao: Kids, do you know how to sing A, B, C?

A: No, we can sing bo, po, mo, fo.

Gao: Let me teach you how to sing "Old McDonald had a farm," all right? "Old McDonald had a farm, E-I-E-I-O, and on his farm he had some chicks, E-I-E-I-O…"

B: Teacher, we have a dog at home!

C: We have a cat!

D: There are rats in my house!

Gao: All right! All right! There are cockroaches in my place. Let's keep singing.

小故事 Stories

Read the following tale for your own enjoyment and for your understanding of the highlighted expression that is relevant to the theme of the chapter.

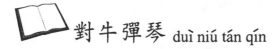 對牛彈琴 duì niú tán qín

❀　　我給他上課，就像對牛彈琴一樣，完全沒用。

彈	tán	to play (an instrument)
琴	qín	musical instrument
古時候	gǔshíhou	ancient times
音樂家	yīnyuèjiā	musician
野外	yěwài	open field
低頭	dītóu	to lower one's head
草	cǎo	grass
曲子	qǔzi	tune, song
錯	cuò	wrong
對象	duìxiàng	object, target

　　古時候有一個很有名的音樂家，他的琴彈得非常好。當天氣好的時候，他就把琴帶到野外去彈。

　　有一天，他看見一頭牛低著頭在吃草，他就很高興地給這頭牛彈起好聽的曲子來。雖然他彈得很認真，可是那頭牛還是低著頭吃草，好像根本沒聽到一樣。

　　這個音樂家很生氣。別人就對他說：「不要生氣了，不是你彈的曲子不好聽，是你選錯了聽曲子的對象啊！」

✎ 對牛彈琴的意思是＿＿＿＿＿＿＿＿＿＿＿＿＿＿＿＿＿＿＿

对牛弹琴 duì niú tán qín

❀ 我给他上课，就象对牛弹琴一样，完全没用。

古时候有一个很有名的音乐家，他的琴弹得非常好。当天气好的时候，他就把琴带到野外去弹。

有一天，他看见一头牛低着头在吃草，他就很高兴地给这头牛弹起好听的曲子来。虽然他弹得很认真，可是那头牛还是低着头吃草，好象根本没听到一样。

弹	tán	to play (an instrument)
琴	qín	musical instrument
古时候	gǔshíhou	ancient times
音乐家	yīnyuèjiā	musician
野外	yěwài	open field
低头	dītóu	to lower one's head
草	cǎo	grass
曲子	qǔzi	tune, song
错	cuò	wrong
对象	duìxiàng	object, target

这个音乐家很生气。别人就对他说："不要生气了，不是你弹的曲子不好听，是你选错了听曲子的对象啊！"

✎ 对牛弹琴的意思是_____

漢字 Characters

Study the following selected characters for further enrichment of your writing and vocabulary.

羽 yǔ 'feather'
+ 番 fān
phonetic

翻

翻譯	fānyì	to translate, to interpret
翻車	fānchē*	to turn over a vehicle
翻船	fānchuán*	to capsize

A: 你會翻譯嗎？

B: 中翻英還可以，英翻中不行。

fān 18
to turn over, to translate

言 yán 'words'
+ 睪 yì
phonetic

译

口譯	kǒuyì*	oral interpretation
音譯	yīnyì*	transliteration
直譯	zhíyì*	to translate literally

A: 你會不會口譯？

B: 可以試試，不過大概只能直譯。

Compare: 幸 xìng

yì 20
to translate, to interpret

門 mén 'door' +
兌 duì 'joy'
phonetic—
passing through
a door to
experience
something new
and pleasant

阅

| 閱讀 | yuèdú | to read |
| 閱讀測驗 | yuèdú cèyàn* | reading comprehension test |

A: 你這一次閱讀測驗考得怎麼樣？

B: 不太好，我閱讀能力還不行。

Compare: 開 kāi 關 guān

yuè 15
to read, to review

言 yán 'words'
+ 賣 mài
phonetic

读

| 讀書 | dúshū* | to read, study |
| 讀物 | dúwù* | reading matter |

A: 你喜歡讀書嗎？都看些什麼？

B: 我喜歡看兒童讀物。

Compare: 續 xù

dú 22
to read (aloud)

竹 zhú 'bamboo'
+ 間 jiān
phonetic—
originally meant
bamboo strips for
writing on, a brief
note, short and
simple

簡歷	jiǎnlì	résumé, curriculum vitae
簡單	jiǎndān	simple, uncomplicated
簡直	jiǎnzhí*	simply, really
簡體字	jiǎntǐzì	simplified characters

A: 我為什麼找不到工作？

B: 你的簡歷太簡單了，簡直沒說什麼。

簡

jiǎn 18
simple, brief, bamboo
slips

垂 chuí
'branches
hanging down'
+ 左 zuǒ 'left
hand'—the left
hand is unlike,
and inferior to,
the right hand

差不多	chàbuduō	almost, good enough
差別	chābié*	difference
郵差	yóuchāi*	postmaster

A: 你的中文水平跟他的差不多。

B: 哪裏，還差得遠呢！

Compare: 著 zhe

差

chà, chā, chāi 9
inferior, poor, to differ, to
lack

Picture of a net
for catching
birds, with 田
tián 'field' at the
top

| 畢業 | bìyè | to graduate |
| 畢業生 | bìyèshēng* | graduate |

A: 他是什麼時候畢業的？

B: 他是九八年的畢業生。

毕

bì 10
to finish, to accomplish

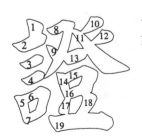

言 yán 'words'
+ 登 dēng
phonetic

證書	zhèngshū	certificate, credentials
簽證	qiānzhèng	visa
圖書證	túshūzhèng*	library card
學生證	xuéshēng zhèng*	student I.D.

A: 去那兒借書需要什麼？

B: 你有圖書證嗎？沒有的話，學生證
　　也行。

证

zhèng 19
to prove, proof,
credentials

Compare: 燈 dēng

扌 shǒu 'hand'
+ 隹 zhuī
phonetic

推

| 推薦信 | tuījiànxìn | letter of recommendation |
| 推薦 | tuījiàn | to recommend |

A: 你能不能幫我寫一封推薦信？

B: 可以，把你推薦給哪個公司？

Compare: 誰 shéi

tuī 11
to push, to infer, to
decline, to delay

衤 yī 'clothing'
+ 甫 fǔ
phonetic

补

補習班	bǔxíbān	supplemental program
補習	bǔxí*	to take lessons after work
補品	bǔpǐn	tonic
補考	bǔkǎo*	to make up a missed exam

A: 他不是在補習班補習嗎？

B: 對啊！可是他常缺課，整天要老師幫
　 他補考。

bǔ 12
to mend, to fill, to
nourish, supplementary

缶 fǒu 'dish' +
夬 guài 'break
through'
phonetic

缺

缺人	quērén*	to be short of hands
缺課	quēkè*	to miss class
缺點	quēdiǎn	shortcoming, defect

A: 這個學生有什麼缺點？

B: 他最大的缺點就是缺課太多。

Compare: 快 kuài

quē 10
to lack, vacancy

石 shí 'stone' +
宛 wǎn
phonetic

碗

飯碗	fànwǎn*	rice bowl, job
金飯碗	jīnfànwǎn	well-paying job
鐵飯碗	tiěfànwǎn*	secure job

A: 在大學教書怎麼樣？

B: 不是個金飯碗，不過倒是個鐵飯碗。

wǎn 13
bowl

木 mù 'tree' +
子 zǐ 'child'—
the tree of the
children

行李	xínglǐ	luggage, baggage
李子	lǐzi*	plum
桃李滿 天下	táolǐ mǎn tiānxià	to have pupils everywhere

A: 她帶那麼多行李，真不怕麻煩！

B: 她桃李滿天下，到處都有人接送。

lǐ 7
plum, Surname

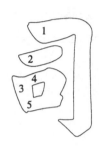

司 is 后 hòu
'queen'
backwards

公司	gōngsī	company, corporation
司機	sījī	driver
官司	guānsī*	lawsuit

A: 那個司機整天跟人打官司。

B: 一定給他的公司找了很多麻煩。

Compare: 詞 cí

sī 5
to manage, department

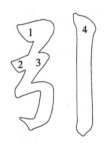

弓 gōng 'bow'
+ 丨 'string'—
draw towards
oneself the
string of a bow

引起	yǐnqǐ	to give rise to, to lead to
吸引	xīyǐn	to attract, to draw
吸引力	xīyǐnlì*	attraction

A: 他上課的時候能引起學生的興趣嗎？

B: 他的故事很能吸引大家的注意。

yǐn 4
to draw, to lead, to cite,
preface

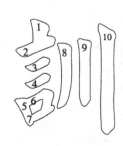

言 yán 'words'
+ 川 chuān
'river'—a flow
of words,
instruct,
admonish

訓練	xùnliàn	to train, to drill
受訓	shòuxùn*	to receive training
短訓班	duǎnxùnbān*	short-term training course

A: 你在短訓班受過訓嗎？

B: 去年冬天我受過一週的教學訓練。

xùn 10
to lecture, to train,
teachings

亻 rén 'person' +
聿 yù phonetic
+ 灬 huǒ 'fire' +
皿 mǐn 'bowl,
brazier in which
the fire burns'—
ashes, ended,
finished

儘管	jǐnguǎn	even though
儘量	jǐnliàng*	(drink/eat) to the full
儘快	jǐnkuài*	as quickly as possible

A: 請你儘快把這件事搞好。

B: 好，我會儘量在這一兩天內做完。

Compare: 盡 jǐn

尽

jǐn 16
utmost, within limits
of

止 zhǐ 'stop' +
匕 'a person
standing, facing
to the right'—
the place wherer
a person has
stopped; here,
this

因此	yīncǐ	therefore, consequently
彼此	bǐcǐ*	each other, one another
從此	cóngcǐ*	thereupon

A: 他們彼此都不喜歡對方 duìfāng 'the other
party'，因此就分手了。

B: 他們從此不再見面了嗎？

Compare: 些 xiē　嘴 zuǐ　紫 zǐ

此

cǐ 6
this

The seal script
contains 丂 qiǎo
exclamation,
analysis of the
rest doubtful

在乎	zàihu	to care about, to mind
似乎	sìhū*	it seems, as if
幾乎	jīhū	almost, nearly

A: 那個學生似乎不在乎他的成績。

B: 對，他幾乎一個星期沒來上課了。

乎

Compare: 呼 hū

hū 5
to, at, with, than

Picture of a
sheep's head;
horns at the top,
nose at the
bottom

山羊	shānyáng*	goat
放羊	fàngyáng*	to herd sheep
羊毛	yángmáo*	sheep's wool, fleece

A: 那個放羊的孩子在做什麼？

B: 他在剪 jiǎn 'cut (with scissors)' 羊毛。

羊

Compare: 美 měi　洋 yáng　樣 yàng　鮮 xiān

yáng 6
sheep

語法和用法 Grammar and Usage

Pay attention to the function of the structure and then study the example sentences.

1. Raising an additional point

~ to reach an (additional) point

A···；至於B 就···了	...；zhìyú...jiù...le	as for (this) (prep.); as regards; as far as B is concerned

我日常對話和閱讀還可以，可是寫的能力不強，**至於**翻譯就更不行了。

1. 你在北京留學，吃的、住的怎麼樣？

   你在北京留学，吃的、住的怎么样？

   You study abroad in Beijing. What do you think of the food and housing conditions?

   吃的都很有特色，至於住的就不那麼舒服了。

   吃的都很有特色，至于住的就不那么舒服了。

   Everything I eat is very unique. As far as living conditions go, they are not very comfortable.

2. 你覺得快餐怎麼樣？

   你觉得快餐怎么样？

   How do you feel about fast food?

   吃快餐很省時間，至於營養 yíngyǎng 就不太豐富 fēngfù 'rich' 了。

   吃快餐很省时间，至于营养就不太丰富了。

   Having fast food saves time, but as far as the nutrition is concerned, it is not very nourishing.

3. 很多人都認為在美國生活非常貴。

   很多人都认为在美国生活非常贵。

   Many people think that it would be very expensive to live in the U.S.

   這很難說，其實日用品很便宜，至於其他東西就比較貴了。

   这很难说，其实日用品很便宜，至于其他东西就比较贵了。

   It's hard to say. Actually, daily goods are cheap. As far as other things go, they are more expensive.

This pattern 至於 is often used to raise an additional point or refer to a change in topic from the one indicated in the preceding statement. Don't confuse this with 關於 (L3,

G6) or 由於 (L16, G3). Very often, in this pattern, the comment concerning B is somewhat negative, with or without a negative marker. The gist is more or less this: "A is OK, but as for B, it's not that good/satisfying."

2. Expressing invariability

(O)S再(怎麼)V 也V不 complement	zài (zěnme)…yě…bù…	No matter how much effort S puts into (O), the result is the same.
(O)再(怎麼)V S 也V不 complement		
effort result		

我想**再怎麼**教**也**教不好，很沒有成就感……

1. 你覺得中文最難的　　你觉得中文最难的　　What do you consider to
   部分是什麼？　　　　部分是什么？　　　　be the hardest part of
   　　　　　　　　　　　　　　　　　　　studying Chinese?

   是聲調，再怎麼練　　是声调，再怎么练　　It's the tones. No matter
   習我也發不好，我　　习我也发不好，我　　how I practice, I can't get
   快氣死了。　　　　　快气死了。　　　　　them right. It makes me
   　　　　　　　　　　　　　　　　　　　furious.

2. 中國有那麼多好吃　　中国有那么多好吃　　There are so many treats
   的點心和補品，你　　的点心和补品，你　　and tonic foods in China.
   想他回來的時候會　　想他回来的时候会　　Do you think he will be
   不會很胖？　　　　　不会很胖？　　　　　very fat when he comes
   　　　　　　　　　　　　　　　　　　　back?

   當然不會，他是那　　当然不会，他是那　　Of course not. He is the
   種再怎麼吃也吃不　　种再怎么吃也吃不　　type of person who will
   胖的人。　　　　　　胖的人。　　　　　　never get fat no matter
   　　　　　　　　　　　　　　　　　　　what he eats.

3. 你剛剛睡醒，為什　　你刚刚睡醒，为什　　You just woke up. Why
   麼還打瞌睡？　　　　么还打瞌睡？　　　　are you still yawning?

   為了準備考試，我　　为了准备考试，我　　In order to prepare for the
   已經兩天沒好好休　　已经两天没好好休　　test, I haven't slept well in
   息了，現在再怎麼　　息了，现在再怎么　　two days. Now no matter
   睡也睡不夠。　　　　睡也睡不够。　　　　how much I sleep, it's still
   　　　　　　　　　　　　　　　　　　　not enough.

This pattern 再(怎麼) … 也 is used to express an unchangeable outcome and often occurs with 不. The object, understood within context, is frequently dropped. The two verbs in this pattern can be the same verb or two different verbs. "再 (怎麼) V" emphasizes the effort one has put into something; "也 V不complement" shows the result. Different verbs go with different resultative complements, such as 睡不夠、睡不着、教不好、教不會, etc. Compare this with 不管/無論…都/也/還 (L2, G1).

强调
jiǎo   emphasize

3. Expressing a consequence

(reason) 於是/因此S就V了	…yúshì/yīncǐ…jiù…le	(reason), as a result S V

很沒有成就感，**於是**就把那份工作辭了。

1. 你為什麼要去中國 旅遊呢？

   你为什么要去中国 旅游呢？

   Why do you want to travel to China?

   朋友說中國有很多 值得參觀的名勝古 蹟，於是我就決定 去中國了。

   朋友说中国有很多 值得参观的名胜古 迹，于是我就决定 去中国了。

   My friends said that China has many historical relics that are worth visiting. That's why I decided to go to China.

2. 他的成績很普通 pǔtōng，怎麼可以進 那家有名的大公 司？

   他的成绩很普通， 怎么可以进那家有 名的大公司？

   His grades are average. How could he get into that famous big company?

   他請了一個有名的 商人給他寫了一封 推薦信，於是他就 得到那份工作了。

   他请了一个有名的 商人给他写了一封 推荐信，于是他就 得到那份工作了。

   He asked a famous businessman to write him a letter of recommendation, and as a result he got the job.

3. 在中國為什麼有人 吃狗肉？

   在中国为什么有人 吃狗肉？

   Why do people eat dog meat in China?

   有人說狗肉是補 品，於是大家就開 始吃狗肉了。

   有人说狗肉是补 品，于是大家就开 始吃狗肉了。

   Because some say dog meat is a tonic food, so everyone has started eating dog meat.

於是/因此 indicates a cause-effect relationship between what precedes and what follows. Different from 因為…所以, 於是/因此 follows the condition. Also, the clauses before and after 於是/因此 refer to actual events, not abstractions. 於是/因此 is much more formal than 因為…所以.

4. Expressing an assumed condition

| 既然…, (那) (S) 就…吧！ | jìrán…, (nà)…jiù…ba | Since (it is the case)…, then |
| 既然…, QW…呢？ | jìrán…, …ne | Now that…, why (not)… |

既然家教不行，**那就**教補習班**吧**！

1. 我根本不喜歡我現在的工作，我該怎麼辦呢？　　我根本不喜欢我现在的工作，我该怎么办呢？　　I simply don't like my current job. What should I do?

既然不喜歡，就把它辭了吧！　　既然不喜欢，就把它辞了吧！　　Since you don't like it, just quit.

2. 我聽不少人說日本車又省油又不容易壞。　　我听不少人说日本车又省油又不容易坏。　　I heard many people say that Japanese cars both save fuel and do not break down easily.

既然日本車這麼好，那我就買日本車好了。　　既然日本车这么好，那我就买日本车好了。　　Since Japanese cars are so good, I will buy a Japanese car.

3. 在北京待了半年，我已經習慣了這兒的生活，真捨不得離開。　　在北京待了半年，我已经习惯了这儿的生活，真舍不得离开。　　I have been in Beijing for half a year. I'm used to it here, and would hate to leave.

既然你喜歡北京，那為什麼不留在那兒呢？　　既然你喜欢北京，那为什么不留在那儿呢？　　Since you like Beijing, then why don't you stay there?

The clause with 既然 "given the fact that…; since…" often states a given situation, and the following clause states a response, either in the form of a statement or a question. If it's a statement, it often contains the adverb 就 after the subject and 吧 or 好了 at the end of the main clause. Remember that it expresses an assumed condition, not a causal relationship 因為…所以. Don't confuse this with 即使…也 (L10, G4).

5. Expressing abstract effect

A引起B的N	yǐnqǐ …de…	A draws/brings out B's N
A引不起B的N	yǐnbùqǐ …de…	A can't draw/bring out B's N
A不會引起B的N	búhuì yǐnqǐ …de…	A won't draw/bring out B's N

最好的是不管我做什麼，都能**引起**他們**的興趣**。

1. 聽說北京的出租車司機很有意思，是嗎？

   听说北京的出租车司机很有意思，是吗？

   I heard that taxi drivers in Beijing are very interesting, aren't they?

   對啊！他們特別喜歡聊天，而且什麼都可以引起他們的關心。

   对啊！他们特别喜欢聊天，而且什么都可以引起他们的关心。

   Yes. They particularly like to chat, and moreover, everything draws their interest.

2. 為什麼最近大家工作的時候，好像都不太高興？

   为什么最近大家工作的时候，好象都不太高兴？

   Why doesn't anyone seem very happy at work lately?

   公司沒有提高tígāo 'to raise' 薪水，引起了大家的不滿bùmǎn。

   公司没有提高薪水，引起了大家的不满。

   The company didn't give people a raise, causing their dissatisfaction.

3. 今天的晚會大家都穿得很漂亮嗎？

   今天的晚会大家都穿得很漂亮吗？

   Did everyone dress up nicely for tonight's party?

   當然了，要不然就引不起別人的注意。

   当然了，要不然就引不起别人的注意。

   Of course—otherwise they wouldn't be able to draw others'attention.

The verb 引起 takes on a limited number of abstract nouns (e.g., 興趣/注意/同情/不滿). Further study of Chinese requires one to take note of this kind of lexical collocation. Note that the negative form is often 引不起 or 不會引起, and the former cannot be used with 不滿. Compare this with 受到 (L8, G6).

6. Expressing emphasis

S 可 Adj 了	kě …le	S is quite Adj
S 可 V(O) 了		S finally V(O)
S 可 AuxV 了		S really likes/wants/knows how to V

我現在「桃李滿天下」，學生**可**多**了**！

1. 聽說你假期裏去參觀了長城，你覺得怎麼樣？

   听说你假期里去参观了长城，你觉得怎么样？

   I heard that you went to visit the Great Wall during the break. How was it?

   長城可漂亮，可偉大了！

   长城可漂亮，可伟大了！

   The Great Wall is so beautiful, so magnificent!

2. 他下午做什麼了？

   他下午做什么了？

   What did he do this afternoon?

   他下午打了兩場籃球，又跑了一個小時的步，他可累壞了。

   他下午打了两场篮球，又跑了一个小时的步，他可累坏了。

   He played two games of basketball, and then jogged for an hour. He is quite exhausted.

3. 為了找工作，你已經發出很多簡歷了，有什麼好消息嗎？

   为了找工作，你已经发出很多简历了，有什么好消息吗？

   In order to land a job, you sent out a lot of résumés. Any good news?

   今天剛來的好消息，唉！我可找到工作了。

   今天刚来的好消息，唉！我可找到工作了。

   Oh, good news just came today! I finally found a job.

4. 你可睡醒了，小高已經等了你兩個小時了。

   你可睡醒了，小高已经等了你两个小时了。

   You finally woke up. Xiao Gao has been waiting for you for two hours.

   那可真對不起，這一覺我睡得可好了。

   那可真对不起，这一觉我睡得可好了。

   I'm really sorry about that, but I was having such a good sleep.

5. 她的孩子會說話了   她的孩子会说话了   Has her child started
嗎？   吗？   talking yet?

她可會說話了，真   她可会说话了，真   She really knows how to
是人見人愛啊。   是人见人爱啊。   talk. Everyone thinks she
is adorable.

In this pattern, 可/可是 is an adverb which must precede an adjective, auxiliary verb 喜歡/想/會 or a verb phrase. 了 often occurs at the end of the sentence. "可…了" is used to emphasize the quality expressed by the adjective or condition/attitude of the subject of the sentence.

文化點滴 Culture Notes

1. **Animal sounds**: Different places and cultures "hear" animal sounds differently. The following is a list contrasting Chinese and American ways of transcribing animal sounds.

Animal	Sounds in Chinese		Pinyin	Sounds in English
Cat	喵喵	喵喵	miāomiāo	meow
Cow	哞哞	哞哞	mōumōu	moo
Dog	汪汪	汪汪	wāngwāng	woof, bowwow
Duck	呱呱	呱呱	guāguā	quack
Hen	咯咯	咯咯	gēgē	bawk bawk
Mouse	吱吱	吱吱	zīzī	squeak
Pig	吭哧	吭哧	kēngchi	oink
Rooster	喔	喔	wō	cock-a-doodle-doo
Sheep	咩咩	咩咩	miēmiē	baaah

2. **Supplemental studies programs**: Who can say whether the Taiwan people's love of extra nourishment or tonic foods is less strong than their desire for supplemental education? Regardless, there are schools for supplemental studies programs 補習班 bǔxíbān everywhere. In fact, there are streets called 補習街 because the whole street has nothing but 補習班. There are all kinds of supplemental studies programs. Whether it is schoolchildren who want to study English, high school graduates who want to pass the joint entrance examination, college students who want to take a TOEFL test, or adults who want to learn more about computing, there are supplemental studies programs for everyone.

3. **Work in mainland China**: In the past, college graduates in mainland China were assigned to different units 單位 dānwèi to work. The work unit decided and arranged most of their living conditions, including where they should live. Being fired or changing one's job was unheard of. People love to have "iron rice bowls" 鐵飯碗 tiěfànwǎn, because they are unbreakable. On the other hand, to eat food prepared in a large cauldron

(the same as everyone else) 吃大鍋飯 chī dàguōfàn lacks competitiveness and thus productivity. Therefore, the Chinese government has changed its policy recently and now college graduates have to look for jobs themselves. There are also many workers, after being laid off from the government agencies, who start their own business as individual entrepreneurs.

4. **Résumé**: The Chinese résumé 簡歷 jiǎnlì <PRC> 履歷 lǚlì <TW> is not much different from the English one. Below is a sample, for someone who wants to teach English in China.

姓名	王大中
性別	男
年齡	24
婚姻狀況	未婚
通訊地址	美國印第安那州，布魯明頓市，東三街，2305號B1
工作經歷	
2000.8-2001.5	印第安那布魯明頓大學東亞系助教
1999.8-2000.4	印第安那布魯明頓大學東亞文化中心學生聯絡員
教育背景	
1991-1997	俄亥俄州辛辛那提市立中學
1997.8-2001.5	印第安那布魯明頓大學東亞系本科
	主修：東亞研究
	副修：歷史
語言特長	中文（日常對話）
	西班牙文（流利）
	英文（母語）
興趣愛好	籃球、游泳、讀書、旅行

5. **Application letter**: Although there are many ways to write an application letter 求職信 qiúzhíxìn, here is a simple sample:

尊敬的王主任：

　　我是一名美國印第安那布魯明頓大學的學生，我叫王大中。我在校的專業是東亞研究。經過四年本科學習，已在今年暑假順利畢業，並獲得

尊敬的王主任：

　　我是一名美国印第安那布鲁明顿大学的学生，我叫王大中。我在校的专业是东亚研究。经过四年本科学习，已在今年暑假顺利毕业，并获得

學士學位。

從小我就對中國非常好奇。在大學學習的時候，我修了很多介紹中國和亞洲文化、歷史的課。同時，我也認識了不少中國來的同學，這讓我對現在的中國有很深的了解。

我聽說中國最近幾十年來，各大高校都需要英語人才。我對英語教學的工作，特別是教中國人英文有很大的興趣。英語是我的母語，我發音清楚，熟悉語法，在大學裏做過幾位中國同學的英語家教，他們都非常滿意。

為了能教好英語，我已經閱讀了一些英語教學的書，而且和學校的幾位教授討論了一些關於教中國人英語的問題。我相信我一定能很快適應您那裏的工作環境，並滿足你們英語教學的要求。希望能有機會對貴校的英語教學做出一點兒貢獻。

隨信附上我的個人簡歷和三封推薦信。此致
敬禮！

王大中
二○○三年三月五日

学士学位。

从小我就对中国非常好奇。在大学学习的时候，我修了很多介绍中国和亚洲文化、历史的课。同时，我也认识了不少中国来的同学，这让我对现在的中国有很深的了解。

我听说中国最近几十年来，各大高校都需要英语人才。我对英语教学的工作，特别是教中国人英文有很大的兴趣。英语是我的母语，我发音清楚，熟悉语法，在大学里做过几位中国同学的英语家教，他们都非常满意。

为了能教好英语，我已经阅读了一些英语教学的书，而且和学校的几位教授讨论了一些关于教中国人英语的问题。我相信我一定能很快适应您那里的工作环境，并满足你们英语教学的要求。希望能有机会对贵校的英语教学做出一点儿贡献。

随信附上我的个人简历和三封推荐信。此致
敬礼！

王大中
二○○三年三月五日

歌兒 Songs

老王與老李
Old Wang and Old Li

Moderato

詞：劉雅詩　曲：馬定一

1. 我　有一個自　己的　英文補習班，　　公司不大薪　水不高
   Wǒ　yǒu yí ge zì　jǐ de　Yīngwén bǔ xí bān,　　gōng sī bú dà, xīn shuǐ bù gāo,
   I have an English school of my own.　　　　It's not big, and the salary is not high,

2. 人　人都說公　司的　工作金飯碗，　　白　天看報打　打瞌睡
   Rén　rén dōu shuō gōng sī de　gōngzuò jīn fàn wǎn,　　bái tiān kàn bào dǎ da kēshuì
   Everyone says that company work is a gold mine. Reading the newspaper all day and taking naps,

1. 可是很　多　事　要辦。　英文翻譯閱　讀各種訓練課程
   kě shì hěn　duō　shì　yào bàn, Yīngwén fānyì yuèdú gèzhǒng xùnliàn kèchéng
   but there's a lot to do.　　　English translation, reading, and all kinds of training fill

2. 沒有什　麼　事　好辦。　可是我卻覺　得日常工作其實
   méi yǒu shén　me　shì　hǎo bàn,　kěshì wǒ què jué de rìcháng gōngzuò qíshí
   with few things to do.　　　Yet, I feel that daily business affairs are

1. 都很滿。家　長　們　望子成龍每天　接送小　孩，雖然我　常　常　忙到
   dōu hěn mǎn. Jiāzhǎngmen wàngzǐchénglóng měitiān jiēsòng xiǎohái.　Suírán　wǒ chángcháng mángdào
   the schedule.　With high hopes for their children, parents drop them off and pick them up each day.

2. 都很難。想　法　對　動作要快東西　還不能　亂，經理　還常　常　不時
   dōu hěn nán. Xiǎngfǎ　duì, dòngzuò yào kuài, dōngxi hái bù néng luàn. Jīnglǐ hái　chángcháng bùshí
   hard to handle. One's scheme must be correct, one's action decisive and nothing can get out of order. The
   manager from time to time

1. 沒時間吃飯。　想　要桃李滿　天下　一　點　都不困　難。
   méi shíjiān chīfàn.　Xiǎng yào táolǐ mǎn　tiānxià　yìdiǎn dōu bù kùn nán.
   Although I'm often so busy that I don't have time to eat, having students all over the place is not hard at all.

2. 找我去面談。　就怕叫我　辭職　嚇得我一身　汗。
   zhǎo nǐ qù miàntán.　Jiù pà jiào wǒ cí zhí xià de wǒ yì shēn hàn.
   asks me for a discussion. I fear he's going to tell me I'm fired. It scares me so much that I sweat all over.

第十五課

Theme Face and Friendship

Communicative Objectives
- Making a phone call
- Giving and responding to an invitation
- Talking with a boss
- Asking a favor

Focus on Characters
- 裝丟騙傷、篇章矛盾、鄰童彈琴、藉助段板、希寧台室

Grammar Focus
- 從 Time When 起/開始SVO
- …，S倒(是) V/Adj
- 拿(人/方面)來說
- 白V(了)
- 寧可V₁(O₁) 也不V₂(O₂)
- 一方面…(另)一方面…

怎麼做才算給面子？

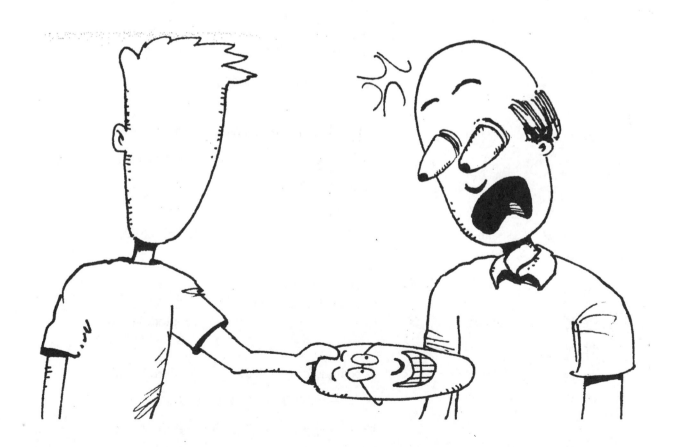

生詞 Vocabulary

Study the following words for their pronunciation and meaning. When an area is shaded, guess at the meaning of the word based on its constituent characters and then fill in the blank. Read the usage of words and related terms (antonyms, synonyms, compounds sharing the constituent characters, etc.) and try to answer the sample questions in Chinese. Note that proper nouns and incidental terms are not numbered.

◎By Order of Appearance

1. 面子　　miànzi　　N　　face *pride/respect*　　[surface-suffix]

   面子大；給……面子

   這兒誰很要面子？

   这儿谁很要面子？

2. 打通　　dǎtōng　　RV　　*to get through (phone call)* [hit-open]

   為什麼你家的電話老打不通？

   为什么你家的电话老打不通？

3. 接　　jiē　　V　　to pick up (phone call), to welcome

   接電話/人/球/信　　↔回電話/信

   你在家為什麼不接電話？

   你在家为什么不接电话？

4. 留言　　liúyán　　VO　　*to leave message* [leave-words]

   給……留言　→留言機 liúyánjī 'answering machine'

   誰常給你留言？

   谁常给你留言？

5. 小孩兒　　xiǎoháir　　N　　child　　[small-child]
   小孩儿

6. 倒　　dào　　Adv　　instead, actually, contrary to what was said/thought

7. 炸彈　　zhàdàn　　N　　bomb　　[explode-bullet]
   炸弹

8. 受傷　　shòushāng　　VO　　to be injured/wounded　　[endure-harm]
   受伤

   昨天車子出事，有沒有人受傷？

   昨天车子出事，有没有人受伤？

9. 兒子　　érzi　　N　　son　　[son-suffix]
   儿子

10.	喜酒	xǐjiǔ	N	*wedding feast* [happy-wine]
				喝喜酒；吃喜糖táng；辦喜事
				你什麼時候請我喝喜酒啊？
				你什么时候请我喝喜酒啊？
11.	請假	qǐngjià	VO	to ask for leave [request-vacation]
	请假			跟人請病假/事假
				我生病，得跟誰請病假？
				我生病，得跟谁请病假？
12.	鄰居	línjū	N	neighbor [adjacent-residence]
	邻居			
13.	客人	kèren	N	visitor, guest [guest-person]
14.	紅包	hóngbāo	N	red paper bag with gift money [red-envelop]
	红包			
15.	裝	zhuāng	V	to pack, to hold, to install
	装			裝紅包/東西/箱子xiāngzi vs. 收拾行李
				這杯子bēizi裏裝的是什麼？
				这杯子里装的是什么？
16.	丟臉	diūliǎn	VO	to lose face [lose-face] *embarassed lashamed*
	丢脸			
17.	直接	zhíjiē	Adj/	*frank, direct* direct, immediate [straight-connect]
			Adv	說話/做事很直接 ↔間接jiànjiē
				你覺得中國人說話不太直接嗎？
				你觉得中国人说话不太直接吗？
18.	老板	lǎobǎn	N	boss [prefix-board]
19.	教室	jiàoshì	N	classroom [teach-room]
20.	當時	dāngshí	Adv	at that time, then [that-time]
	当时			當時你為什麼不跟他分手？
				当时你为什么不跟他分手？
21.	例子	lìzi	N	example, case [instance-suffix]

luosuo

Characters with Many Strokes

彈 傷 喜 假 鄰 裝 臉 接 當 例

| 22. | 說明
说明 | shuōmíng | V/N | to explain, illustration | [say-clear] |

說明……用法/觀點/做法　　→說明書

請你說明一下這個東西的用法。

请你说明一下这个东西的用法。

| 23. | 同事 | tóngshì | N | Colleague | [same-job] |

→同學、同屋　　vs.室友、筆友、網友

你喜歡你的同事嗎？

你喜欢你的同事吗？

| 24. | 篇 | piān | M | piece of writing | |

這學期你寫了幾篇文章？

这学期你写了几篇文章？

| 25. | 文章 | wénzhāng | N | essay, article | [literary-chapter] |
| 26. | 順便
顺便 | shùnbiàn | Adv | conveniently, in passing | [follow-convenience] |

你出門順便幫我買些東西吧？

你出门顺便帮我买些东西吧？

| 27. | 利用 | lìyòng | V | to use, to take advantage of | [profit-use] |

利用機會/時間/假期

週末時你會利用時間做什麼？

周末时你会利用时间做什么？

| 28. | 寧可
宁可 | nìngkě | Adv | would rather, better | [prefer-approve] |
| 29. | 幫助
帮助 | bāngzhù | N/V | help, to assist [help-aid] | |

誰常常幫助你？

谁常常帮助你？

| 30. | 請客
请客 | qǐngkè | VO | to treat someone to | [invite-guest] |

什麼時候你會請客？

什么时候你会请客？

| 31. | 藉口
借口 | jièkǒu | N | excuse | [borrow-mouth] |

找/用……做藉口

你找什麼做藉口不跟他去約會？

你找什么做借口不跟他去约会？

| 32. | 騙
骗 | piàn | V | to deceive, to cheat, to swindle | |

騙人、受騙 shòupiàn　　vs. 上……的當

局　jú　dethis or bureau

騙子 trap

皇帝　huáng yì emperor

广告　advertisement　guǎng gào

你有過受騙上當的經驗嗎？

你有过受骗上当的经验吗？

| 33. | 方法 | fāngfǎ | N | method, means | [way-law] |

→辦法、看法、做法

你用什麼方法來學中文？

你用什么方法来学中文？

| 34. | 怪 | guài | V | to blame | |

你的同屋常怪你什麼？

你的同屋常怪你什么？

| 35. | 段 | duàn | M | period (of time), paragraph (of article) | |

| 36. | 矛盾 | máodùn | Adj/ N | contradictory, contradiction | [spear-shield] |

你的心裏什麼時候覺得很矛盾？

你的心里什么时候觉得很矛盾？

| 37. | 方面 | fāngmiàn | N | aspect, side [region-side] | |

這／那／各／許多／一方面

誰在各方面都很有能力？

谁在各方面都很有能力？

| 38. | 懷疑 怀疑 | huáiyí | V/N | to doubt, suspect | [think of-doubt] |

他為什麼總是受到大家的懷疑？

他为什么总是受到大家的怀疑？

| 39. | 真正 | zhēnzhèng | Adj | genuine, real | [real-straight] |

真正的朋友／原因

誰是你真正的朋友？

谁是你真正的朋友？

| 40. | 目的 | mùdì | N | purpose, aim, goal | [eye-target] |

他這麼做究竟有什麼目的？

他这么做究竟有什么目的？

| 41. | 究竟 | jiūjìng | Adv | actually, after all, in the end | [investigate-limit] |

Characters with Many Strokes

篇　章　順　寧　幫　藉　騙　段　懷　疑

◎By Grammatical Categories

Nouns/Pronouns

篇	piān	piece of writing	小孩兒	xiǎoháir	child
段	duàn	period (of time), paragraph (of article)	兒子	érzi	son
文章	wénzhāng	essay, article	客人	kèren	visitor, guest
例子	lìzi	example, case	鄰居	línjū	neighbor
面子	miànzi	face	老板	lǎobǎn	boss
方面	fāngmiàn	aspect, side	同事	tóngshì	colleague
方法	fāngfǎ	method, way, means	教室	jiàoshì	classroom
藉口	jièkǒu	excuse	炸彈	zhàdàn	bomb
目的	mùdì	purpose, aim, goal	紅包	hóngbāo	red paper bag with gift money
幫助	bāngzhù	help, to assist	喜酒	xǐjiǔ	wedding feast

Verbs/Stative Verbs/Adjectives

騙	piàn	to deceive, to cheat, to swindle	請假	qǐngjià	to ask for leave
怪	guài	to blame	請客	qǐngkè	to treat sb. (to meal/show/etc.)
裝	zhuāng	to pack, to hold, to install	留言	liúyán	to leave message
接	jiē	to pick up (phone call), to welcome	丟臉	diūliǎn	to lose face
打通	dǎtōng	to get through (phone call)	受傷	shòushāng	to be injured/wounded
利用	lìyòng	to use, to take advantage of	真正	zhēnzhèng	genuine, true, real
說明	shuōmíng	to explain, illustration	直接	zhíjiē	direct, immediate
懷疑	huáiyí	to doubt, suspect	矛盾	máodùn	contradictory, contradiction

Adverbs and Others

倒	dào	instead, actually, contrary to what was said/thought	寧可	nìngkě	would rather, better
當時	dāngshí	at that time, then	究竟	jiūjìng	actually, after all, in the end
順便	shùnbiàn	conveniently, in passing			

◎By Pinyin

Entries with * indicate lexical items used in Mini-Dialogues and of possible interest for supplemental study.

bāngzhù	帮助	to help, to assist	máodùn	矛盾	contradictory, contradiction
dāngshí	当时	at that time, then	miànzi	面子	face
dào	倒	instead, actually, contrary to what was said/thought	mùdì	目的	purpose, aim, goal
			nìngkě	宁可	would rather, better
dǎtōng	打通	to get through (phone call)	piān	篇	piece of writing
diūliǎn	丢脸	to lose face	piàn	骗	to deceive, to cheat, to swindle
duàn	段	period (of time), paragraph (of article)	qǐngjià	请假	to ask for leave
érzi	儿子	son	qǐngkè	请客	to treat sb. (to meal/show/etc.)
fàndiàn*	饭店	hotel, restaurant	qǐngtiě*	请帖	invitation card
fāngfǎ	方法	method, means	ruǎntǐ*	软体	<TW> software
fāngmiàn	方面	aspect, side	shídài*	时代	times, age, era
guài	怪	to blame	shòushāng	受伤	to be injured/wounded
hóngbāo	红包	red paper bag with gift money	shùnbiàn	顺便	conveniently, in passing
huáiyí	怀疑	to doubt, to suspect	shuōmíng	说明	to explain, illustration
jiàoshì	教室	classroom	tóngshì	同事	colleague
jiē	接	to pick up (phone call), welcome	wǎngzhàn*	网站	website
jièkǒu	借口	excuse	wénzhāng	文章	essay, article
jiūjìng	究竟	actually, after all, in the end	xiǎoháir	小孩儿	child
kèren	客人	visitor, guest	xǐjiǔ	喜酒	wedding feast
lǎobǎn	老板	boss	zhàdàn	炸弹	bomb
línjū	邻居	neighbor	zhànxiàn*	占线	the (phone) line is busy
liúyán	留言	to leave message	zhēnzhèng	真正	genuine, true, real
lìyòng	利用	to use, to take advantage of	zhíjiē	直接	direct, immediate
lìzi	例子	example, case	zhuāng	装	to pack, to hold, to install

課文 Text

Use the following questions to guide your reading of the text.

1. 最近什麼事讓小高頭疼？

2. 小高和他的老板有過什麼誤會？

3. 為什麼別人請小高吃飯的時候，他心裏總是很矛盾？

德中：

　　我上個星期給你打了幾次電話，都沒打通，後來打通了，又沒有人接，只好留言。前天聽小王說，你[1]從二月起就在一家兒童英語補習班工作，怪不得這麼忙。教小孩兒英文好玩嗎？最近有什麼有趣的事兒？說來聽聽。

美英上

美英：

　　最近有趣的事沒有，不過頭疼的問題[2]倒不少！上個星期我收到了一個「紅色炸彈」，別緊張，我沒受傷。原來我的鄰居張先生的兒子要結婚，請我去喝喜酒。本來我不想去，因為我有課，得請假，而且我和他並不特別熟。可是聽說有些人覺

得結婚的時候，客人來得越多越有面子，如果我不去，他可能以為我不給他面子呢！後來又聽說我去還得送紅包，問題是紅包得裝多少錢呢？怎麼做才算給面子？真麻煩！

　　我發現中國人因為怕自己或別人丟臉，說話常常不太直接，害得我們老外常常誤會他們的意思。[3]**拿**我補習班的老板**來說**，有一次我告訴他，我們的教室需要裝一台電腦，當時他說：「好！好！我研究、研究。」我以為他同意了，哪知道這就是「不行」的意思。害得我[4]**白高興了**半天。

　　還有一個例子可以說明，和中國人交朋友真不容易！有一次，一個同事請我去他家吃飯，我高興極了。我們剛開始的時候，談得很愉快，沒想到最後他拿出一篇文章來，請我「順便」幫他改改。當時我心裏很生氣，覺得被人利用了。我[5]**寧可**這個同事一開始的時候，就告訴我他需要我的幫助，**也不**希望他用請客的藉口來騙我。當然我後來明白了，這就是中國人辦事、交朋友的方法，我不應該怪他。不過以後好長一段時間，有人請我吃飯，我心裏就很矛盾：[6]**一方面**高興交了個朋友，**另一方面**又懷疑他們真正的目的究竟是什麼。時間不早了，下次再聊吧！

德中上

课文 Text

Use the following questions to guide your reading of the text.

1. 最近什么事让小高头疼？

2. 小高和他的老板有过什么误会？

3. 为什么别人请小高吃饭的时候，他心里总是很矛盾？

德中：

我上个星期给你打了几次电话，都没打通，后来打通了，又没有人接，只好留言。前天听小王说，你[1]从二月起就在一家儿童英语补习班工作，怪不得这么忙。教小孩儿英文好玩吗？最近有什么有趣的事儿？说来听听。

美英上

美英：

最近有趣的事没有，不过头疼的问题[2]倒不少！上个星期我收到了一个"红色炸弹"，别紧张，我没受伤。原来我的邻居张先生的儿子要结婚，请我去喝喜酒。本来我不想去，因为我有课，得请假，而且我和他并不特别熟。可是听说有些人觉得结婚的时候，客人来得越多越有面子，如果我不去，他可能以为我不给他面子呢！

后来又听说我去还得送红包，问题是红包得装多少钱呢？怎么做才算给面子？真麻烦！

　　我发现中国人因为怕自己或别人丢脸，说话常常不太直接，害得我们老外常常误会他们的意思。[3]拿我补习班的老板来说，有一次我告诉他，我们的教室需要装一台电脑，当时他说："好！好！我研究、研究。"我以为他同意了，哪知道这就是"不行"的意思。害得我[4]白高兴了半天。

　　还有一个例子可以说明，和中国人交朋友真不容易！有一次，一个同事请我去他家吃饭，我高兴极了。我们刚开始的时候，谈得很愉快，没想到最后他拿出一篇文章来，请我"顺便"帮他改改。当时我心里很生气，觉得被人利用了。我[5]宁可这个同事一开始的时候，就告诉我他需要我的帮助，也不希望他用请客的借口来骗我。当然我后来明白了，这就是中国人办事、交朋友的方法，我不应该怪他。不过以后好长一段时间，有人请我吃饭，我心里就很矛盾：[6]一方面高兴交了个朋友，另一方面又怀疑他们真正的目的究竟是什么。时间不早了，下次再聊吧！

　　　　　　　　　　　　　　　　　　　　　　　　　　德中上

小對話 Mini-Dialogues

Read the supplementary dialogues for a better understanding of the text. See if you can memorize one and perform it in class.

(1) Making a phone call

Lin:	小王，台北和這兒差多少個小時？
Wang:	十二個吧！你晚上給他打電話，就是他那兒的上午。
Lin:	好吧！我今晚試試。
	（打電話）
Wang:	怎麼？都打不通嗎？是不是佔線 zhànxiàn？還是沒撥區號 qūhào 02？
Lin:	我撥了，現在通了，可是沒人接。我留言好了。

小王，台北和这儿差多少个小时？

十二个吧！你晚上给他打电话，就是他那儿的上午。

好吧！我今晚试试。

（打电话）

怎么？都打不通吗？是不是占线？还是没拨区号02？

我拨了，现在通了，可是没人接。我留言好了。

Lin: Xiao Wang, what is the time difference between here and Taipei?

Wang: Twelve hours! If you call him in the evening, it will be morning where he is.

Lin: All right, I will give him a call tonight.

(Making a phone call)

Wang: What happened? Can't you get through? Is the line busy or did you not dial the area code "02"?

Lin: I dialed that. Now I got through, but no one's answering. I think I'll leave a message.

(2) Giving and responding to an invitation

A:	小高，下星期六有空嗎？	小高，下星期六有空吗？
Gao:	張先生，什麼事？	张先生，什么事？
A:	我兒子要結婚了，歡迎你來喝喜酒，這是請帖qǐngtiě。	我儿子要结婚了，欢迎你来喝喜酒，这是请帖。
Gao:	謝謝！什麼時候？	谢谢！什么时候？
A:	晚上六點在「來來飯店fàndiàn」。	晚上六点在"来来饭店"。
Gao:	好，沒事的話，我一定去。	好，没事的话，我一定去。

A: Xiao Gao, are you free next Saturday?

Gao: Mr. Zhang, what's going on?

A: My son is going to get married. Please come to his wedding banquet. This is the invitation.

Gao: Thanks! What time is it?

A: It will be 6:00 p.m. at the "Lai Lai hotel."

Gao: O.K. I will go if I'm free.

(3) Talking with a boss

Gao:	老板，現在有很多兒童學英語的軟體ruǎntǐ。我們應該裝一台電腦了。	老板，现在有很多儿童学英语的软体。我们应该装一台电脑了。
A:	那些軟體有用嗎？	那些软体有用吗？
Gao:	有總比沒有好。現在是「電腦時代shídài」了！	有总比没有好。现在是"电脑时代"了！
A:	好！好！我研究、研究。	好！好！我研究、研究。
Gao:	太好了，我可以上網，找些美國的兒童網站wǎngzhàn了。	太好了，我可以上网，找些美国的儿童网站了。

Gao:　Sir, nowadays there are many software programs that help children learn English. We should have a computer.

A:　Is that software useful?

Gao:　It's always better to have some than none. This is the "computer age."

A:　Fine, fine. I will study this.

Gao:　That's great. I will log on and find some U.S. web sites for children.

(4) Asking a favor

A:　小高，這個週末來我家吃飯怎麼樣？

Gao:　好啊！有什麼事嗎？

A:　沒什麼，咱們是同事，聊聊天嘛！（在家裏）這些都是家常菜，不要客氣，自己來。

Gao:　那我就不客氣了。真不好意思，害你忙了半天。

A:　哪兒的話，等一下請你幫我改一篇英文作文，怎麼樣？

A:　小高，这个周末来我家吃饭怎么样？

好啊！有什么事吗？

zán (we)
没什么，咱们是同事，聊聊天嘛！（在家里）这些都是家常菜，不要客气，自己来。

那我就不客气了。真不好意思，hài 害你忙了半天。

哪儿的话，等一下请你帮我改一篇英文作文，怎么样？

a piece of

A:　Xiao Gao, would you like to come over for dinner this weekend?

Gao:　Fine! Is there a special occasion?

A:　Nothing. We are colleagues. Let's have a chat. (At home) These are all homemade dishes. Don't be so polite. Help yourself.

Gao:　Then I won't be polite. I'm really embarrassed. I've caused you such trouble.

A:　Think nothing of it. After this, how about helping me correct an English essay?

小故事 Stories

Read the following tale for your own enjoyment and for your understanding of the highlighted expression that is relevant to the theme of the chapter.

 自相矛盾 zì xiāng máodùn

❀ 他一邊兒說自己不講面子，一邊兒又怕晚會來的人少，太丟臉，真是自相矛盾。

從前有一個人在市場上賣東西。他拿起一隻矛，對大家說：「你們看，我的矛是世界上最好、最利的。不管多硬的東西，都能刺穿。」

過了一會兒，他拿起一面盾，又對周圍的人說：「你們看，我的盾是世界上最好、最硬的。什麼東西都刺不穿它。」這時旁邊有一個人突然說：「如果拿你的矛去刺你的盾，結果會怎麼樣呢？」這個賣東西的人聽了，一句話也說不出來。

市場	shìchǎng	market
矛	máo	spear
利	lì	sharp
硬	yìng	hard
刺穿	cìchuān	to pierce through
盾	dùn	shield
周圍	zhōuwéi	around, round

✎ 自相矛盾的意思是＿＿＿＿＿＿＿＿＿＿＿＿＿＿＿＿＿＿＿＿＿

自相矛盾 zì xiāng máodùn

✿ 他一边儿说自己不讲面子，一边儿又怕晚会来的人少，太
丢脸，真是自相矛盾。

从前有一个人在市场上卖东西。他拿
起一只矛，对大家说："你们看，我的矛
是世界上最好、最利的。不管多硬的东
西，都能刺穿。"

过了一会儿，他拿起一面盾，又对周

市场	shìchǎng	market
矛	máo	spear
利	lì	sharp
硬	yìng	hard
刺穿	cìchuān	to pierce through
盾	dùn	shield
周围	zhōuwéi	around, round

围的人说："你们看，我的盾是世界上最好、最硬的。什么东西都
刺不穿它。"这时旁边有一个人突然说："如果拿你的矛去刺你的
盾，结果会怎么样呢？"这个卖东西的人听
了，一句话也说不出来。

漢字 Characters

Study the following selected characters for further enrichment of your writing and vocabulary.

衣 yī
'clothing' + 壯 zhuàng
phonetic

裝

包裝	bāozhuāng*	to pack, packing
包裝紙	bāozhuāngzhǐ*	wrapping paper
西裝	xīzhuāng*	Western-style clothes

A: 那家商店的東西怎麼樣？
B: 不太好，可是都包裝得很漂亮。

zhuāng 13
to act, to pretend

丿 'a falling stroke' + 去 qù
'go away'—to drop away

丟

| 丟臉 | diūliǎn | to lose face |
| 丟掉 | diūdiào* | to lose, throw away |

A: 把這些東西丟掉，放這兒太丟臉了。
B: 能用就用，別浪費。

Compare: 去 qù

diū 6
to lose, to discard

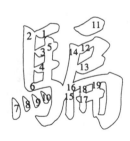

馬 mǎ 'horse' + 扁 biǎn
phonetic—to vault on a horse, cheat, swindle

骗

騙人	piànrén*	to deceive people
騙子	piànzi*	swindler, cheat
受騙	shòupiàn*	to be deceived

A: 你為什麼說他是個大騙子？
B: 因為他到處騙人，我也受過騙。

Compare: 偏 piān 篇 piān

piàn 19
to deceive, to fool

亻 rén 'person' + 矢 shǐ
'arrow' + 昜 yáng phonetic

伤

| 受傷 | shòushāng | to be wounded |
| 傷口 | shāngkǒu* | wound, cut |

A: 你受傷了嗎？嚴不嚴重？
B: 沒有什麼，只有一個小傷口。

Compare: 場 chǎng 湯 tāng

shāng 13
to injure, wound

竹 zhú
'bamboo' + 扁
biǎn phonetic/a
冊 document
hung on a 戶
door—bamboo
strips that were
used for writing
on

piān 15
piece of writing, sheet

一篇文章　　yì piān wénzhāng　　an article
短篇小說　　duǎnpiān xiǎoshuō*　short story
A: 那篇文章怎麼樣？
B: 還行，寫得很清楚。

Compare: 偏 piān　遍 biàn　騙 piàn

音 yīn 'sound' +
十 shí 'ten'—a
section of music,
or a verse or
chapter of poetry

zhāng 11
chapter, rules, stamp,
badge

文章　　　wénzhāng　　　article, essay
印章　　　yìnzhāng*　　　seal, stamp
第一章　　dì-yī zhāng*　　chapter one
A: 那個長篇小說怎麼樣？
B: 第一章還可以，後面的部分不太好。

Picture of a spear
or lance

máo 5
spear, lance

矛盾　　　　máodùn　　　　contradiction
自相矛盾　　zìxiāng- máodùn*　to contradict
　　　　　　　　　　　　　　　　oneself
A: 你這麼做，實在是自相矛盾。
B: 我知道，我心裏也很矛盾。

Compare: 務 wù　柔 róu　橘 jú

目 mù 'a picture
of a buckler' +
十 shí 'a handle'
+ 厂 'covering,
shielding'

dùn 9
shield

矛盾百出　　máodùn- bǎichū*　full of
　　　　　　　　　　　　　　　　contradictions
A: 這篇報告寫得怎麼樣？
B: 矛盾百出，需要好好地改一改。

阝 yì 'city' +
粦 lín phonetic

邻

lín 14
neighbor, community,
near

鄰居　　　　línjū　　　　　neighbor

A: 你的鄰居是做什麼的？

B: 不知道，我們從來沒說過話。

Compare: 憐 lián

辛 xīn
'suffering' + 重
chóng phonetic
—a servant,
boy or girl
under 15 years
of age, young

童

tóng 12
children

兒童　　　　értóng　　　　children
童話　　　　tónghuà*　　　fairy tales
神童　　　　shéntóng*　　　child prodigy

A: 為什麼大家說他是個神童？

B: 因為才八歲，他居然寫了個童話。

Compare: 鐘 zhōng

弓 gōng 'bow'
+ 單 dān
phonetic—to
shoot, strike,
bullet

弹

tán, dàn 15
to shoot, to flip, to
play, bullet

炸彈　　　　zhàdàn　　　　bomb
子彈　　　　zǐdàn*　　　　bullet, cartridge
原子彈　　　yuánzǐdàn*　　atomic bomb
彈吉他　　　tán jítā*　　　to play guitar

A: 你收到「紅色炸彈」，有沒有受傷？

B: 身體沒有，但是錢包「受重傷」。

王 yù 'jade' +
今 jīn phonetic
—several pieces
of jade,
anciently
suspended to
form a kind of
harpsichord

琴

qín 12
musical instrument

鋼琴　　　　gāngqín　　　　piano
口琴　　　　kǒuqín*　　　　harmonica
小提琴　　　xiǎotíqín　　　violin
中提琴　　　zhōngtíqín*　　viola
大提琴　　　dàtíqín*　　　　cello

A: 你會拉小提琴嗎？

B: 不會，但是我會彈鋼琴。

艹 cǎo 'grass' +
耤 jí phonetic

jiè 17
to borrow, to lend, to
make use of

藉口	jièkǒu	excuse, pretext
藉機	jièjī*	to seize an opportunity

A: 他又去參加晚會，這次是什麼藉口？

B: 剛找到工作，他藉機慶祝一下。

力 lì 'strength'
+ 且 qiě
phonetic

zhù 7
to help, to assist

幫助	bāngzhù	to help, assist
互助	hùzhù*	to help each other
助教	zhùjiào*	teaching assistant

A: 你有問題，可以請助教幫助你。

B: 她說我們同學應該互助合作。

Compare: 租zū 組zǔ 祖zǔ

丨 + 殳 shū
'beat'—
something long
cut in four
sections by
beating

duàn 9
section, paragraph

第一段	dì-yī duàn	first paragraph

A: 老師，這篇作文要多長？

B: 最少三段。

Compare: 鍛duàn

木 mù 'wood'
+ 反 fǎn
phonetic

bǎn 8
board, hard

老板	lǎobǎn	shopkeeper, boss
黑板	hēibǎn*	blackboard
地板	dìbǎn*	floor
天花板	tiānhuābǎn*	ceiling

A: 你的老板怎麼樣？

B: 省錢省得要命，地板、天花板都舊了
還不換huàn 'change'。

巾 jīn 'woven material' + 'loose meshes' —loose, rare, seldom, to hope

希

| 希望 | xīwàng | to hope, wish |

A: 你希望當助教嗎？

B: 對，我很需要教書經驗。

xī 7
to hope, rare, scarce

宀 mián 'roof' + 心 xīn 'heart' + 皿 mǐn 'dish' + 丁/丂 qiǎo 'rest'—peace, to prefer a house, a heart, and a cup

宁

| 寧可 | nìngkě | would rather, better |
| 寧願 | nìngyuàn* | would rather, better |

A: 我寧可多付一點錢也不要跟她住。

B: 她真的那麼讓人討厭嗎？

nìng, níng 14
to prefer, rather, peaceful

厶 'breath' + 口 kǒu 'mouth'— the mouth exhaling a breath: to speak to make one's self known, I

台

台灣	Táiwān	Taiwan
電台	diàntái*	broadcasting station
電視台	diànshìtái*	TV station

A: 你想找什麼工作？

B: 在電台或者電視台工作都不錯。

Compare: 始 shǐ 治 zhì 抬 tái

tái 5
platform, stand, table, you

宀 mián 'roof' + 至 zhì 'an arrow arriving at its target' phonetic

室

| 教室 | jiàoshì | classroom |
| 辦公室 | bàngōngshì* | office |

A: 你的教室裏有沒有電腦？

B: 沒有，辦公室有。

Compare: 到 dào 家 jiā 宿 sù

shì 9
room, house

語法和用法 Grammar and Usage

Pay attention to the function of the structure and then study the example sentences.

1. Expressing the continuation of an action from its origin

從Time When起/開始SVO S從Time When起/開始VO	cóng…qǐ /kāishǐ…	starting from; since (a point in time)

前天聽小王說，你**從**二月**起**就在一家兒童英語補習班工作。

1. | 你的中文這麼好，一定學了很久jiǔ 'long time' 吧！ | 你的中文这么好，一定学了很久吧！ | Your Chinese is so good. You must have studied it for a long time. |
   | --- | --- | --- |
   | 我從上個學期才開始學中文，所以其實還很不好。 | 我从上个学期才开始学中文，所以其实还很不好。 | I didn't start studying Chinese till last semester, so actually I am not very good at it at all. |

2. | 我昨天從早上起就給你打電話，可是一直沒人接，你去哪兒了？ | 我昨天从早上起就给你打电话，可是一直没人接，你去哪儿了？ | Yesterday morning I started calling you, but no one answered the phone. Where did you go? |
   | --- | --- | --- |
   | 我去機場接朋友，可是飛機晚點了，我從早上八點開始，等到中午十二點。 | 我去机场接朋友，可是飞机晚点了，我从早上八点开始，等到中午十二点。 | I went to the airport to pick up a friend, but the plane was late. I waited from eight o'clock in the morning till noon. |

3. | 你知道中國是什麼時候出現chūxiàn 'to appear' 個體戶的嗎？ | 你知道中国是什么时候出现个体户的吗？ | Do you know when those individual entrepreneurs first appeared in China? |
   | --- | --- | --- |
   | 應該是從一九七八年開始出現的。 | 应该是从一九七八年开始出现的。 | They should have first appeared in 1978. |

The pattern 從…起 indicates the origin of a time when an action starts to take place. It can precede or follow the subject. Compare this with 自從 VO以後 (L4, G1).

[handwritten margin notes: inverted stand 倒立 hand/head stand; drive backward 倒车]

2. Expressing contrariety

O S₁ V, S₂倒(是) V/Adj	…dào (shi)…	actually; on the contrary; instead

最近有趣的事沒有，不過頭疼的問題**倒**不少！

1. 今年天氣怎麼樣？雪下得多不多？   今年天气怎么样？雪下得多不多？   How was the weather this year? Was there a lot of snow?

   雪下得不多，雨倒下了不少。   雪下得不多，雨倒下了不少。   There wasn't much snow, but it rained a lot instead.

2. 動物園好玩嗎？看到大熊貓了嗎？   动物园好玩吗？看到大熊猫了吗？   Is it fun to go to the zoo? Did you see any giant pandas?

   大熊貓我沒看到，無尾熊wúwěixióng我倒看到了三隻。   大熊猫我没看到，无尾熊我倒看到了三只。   I didn't see any giant pandas. Instead, I saw three koala bears.

3. 她真漂亮！   她真漂亮！   She is really beautiful.

   我倒是覺得她那個不愛說話的妹妹更可愛。   我倒是觉得她那个不爱说话的妹妹更可爱。   Actually I think that her quiet little sister is cuter.

倒(是) is an adverb used to convey something contrary to what was said or thought. It often defies expectation or common sense, e.g., "他没吃藥，病倒好了" or "妹妹倒比姐姐高." In such cases, it is similar to the function of 反而. Compare it with 不但沒/不…反而… (L5, G3) and 居然 (L2, G5). However, when the meaning is simply to contradict what has been previously said, it is similar to 才 (L17, G6) and 是…而不是 (L20, G4).

3. Expressing an aspect or perspective to illustrate a point

（就）拿person/aspect來說， (comment)	(jiù)ná…láishuō,…	(Just) taking the person/aspect as an example, … as for…, concerning…, take…

拿我補習班的老板**來說**，有一次我告訴他，我們的教室需要裝一台電腦……

1. 在國外留學，有什麼不習慣的地方嗎？

   在国外留学，有什么不习惯的地方吗？

   Is there anything unfamiliar about studying abroad?

   可多了，拿語言來說吧，這是最大的問題。

   可多了，拿语言来说吧，这是最大的问题。
   ná yǔ yán lái

   A lot. As for the language, that's the biggest problem.

2. 聽說印大在美國中西部很有名？

   听说印大在美国中西部很有名？

   I heard that I.U. is well known in the Midwest.

   沒錯，拿商學院 shāngxuéyuàn 來說，每年都吸引了很多學生。

   没错，拿商学院来说，每年都吸引了很多学生。

   That's right. Take the business school as an example, they attract a lot of students every year.

3. 你覺得東方人一定比西方人愛面子嗎？

   你觉得东方人一定比西方人爱面子吗？

   Do you think East Asians necessarily like to keep up appearances more than Westerners?

   不一定，拿我來說，我覺得自己有時候比東方人更怕丟臉。

   不一定，拿我来说，我觉得自己有时候比东方人更怕丢脸。

   Not necessarily. Take me as an example. I feel sometimes that I am even more afraid of losing face than East Asians.

The pattern 拿…來說 means to "take…as the focus or point of departure in saying something." Therefore, for context, a general statement often precedes it (e.g., 住宿舍沒有住校外那麼好). One uses this pattern to give a specific example (e.g., 拿吃的來說，宿舍的飯又貴又難吃). Don't confuse this pattern with 拿A跟B比較 (L12, G5).

4. Expressing the futility of an action

白 V(了)	bái... (le)	V in vain

我以為他同意了，哪知道這就是「不行」的意思。害得我**白高興了**半天。

1.	好消息！老師病了，所以今天沒有考試。	好消息！老师病了，所以今天没有考试。	Good news! The teacher is sick, so we have no test today.
	白準備了，早知道我就可以去喝朋友的喜酒了。	白准备了，早知道我就可以去喝朋友的喜酒了。	I prepared for nothing. If I had known this beforehand, I would have gone to my friend's wedding banquet.
2.	他答應幫我買一本書，可是到現在也沒買來。	他答应帮我买一本书，可是到现在也没买来。	He promised to buy me a book, but he hasn't bought it yet.
	那你白請他吃飯了。	那你白请他吃饭了。	Then you wasted your money treating him to dinner.
3.	儘管我在補習班學了三個月英文，可是我還是不敢說英文。	尽管我在补习班学了三个月英文，可是我还是不敢说英文。	Even though I studied English for three months in an accelerated program, I still don't dare speak English.
	那你補習班白上了，錢也白花了。	那你补习班白上了，钱也白花了。	Then you went to the school for nothing, and wasted all of your money as well.

The usage of 白 in this chapter means to "do something in vain." There is often a 了 at the end of the sentence, as it denotes a change in status.

5. Expressing the least objectionable alternative

寧可 V₁(O₁)也不 V₂(O₂)	nìngkě... yěbù...	rather do V₁O₁ than do V₂O₂ (V₁O₁ is reluctantly preferred)

我**寧可**這個同事一開始的時候，就告訴我他需要我的幫助，**也不**希望他用請客的藉口來騙我。

1. | 你想不想試一試中國人喜歡的豬腳、狗肉什麼的？ | 你想不想试一试中国人喜欢的猪脚、狗肉什么的？ | Would you like to try the pig's feet and dog meat that the Chinese like so much? |

   我寧可餓死也不吃那些東西。　我宁可饿死也不吃那些东西。　I would rather die of hunger than eat those things.

2. | 你爸爸認識那麼多朋友，讓他拉拉關係，你一定能找到一個好工作。 | 你爸爸认识那么多朋友，让他拉拉关系，你一定能找到一个好工作。 | Your father knows so many friends. Let him make some contacts. You will certainly find a good job. |

   我寧可靠自己的能力找一個普通 pǔtōng 的工作，也不讓爸爸走後門。　我宁可靠自己的能力找一个普通的工作，也不让爸爸走后门。（kào）　I would rather depend on my own ability to find an ordinary job, than have my father go through the back door for me.

3. | 我很想請那個女孩和我去散步，可是她不同意的話，我會很丟臉。 | 我很想请那个女孩和我去散步，可是她不同意的话，我会很丢脸。 | I would really like to ask that girl out for a walk. But if she refused me, I would lose face. |

   面子那麼重要嗎？寧可失去 shīqù 'to lose' 她，也不能失去面子？　面子那么重要吗？宁可失去她，也不能失去面子？　Is your face so important? Would you rather lose her than lose your face?

The pattern 寧可 A 也不 B is used to indicate one's preference of $V_1(O_1)$, the lesser of two evils. V_1O_1 and V_2O_2 are typically something severe and deplorable, and neither is the desirable choice of the speaker, if she or he has other options. Yet, if the speaker is forced to make a choice between two unwanted things, V_1O_1 is preferable. Therefore, it's semantically odd to say 我寧可吃雞肉也不吃狗肉 though syntactically it's all right. In this case, it would be more appropriate to say 我寧可餓死也不吃狗肉. To describe a student who hates to do homework, one may say 他寧可被老師打也不做功課.

6. Expressing different aspects

一方面…(另)一方面…	yìfāngmiàn…(lìng) yìfāng miàn	on the one hand…, on the other hand

一方面高興交了個朋友，**另一方面**又懷疑他們真正的目的究竟是什麼。

1. 中國人辦喜事的時候，為什麼請那麼多客人呢？

    中国人办喜事的时候，为什么请那么多客人呢？

    Why do Chinese invite so many guests when they have a wedding ceremony?

    我想一方面是人多熱鬧，另一方面是人多主人會很有面子。

    我想一方面是人多热闹，另一方面是人多主人会很有面子。

    I think it is because on the one hand, the more people you have the more festive it is, and on the other hand, when there are a lot of people the host feels important.

2. 你去中國留學真正的原因是什麼？

    你去中国留学真正的原因是什么？

    What is your real reason for going to China to study?

    一方面是學好中文，另一方面是為了直接了解中國文化。

    一方面是学好中文，另一方面是为了直接了解中国文化。

    On the one hand, I want to study Chinese well; on the other hand, I want to understand Chinese culture firsthand.

3. 參加旅行團有什麼好處、壞處？

    参加旅行团有什么好处、坏处？

    What are the advantages and disadvantages of joining a tour group?

    一方面由旅行團安排事情可以省很多麻煩，但另一方面卻少了自由。

    一方面由旅行团安排事情可以省很多麻烦，但另一方面却少了自由。

    On the one hand, the tour group will save you a lot of trouble in arranging things. On the other hand, you will have less freedom.

This pattern expresses two concerns that occur simultaneously. There is often 又/也/卻 in the clause with 另一方面. Compare this with 一來…二來 (L6, G3) when one wants to enumerate reasons, and with 一邊兒…一邊兒 when one wants to describe two actions occurring simultaneously.

文化點滴 Culture Notes

1. **Wedding ceremony**: In a traditional Chinese wedding, one can expect to have a feast of at least ten to twelve dishes, starting with assorted cold dishes 冷盤 lěngpán, then hot dishes 熱菜 rècài, and Chinese style desserts such as 八寶飯 bābǎofàn. While guests are enjoying the food to their hearts' delight, the bride and groom walk around making numerous toasts to guests at their tables. In Taiwan, the bride will also change her clothes frequently during the feast, almost as if she were a model in a fashion show. When the feast is over, the newlyweds stand at the door to see the guests out, but some, mostly close friends and classmates, may stay to tease the newlyweds with all kinds of tricks. The havoc of a Chinese wedding party is nicely depicted in the film *The Wedding Banquet* 喜宴 xǐyàn, by Ang Lee.

2. **Red envelopes**: In Chinese society, the red envelope 紅包 hóngbāo, a gift of money, serves many purposes. It can be used as a congratulatory gift for all manner of auspicious events, such as a New Year's gift given by adults to children, a "small consideration" to the doctor before surgery or the birth of a child, as an expression of a boss's appreciation to his employees, or for the bride and groom at their wedding ceremony.

3. **Taking someone out**: It may not be an exaggeration to say that most of the Chinese business deals are negotiated over a meal. In fact, getting together for lunch or dinner is one of the most popular activities for friends and co-workers as well. It is said that the money spent on food each year in Taiwan could build several highways. Although going Dutch treat is popular among young people, it is still common to see people fighting over who pays the bill in a restaurant.

4. **Asking for leave**: There are different kinds of leave one can request. The following is a sample of notes asking for a leave of absence 請事假 qǐng shìjià.

劉老師：	刘老师：
我父親從美國來看我，明天上午到台北，我想去機場接他，不能來上課，請准zhǔn假一天。	我父亲从美国来看我，明天上午到台北，我想去机场接他，不能来上课，请准假一天。
學生 高德中上	学生 高德中上
二○○三年三月十日	二○○三年三月十日

歌兒 Songs

面子問題
The Face Problem

Allegretto　　　　　　　　　　　　　　　　詞：劉雅詩　　曲：馬定一

1. 那　天　我　接到　鄰　居的紅色炸彈，這　下子　可　真是
   Nà　tiān　wǒ　jiēdào　lín　jū de hóngsè zhàdàn, zhè　xiàzi　kě　zhēnshì
   The day I received a "red bomb" from my neighbor,　　well, it really

2. 同　事　問　我和　鄰　居是不是很熟，如果我　不吃　喜酒
   Tóng　shì　wèn　wǒ hé　lín　jū shìbúshì hěn shú, rúguǒ wǒ　bù chī xǐjiǔ
   My colleague asks me whether or not I'm very well acquainted with this neighbor. If I don't go to the banquet,

1. 讓　我　左右為難。要　請假　參　加　會對不起我　老板。
   ràng　wǒ　zuǒyòu wéinán.　Yào　qǐngkè　cān　jiā,　huì duìbùqǐ wǒ　lǎobǎn.
   put me in a bind.　To ask for time off to attend the wedding banquet would let my boss down.

2. 可　以　找　藉口。先　送個　紅　包　鄰居面子就　很夠。
   kě　yǐ　zhǎo　jièkǒu.　Xiān　sòng ge　hóng　bāo, línjū miànzi jiù hěn gòu.
   I can find an excuse.　First give him a red envelope, then he will save face.

1. 不　參加　客人　很少　鄰　居　會丟臉。我心裏矛　盾　不知道該怎
   Bù　cānjiā kèrén hěn shǎo lín　jū　huì diūliǎn. Wǒ xīnlǐ máo dùn bù zhīdào gāi zěn
   Not to attend would mean fewer guests and my neighbor would lose face. I'm so perplexed, I don't know

2. 再　說聲恭　喜　可惜自己　沒有空，要不然一　定　找時間去喝
   Zài shuōshēng gōng　xǐ　kěxí zìjǐ　méiyǒu kòng. Yàobùrán yídìng zhǎoshíjiān qù hē
   Then say congratulations and it's a pity you don't have spare time. Otherwise you would certainly

1. 麼辦，只好　問　問　我　同　事　順　便　吃　個　飯。
   mebàn. Zhǐ hǎo wèn　wèn　wǒ　tóngshì　shùnbiàn　chī　ge　fàn.
   what to do. The only choice is to ask my colleague, in passing, to get together for dinner.

2. 喜酒，祝　福　新　婚　小　夫　婦　幸　福　常　左　右。
   xǐjiǔ. Zhù fú　xīn　hūn xiǎo fū　fù　xìng　fú　cháng zuǒ yòu.
   go to the banquet and bless the newlyweds with happiness forever.

✍　我的問題：

✍　我的學習方法：

第十六課

Theme Social Trends and Problems

Communicative Objectives
- Talking about activism
- Talking about the price of goods
- Talking about crime
- Talking about the U.S.

Focus on Characters
- 危險展示、豐富普遍、青蘋光筆、隨緣批價、抱財冒聞

Grammar Focus
- S動不動就VO
- S一會兒…一會兒…
- B是由於/因為A(的緣故/關係)
- …，光是A就…
- (要到)/(直到)…S才…
- 各V各的(O)

哪兒有「桃花源」呢？

生詞 Vocabulary

Study the following words for their pronunciation and meaning. When an area is shaded, guess at the meaning of the word based on its constituent characters and then fill in the blank. Read the usage of words and related terms (antonyms, synonyms, compounds sharing the constituent characters, etc.) and try to answer the sample questions in Chinese. Note that proper nouns and incidental terms are not numbered.

◎By Order of Appearance

1. 桃花源　Táohuāyuán　N　utopia　[peach-blossom-origin]

2. 一陣子　yízhènzi　N/ M　a while, a short period of time　[one-battle array-suffix]

　　一阵子　*前、这、过*　這/前一陣子

　　1 mnth 5 mnth 3 days　你這一陣子忙不忙？

　　你这一阵子忙不忙？

3. 新聞　xīnwén　N　news　[new-hear]

　　头条 新闻 = headline / top story　報上/電視新聞；頭條 tóutiáo 'number one' 新聞

　　tou tiao　今天報上的頭條新聞是什麼？

　　今天报上的头条新闻是什么？

4. 批　pī　M　batch, lot, group　*一批*

5. 偷渡　tōudù　*客*　V　to steal across international　[secretly-ferry across]
　　illegal immigrant　border

　　很多人從墨西哥 Mòxīgē 偷渡到哪兒去？

　　很多人从墨西哥偷渡到哪儿去？

6. 國家　guójiā　N　country, state, nation　[country-family]

　　国家

　　現在哪些國家有很多偷渡客？

　　现在哪些国家有很多偷渡客？

卖○

做 ↗ 7. 生意　shēngyi　N　business, trade　[bear-idea]

8. 發財　fācái　VO　to get rich　[expand-wealth]

　　发财　*发一笔财*

9. 筆　bǐ　M　measure word for money

　　笔

　　現在做什麼生意可以發一筆大財？

　　现在做什么生意可以发一笔大财？

10. 冒　mào　V　to risk, to brave

　　冒……的危險/大雨V

　　→冒險 màoxiǎn 'to take a risk'

　　你冒著大雨出去做什麼？

排队 que
pái dùi

（handwritten top margin: 冒着 生命的危险）

你冒着大雨出去做什么？

| 11. | 生命 | shēngmìng | N | (physical) life | [life-life] |

在你生命中哪些事最重要？
在你生命中哪些事最重要？

（handwritten: 风险 risk）

| 12. | 危险
危险 | wēixiǎn | N/
Adj | danger, dangerous | [danger-risk] |

（handwritten: qián 潜 水 diving）

↔安全
美國哪個城市最危險？
美国哪个城市最危险？

| 13. | 不滿
不滿 | bùmǎn | Adj | displeased | [not-satisfied] |

（handwritten left: S 對……不滿）

對……很不滿/很滿意；心裏很不滿 *（handwritten: secretly hold a grudge）*
你對什麼事情很不滿？
你对什么事情很不满？

| 14. | 現象
现象 | xiànxiàng | N | phenomenon | [show-appearance] |

（handwritten: pǔbiàn xiànxiàng → common use）

| 15. | 普遍 | pǔbiàn | Adj | universal, widespread | [common-everywhere] |

在哪兒偷渡的現象很普遍？
在哪儿偷渡的现象很普遍？

16.	老百姓	lǎobǎixìng	N	common people, civilians	[prefix-numerous-surname]
17.	動不動 动不动	dòngbudòng	Adv	easily, at the slightest provocation	[move-not-move]
18.	遊行 游行	yóuxíng	V/N	to demonstrate, parade	[rove-travel]

那些人為了什麼來遊行示威？
那些人为了什么来游行示威？ *（handwritten: 示花游行; show-power）*

| 19. | 示威 | shìwēi | VO/N | to march, demonstration | [show-threat] |
| 20. | 抱怨 | bàoyuàn | V | to complain, to grumble | [hold in arms-blame] |

跟/向（人）抱怨（事）
學生常喜歡抱怨什麼？
学生常喜欢抱怨什么？

Characters with Many Strokes

源 陣 偷 渡 筆 險 普 遍 威 怨

21.	物價 物价	wùjià	N	commodity prices	[thing-price]
				→油價、房價	
22.	漲 涨	zhǎng	V	to rise, to go up	
				今年的學費又漲了多少？	
				今年的学费又涨了多少？	
23.	股票	gǔpiào	N	stock	[share-certificate]
24.	跌	diē/dié	V	to fall, to tumble	
				最近哪裏的股票跌得很慘？	
				最近哪里的股票跌得很惨？	
25.	豐富 丰富	fēngfù	Adj/ V	rich, enrich	[abundance-rich]
				食物/經驗豐富	
				什麼可以豐富你的生活經驗？	
				什么可以丰富你的生活经验？	
26.	由於 由于	yóuyú	Prep	owing/due/thanks to	[via-that]
27.	升學 升学	shēngxué	VO	to enter higher school	[ascend-study]
28.	壓力 压力	yālì	N	pressure	[push down-power]
				升學/考試/工作壓力	
				你現在受到什麼樣的壓力？	
				你现在受到什么样的压力？	
29.	競爭 竞争	jìngzhēng	N/V	competition, to compete	[compete-vie]
30.	激烈	jīliè	Adj	intense, fierce	[sharp-strong]
				競爭/討論/比賽激烈	
				你們同學之間的競爭激烈嗎？	
				你们同学之间的竞争激烈吗？	
31.	緣故 缘故	yuángù	N	cause, reason	[cause-cause]
32.	安全	ānquán	Adj/ N	safe, security	[quiet-whole]
33.	青少年	qīng-shào nián	N	the young generation	[green-little-age]
				你了解現代青少年的問題嗎？	

你了解現代青少年的問題嗎？

34.	犯罪	fànzuì	N/	crime, to commit a crime	[offend-guilt]
			VO	為什麼青少年犯罪越來越多？	
				为什么青少年犯罪越来越多？	
35.	隨便 隨便	suíbiàn	Adv/ V	carelessly, to do as one pleases 隨（人的）便；隨便吃	[follow-convenience]

"I don't care" → just word
polite

你怎麼可以隨便亂說話呢？
你怎么可以随便乱说话呢？

| 36. | 開槍
开枪 | kāiqiāng | VO | to shoot | [fire-gun] |
| 37. | 隨著 | suízhe | Prep | along with, in the wake of | [follow-particle] |

☆ 隨着 +N 的 fazhan/bianhua 隨著……的發展/變化/到來

| 38. | 發展
发展 | fāzhǎn | N/V | development, to develop | [begin-expand] |

現在什麼發展得很快？
现在什么发展得很快？

| 39. | 變化
变化 | biànhuà | N | change [change-transform] | |

有/產生 chǎnshēng……的變化

| 40. | 吃虧
吃亏 | chīkuī | VO | to suffer loss | [suffer-lose] |

你昨天吃了誰的虧？
你昨天吃了谁的亏？

41.	光是	guāngshì	Adv	merely, just	[only-this]
42.	直到	zhídào	Prep/ Adv	until, up to	[straight-to]
43.	神話 神话	shénhuà	N	Myth, mythology	[god-story]

你覺得什麼是個神話？
你觉得什么是个神话？

| 44. | 國外
国外 | guówài | N | external, overseas, abroad | [country-outside] |
| 45. | 蘋果
苹果 | píngguǒ | N | apple | [apple-fruit] |

Characters with Many Strokes

壓　競　激　罪　隨　槍　展　變　虧　蘋

◎By Grammatical Categories

Nouns/Pronouns

筆	bǐ	measure word for money	青少年	qīng-shàonián	youths
批	pī	batch, lot, group	新聞	xīnwén	news
發展	fāzhǎn	development, to develop	神話	shénhuà	myth, mythology
變化	biànhuà	change	生命	shēngmìng	(physical) life
犯罪	fànzuì	crime, to commit a crime	生意	shēngyi	business, trade
危險	wēixiǎn	danger, dangerous	股票	gǔpiào	stock
競爭	jìngzhēng	competition, to compete	物價	wùjià	commodity prices
國家	guójiā	country, state, nation	現象	xiànxiàng	phenomenon
國外	guówài	external, overseas, abroad	壓力	yālì	pressure
蘋果	píngguǒ	apple	緣故	yuángù	cause, reason
老百姓	lǎobǎixìng	common people, civilians	桃花源	Táohuāyuán	utopia
			一陣子	yízhènzi	a while, a short period of time

Verbs/Stative Verbs/Adjectives

漲	zhǎng	to rise, to go up	升學	shēngxué	to enter higher school
跌	diē/dié	to fall, to tumble	發財	fācái	to get rich
冒	mào	to risk, to brave	吃虧	chīkuī	to suffer loss, to come to grief
偷渡	tōudù	to steal across international border	不滿	bùmǎn	dissatisfied
抱怨	bàoyuàn	to complain, to grumble	普遍	pǔbiàn	universal, widespread
開槍	kāiqiāng	to shoot	激烈	jīliè	intense, fierce
示威	shìwēi	to march, demonstration	安全	ānquán	safe, security
遊行	yóuxíng	to demonstrate, parade	豐富	fēngfù	rich, enrich

Adverbs and Others

動不動	dòngbudòng	easily, at the slightest provocation	光是	guāngshì	merely, just
由於	yóuyú	owing/due/thanks to	隨著	suízhe	along with, in the wake of
隨便	suíbiàn	carelessly, casually, to do as one pleases	直到	zhídào	until, up to

◎By Pinyin

Entries with * indicate lexical items used in Mini-Dialogues and of possible interest for supplemental study.

ānquán	安全	safe, security	pī	批	batch, lot, group
bàoyuàn	抱怨	to complain, to grumble	pǔbiàn	普遍	universal, widespread
biànhuà	变化	change	qīng-shàonián	青少年	young people and teenagers, youths
bǐ	笔	measure word for money	shēngmìng	生命	(physical) life
bùmǎn	不满	dissatisfied	shēngxué	升学	to enter higher school
chīkuī	吃亏	to suffer loss, to come to grief	shēngyi	生意	business, trade
dàijià*	代价	price, cost	shénhuà	神话	myth, mythology
diē/dié	跌	to fall, to tumble	shìwēi	示威	to march, demonstration
dòngbudòng	动不动	easily, at the slightest provocation	suíbiàn	随便	carelessly, casually, to do as one pleases
fācái	发财	to get rich	suízhe	随着	along with, in the wake of
fànzuì	犯罪	crime, to commit a crime	táifēng*	台风	typhoon
fāzhǎn	发展	development, to develop	Táohuāyuán	桃花源	utopia
fēngfù	丰富	rich, enrich	tōudù	偷渡	to steal across international border
guāngshì	光是	merely, just			
guójiā	国家	country, state, nation	wēixiǎn	危险	danger, dangerous
guówài	国外	external, overseas, abroad	wùjià	物价	commodity prices
gǔpiào	股票	stock	xiànxiàng	现象	phenomenon
jīliè	激烈	intense, fierce	xīnwén	新闻	news
jìngzhēng	竞争	competition, to compete	yālì	压力	pressure
júzi*	桔子	orange	yízhènzi	一阵子	a while, a short period of time
kāiqiāng	开枪	to shoot	yóuxíng	游行	to demonstrate, parade
lǎobǎixìng	老百姓	common people, civilians	yóuyú	由于	owing/due/thanks to
liàng*	辆	measure word for cars	yuángù	缘故	cause, reason
mào	冒	to risk, to brave	zhǎng	涨	to rise, to go up
píngguǒ	苹果	apple	zhídào	直到	until, up to

課文 Text

Use the following questions to guide your reading of the text.

1. 小高不明白什麼問題？

2. 小高看到台灣的社會有什麼現象？

3. 小李覺得大陸的社會這幾年有什麼現象？他的看法是什麼？

小李：

你這一陣子忙嗎？有機會上網看看新聞嗎？最近又有一批大陸人，在偷渡到其他國家的路上死了，真慘！聽說他們在國內的生活都很不錯，很多是做生意、發了財的人，所以才能付那一大筆偷渡的錢。我真不明白他們為什麼要冒生命的危險，離開自己的地方呢？是為了找「桃花源」嗎？哪兒有「桃花源」呢？

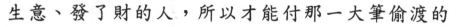

對現實不滿的現象在台灣也很普遍。這兒的老百姓[1]動不動就去遊行示威，[2]一會兒抱怨物價漲得太厲害、一會兒抱怨股票跌得太快。不管什麼原因，好像都可以引起不滿。儘管人們的生活比從前豐富多了，

即使 … 也 …
even if …

富有～錢

但是大家還是想出國、移民，即使自己不走，也要送孩子出去做個「小留學生」。有人說這是[3]**由於**台灣的升學壓力太大、競爭太激烈**的緣故**，有人說是由於社會不安全、青少年犯罪問題嚴重的關係，難道他們不知道美國的教育也有很多問題，有些孩子也在校園內隨便開槍殺人嗎？

德中上

 小高：

　　這些年來隨著經濟的發展，大陸各方面都有了很大的變化。可以說人人怕吃虧，一切向「錢」看吧！很多人以為國外有很多賺錢的機會，而且生活水平比國內高得多，所以只要有一點兒辦法的人都爭著出國，每年[4]**光是**申請到國外留學的人**就**不知道有多少。我自己沒來美國以前，也以為這兒是全世界最好的地方，[5]**直到**來了以後**才**知道，很多東西都是神話，這兒窮人的生活可能比國內的還慘呢！在我看來，國內、國外[6]**各有各的**問題，但是中國人在國外再找也找不到「桃花源」，有的只是「蘋果園」吧！

李明上

课文 Text

Use the following questions to guide your reading of the text.

1. 小高不明白什么问题？

2. 小高看到台湾的社会有什么现象？

3. 小李觉得大陆的社会这几年有什么现象？他的看法是什么？

 小李：

你这一阵子忙吗？有机会上网看看新闻吗？最近又有一批大陆人，在偷渡到其他国家的路上死了，真惨！听说他们在国内的生活都很不错，很多是做生意、发了财的人，所以才能付那一大笔偷渡的钱。我真不明白他们为什么要冒生命的危险，离开自己的地方呢？是为了找"桃花源"吗？

哪儿有"桃花源"呢？

对现实不满的现象在台湾也很普遍。这儿的老百姓[1]动不动就去游行示威，[2]一会儿抱怨物价涨得太厉害、一会儿抱怨股票跌得太快。不管什么原因，好象都可以引起不满。尽管人们的生活比从前丰富多了，但是大家还是想出国、移民，即使自己不走，也要送孩子出去做个"小留学生"。有人说这是[3]由于台湾的升学压力太大、竞争太激烈的缘故，有人说是由

于社会不安全、青少年犯罪问题严重的关系，难道他们不知道美国的
教育也有很多问题，有些孩子也在校园内随便开枪杀人吗？

德中上

小高：

    这些年来随着经济的发展，大陆各方面都有了很大的变化。可
以说人人怕吃亏，一切向"钱"看吧！很多人以为国外有很多赚钱的
机会，而且生活水平比国内高得多，所以只要有一点儿办法的人都争
着出国，每年⁴**光是**申请到国外留学的人**就**不知道有多少。我自己没
来美国以前，也以为这儿是全世界最好的地方，⁵**直到**来了以后**才**知
道，很多东西都是神话，这儿穷人的生活可能比国内的还惨呢！在我
看来，国内、国外⁶**各有各的**问题，但是中国人在国外再找也找不到
"桃花源"，有的只是"苹果园"吧！

李明上

小對話 Mini-Dialogues

Read the supplementary dialogues for a better understanding of the text. See if you can memorize one and perform it in class.

(1) Talking about activism

Gao: 今天有什麼新聞？

今天有什么新闻？

A: 又有人示威遊行，光是台北火車站前面就擠了兩百人。

又有人示威游行，光是台北火车站前面就挤了两百人。

Gao: 難怪今天到處塞車。這兒的老百姓動不動就抱怨，太過分了！

难怪今天到处塞车。这儿的老百姓动不动就抱怨，太过分了！

A: 我倒覺得這是個好現象，把自己的不滿說出來，社會才能進步啊！

我倒觉得这是个好现象，把自己的不满说出来，社会才能进步啊！

Gao: Is there any news today?

A: People demonstrated again. There were two hundred people crowded in front of the Taipei train station alone.

Gao: No wonder there were traffic jams all over today. The people here complain with or without the slightest provocation. It's getting out of hand!

A: On the contrary—I think it's a good trend. Only after people express their discontent can society make progress.

(2) Talking about the price of goods

Gao: 這橘子 júzi 多少錢一斤？

这桔子多少钱一斤？

A: 五十塊。

五十块。

Gao: 怎麼又漲價了？上個星期不是四十塊一斤嗎？

怎么又涨价了？上个星期不是四十块一斤吗？

A:　　颱風táifēng剛過嘛！　　　　　　台风刚过嘛！

Gao:　颱風對橘子有影響嗎？你們賺　　颱风对桔子有影响吗？你们赚
　　　錢也賺得太屬害了吧！　　　　　钱也赚得太厉害了吧！

A:　　我們只是做小生意的，能賺什　　我们只是做小生意的，能赚什
　　　麼錢。　　　　　　　　　　　　么钱。

Gao:　How much is this orange per *jin*?

A:　　Fifty dollars.

Gao:　How come the price went up again?
　　　Wasn't it forty dollars per *jin* last week?

A:　　A typhoon just hit.

Gao:　Does a typhoon have an impact on oranges?
　　　You are too good at making money.

A:　　We're just small businessmen. What kind
　　　of money can we earn?

(3) Talking about crime

A:　　你聽說了沒有？前一陣子又有　　你听说了没有？前一阵子又有
　　　一些青少年騎機車出去，隨便　　一些青少年骑机车出去，随便
　　　殺人。　　　　　　　　　　　　杀人。

Gao:　這麼可怕，為什麼現在青少年　　这么可怕，为什么现在青少年
　　　犯罪的問題這麼嚴重呢？是因　　犯罪的问题这么严重呢？是因
　　　為升學壓力太大了嗎？　　　　为升学压力太大了吗？

A:　　這幾年大學已經比從前多多　　这几年大学已经比从前多多
　　　了，我看都是受了電視不好的　　了，我看都是受了电视不好的
　　　影響。　　　　　　　　　　　　影响。

Gao:　我想這些孩子都沒有受到好的　　我想这些孩子都没有受到好的
　　　照顧，他們的家庭多半兒都有　　照顾，他们的家庭多半儿都有
　　　問題。　　　　　　　　　　　　问题。

A:　　Have you heard? A while back, there were some young men out riding their
　　　motorcyles and killing people at random.

Gao:　That's terrible. Why has the problem of juvenile deliquency become so serious these
　　　days? Is it because the pressure to get into college is too great?

A: There are a lot more colleges
      these past few years. I
      think it's all because of
      the negative influence
      they get from
      television.

Gao: I think none of these
      children received a good
      upbringing. Most of their
      families have problems.

(4) Talking about the U.S.

A: 聽說美國每個家庭都有兩輛liàng   听说美国每个家庭都有两辆车，
      車，都住在大房子裏！   都住在大房子里！

Gao: 不一定，沒有車的人也不少。   不一定，没有车的人也不少。

A: 聽說那兒到處是機會，誰都能   听说那儿到处是机会，谁都能
      成功。   成功。

Gao: 在中國也好，在美國也好，成功   在中国也好，在美国也好，成功
      都是要付代價dàijià的。   都是要付代价的。

A: 不管什麼代價我都要去看看。   不管什么代价我都要去看看。

Gao: 我看你美國電影看得太多，被好   我看你美国电影看得太多，被好
      萊塢Hǎoláiwū「洗腦」xǐnǎo了！   莱坞"洗脑"了！

A: I heard that every U.S. household has two cars and a big house.

Gao: Not necessarily. There are also quite a few people without cars.

A: I heard that there are opportunities everywhere. Everyone can be suceessful.

Gao: Whether in China or in the U.S., there is a price you must pay
      for success.

A: No matter what the price, I want to go there and
      see.

Gao: I think you have seen too many U.S. movies,
      and been "brainwashed" by Hollywood!

小故事 Stories

Read the following tale for your own enjoyment and for your understanding of the highlighted expression that is relevant to the theme of the chapter.

 世外桃源 shìwài táoyuán

❀ 這個地方這麼美、這麼好，真是個世外桃源啊！

很久以前，有一個打魚的人划著小船，順著一條小河往上走。河的兩邊都是桃樹，桃花兒在天上飛，美極了！後來他發現桃樹沒了、河也沒了。前面有一個山，山下有一個洞。

他走進洞裏，看見那兒有很多房子和田地，房子前面有雞、有狗，人們在田裏工作，都很快樂的樣子。他們看見這個打魚的，都很吃驚，問他是怎麼來的，又請他去家裏喝酒、吃飯。這些人說，他們

桃源	táoyuán	peach-blossom spring
打魚的	dǎyúde	fisherman
船	chuán	boat
河	hé	river
桃樹	táoshù	peach tree
洞	dòng	cave
田地	tiándì	field, farmland
雞	jī	chicken
祖先	zǔxiān	ancestor
逃	táo	to flee, to escape
避難	bìnàn	to take refuge
朝代	cháodài	dynasty
村子	cūnzi	village
記號	jìhào	mark, sign

的祖先在五六百年以前就逃到這兒來避難，後來就一直沒有出去過。他們不知道現在外頭是哪個朝代了。住了幾天，打魚的要回家了，村子裏的人請他不要把這個地方告訴別人。

打魚的回去的時候，在路上做了很多記號。可是他想再回來的時候，不知道為什麼記號都不見了，也找不到那條路了。

✐ 世外桃源的意思是＿＿＿＿＿＿＿＿＿＿＿＿＿＿＿＿＿＿

世外桃源 shìwài táoyuán

❀ 这个地方这么美、这么好，真是个世外桃源啊！

桃源	táoyuán	peach-blossom spring
打鱼的	dǎyúde	fisherman
船	chuán	boat
河	hé	river
桃树	táoshù	peach tree
洞	dòng	cave
田地	tiándì	field, farmland
鸡	jī	chicken
祖先	zǔxiān	ancestor
逃	táo	to flee, to escape
避难	bìnàn	to take refuge
朝代	cháodài	dynasty
村子	cūnzi	village
记号	jìhào	mark, sign

　　很久以前，有一个打鱼的人划着小船，顺着一条小河往上走。河的两边都是桃树，桃花儿在天上飞，美极了！后来他发现桃树没了、河也没了。前面有一个山，山下有一个洞。

　　他走进洞里，看见那儿有很多房子和田地，房子前面有鸡、有狗，人们在田里工作，都很快乐的样子。他们看见这个打鱼的，都很吃惊，问他是怎么来的，又请他去家里喝酒、吃饭。这些人说，他们的祖先在五六百年以前就逃到这儿来避难，后来就一直没有出去过。他们不知道现在外头是哪个朝代了。住了几天，

打鱼的要回家了，村子里的人请他不要把这个地方告诉别人。

　　打鱼的回去的时候，在路上做了很多记号。可是他想再回来的时候，不知道为什么记号都不见了，也找不到那条路了。

漢字 Characters

Study the following selected characters for further enrichment of your writing and vocabulary.

危

人 rén person standing over a 厂 cliff

wēi 6
danger

危機　　wēijī*　　crisis

A: 你為什麼要去打工？

B: 我最近有「經濟危機」。

Compare: 脆cuì 跪guì

險

阝fù 'hill' + 僉 qiān phonetic

xiǎn 15
vicious, danger

危險　　wēixiǎn　　dangerous, perilous
保險　　bǎoxiǎn*　　insurance, safe
冒險　　màoxiǎn　　to take risks/chances

A: 這種工作很危險，整天要去冒險。

B: 所以保險特別重要。

Compare: 臉liǎn

展

尸 shī 'body' + 㞡 phonetic

zhǎn 10
to spread out, exhibit

發展　　fāzhǎn　　to develop, to grow
書展　　shūzhǎn*　　book exhibition
影展　　yǐngzhǎn*　　film festival/fair

A: 現在中國的電影發展得怎麼樣？

B: 很快，在很多大小影展上都受到歡迎。

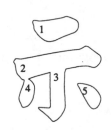

示

丅 an altar with dripping sacrifices on it— prognostic, indicate, inform

shì 5
to show, to indicate

示威　　shìwēi　　demonstration
表示　　biǎoshì*　　to show, to express, to indicate

A: 最近很多學生在校園內示威。

B: 他們是要跟學校表示他們的不滿嗎？

Compare: 宗zōng 票piào 標biāo 際jì

丰 a leafy bough was doubled + 山 shān + 豆 dòu —picture of a blossom, a bouquet

丰

fēng 18
abundance

| 豐富 | fēngfù | rich, abundant, to enrich |
| 豐收 | fēngshōu* | bumper harvest |

A: 聽說加州的水果很豐富。
B: 今年特別好，因為他們豐收。

宀 mián 'roof' + 畐 fú 'abundance'

富

fù 12
wealthy, abundant

富有	fùyǒu*	to be rich/wealthy
富強	fùqiáng*	prosperous and strong
財富	cáifù*	wealth, riches

A: 他家很富有。
B: 國家不富強，個人有再多財富也沒用。

Compare: 福 fú

並 bìng 'together' + 日 rì 'sun'—taken together all the places where the sun shines

普

pǔ 12
common

普遍	pǔbiàn	universal, widespread
普通	pǔtōng	ordinary, common
普通話	pǔtōnghuà	Mandarin Chinese
吉普車	jípǔchē*	<loan> Jeep

A: 這兒普通人都開小汽車。
B: 對啊！連吉普車也很普遍。

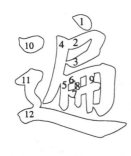

辶 cuò 'go' + 扁 biǎn phonetic—to go around, all around, a time, universal

遍

biàn 12
all over, (for occurrences)

| 遍地 | biàndì* | everywhere |
| 走遍 | zǒubiàn* | to travel throughout |

A: 這兒遍地垃圾，怎麼沒有人管？
B: 對啊！我走遍各地，還沒看過這麼髒的地方。

Compare: 篇 piān

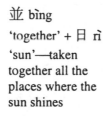

生 shēng 'life'
+ 月／丹 dān
'red'—the hue
of growing
plants

青少年	qīngshàonián	youths
青年	qīngnián*	young people
青菜	qīngcài*	green vegetables

A: 現在的青少年喜歡些什麼？

B: 我不清楚，我已經「人到中年」了。

Compare: 請 qǐng　情 qíng　清 qīng　晴 jīng

qīng 8
green, blue, not ripe,
young

⺿ cǎo 'plant'
+ 頻 pín
phonetic

| 蘋果 | píngguǒ | apple |

A: 那個孩子喜歡吃什麼水果？

B: 他喜歡吃蘋果。

píng 19
apple

Originally 火
huǒ 'fire' over
人 rén 'person'

光是	guāngshì	merely, just
眼光	yǎnguāng*	sight, vision, view
月光	yuèguāng*	moonlight

A: 我的眼光怎麼樣？

B: 不錯，這套西裝光是褲子就要美金一
百塊。

Compare: 先 xiān

guāng 6
light, honor, used up,
merely

竹 zhú
'bamboo' + 聿
yù: a ⺕ hand
holding a ｜
brush and
writing 二
strokes

筆記本	bǐjìběn*	notebook
筆友	bǐyǒu*	pen pal
毛筆	máobǐ*	writing brush
鉛筆	qiānbǐ*	pencil

A: 你在筆記本上寫什麼？

B: 我給我的筆友寫信。

bǐ 12
pen, stroke, (measure
word for money)

辶 chuò 'go' +
隋 suí phonetic

隨

隨便	suíbiàn	casually, carelessly
隨時	suíshí	at any time, at all times
隨地	suídì	anywhere, everywhere
隨身	suíshēn*	(take/have) with oneself

A: 他總是隨身帶個手機'cellular phone'。
B: 所以能隨時隨地跟朋友打電話。

suí 14
to follow, as soon as

糸 sī 'silk
thread' + 象
tuǎn phonetic

緣

| 緣故 | yuángù | cause, reason |

A: 你為什麼昨天沒來上課？
B: 因為下雪的緣故，我趕不上公車。

Compare: 綠 lǜ

yuán 15
cause, reason, fate,
edge

扌 shǒu 'hand'
+ 比 bǐ
phonetic

批

大批	dàpī*	large batch of
批評	pīpíng*	to criticize, criticism
批發	pīfā*	wholesale

A: 這種東西跟批發商買，比較便宜。
B: 別總是批評我浪費。

pī 7
batch, group, slap,
criticize

亻 rén 'person'
+ 賈 jiǎ
phonetic

价

物價	wùjià	commodity prices
跌價	diējià	to go down in price
講價	jiǎngjià*	to bargain
價錢	jiàqián*	price

A: 你的價錢太高了，算我半價怎麼樣？
B: 你真會講價。

jià 15
price, value

扌 yú 'hand' +
包 bāo 'wrap'
—to wrap your
arms around,
embrace

抱

| 抱怨 | bàoyuàn | to complain, to grumble |
| 抱不平 | bào bùpíng* | to be outraged by an injustice (done to sb. else) |

A: 最近老百姓有什麼抱怨？

B: 很多人為農民抱不平。

bào 8
to hold in arms, to
cherish

貝 bèi 'money'
+ 才 cái
'ability'

財

| 發財 | fācái | to get rich |
| 財產 | cáichǎn* | property |

A: 聽說他最近發了一筆大財。

B: 對！他財產多得連自己都搞不清楚。

cái 10
wealth, riches

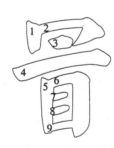

日 mào 'cover'
+ 目 mù 'eye'
—to go with
covered eyes

冒

冒險	màoxiǎn	to take risks/chances
冒火	màohuǒ*	to flare up
感冒	gǎnmào	to catch cold, cold

A: 他很喜歡冒險，一點兒也不怕受傷。

B: 怪不得他的父母常常冒火。

Compare: 帽 mào

mào 9
to emit, to risk, to
pretend to be

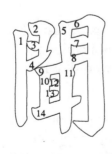

An 耳 ěr ear
listening at a 門
mén door; 門
is also phonetic

聞

新聞	xīnwén	news
舊聞	jiùwén*	past events, old matters
趣聞	qùwén*	interesting news/anecdotes
難聞	nánwén*	smell bad

A: 我告訴你一個趣聞！

B: 別說了，你的新聞都是「舊聞」。

Compare: 問 wèn 悶 mèn

wén 14
to hear, to smell, news,
famous

語法和用法 Grammar and Usage

Pay attention to the function of the structure and then study the example sentences.

1. Expressing an unfavorable tendency

S 動不動就VO	...dòngbúdòng jiù...	S VO at every possible moment; S is apt to do sth. negative

這兒的老百姓**動不動就**去遊行示威……

1. 小高昨天向我抱怨他的工作壓力太大，他快受不了了。

   小高昨天向我抱怨他的工作压力太大，他快受不了了。

   Xiao Gao complained to me yesterday that the pressure of his job was too much. He was about to burn out.

   他就是這樣，動不動就抱怨，好像對什麼都不滿。

   他就是这样，动不动就抱怨，好像对什么都不满。

   He is just like that, complaining at the slightest provocation. He seems to be unsatisfied with everything.

2. 我的飛機下午兩點才起飛，為什麼這麼早就出發？

   我的飞机下午两点才起飞，为什么这么早就出发？

   My plane leaves at two o'clock in the afternoon. Why should I leave so early?

   這裏動不動就塞車，不早點兒走你的機票可能會白買了。

   这里动不动就塞车，不早点儿走你的机票可能会白买了。

   There can be a traffic jam here at any time. If you don't leave early, your plane ticket may have been purchased in vain.

3. 報上說佛州 Fózhōu 有一個少年開槍殺了他的老師。

   报上说佛州有一个少年开枪杀了他的老师。

   The newspaper said that there was a child in Florida who shot his teacher.

   最近校園真不安全，動不動就有人犯罪。

   最近校园真不安全，动不动就有人犯罪。

   Lately the schools are not very safe; people are committing crimes all the time.

動不動 is used to indicate a ready tendency to do something negative. Therefore, it always occurs with 就 and the verbs follow are often something like 抱怨、吵架、罵人、開槍、塞車、遊行、哭. It would be odd to say this: 你可以動不動就省些錢，不買衣服。

2. Expressing a rapid fluctuation of events

| S一會兒…一會兒… | yìhuǐr…yìhuǐr… | now…now; one moment…the next |

一**會兒**抱怨物價漲得太屬害、一**會兒**抱怨股票跌得太快。

1. 買股票很容易發財，你想不想試一試？

   买股票很容易发财，你想不想试一试？

   It's easy to get rich buying stocks. Do you want to give it a try?

   股票一會兒漲，一會兒跌，我不想冒險。

   股票一会儿涨，一会儿跌，我不想冒险。 *xiǎn*

   The stocks rise at one moment and tumble the next. I don't want to take the chance.

2. 等我看完今天的新聞以後，我們再去吃飯，好嗎？

   等我看完今天的新闻以后，我们再去吃饭，好吗？

   Wait until I finish reading today's news and then we will go to eat, all right?

   現在的新聞一會兒是老百姓遊行，一會兒是青少年犯罪，真不明白有什麼吸引人的地方。

   现在的新闻一会儿是老百姓游行，一会儿是青少年犯罪，真不明白有什么吸引人的地方。 *xī yǐn*

   Nowadays the news is either about people's demonstrations or about kids committing crimes. I don't understand what's so great about listening to the news.

3. 你們決定好春假去什麼地方旅行了嗎？

   你们决定好春假去什么地方旅行了吗？

   Have you decided to go anywhere for spring break?

   我們一會兒想去看名勝古蹟，一會兒想去參觀博物館，所以到現在還沒有決定究竟去哪兒。

   我们一会儿想去看名胜古迹，一会儿想去参观博物馆，所以到现在还没有决定究竟去哪儿。

   We want to visit historical sites one moment, and museums the next, so we haven't really decided where to go yet.

一會兒…一會兒 is used to indicate the swiftness of change in circumstances. So, it can be used to describe the fluctuation of stocks, change of climate, the busy state one is in, e.g., 她一會兒做飯，一會兒洗碗，忙得很。Compare this with the sentence 她一邊兒做飯，一邊兒洗碗 which stresses the concurrence of two events.

3. Expressing causation

result B是由於/因為A reason （的緣故/關係） 由於A（的緣故/關係），　所以B	…shì yóuyú/yīnwéi…　（de yuángù/guānxi） yóuyú…(de yuángù/guānxi),　suǒyǐ…	B because (of …reason) Due to A, B…

有人說這是**由於**台灣的升學壓力太大、競爭太激烈**的緣故**……

1. 我們才幾天沒見，你怎麼突然瘦了這麼多？

   我们才几天没见，你怎么突然瘦了这么多？

   We haven't seen each other for a few days. How come you have lost so much weight?

   由於學習壓力太大，所以我才累成這樣。

   由于学习压力太大，所以我才累成这样。

   It's because I've been so tired from the overly great pressure to study.

2. 我覺得住在你對面的人很好，可是你為什麼從來不和他來往 láiwǎng 'dealings'？

   我觉得住在你对面的人很好，可是你为什么从来不和他来往？

   I think the guy who lives across from you is nice, so why haven't you gotten to know him yet?

   由於他剛來的時候，我吃過他的虧 kuī，所以決定不和他來往。

   由于他刚来的时候，我吃过他的亏，所以决定不和他来往。

   Because he tricked me when he first came, so I have decided not to have anything to do with him.

3. 這兒的老百姓為什麼動不動就示威遊行？

   这儿的老百姓为什么动不动就示威游行？

   Why do the people here go on strike all of the time?

   他們這樣做是由於最近犯罪很普遍，人們覺得不安全。

   他们这样做是由于最近犯罪很普遍，人们觉得不安全。

   They did so because lately crime is quite common. People don't feel secure.

4.　昨天你的電話總是
　　佔線 zhànxiàn，你一
　　直在和別人聊天
　　嗎？

　　昨天你的电话总是
　　占线，你一直在和
　　别人聊天吗？

Yesterday your line was always busy. Were you chatting with someone the whole time?

　　沒有啊！電話佔線
　　可能是因為我用電
　　腦上網的緣故吧！

　　没有啊！电话占线
　　可能是因为我用电
　　脑上网的缘故吧！

No. It was busy probably because I was online.

5.　中國人為什麼覺得
　　結婚的請帖 qǐngtiě 是
　　「紅色炸彈」？

　　中国人为什么觉得
　　结婚的请帖是"红
　　色炸弹"？

Why do Chinese people think that the invitation for a wedding banquet is a "red bomb"?

　　這是因為喝喜酒就
　　要送紅包的緣故，
　　所以大家都怕朋友
　　結婚。

　　这是因为喝喜酒就
　　要送红包的缘故，
　　所以大家都怕朋友
　　结婚。

This is because at the banquet you need to give money as a gift, so everyone is afraid of their friends' weddings.

6.　我發現很多人比較
　　喜歡買日本車，不
　　知道為什麼？

　　我发现很多人比较
　　喜欢买日本车，不
　　知道为什么？

I found that many people like to buy Japanese cars. I don't know why.

　　大概是因為日本車
　　省油的緣故吧！

　　大概是因为日本车
　　省油的缘故吧！

It's probably because Japanese cars are more fuel-efficient.

In this pattern, B is the result and A is the cause. 由於/因為 can be used in either a clause or a simple sentence. 由於 often occurs in the first clause of a compound sentence, and in this case the cause precedes the result, e.g., 由於國內競爭太激烈，他想去外國念書. When 由於 occurs in a simple sentence, the result precedes the cause and "…的緣故/關係/結果" often occurs at the end of the cause, e.g., 他想去外國念書是由於國內競爭太激烈的緣故. 由於 is also much more formal than 因為…所以.

4.　Expressing a maximal degree by a minimal example

（general comments），光是A就…	…guāngshì…jiù…	（general comments), only considering A, it is…

每年光是申請到國外留學的人就不知道有多少。

"活到老，学到老"

1. 外國學生到美國留學貴不貴？

   外国学生到美国留学贵不贵？

   Is it expensive for foreign students to study in the U.S.?

   貴死了，每年光是學費就要一萬多美金 měijīn。

   贵死了，每年光是学费就要一万多美金。 *10,000*

   It's terribly expensive. It costs more than ten thousand U.S. dollars annually just for tuition.

2. 我雖然沒去過台北，但很多人都說台北的交通問題非常嚴重，是嗎？

   我虽然没去过台北，但很多人都说台北的交通问题非常严重，是吗？

   Although I have never been to Taipei, many people say that Taipei's traffic problem is very serious, is that right?

   對啊！台北街上的車多死了，光是機車就把馬路 mǎlù 擠滿了。

   对啊！台北街上的车多死了，光是机车就把马路挤满了。 *road*

   Right. There are so many cars on the streets of Taipei. Motorcycles alone fill the streets.

3. 中文和英文很不一樣，學起來一定很難吧！

   中文和英文很不一样，学起来一定很难吧！

   Chinese and English are quite different. It certainly must be very difficult to study Chinese.

   當然了，光是中文的聲調就讓我非常頭疼。

   当然了，光是中文的声调就让我非常头疼。 *shēng diào*

   Of course. Chinese tones alone have caused me a lot of headaches.

The pattern 光是…就 is used to give an example to illustrate a point raised in the preceding statement. 光 literally means "merely, just," so this pattern emphasizes that just this one example is enough to underscore the point. Therefore, what goes between 光是…就 is often one aspect of the previous statement, e.g., 中文課的功課很多，光是作文就要寫四篇。這個圖書館很大，光是中文書就有一萬本。

5. Expressing the later-than-expected occurrence of an event

（要到）…S才…	(yàodào)…cái	S V as late as… (then: in the future)
（直到）…S才…	(zhídào)…cái	S V as late as… (then: past/future)

投票 Imelda Marcos

直到來了以後，**才**知道很多東西都是神話，這兒窮人的生活可能比國內的還慘呢！

1. 你從什麼時候開始對中文有興趣的？	你从什么时候开始对中文有兴趣的？	When did you start to have an interest in Chinese?
直到上大學以後，我才開始學中文。	直到上大学以后，我才开始学中文。	Not until I went to college did I start to study Chinese.
2. 大熊貓的數量shùliàng越來越少，中國政府正在保護他們。	大熊猫的数量越来越少，中国政府正在保护他们。	The number of giant pandas is decreasing. The Chinese government is trying to protect them.
要到動物快要絕種的時候，政府才知道要保護。	要到动物快要绝种的时候，政府才知道要保护。	Not until they were almost extinct did the government understand that it must protect them.
3. 昨天我一直給旅行社打電話，可是總是佔線，怎麼回事？	昨天我一直给旅行社打电话，可是总是占线，怎么回事？	I tried all day yesterday to call the travel agency, but the line was always busy. What was the matter?
要到下午四點以後打，才能打通。	要到下午四点以后打，才能打通。	Only if you call them after four o'clock in the afternoon will you be able to get through.

This pattern 要到/直到…才 indicates that one won't carry out an action until some time later than expected. Note that if the event occurred in the past, one uses only 直到…才. Also 才 always occurs after the subject. Thus, never say something like 直到一個星期以後，才我知道考試的結果. What goes after 要到/直到 can be a point in time (e.g., 明年、上個星期), time span (e.g., 三個月以後), or an event (e.g., 放假以後).

6. Expressing discreteness

各V各的(O)	gè…gè de…	Each does it in his/her own way

在我看來，國內、國外**各有各的**問題……

1. 你覺不覺得我們兩個老板好像有點兒矛盾？

你觉不觉得我们两个老板好象有点儿矛盾？

Don't you think that there is some conflict between our two bosses?

這還看不出來？每次開會的時候，他們都各說各的，從來沒同意過對方的觀點guāndiǎn。

这还看不出来？每次开会的时候，他们都各说各的，从来没同意过对方的观点。

Who can't see that? Each time there is a meeting, they each say their piece without ever agreeing with the other's point of view.

2. 在台北可以吃到各地的點心，你最喜歡的是什麼？

在台北可以吃到各地的点心，你最喜欢的是什么？

You can have all sorts of dishes in Taipei. What is your favorite?

這很難說，每種點心都各有各的特色。

这很难说，每种点心都各有各的特色。

It's hard to say. Every dish has its own special flavor.

3. 考試的時候，老師總是說：「大家各寫各的，不要看別人的。」

考试的时候，老师总是说："大家各写各的，不要看别人的。"

At exams, teachers always say, "everyone write your own work, don't look at others'."

老師們都各有各的要求，但這一點永遠yǒngyuǎn 'forever'是一樣的。

老师们都各有各的要求，但这一点永远是一样的。

All teachers have their own requirements, but that's the one point that's always the same (i.e., they all demand no cheating).

各V各的 is used to indicate that people do their own thing. The object is often dropped if it can be understood from context. If the object is present, it follows 的. So, one can say 各吃各的 or各吃各的飯. "Go Dutch" in Chinese is 各付各的.

文化點滴 Culture Notes

1. **Little overseas students**: Some well-to-do families in Taiwan, with hopes of freeing their children from the pressures from numerous exams and tests, send their children abroad to study, usually to the U.S. It is believed that Western or American education is the best system and will bring out the potential of their children. In many cases, these children 小留學生 xiǎoliúxuéshēng are left to be cared for by friends, relatives, or even others less familiar to them.

2. **Repeal of martial law in Taiwan**: Since the repeal of martial law in 1987, Taiwan has undergone a lot of changes toward a more open, pluralistic, and democratic society. Years back, one rarely heard of protests and demonstrations. The media and newspapers were tightly controlled by the government. Now, people are free to voice their discontent and debate every issue. In 2000, the candidate from the Opposition Party 民進黨 Mínjìndǎng, for the first time in over fifty years, defeated the candidate from the Ruling Party 國民黨 Guómíndǎng and took the presidency.

歌兒 Songs

桃花源
Utopia

Andante

詞：劉雅詩　曲：馬定一

1. 我　們　心　中　都　有　桃　花　源，　那　地　方　找
   Wǒmen　xīn zhōng dōu　yǒu　Táohuāyuán,　　nà dìfang zhǎo
   We all have utopia in our minds.　　　　　　In that place

2. 這　種　地　方　只　是　個　神　話，　新　聞　裏　免
   Zhè　zhǒng dìfang　zhǐ　shì　ge　shénhuà,　　xīnwén lǐ miǎn
   This kind of place is only a myth.　　　　　There is always

1. 不　到　壓　力　犯　罪　危　險。　百姓　平安幸福　沒有什麼
   bu dào yā　lì　fànzuì　wēixiǎn.　　Bǎixìng píng'ān xìngfú méiyǒu shénme
   no stress, crime, or danger can be found.　People have peace and happiness and no

2. 不　了　會　有　打　打　殺　殺。　股票　隨著經濟　也會跌跌
   buliǎo huì　yǒu　dǎdǎ　shāshā.　　Gǔpiào suízhe jīng jǐ　yě huì diēdiē
   fighting and killing in the news.　　Stocks also rise and

1. 抱　怨。　鳥　語花香　到　處　是　公　園。小　孩　兒　快　樂
   bào　yuàn.　Niǎo yǔ huā xiāng dàochù shì gōng　yuán. Xiǎoháir　kuàilè
   complaints.　Birds chirp, flowers are fragrant, and parks are everywhere.　Children grow up happily

2. 漲　漲。　物　價　每　天　會　上　上　下　下。　生　活　裏　總　是
   zhǎngzhǎng Wù jiā měi tiān　huì　shàng shàng xià xià.　Shēnghuó lǐ　zǒng shì
   fall with the economy.　The price of goods fluctuates every day.　There is always fierce competition

1. 長　大　成　為青少　年，　人　人　發財生　命　財産　都　安　全。
   zhǎngdà　chéngwéi qīngshào nián.　Rénrén　fācái shēngmìng cáichǎn dōu ānquán.
   and become teenagers.　Everyone can make a fortune and life and property are safe.

2. 競　爭　激　烈多變　化，　努　力　工　作國　家　發　展靠大家。
   jìngzhēng　jīliè duō biànhuà.　Nǔlì　gōngzuò guójiā fāzhǎn kào dàjiā.
   and many changes in our lives.　We need to work hard because our country's development depends on us all.

第十七課

Theme Philosophy and Religion

Communicative Objectives
- Talking about the weather
- Talking about the Tomb Sweeping festival
- Talking about *feng shui*
- Talking about lucky numbers

Grammar Focus
- S Adj 起來(了)/V起(O)來(了)
- V_1著V_1著，S(忽然)就V_2起(O)來了
- 無所不V/無N不V
- 凡事都…
- A對B(沒)有利/(沒)有好處
- S才…(呢)

Focus on Characters
- 暖陽深颳、祖先宗族、拜神鬧鬼、忽漸衝數、凡迷哲際

活著是為了什麼？

1.

2.

3.

4.

5.

6.

FIN.

生詞 Vocabulary

Study the following words for their pronunciation and meaning. When an area is shaded, guess at the meaning of the word based on its constituent characters and then fill in the blank. Read the usage of words and related terms (antonyms, synonyms, compounds sharing the constituent characters, etc.) and try to answer the sample questions in Chinese. Note that proper nouns and incidental terms are not numbered.

◎By Order of Appearance

1.	漸漸	jiànjiàn	Adv	gradually	
	渐渐				
2.	暖和	nuǎnhuo	Adj	(nice and) warm	[warm-mild]
				天氣暖和/涼快 liángkuài 'cool' /熱/冷	
				這兒幾月天氣會暖和起來？	
				这儿几月天气会暖和起来？	
3.	颳風	guāfēng	VO	the wind is blowing	[blow-wind]
	刮风			這兒冬天常颳大風嗎？	
				这儿冬天常刮大风吗？	
4.	太陽	tàiyáng	N	sun, sunshine	[great-sun]
	太阳			曬太陽 shài tàiyáng 'to have a suntan' 對身體好嗎？	
				晒太阳对身体好吗？	
5.	忽然	hūrán	Adv	suddenly	[suddenly-so]
				她怎麼說著說著忽然就哭了？	
				她怎么说着说着忽然就哭了？	
6.	看熱鬧	kàn rènao	VO	to go where crowds are (for fun/excitement)	[look-hot-noisy]
	看热闹				
7.	拜	bài	V	to worship, to honor	
				你過年的時候，去誰家拜年？	
				你过年的时候，去谁家拜年？	
8.	神	shén	N	god, supernatural, magical	
	財神	cáishén	N	god of fortune	[fortune-god]
	财神				
9.	海	hǎi	N	sea	
	媽祖	Māzǔ	N	heavenly queen	[mother-ancestor]
	妈祖				

忽 + adj1 + 忽 + adj2 unpredictable

adj1 <-> adj2 opposites

10.	廟 庙	miào	N	temple	寺 庙 buddha temple sì miào
11.	信教	xìnjiào	VO	to be religious	[believe-religion]
				你信什麼教？	
				你信什么教？	
	清明節 清明节	Qīngmíng jié	N	"Tomb Sweeping" Day	[pure-clear-festival] 扫墓 sǎo mù to sweep tombs
12.	祖先	zǔxiān	N	ancestors	[ancestor-elder generation]
				你的祖先是從哪兒來的？	
				你的祖先是从哪儿来的？	
	灶君	Zàojūn	N	kitchen god	[stove-supreme ruler]
13.	好運 好运	hǎoyùn	N		[good-luck]
				你相信什麼會給你帶來好運？	恶 运
				你相信什么会给你带来好运？	è bad luck
14.	鬼	guǐ	N	ghost	
15.	友好	yǒuhǎo	Adj	friendly	[friend-good]
				你來這兒的時候，誰對你很友好？	
				你来这儿的时候，谁对你很友好？	
	唐朝	Tángcháo	N	Tang dynasty (618–907)	
16.	服務 服务	fúwù	V/N	to serve, service	[serve-business] 为。。服务 to serve for this
				為人/社會/國家服務	
				你覺得他們的服務態度怎麼樣？	
				你觉得他们的服务态度怎么样？	
17.	也許 也许	yěxǔ	Adv	perhaps, probably	[also-maybe]
18.	民族	mínzú	N	ethnic minority/group, nation	[people-clan]
	孔孟	Kǒng Mèng	N	Confucius and Mencius	
19.	儒家	Rújiā	N	Confucian school	[Confucian-school of thought]

Characters with Many Strokes

漸 暖 陽 然 熱 鬧 廟 務 族 儒

còu
凑 put together eg. 热闹

20.	思想	sīxiǎng	N	thought, thinking, ideology	[think-think]

→思想家 sīxiǎngjiā 'thinker'

誰是二十世紀最偉大的思想家？

谁是二十世纪最伟大的思想家？

21.	深	shēn	Adj	deep	
22.	實際 实际	shíjì	Adj/ N	practical, reality	[true-boundary]

做人很實際　　→實際上

你覺得自己的想法很實際嗎？

你觉得自己的想法很实际吗？

[handwritten: 多+N 都+Adj]

[handwritten: 实际上 = in fact,...]

23.	凡事	fánshì	N	everything	[ordinary-thing]
	老莊 老庄	Lǎo-Zhuāng	N	Laozi and Zhuangzi	
24.	哲學 哲学	zhéxué	N	philosophy	[philosophy-study]

→哲學家 zhéxuéjiā *[handwritten: philosopher]*

你最喜歡的哲學家是誰？

你最喜欢的哲学家是谁？

25.	傳統 传统	chuántǒng	Adj/ N	traditional, tradition	[pass on-system]

[handwritten: Zhongjiao chuantong]

26.	宗教	zōngjiào	N	religion	[clan-teach]
27.	有利	yǒulì	Adj/ VO		[have-benefit]

=有好處

28.	佛教	Fójiào	N	Buddhism	[Buddha-religion]
29.	道教	Dàojiào	N	Daoism (as a religion)	[way-religion]
30.	基督教	Jīdūjiào	N	Christianity	[Christ-religion]
31.	天主教	Tiānzhǔjiào	N	Catholicism	[heaven-master-religion]
32.	回教	Huíjiào	N	Islam	[Muslim-religion]

=伊斯蘭教 yīsīlánjiào

33.	衝突 冲突	chōngtū	N	conflict, clash	[collide-dash forward]

[handwritten: Past]

和……有很大的衝突

[handwritten: A和B有過很大的]

你和誰有過很大的衝突？

你和谁有过很大的冲突？

34.	種族 种族	zhǒngzú	N	race, ethnic group	[race-clan]

種族歧視/問題/衝突

[handwritten: 拜访谁 fang — Formally visit]

[handwritten: 公元前 B.C.E.]

fire chicken = turkey
huo ji

tuzi = bunny

什麼地方種族歧視的問題很嚴重？

什么地方种族歧视的问题很严重？

熔爐 熔炉	rónglú	N	melting pot	[smelt-furnace]

also 溶 róng for cold melting 火容 for melting at high temp

拼盤 拼盘	pīnpán	N	assorted cold dishes, hors d'oeuvres	[piece together-dish]
35. 迷信	míxìn	V/N	to have blind faith in, superstition	[enchanted-faith]

to get lost

美國人有些什麼樣的迷信？

美国人有些什么样的迷信？

36. 風水 风水	fēngshui	N		[wind-water]

看風水 →風水先生

這個地方的風水怎麼樣？

这个地方的风水怎么样？

37. 數字 数字	shùzì	N	numeral, digit	[number-character]
38. 算命	suànmìng	N/ VO	fortune-telling, to tell fortune	[count-fate]
39. 年輕人 年轻人	niánqīngrén	N	young people	[age-young-people]

→中年人、老人   *中年人*
                        老年人

中國的年輕人崇拜什麼人？

中国的年轻人崇拜什么人？

40. 崇拜	chóngbài	V	to worship	[sublime-salute]

對……很崇拜；崇拜……；崇拜的對象

美國的年輕人對什麼很崇拜？

美国的年轻人对什么很崇拜？

41. 簡單 简单	jiǎndān	Adj	simple, ordinary	[simple-single]
42. 晚安	wǎn'ān	IE	Good night!	[night-peace]

Characters with Many Strokes

實 際 傳 基 督 衝 種 數 崇 簡

◎By Grammatical Categories

Nouns/Pronouns

海	hǎi	sea	民族	mínzú	ethnic minority/group, nation
太陽	tàiyáng	sun, sunshine	種族	zhǒngzú	race, ethnic group
風水	fēngshui	geomancy	儒家	Rújiā	Confucian school
數字	shùzì	numeral, digit	思想	sīxiǎng	thought, thinking, ideology
算命	suànmìng	fortune-telling	傳統	chuántǒng	traditional, tradition
衝突	chōngtū	conflict, clash	哲學	zhéxué	philosophy
好運	hǎoyùn	good luck	宗教	zōngjiào	religion
凡事	fánshì	everything	佛教	Fójiào	Buddhism
廟	miào	temple	道教	Dàojiào	Daoism (as a religion)
祖先	zǔxiān	ancestors	回教	Huíjiào	Islam
年輕人	niánqīngrén	young people	天主教	Tiānzhǔjiào	Catholicism
鬼	guǐ	ghost	基督教	Jīdūjiào	Christianity
神	shén	god, supernatural, magical			

Verbs/Stative Verbs/Adjectives

拜	bài	to worship	看熱鬧	kàn rènao	to go where crowds are (for fun/excitement)
崇拜	chóngbài	to worship	實際	shíjì	practical, reality
信教	xìnjiào	to be religious	有利	yǒulì	(to be) advantageous
迷信	míxìn	to have blind faith in, superstition	友好	yǒuhǎo	friendly
服務	fúwù	to serve, service	簡單	jiǎndān	simple
颱風	guāfēng	the wind is blowing	深	shēn	deep
暖和	nuǎnhuo	(nice and) warm			

Adverbs and Others

漸漸	jiànjiàn	gradually	也許	yěxǔ	perhaps, probably
忽然	hūrán	suddenly	晚安	wǎn'ān	Good night!

◎By Pinyin

Entries with * indicate lexical items used in Mini-Dialogues and of possible interest for supplemental study.

bài	拜	to worship	nuǎnhuo	暖和	(nice and) warm
chóngbài	崇拜	to worship	páshān*	爬山	to climb mountain
chōngtū	冲突	conflict, clash	qiūtiān*	秋天	autumn
chūntiān*	春天	spring	Rújiā	儒家	Confucian school
chuānghu*	窗户	window	shén	神	god, supernatural, magical
chuántǒng	传统	traditional, tradition	shēn	深	deep
Dàojiào	道教	Daoism (as a religion)	shíjì	实际	practical, reality
fánshì	凡事	everything	shǒujī*	手机	cellular phone
fēngshui	风水	geomancy	shùzì	数字	numeral, digit
Fójiào	佛教	Buddhism	sīxiǎng	思想	thought, thinking, ideology
fúwù	服务	to serve, service	suànmìng	算命	fortune-telling, to tell fortune
guāfēng	刮风	the wind is blowing	tàiyáng	太阳	sun, sunshine
guǐ	鬼	ghost	Tiānzhǔjiào	天主教	Catholicism
hǎi	海	sea	wǎn'ān	晚安	Good night!
hàomǎ*	号码	number	xiàxuě*	下雪	to snow
hǎoyùn	好运	good luck	xiàyǔ*	下雨	to rain
hūrán	忽然	suddenly	xìnjiào	信教	to be religious
Huíjiào	回教	Islam	yěxǔ	也许	perhaps
jiǎndān	简单	simple	yéye*	爷爷	(paternal) grandfather
jiànjiàn	渐渐	gradually	yǒuhǎo	友好	friendly
Jīdūjiào	基督教	Christianity	yǒulì	有利	(to be) advantageous
kàn rènao	看热闹	to go where crowds are (for fun/ excitement)	yuànzi*	院子	yard
miào	庙	temple	zhéxué	哲学	philosophy
mínzú	民族	ethnic minority/ group, nation	zhǒngzú	种族	race, ethnic group
míxìn	迷信	superstition, to have blind faith in	zōngjiào	宗教	religion
niánqīngrén	年轻人	young people	zǔxiān	祖先	ancestors

課文 Text

Use the following questions to guide your reading of the text.

1. 小高發現台灣的中國人有什麼特別？

2. 王華覺得小高的看法怎麼樣？

3. 王華覺得中國人對宗教的態度怎麼樣？

 小王：

你們快放春假了嗎？這兒的天氣也漸漸暖和[1]**起來了**，昨天沒颱風、還出太陽，我就上街逛了逛。在路上[2]**走著走著，忽然**看到一大群人，擠在一起，我也跟著去看熱鬧，原來有人在拜神。真有意思，我發現這兒的中國人好像[3]**無所不拜**：作生意的人拜財神，靠海生活的人拜媽祖，想生孩子的夫婦、希望兒女考上大學的父母也都去廟裏拜神，不信教的人到了清明節的時候，也一定會拜自己的祖先。而且中國人信的神無所不在：家裏的門口有門神，廚房有灶君，聽說年底的時候，人們給廚房的神吃一點東西，它就會到天上去幫人說好話，給人帶來好運。總之，中國人和鬼神的關係，好像相當友好，唐朝就有很多女鬼幫助人的故事。而且這兒的神好像是專門為人服務的。你覺得我說的對嗎？你信什麼教呢？你覺得我們活著是為了什麼？

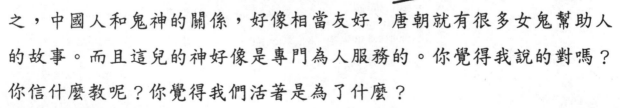

德中上

小高：

　　我覺得你說的很對。對很多西方人來說，人是應該為神服務的，可是中國人的想法正好相反。也許我們這個民族受了孔孟儒家思想的影響太深，太實際了，[4]**凡事都**從自己出發，好像把現在的生活搞好就行了，不管過去，也不管將來。受了老莊哲學影響的人對生、死更不在乎了，認為一切都是自然的。從這些傳統的思想中可以看出來：在中國，宗教是為人服務的，所以無論什麼教，只要[5]**對人有利**，大家就能接受。怪不得佛教、道教、基督教、天主教、回教，各種教在中國

都有人信，而且互相之間很少有矛盾、衝突。

　　如果說美國是個種族的大熔爐，中國就是個宗教的大拼盤！不過現代人可能更「迷信」風水、數字和算命呢！而且在許多年輕人的眼中，歐、美、日的明星[6]**才**是他們真正「崇拜」的對象。你問我信什麼教呢？我的回答很簡單：「睡覺」。晚安！

　　　　　　　　　　　　　　　　　　　　　　　王華上

课文 Text

Use the following questions to guide your reading of the text.

1. 小高发现台湾的中国人有什么特别？

2. 王华觉得小高的看法怎么样？

3. 王华觉得中国人对宗教的态度怎么样？

 小王：

你们快放春假了吗？这儿的天气也渐渐暖和[1]起来了，昨天没刮风、还出太阳，我就上街逛了逛。在路上[2]走着走着，忽然看到一大群人，挤在一起，我也跟着去看热闹，原来有人在拜神。真有意思，我发现这儿的中国人好象[3]无所不拜：作生意的人拜财神，靠海生活的人拜妈祖，想生孩子的夫妇、希望儿女考上大学的父母也都去庙里拜神，不信教的人到了清明节的时候，也一定会拜自己的祖先。而且中国人信的神无所不在：家里的门口有门神，厨房有灶君，听说年底的时候，人们给厨房的神吃一点东西，它就会到天上去帮人说好话，给人带来好运。总之，中国人和鬼神的关系，好象相当友好，唐朝就有很多女鬼帮助人的故事。而且这儿的神好象是专门为人服务的。你觉得我说的对吗？你信什么教呢？你觉得我们活着是为了什么？

德中上

小高：

　　我觉得你说的很对。对很多西方人来说，人是应该为神服务的，可是中国人的想法正好相反。也许我们这个民族受了孔孟儒家思想的影响太深，太实际了，⁴凡事都从自己出发，好象把现在的生活搞好就行了，不管过去，也不管将来，受了老庄哲学影响的人对生、死更不在乎了，认为一切都是自然的。从这些传统的思想中可以看出来：在中国，宗教是为人服务的，所以无论什么教，只要⁵对人有利，大家就能接受。怪不得佛教、道教、基督教、天主教、回教，各种教在中国都有人信，而且互相之间很少有矛盾、冲突。

　　如果说美国是个种族的大熔炉，中国就是个宗教的大拼盘！不过现代人可能更"迷信"风水、数字和算命呢！而且在许多年轻人的眼中，欧、美、日的明星⁶才是他们真正"崇拜"的对象。你问我信什么教呢？我的回答很简单："睡觉"。晚安！

王华上

中国　宗教
　　　∟→是为人服务的。
　　　　　∟→所以都有人信，没有矛盾

小對話 Mini-Dialogues

Read the supplementary dialogues for a better understanding of the text. See if you can memorize one and perform it in class.

(1) Talking about the weather

Gao: 今天的天氣不錯。   今天的天气不错。

A: 是啊！真難得，不冷也不熱。   是啊！真难得，不冷也不热。

Gao: 前一陣子熱得要命，真不像春   前一阵子热得要命，真不像春
      天chūntiān。   天。

A: 我也怕熱。其實這兒沒有春   我也怕热。其实这儿没有春
      天、秋天qiūtiān，只有夏天、冬   天、秋天，只有夏天、冬天。
      天。

Gao: 聽說這兒冬天不下雪xiàxuě，應   听说这儿冬天不下雪，应该不
      該不冷吧！   冷吧！

A: 雖然不下雪，可是常下雨xiàyǔ，   虽然不下雪，可是常下雨，还
      還是挺冷的。   是挺冷的。

tǐng
(very)

Gao: The weather is nice today.

A: That's right. How unusual. It's not cold
      and not hot, either.

Gao: It's been so hot the last few days, not like
      spring at all.

A: I don't like hot weather, either. Actually,
      there is no spring or autumn here, only
      summer and winter.

Gao: I heard that it doesn't snow here in the
      winter. It ought not be too cold, I
      suppose.

A: Although it doesn't snow, it rains a lot. It's still pretty cold.

(2) Talking about the Tomb Sweeping festival

Mom: 四月五號就是清明節了，你看
      是星期幾？

是不是要給爺爺yéye掃墓sǎomù？
Child: 是不是要給爺爺yéye掃墓sǎomù？
      我們這一次還帶酒和水果嗎？

Mom: 對，我們該去看爺爺了。

Child: 好啊！我最喜歡去山上玩了。

Mom: 我們是要去掃墓，不是去爬山
      páshān啊！

四月五号就是清明节了，你看
是星期几？

是不是要给爷爷扫墓？我们这
一次还带酒和水果吗？

对，我们该去看爷爷了。

好啊！我最喜欢去山上玩了。

我们是要去扫墓，不是去爬山
啊！

Mom: April fifth is the Tomb Sweeping Festival.
       See which day of the week it is.

Child: Are we going to sweep our grandpa's tomb?
       Will we bring wine and fruit with us this time?

Mom: Yes, we have to go see grandpa.

Child: Great! Going to the mountains for some fun
       is my favorite thing to do.

Mom: We are going there to sweep the tomb, not to
       take a hike.

(3) Talking about *feng shui*

Gao: 你看這個房子怎麼樣？

A: 一出門就對著路口，風水不太
     好。

Gao: 風水怎麼不好？這兒窗戶
     chuānghu又多又大，一開窗就有
     風，院子yuànzi裏還有游泳池，
     水也不少。

A: 別開玩笑了！你最近成績怎麼
     樣？

你看这个房子怎么样？

一出门就对着路口，风水不太
好。

风水怎么不好？这儿窗户又多
又大，一开窗就有风，院子里
还有游泳池，水也不少。

别开玩笑了！你最近成绩怎么
样？

Gao: 不太好，可能是我房間的「風水」不對！

不太好，可能是我房间的"风水"不对！

Gao: What do you think of this house?

A: It faces the entrance of a road as soon as you get out of the door. The *feng shui* is not good.

Gao: Why isn't the *feng shui* good? The windows here are both many and large. As soon as you open a window, the wind comes in. There is also a swimming pool in the yard—no shortage of water.

A: Stop kidding. How are your grades at school lately?

Gao: Not so good. Perhaps it's because the "*feng shui*" of my room is bad.

(4) Talking about lucky numbers

A: 聽說，你也有個手機 shǒujī？

听说，你也有个手机？

B: 現在誰沒有「大哥大」啊？

现在谁没有"大哥大"啊？

A: 你那不是「大哥大」，是「大姐大」。什麼號碼 hàomǎ？

你那不是"大哥大"，是"大姐大"。什么号码？

B: 你猜猜？再好也沒有了。

你猜猜？再好也没有了。　不能再好了。

A: 小姐，我怎麼猜得著？

小姐，我怎么猜得着？

B: 八八八，一七八八（發、發、發，一切發、發）。

八八八，一七八八（发、发、发，一切发、发）。

A: I heard that you have a cellular phone too.

B: Nowadays who doesn't have a "Great Big Brother"?

A: Yours is not "Great Big Brother." It's "Great Big Sister." What's your number?

B: Guess. It's couldn't possibly be better.

A: My lady, how could I possibly guess?

B: Eight, eight, eight, one, seven, eight, eight (prosper, prosper, prosper, everything is prospering, prosper.)

小故事 Stories

Read the following tale for your own enjoyment and for your understanding of the highlighted expression that is relevant to the theme of the chapter.

 杞人憂天 Qǐ rén yōu tiān

❀ 你應該好好過日子，不要總是杞人憂天。

從前杞國有一個人，老怕天塌下來，怕地垮下去。他飯也不想吃，覺也不敢睡，什麼事兒都不想做。

他的朋友對他說：「天是很厚很厚的大氣，就算塌下來，你也不會被壓傷。地上到處都有泥土，你每天在泥土上走來走去，為什麼擔心它會垮下去呢？」

那個人聽了朋友的話以後，好不容易才放心了。

杞	Qǐ	name of a state
憂	yōu	to worry
塌	tā	to cave in, to fall down
垮	kuǎ	to collapse
厚	hòu	thick
大氣	dàqì	atmosphere
壓傷	yāshāng	to press and hurt
泥土	nítǔ	earth, soil
放心	fàngxīn	to feel relieved

✎ 杞人憂天的意思是＿＿＿＿＿＿＿＿＿＿＿＿＿＿＿

杞人忧天 Qǐ rén yōu tiān

❀　你应该好好过日子，不要总是杞人忧天。

从前杞国有一个人，老怕天塌下来，怕地垮下去。他饭也不想吃，觉也不敢睡，什么事儿都不想做。

他的朋友对他说："天是很厚很厚的大气，就算塌下来，你也不会被压伤。地上到处都有泥土，你每天在泥土上走来走去，为什么担心它会垮下去呢？"

那个人听了朋友的话以后，好不容易才放心了。

杞	Qǐ	name of a state
忧	yōu	to worry
塌	tā	to cave in, to fall down
垮	kuǎ	to collapse
厚	hòu	thick
大气	dàqì	atmosphere
压伤	yāshāng	to press and hurt
泥土	nítǔ	earth, soil
放心	fàngxīn	to feel relieved

✎杞人忧天的意思是＿＿＿＿＿＿＿＿＿＿＿＿＿＿

漢字 Characters

Study the following selected characters for further enrichment of your writing and vocabulary.

日 rì 'sun' +
爰 yuán 'drag'
—warm, when
the sun is
dragging on

暖

暖和	nuǎnhuo	(nice and) warm
暖氣	nuǎnqì*	central heating
保暖	bǎonuǎn*	to keep warm

A: 這兒很暖和，不用暖氣。

B: 不開暖氣，就要多穿點衣服保暖。

nuǎn 13
warm, to warm up

阝 fù 'hill' +
日 rì 'sun' +
勿 wù 'rays
coming down'

阳

太陽	tàiyáng	sun
陽光	yángguāng*	sunshine
陽傘	yángsǎn*	parasol, sunshade

A: 這兒的太陽很大！

B: 對皮膚 pífu 'skin' 很不好，你要陽傘嗎？

Compare: 湯 tāng 揚 yáng 易 yì

yáng 11
sun, in relief, overt

Deep 氵 shuǐ
water, deep 穴
xuè hole, and
deep 木 mù
forest; 穴 is
missing the dot
on top

深

| 深夜 | shēnyè* | deep in the night |
| 深山 | shēnshān* | remote mountains |

A: 我昨天晚上搞到深夜才睡。

B: 是不是老師要你看的書太深了？

shēn 11
deep, profound

風 fēng 'wind'
+ 舌 shé
phonetic

刮

| 颳風 | guāfēng | the wind blows |

A: 今天天氣怎麼樣？

B: 風颳得很大，得穿風衣才行。

Compare: 活 huó 話 huà

guā 15
to scrape, to blow

衤 shì 'altar' +
且 qiě phonetic

祖

zǔ 9
grandfather, ancestor

祖先	zǔxiān	ancestors, forebears
祖父	zǔfù*	(paternal) grandfather
祖母	zǔmǔ*	(paternal) grandmother
外祖母	wàizǔmǔ*	maternal grandmother

A: 你的祖先是從哪兒來的？

B: 祖父從德國來，祖母從法國來，再上
去就不知道了。

Compare: 租zū 組zǔ

止 zhǐ 'foot-
print with the
toes pointing
upward' + 儿 /
人 rén 'person'
—following the
footsteps of
those who went
first

先

xiān 6
before, earlier, first,
ancestor

先生	xiānsheng	teacher, Mr., husband
首先	shǒuxiān*	first, first of all
事先	shìxiān*	in advance, beforehand

A: 她出去事先沒有告訴她的先生嗎？

B: 沒有，所以他那麼生氣。

Compare: 洗xǐ 贊zàn 告gào 牛niú

宀 mián 'roof'
+ 示 shì
'altar'—the
house for
religious rites:
ancestral temple

宗

zōng 8
ancestor, clan, sect

| 宗教 | zōngjiào | religion |
| 教宗 | jiàozōng* | Pope |

A: 你對宗教有研究嗎？

B: 現在沒有什麼研究。

Compare: 綜zòng 棕zōng

扩 yǎn 'flag' +
矢 shǐ 'arrow'
—military unit,
clan

族

zú 11
clan, race, tribe, group

民族	mínzú	ethnic minority/group
種族	zhǒngzú	race, ethnic group
家族	jiāzú*	clan, family
貴族	guìzú*	noble, aristocrat

A: 你覺得種族歧視還很嚴重嗎？

B: 對，少數民族還是會受到歧視。

Originally 手
手 two hands
over 下 down
—to honor with
two hands held
down

拜

拜佛	bàifó*	to worship Buddha
拜年	bàinián*	to pay New Year's call
拜訪	bàifǎng*	to pay visit, call on

A: 春節的時候，你去誰家拜年？
B: 我總是去拜訪我從前的老師。

bài 9
to salute, to honor, to
worship

礻 shì 'altar' +
申 shēn
phonetic

神

精神	jīngshén*	spirit, mind
留神	liúshén*	to be careful, to take care
神話	shénhuà	mythology, myth

A: 你精神不太好，開車要留神。
B: 別擔心。

shén 9
god, spirit, energy,
clever

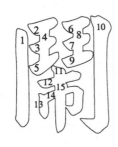

鬥 dòu 'fight'
+ 市 shì
'market'—fight
in the market

鬧

熱鬧	rènao	lively, excitement
看熱鬧	kànrènao	to go where crowds are
鬧笑話	nàoxiàohuà	to make a fool of oneself

A: 這兒為什麼這麼熱鬧？
B: 有個人鬧了個笑話。

nào 15
to make a noise, to
suffer from

Picture of a
ghost

鬼

搞鬼	gǎoguǐ*	be up to some mischief
有鬼	yǒuguǐ*	There is sth. fishy (going on)
酒鬼	jiǔguǐ*	drunkard, alchoholic
小氣鬼	xiǎoqìguǐ*	miser, penny-pincher

A: 那個小氣鬼這一陣子在搞什麼鬼？
B: 誰知道，我看他心裏有鬼。

Compare: 塊 kuài 醜 chǒu

guǐ 9
ghost, spirit, dirty trick

心 xīn 'heart' +
勿 wù phonetic

| 忽然 | hūrán | suddenly |
| 忽視 | hūshì* | to ignore, to overlook |

A: 他走了，忽然又回過頭來。

B: 他想跟你說什麼嗎？

hū 8
to neglect, to disdain,
suddenly

氵 shuǐ 'water'
+ 斬 zhǎn
'chop' phonetic
—water
gradually
chopping up a
car by making it
rust

| 漸漸 | jiànjiàn | gradually, little by little |
| 逐漸 | zhújiàn* | gradually, by degrees |

A: 天漸漸黑了，街上的車也逐漸少了。

B: 這正是出去散步的好時候呢！

jiàn 14
gradually, by degrees

行 xíng 'walk'
+ 重 zhòng
'heavy'
phonetic

| 衝突 | chōngtū | conflict, clash |
| 衝動 | chōngdòng* | impulse, be impetuous |

A: 他常跟人起衝突嗎？

B: 他做事很衝動，衝突是免不了的。

chōng, chòng 15
to rush, clash, towards

婁 lóu 'go bad'
+ 攴 pū
'beat'—
clapping,
tapping
rythmically to
facilitate
counting

數字	shùzì	numeral, digit
數學	shùxué*	mathematics
多數	duōshù*	majority
分數	fēnshù*	mark, score, grade

A: 奇怪，這次考試多數人都考得很好。

B: 會不會是分數算錯了？

shù, shǔ 15
number, to count, to
scold

丶 'a dot representing unity' + 几 'decline, on the contrary, but'

凡

fán 3
ordinary, all

| 凡事 | fánshì | everything |
| 凡是 | fánshì | every, any, all, whatever |

A: 凡是人都會犯錯。

B: 但是你不能凡事都一錯再錯啊！

Compare: 風 fēng 築 zhù 贏 yíng

辶 chuò 'go' + 米 phonetic

迷

mí 9
confused, enchanted, fan

迷信	míxìn	superstition, blind faith
迷人	mírén*	charming, enchanting
迷路	mílù*	to get lost
歌迷	gēmí*	fan (of a singer)

A: 台灣很多人迷信什麼？

B: 迷信風水和數字。

Compare: 謎 mí

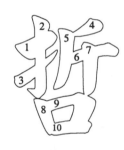

口 kǒu 'mouth' + 折 zhé phonetic

哲

zhé 10
philosophy

哲學	zhéxué	philosophy
哲學家	zhéxuéjiā*	philosopher
哲學系	zhéxuéxì*	philosophy department

A: 他的專業是什麼？

B: 哲學，他將來想做個哲學家。

Compare: 折 zhé

阝 fù 'hill' + 祭 jì phonetic

际

jì 13
border, occasion, among

實際	shíjì	reality, practical
實際上	shíjìshang*	as a matter of fact
國際	guójì*	international

A: 聽說他很不實際，跑去學文學。

B: 實際上他學的是國際貿易 màoyì 'trade'。

語法和用法 Grammar and Usage

Pay attention to the function of the structure and then study the example sentences.

1. Expressing the arising of an action or state

S Adj 起來（了）	…qǐ lái (le)	S starts to be Adj
S（沒）Adj（不）起來	(méi)…(bù) qǐ lái	S didn't/doesn't start to…
S V 起（O）來（了）	… qǐ (…) lái (le)	S starts to V(O)
S（沒）V（不）起（O）來	(méi)…(bù) qǐ (…) lái	S didn't/doesn't start to…

這兒的天氣也漸漸暖和**起來了**，昨天沒颱風、還出太陽，我就上街逛了逛。

1. 現在他的身體怎麼樣？

    現在他的身体怎么样？

    How is his health now?

    慢慢好起來了，再過幾天就可以回來工作了。

    慢慢好起来了，再过几天就可以回来工作了。

    He is starting to get better. In a few days he should be able to come back to work.

2. 最近在圖書館學習的人怎麼多起來了？

    最近在图书馆学习的人怎么多起来了？

    How come there are getting to be so many people in the library now?

    期末考試快到了，大家都緊張起來了。

    期末考试快到了，大家都紧张起来了。

    The final exam is coming. Everyone is starting to get nervous.

3. 你怎麼吃這麼多？不怕胖嗎？

    你怎么吃这么多？不怕胖吗？

    How come you ate so much? Aren't you afraid of gaining weight?

    沒關係，我這個人怎麼吃也胖不起來。

    沒关系，我这个人怎么吃也胖不起来。

    No problem. I'm the type who never gets fat no matter how much I eat.

4. 你為什麼不去找她談談？

    你为什么不去找她谈谈？

    Why don't you go find her and talk with her?

| 她太囉唆，說起話來，沒完沒了。 | 她太罗唆，说起话来，没完没了。 | She is too longwinded. When she starts to talk, she doesn't know when to stop. |

不能停下来

起來 literally means "to get up." When placed after an adjective or verb, it indicates the start and continuation of a state or action. If the verb takes an object, it should be placed between 起 and 來. There is often a 了 at the end of the sentence. Note that to negate the arising of an action/state in the past, the negative marker 沒 should be used and it is placed before the adjective or verb. To negate the arising of an action/state at present, the marker 不 should be used and it is placed after the adjective or verb (see example 3). Compare this pattern with the use of 起來 in a sensory reaction (L1, G3).

2. Expressing an (inexplicable) change of state

| (S₁) V₁著V₁著, S₁/S₂ (忽然)就V₂起(O)來了 | ...zhe... zhe...(hūrán) jiù...qǐ... lái le | While (S₁) is in the middle of doing V₁, S₁/S₂ (suddenly) starts to V₂ |

在路上走著走著，忽然看到一大群人，擠在一起，我也跟著去看熱鬧……

1.	她怎麼了？不是在說故事嗎？	她怎么了？不是在说故事吗？	What happened to her? She was telling a story, wasn't she?
	誰知道？她說著說著，忽然就哭起來了。	谁知道？她说着说着，忽然就哭起来了。	Who knows? She was talking and then suddenly started to cry.
2.	那些孩子不是在跑步嗎？	那些孩子不是在跑步吗？	Those children are running, aren't they?
	對啊！他們跑著跑著，忽然就唱起歌兒來了。	对啊！他们跑着跑着，忽然就唱起歌儿来了。	Yes, they are. As they were running, they suddenly started to sing.
3.	剛才外面下雨，你還出去！	刚才外面下雨，你还出去！	It was raining outside a moment ago and you went out anyway.
	沒事，走著走著，	沒事，走着走着，	It wasn't a problem.

我

雨就停了。	雨就停了。 S2	While I was walking, the rain let up.

This pattern conveys a change in the state of something. The use of 忽然 indicates a swift or unexpected change. There is often 了 at the end of the sentence. Remember that V₁ should be one syllable and if V₂ takes an object, it should be placed between 起 and 來. Sometimes there might be two different subjects involved, as in example 3.

3.   Expressing universality with double negation

無所不V 聊	wú suǒ bù…	There is nothing that S does not
無N不V	wú…bù …	There is no N that does not V

（handwritten: 无）

真有意思，我發現這兒的中國人好像**無所不拜**……

1.	那個教授很屬害嗎？	那个教授很厉害吗？	Is that professor really sharp?
	對，她真是無所不知呢。	对，她真是无所不知呢。	Yes, she really knows her stuff.
2.	你跟你的父母無話不說嗎？	你跟你的父母无话不说吗？	Do you talk to your parents about everything?
	媽媽還行，爸爸就不行了。	妈妈还行，爸爸就不行了。	I do with my mom, but not really with my dad.
3.	你不是喜歡她嗎？	你不是喜欢她吗？	You like her, don't you?
	我沒希望了。她跟小王談戀愛的事，現在無人不知了。	我没希望了。她跟小王谈恋爱的事，现在无人不知了。	I have no chance. Now everyone knows that she is dating Xiao Wang.

（handwritten: lián）

The phrase 無所不 takes on a limited number of one syllable verbs to form idiom-like formal expressions, e.g., 知/能/在/行/談. The 無…不 double negation structure also takes on a closed list of one syllable nouns and verbs to form stylized expressions, e.g., 無人不知/無話不談/無惡不做. Don't put 所 and nouns together, e.g., 無所人不認識他.

（handwritten: A, 无人不知, = everyone knows A）

4. Expressing total inclusiveness

| 凡事都… | fánshì dōu... | all, everything, in every aspect/matter/issue... |

也許我們這個民族受了孔孟儒家思想的影響太深，太實際了，**凡事都**從自己出發……

1. 我走了，到了再給你來信。

   我走了，到了再给你来信。

   I'll leave now. When I get there, I will write you a letter.

   你一個人在外，凡事都得小心點兒。

   你一个人在外，凡事都得小心点儿。

   You are alone away from home. You must be somewhat careful about everything.

2. 她聽父母的話嗎？

   她听父母的话吗？

   Did she listen to her parents?

   聽，她凡事都先跟父母商量再做。

   听，她凡事都先跟父母商量再做。

   Yes, she first discusses everything with her parents before she does anything.

3. 我又忘了帶我的功課來。

   我又忘了带我的功课来。

   I forgot to bring my homework again.

   你凡事都應該寫下來，才不容易忘記。

   你凡事都应该写下来，才不容易忘记。

   You should write down everything, so that it won't be so easy to forget.

凡事 means 'everything,' so it always occurs with 都. But note that 都 follows the subject when 凡事 is placed at the beginning of the sentence. For example, one can say 凡事我都自己來 or 我凡事都自己來, but not 凡事都我自己來. Compare this with 凡是…都 (L19, G1).

5. Expressing the benefit/detriment of one thing to another

| A對B（沒）有利 | duì…(méi)yǒulì | A is (not) advantageous to B |
| A對B（沒）有好處 | duì…(méi)yǒu hǎochù | A (doesn't) benefits B |

無論什麼教，只要**對人有利**，大家就能接受。

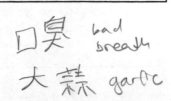

坏处

口臭 bad breath

大蒜 garlic

1.	學中文對找工作有 好處嗎？	学中文对找工作有 好处吗？	Is studying Chinese good for finding a job?

1. 學中文對找工作有好處嗎？ / 学中文对找工作有好处吗？ — Is studying Chinese good for finding a job?

有很大的好處。 / 有很大的好处。 — It is very advantageous.

2. 你為什麼反對我跟他在一起？ / 你为什么反对我跟他在一起？ — Why do you oppose my being with him?

跟那種人交朋友對你沒有利。 / 跟那种人交朋友对你没有利。 — It does you no good to be associated with that kind of person.

3. 你家怎麼連電視都沒有？ / 你家怎么连电视都没有？ — Why don't you even have a TV at home?

看電視對孩子沒有好處。 / 看电视对孩子没有好处。 — Watching TV is not good for children.

In this pattern A is the benefactor and B the beneficiary. To say "even more advantageous" in Chinese is 更有利/更有好處, and "of no benefit at all" is 一點兒好處也沒有.

6. Expressing a retort

S才…(呢)	cái…(ne)	contradiction of the previous statement

在許多年輕人的眼中，歐、美、日的明星才是他們真正「崇拜」的對象。

1. 你這麼做，真笨！ / 你这么做，真笨！ — You are really stupid to do it this way.

我不笨，你才笨呢！ / 我不笨，你才笨呢！ — I am not stupid. You are the one that is stupid.

2. 我家很大，有三個房間！ / 我家很大，有三个房间！ — My house is big. We have three rooms!

我家才大呢！我們 / 我家才大呢！我们 — The real big one is mine.

有 三 個 游 泳 池 yóuyǒngchí。	有三个游泳池。	We have three swimming pools.
3. 你的鼻子很大！	你的鼻子很大！	Your nose is big!
你的鼻子才大呢！	你的鼻子才大呢！	Yours is the one that is big!

才 is used to contradict or defy a view or suggestion just expressed by others. There is often a 呢 at the end of the sentence. Remember that 才 precedes the verb, so never say something like 才狗是人們的好朋友. This usage of 才 is often expressed in English merely with rising intonation.

文化點滴 Culture Notes

1. **Tomb Sweeping Festival**: Tomb Sweeping Festival, 清明節 Qīngmíngjié, is observed in early spring (106th day after the winter solstice), and usually falls on April 5. Qing Ming, literally meaning clear/pure and bright, is a period to remember, honor and pay respect to one's deceased ancestors and family members. Rituals include weeding the grave area, cleaning the headstone, offering incense, flowers, wine, and fruit, and burning imitation paper money for the deceased to use in the afterlife. The eve of Qing Ming is another holiday, the "cold food" festival 寒食節 Hánshíjié, which is little known now. It is said that in 655 B.C. a man named Jie Zhitui 介之推 saved his lord's life by serving him a piece of flesh from his own leg. The lord later became the ruler of the Jin state, but forgot to pay back the one who'd saved his life. When he learned that Jie and his mother led a secluded life living in the mountains, the lord wanted to offer Jie a government position. Thinking that this would force Jie out, the lord ordered his men to set fire to the mountain. To his regret, Jie remained there and was burnt to death. To commemorate Jie, the lord ordered all fires to be put out and thus began the "cold food festival" because no food could be cooked. A famous poem about Qing Ming (by Du Mu 杜牧 803–852) goes as follows:

清明時節雨紛紛，	清明时节雨纷纷，
路上行人欲斷魂。	路上行人欲断魂。
借問酒家何處有，	借问酒家何处有，
牧童遙指杏家村。	牧童遥指杏家村。

Qīngmíng shíjié yǔ fēnfēn,	The rain kept falling during the Tomb Sweeping festival,
Lùshàng xíngrén yù duàn hún.	Those on the road were heart-stricken.
Jiè wèn jiǔjiā héchù yǒu,	When they asked where one could find a tavern,

Mùtóng yáo zhǐ xìngjiācūn.　　　A shepherd boy pointed toward faraway Xing village.

2. **The Gate Gods:** In China, there used to be a custom of putting drawings of the gate gods 門神 on gates during Chinese New Year. It is said that long ago two brothers, Shen Tu 神茶 and Yu Lei 鬱壘 lived in a peach forest. Both of them were so strong that animals would bow their heads before them. Near the forest lived a monster who had heard that the brothers' magic peaches would turn evil ones into gods. The monster came for the peaches but the brothers refused him. He was so mad that he led more than 300 ghosts to fight against the brothers. Even so, the monster was defeated and ran away. Another fierce battle took place but the brothers won again and the ghosts have never dared to annoy them since. Years later, when the brothers died, people thought they went to Heaven and became gods, serving as guards by the gate of the Heaven. Later people started to hang a peach board with the brothers' names on it on each side of their door with the belief that the branches of peach trees were full of magic. When paper was used, a picture of the brothers was put up instead.

3. **Kitchen God**: In Chinese folk culture, people believe that in every household there is a Kitchen God 灶君 zàojūn, who takes charge of the family's affairs and annually reports to Heaven what the family has done over the past year on the 23rd of the 12th month of the Chinese lunar calendar (when the Spring Festival or Chinese New Year begins). To make sure that the Kitchen God speak well of the family to Heaven, people offer a candy-like sticky cake instead of the usual cows, pigs or sheep. Although this tradition is no longer popular in cities, it is still observed in countryside.

4. **Religions in China**: Some say ancestor worship is the only religion native to China. All others, including, Buddhism, Christianity, Judaism, and Islam, were imported from outside. Confucianism and Daoism originated in China, but they are more philosophies than religions. Confucianism is concerned with human beings, their achievements, interests and relationships, rather than with abstract concepts and problems of theology. It urges the individual to conform to the standards of an ideal social system. Daoism, in contrast, encourages individuals to ignore the dictates of society and seek only to conform to the underlying pattern of the universe, the Dao (or Tao, meaning "way"). In the past, the dominant religions in China were Confucianism, Daoism, and Buddhism, and most Chinese were affected by all three major faiths and thus lacked strong allegiance to a single religion. In addition, Chinese people are very practical in their worship of gods. Different gods are invited for different occasions. When people are short of money, the god of fortune would be the guest at the table of sacrifice. In China, organized religion was officially eliminated after 1949. In 1978 the promulgation of formal religion was again permitted in China, and since 1982 many temples, churches, and mosques have reopened because the constitution allows freedom of religious belief, and protects legitimate religious activities.

5. **Feng shui**: Feng shui 風水, meaning wind and water, is an ancient branch of knowledge in which Chinese draw from science and intuition to express their view of the environment and its influence on one's fortune. People believe that the position and orientation of a

house or any space may be auspicious or inauspicious. Thus, through the knowledge of feng shui and the adjustment of the underlying environmental force (qi 氣), people are able to make themselves more compatible with nature, their surroundings and their own everyday life, so that prosperity, good health, and harmonious relationships can be promoted.

6. **Number:** In every day life of Chinese, numbers are believed to be either auspicious or ominous, depending on their pronounciation. People believe that similar sounds can produce similar results. Therefore, the number "eight" is significant for Cantonese because "eight" and "success" sound very close in Cantonese. People may spend a fortune just to get a license plate ending in "8888," and businessmen would pay a higher price to stay in hotel rooms with lucky numbers like 518 or 688. "Four" is considered an unlucky number because it sounds like "death" in Taiwanese. Therefore, hospitals and hotels in Taiwan normally have no fourth floor. The numbers in the elevator simply skip right from three to five. In general, people prefer even numbers because it is believed that "fortune/happiness comes in pairs." Therefore, at weddings when Chinese give "red envelopes" with gifts of cash, they often give even amounts such as NT$1,200 or NT$3,600 to express auspiciousness. At funerals, on the other hand, people usually give offerings with the last digit being odd, hoping that the ill fortune won't come again. Chinese not only use numbers to appeal for good fortune, they also use them to scold people. The following are a few examples.

Number		Pinyin	English
三八	三八	sānbā	<TW> scatterbrained
十三點	十三点	shísān diǎn	<TW> stupid/silly
二百五	二百五	èrbǎiwǔ	fool
不三不四	不三不四	bù sān bú sì	dubious, shady, neither one thing nor the other, without any order or out of touch

歌兒 Songs

你信什麼教
In What Faith Do You Believe?

Adagio

詞：劉雅詩　　曲：馬定一

1. 也 許 是 因 為 我 越 來 越 老，　　不 知 道 為 什麼
   Yě xǔ shì yīn wéi wǒ yuèlái yuè lǎo,　　bù zhī dào wèishénme
   Perhaps it's because I'm getting older.　　I don't know why

2. 我 想 你 不 是 真 的 要 信 教，　　只 是 愛 去 廟 裏
   Wǒ xiǎng nǐ bú shì zhēnde yào xìn jiào,　　zhǐshì ài qù miào lǐ
   I don't think you really want religion.　　You only like to go worship

1. 忽 然 想 要 信 教。　　可 能 是 因 為 想 要 找 個 依 靠。
   hūrán xiǎng yào xìn jiào.　　Kěnéng shì yīnwèi xiǎng yào zhǎo ge yī kào.
   I suddenly want something to believe.　　Maybe it's because I need something to rely on.

2. 拜 拜 心 安 就 好。　　希 望 神 保 佑 自 己 一 生 到 老。
   bàibài xīn ān jiù hǎo.　　Xīwàng shén bǎoyòu zìjǐ yì shēng dào lǎo.
   at the temple to put yourself at ease, hoping that the gods will bless you for your entire life.

1. 不 管 佛 教 道 教 或 天 主 教，　　還 有 回 教 基 督 教 和
   Bùguǎn Fó jiào, Dàojiào huò Tiānzhǔjiào,　　háiyǒu Huíjiào, Jīdūjiào hé
   No matter whether it's Buddhism, Taoism, or Catholicism, Islam, Christianity or

2. 迷 信 風 水 算 命 樣 樣 不 少，　　傳 統 儒 家 哲 學 思 想
   Míxìn fēngshuǐ suànmìng yàngyàng bù shǎo,　　chuántǒng Rújiā zhéxué sīxiǎng
   Superstition, geomancy, and fortune-telling, [you have tried] them all. Traditional Confucianism

1. 其 他 的 宗 教。　　只 希 望 神 能 保 佑 凡 事 好 運 到。
   qítā de zōngjiào.　　Zhǐ xīwàng shén néng bǎoyòu fánshì hǎoyùn dào.
   the other religions, I only hope that the gods are able to bless us and bring good luck to everything.

2. 早 就 沒 人 要。　　也 許 你 最 想 信 的 宗 教 是 睡 覺。
   zǎo jiù méi rén yào.　　Yě xǔ nǐ zuì xiǎng xìn de zōngjiào shì shuìjiào.
   is no longer what people want. Perhaps the religion you believe in most is sleep.

第十八課

Theme Spoken and Written Languages

Communicative Objectives
- Talking about characters
- Talking about Mandarin in Beijing
- Talking about Mandarin in Taipei
- Talking about a comical dialogue

Grammar Focus
- S不到/沒到…就V
- …的N之一
- 左V右V　都Neg.V/總算Pos.V了
- Sentence才怪
- A比B Adj # 倍
- Adj 就 Adj 在…

Focus on Characters
- 稱讚標準、基礎漲跌、招牌捲播、哈啦嘴繁、永肯倍盲

誰的中文最標準？

生詞 Vocabulary

Study the following words for their pronunciation and meaning. When an area is shaded, guess at the meaning of the word based on its constituent characters and then fill in the blank. Read the usage of words and related terms (antonyms, synonyms, compounds sharing the constituent characters, etc.) and try to answer the sample questions in Chinese. Note that proper nouns and incidental terms are not numbered.

◎By Order of Appearance

高标准，严要求
要求 requirement

1.	標準 标准	biāozhǔn	Adj/ N	standard 拿……做標準；標準高/低 你用什麼標準來要求自己？ 你用什么标准来要求自己？	[mark-norm]
2.	晚飯 晚饭	wǎnfàn	N	supper, dinner	[evening-meal]
3.	操場 操场	cāochǎng	N	practice field *playground*	[drill exercise-field]
4.	鬧笑話 闹笑话	nào xiàohua	VO	to make a fool of oneself 你昨天鬧了一個什麼笑話？ 你昨天闹了一个什么笑话？	[make-joke]
5.	面前	miànqián	N	⬛⬛⬛⬛⬛⬛ 你在誰的面前說話會很緊張？ 你在谁的面前说话会很紧张？	[face-before]
6.	打招呼	dǎ zhāohu	VO	to greet	[hit-beckon-call]
7.	哈哈	hāhā	ON	haha (sound of laughter)	
8.	稱讚 称赞	chēngzàn	V	to praise 老師常稱讚你們什麼？ 老师常称赞你们什么？	[commend-praise]
9.	教訓 教训	jiàoxun	N/ V	lesson, to lecture sb. 什麼事情給了你一個教訓？ 什么事情给了你一个教训？ 你做錯事的時候，誰常教訓你？ 你做错事的时候，谁常教训你？	[teach-lecture]
10.	大人	dàren	N	⬛⬛⬛⬛⬛⬛	[big-person]
11.	了不起	liǎobuqǐ	Adj	amazing, terrific	[understand-not-up]

瑟瑟发抖
sè sè dǒu shaking out of fear ✓

名词 lesson

论文 paper (acad.)

你覺得哪個球員很了不起？

你觉得哪个球员很了不起？

| 12. | 發音 | fāyīn | N/V | pronunciation, to pronounce | [utter-sound] |

發音

你覺得自己的發音怎麼樣？

你觉得自己的发音怎么样？

發音很好／差／正確 zhèngquè／標準

| 13. | 不停 | bùtíng | Adv | incessantly | [not-stop] |

說個／唱個不停；不停地說／唱

誰整天說個不停，讓你頭疼？

谁整天说个不停，让你头疼？

| 14. | 之一 | zhīyī | Suf | one of | [of-one] |
| 15. | 普通話 | pǔtōnghuà | N | Mandarin Chinese | [common-speech] |

普通话

……很普通　　　→普通人

美國普通老百姓都有什麼？

美国普通老百姓都有什么？

| 16. | 方言 | fāngyán | N | Dialect | [region-language] |
| 17. | 外地人 | wàidìrén | N | non-local people | [outside-place-person] |

→本地人 běndìrén

這兒的本地人說話有口音嗎？

这儿的本地人说话有口音吗？

| 18. | 口音 | kǒuyīn | N | regional accent | [mouth-sound] |

口音很重／不重；有一點兒口音

美國哪個地方的人口音很重？

美国哪个地方的人口音很重？

19.	嘴	zuǐ	N	mouth	
20.	茄子	qiézi	N	eggplant	[eggplant-suffix]
21.	基礎	jīchǔ	N/	foundation, basic	[base-foundation]

基础   Adj　你的中文基礎打得好不好？

你的中文基础打得好不好？

Characters with Many Strokes

標 場 鬧 稱 讚 發 普 嘴 基 礎

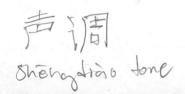

稅 tax
shuì

声調
shēngdiào tone

caisuai = bullshit

22.	舌頭 舌头	shétou	N	tongue	[tongue-suffix]
23.	捲 卷	juǎn	V	to roll, to curl	

捲舌頭/袖子xiùzi 'sleeve'

你發捲舌音有沒有問題？

你发卷舌音有没有问题？

24.	總算 总算	zǒngsuàn	Adv	at long last, finally	[total-count]
25.	啦	la	Part	indicating excitement/doubt (le 了 plus 啊)	
	捲舌音 卷舌音	juǎnshćyīn	N	retroflex	[curl-tongue-sound]
26.	收	shōu	V	to put away, to take back	

收東西/錢/信/衣服

洗好的衣服你收了沒有？

洗好的衣服你收了没有？

| 27. | 廣播
广播 | guǎngbō | N/V | broadcast, to air | [wide-broadcast] |

新聞/電視廣播

你喜歡聽哪一個台的廣播？

你喜欢听哪一个台的广播？

| 28. | 相聲
相声 | xiàngsheng | N | cross talk, comical dialogue | [mutual-sound] |

你聽過中國的相聲嗎？

你听过中国的相声吗？

| 29. | 倍 | bèi | M | times, -fold | |

你覺得中文比英文難嗎？

你觉得中文比英文难吗？

| 30. | 經常
经常 | jīngcháng | Adv | frequently, often | [regular-constant] |

=常常、總是

你經常遇到什麼問題？

你经常遇到什么问题？

| 31. | 書面語
书面语 | shūmiàn yǔ | N | written/literary language | [book-aspect-language] |
| 32. | 口語 | kǒuyǔ | N | spoken/vernacular language | [mouth-language] |

	口语			口語和書面語有什麼不同？	
				口语和书面语有什么不同？	
33.	認真 认真	rènzhēn	Adj/ V	earnest, serious, to take to heart	[consider-true]
34.	基本	jīběn	N/	basic, essential	[base-root]
			Adj	基本上；基本條件	
				找工作有哪些基本條件？	
				找工作有哪些基本条件？	
35.	簡體字 简体字	jiǎntǐzì	N	simplified characters	[simple-form-character]
36.	繁體字 繁体字	fántǐzì	N	traditional characters	[complex-form-character]
37.	招牌	zhāopai	N	shop sign	[beckon-plate]
				你看得懂中文的商店招牌嗎？	
				你看得懂中文的商店招牌吗？	
38.	文字	wénzì	N	characters, script	[writing-character]
				你覺得中國文字難在哪兒？	
				你觉得中国文字难在哪儿？	
39.	文盲	wénmáng	N		[writing-blind]
				→音盲、色盲 sèmáng	
				中國現在有多少文盲？	
				中国现在有多少文盲？	
40.	主要	zhǔyào	Adj	main, principal	[main-vital]
				主要的原因／問題／目的	
				你學中文的主要目的是什麼？	
				你学中文的主要目的是什么？	
41.	肯定	kěndìng	Adv/	definitely, positive, to affirm [consent-fixed]	
			Adj/	她今天肯定會來嗎？	
			V	她今天肯定会来吗？	

Characters with Many Strokes

廣 播 聲 經 基 簡 體 繁 牌

42.　永遠　　　　yǒngyuǎn　　Adv　forever　　　　　　　[perpetually-far]

　　永远 *爱你*

　　　　　　　　　　　　　　　永遠不變/學不完

　　　　　　　　　　　　　　　世界上什麼是永遠不變的？

　　　　　　　　　　　　　　　世界上什麼是永远不变的？

43.　同情　　　　tóngqíng　　V　　to sympathize with　　[same-feeling]

　　　　　　　　　　　　　　　同情（人）

　　　　　　　　　　　　　　　你同情什麼人？

　　　　　　　　　　　　　　　你同情什么人？

Characters with Many Strokes

遠　情

◎By Grammatical Categories

Nouns/Pronouns

倍	bèi	times, -fold	發音	fāyīn	pronunciation, to pronounce
嘴	zuǐ	mouth	相聲	xiàngsheng	cross talk, comical dialogue
舌頭	shétou	tongue	廣播	guǎngbō	broadcast, to air
茄子	qiézi	eggplant	招牌	zhāopai	shop sign
晚飯	wǎnfàn	supper, dinner	教訓	jiàoxun	lesson, to lecture sb.
面前	miànqián	in front of	基礎	jīchǔ	foundation, basic
操場	cāochǎng	practice field	基本	jīběn	basic, essential
大人	dàren	adult	文字	wénzì	characters, script
外地人	wàidìrén	non-local people	文盲	wénmáng	illiterate, illiteracy
普通話	pǔtōnghuà	Mandarin Chinese	書面語	shūmiàn yǔ	written/literary language
方言	fāngyán	dialect	簡體字	jiǎntǐzì	simplified characters
口音	kǒuyīn	regional accent	繁體字	fántǐzì	traditional characters
口語	kǒuyǔ	spoken/vernacular language			

Verbs/Stative Verbs/Adjectives

捲	juǎn	to roll, to curl	打招呼	dǎ zhāohu	to greet
收	shōu	to put away, to take back	了不起	liǎobuqǐ	amazing, terrific
稱讚	chēngzàn	to praise	主要	zhǔyào	main, principal
同情	tóngqíng	to sympathize with	標準	biāozhǔn	standard
鬧笑話	nào xiàohua	to make a fool of oneself	認真	rènzhēn	earnest, serious, to take to heart

Adverbs and Others

不停	bùtíng	incessantly	之一	zhīyī	one of
經常	jīngcháng	frequently, often	啦	la	indicating excitement/ doubt (le 了 plus 啊)
永遠	yǒngyuǎn	forever	哈哈	hāhā	haha (sound of laughter)
總算	zǒngsuàn	at long last, finally			
肯定	kěndìng	<PRC> definitely, positive, to affirm			

◎By Pinyin

Entries with * indicate lexical items used in Mini-Dialogues and of possible interest for supplemental study.

bèi	倍	times, -fold	liǎobuqǐ	了不起	amazing, terrific
biāozhǔn	标准	standard	miànqián	面前	in front of
bùtíng	不停	incessantly	nàoxiàohua	闹笑话	to make a fool of oneself
cāochǎng	操场	practice field	pàomiàn*	泡面	<TW> instant noodles
chēngzàn	称赞	to praise	pǔtōnghuà	普通话	Mandarin Chinese
dǎ zhāohu	打招呼	to greet	qiézi	茄子	eggplant
dàren	大人	adult	rènzhēn	认真	earnest, serious, to take to heart
fāngbiànmiàn*	方便面	<PRC> instant noodles	shétou	舌头	tongue
fāngyán	方言	dialect	shūmiàn yǔ	书面语	written/literary language
fántǐzì	繁体字	traditional characters	shōu	收	to put away, to take back
fāyīn	发音	pronunciation, to pronounce	tóngqíng	同情	to sympathize with
guǎngbō	广播	broadcast, to air	wàidìrén	外地人	non-local people
hāhā	哈哈	haha (sound of laughter)	wǎnfàn	晚饭	supper, dinner
jiǎntǐzì	简体字	simplified characters	wénmáng	文盲	illiterate, illiteracy
jiàoxun	教训	lesson, to lecture sb.	wénzì	文字	characters, script
jīběn	基本	basic, essential	xiàngsheng	相声	cross talk, comical dialogue
jīchǔ	基础	foundation, basic	yǒngyuǎn	永远	forever
jīngcháng	经常	frequently, often	zhāopai	招牌	shop sign
juǎn	卷	to roll, to curl	zhīyī	之一	one of
kěndìng	肯定	<PRC> definitely, positive, to affirm	zhǔyào	主要	main, principal
kǒuyīn	口音	regional accent	zǒngsuàn	总算	at long last, finally
kǒuyǔ	口语	spoken/vernacular language	zuǐ	嘴	mouth
la	啦	indicating excitement/doubt (le 了 plus 啊)			

課文 Text

Use the following questions to guide your reading of the text.

1. 小高最近鬧了一個什麼笑話？他從這件事情中學到什麼？

2. 小高想說標準的漢語，可是他遇到什麼困難？

3. 小高覺得中文難的原因是什麼？

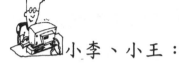小李、小王：

　　昨天我吃過晚飯就到附近一個學校的操場散散步，誰知道出去 [1]沒到三分鐘，我就鬧了一個大笑話。一個很可愛的孩子從我面前走過，我想和他打招呼，就問他：「你吃fèn了沒有？」結果，他哈哈大笑。我剛才也這麼跟人打招呼，有人還稱讚我的中文很不錯呢！這件事情給我的教訓是：一般的中國人，特別是大人，都太客氣了，覺得老外能說幾句中文，就很了不起。所以不管發音、聲調對不對，都不停地稱讚，只有孩子是最老實的。

　　我很希望能說一口標準的中文，去北京留學[2]的原因之一，就是想多聽聽標準的普通話，去了才發現，北京有很多說方言的外地人，說普通話時口音很重，並不標準；但是真正的北京人說起話來，嘴裏卻像有個茄子似的，兒呀兒的，我也聽不太懂。原來很少人說話說得像我的中文老師那樣清楚、明白，從前真應該打好基礎。我在北京把

舌頭[3]**左捲右捲**，**總算**能說出「今兒的事兒多啦」這樣一個句子。可是到了台灣，那兒的人又聽不慣我這種說法，只好把好不容易才練好的捲舌音收起來了。究竟誰的中文最標準？有人叫我去聽廣播、新聞、或相聲，我聽得懂[4]**才怪**！一來他們說得[5]**比**平常人不知道快多少**倍**，二來那些語言中經常有書面語，和口語很不同。也許我太認真了，中國人自己好像也不在乎中文說得標不標準，可能他們覺得他們的英文說得標準更重要呢！

　　大概中文難[6]**就**難**在**「標準」太多！除了聽、說以外，讀、寫也很麻煩。基本上，大陸用的是簡體字，台灣用的是繁體字，可是這也不一定對。實際上有些台灣人為了寫得快，有時也會用幾個簡體字；大陸上的一些商店招牌，有時候也能看到繁體字。我不知道中國文字這麼複雜、這麼困難，是不是中國有很多文盲的主要原因，但是這麼多的「標準」肯定讓學生覺得很吃力、很沒有成就感。我覺得中文要學的東西實在太多了，永遠學不完！你們同情我嗎？

　　　　　　　　　　　　　　　　　　　　　可憐的老外上

课文 Text

Use the following questions to guide your reading of the text.

1. 小高最近闹了一个什么笑话？他从这件事情中学到什么？

2. 小高想说标准的汉语，可是他遇到什么困难？

3. 小高觉得中文难的原因是什么？

 小李、小王：

　　昨天我吃过晚饭就到附近一个学校的操场散散步，谁知道出去[1]没到三分钟，我就闹了一个大笑话。一个很可爱的孩子从我面前走过，我想和他打招呼，就问他："你吃fēn了没有？"结果，他哈哈大笑。我刚才也这么跟人打招呼，有人还称赞我的中文很不错呢！这件事情给我的教训是：一般的中国人，特别是大人，都太客气了，觉得老外能说几句中文，就很了不起。所以不管发音、声调对不对，都不停地称赞，只有孩子是最老实的。

　　我很希望能说一口标准的中文，去北京留学[2]的原因之一，就是想多听听标准的普通话，去了才发现，北京有很多说方言的外地人，说普通话时口音很重，并不标准；但是真正的北京人说起话来，嘴里却象有个茄子似的，儿呀儿的，我也听不太懂。原来很少人说话说得象我的中文老师那样清楚、明白，从前真应该打好基础。我在北京把舌头[3]左卷右卷，总算能说出"今儿的事儿多啦"这样一个句子。可是到了台湾，那儿的人又听不惯我这种说法，只好把好不容易才练好的卷舌音收起来了。究竟谁的中文最标准？有人叫我去听广播、新闻、或相声，我听得懂[4]**才怪**！一来他们说得[5]**比**平常人不知道快多少**倍**，二来那些语言中经常有书面语，和口语很不同。也许我太认真了，中国人自己好象也不在乎中文说得标不标准，可能他们觉得他们的英文说得标准更重要呢！

　　大概中文难[6]**就**难**在**"标准"太多！除了听、说以外，读、写也很麻烦。基本上，大陆用的是简体字，台湾用的是繁体字，可是这也

不一定对。实际上有些台湾人为了写得快，有时也会用几个简体字；大陆上的一些商店招牌，有时候也能看到繁体字。我不知道中国文字这么复杂、这么困难，是不是中国有很多文盲的主要原因，但是这么多的"标准"肯定让学生觉得很吃力、很没有成就感。我觉得中文要学的东西实在太多了，永远学不完！你们同情我吗？

　　　　　　　　　　　　　　　　　　　　　　　可怜的老外上

小對話 Mini-Dialogues

Read the supplementary dialogues for a better understanding of the text. See if you can memorize one and perform it in class.

(1) Talking about characters

A: 我媽媽說，什麼人，寫什麼字。　　我妈妈说，什么人，写什么字。

B: 怪不得我找不到女朋友，我的字太難看了。　　怪不得我找不到女朋友，我的字太难看了。

A: 難看沒關係，寫清楚就行了。　　难看没关系，写清楚就行了。

B: 漢字這麼複雜，怎麼寫清楚？　　汉字这么复杂，怎么写清楚？

A: 那你為什麼不寫簡體字呢？　　那你为什么不写简体字呢？

B: 簡體字雖然簡單，但是不如繁體字有意思、漂亮。你看，「嘴」這個繁體字是不是比較好看？　　简体字虽然简单，但是不如繁体字有意思、漂亮。你看，"嘴"这个繁体字是不是比较好看？

A: 你知道嗎？「嘴」的簡體字跟繁體字是一樣的。　　你知道吗？"嘴"的简体字跟繁体字是一样的。

A: My mother said you can tell what kind of person someone is by the way they write their characters.

B: No wonder I can't find a girlfriend. My characters look awful.

A: It doesn't matter if they look bad. As long as you write them clearly, it will be fine.

B: Chinese characters are so complicated. How do you write them clearly?

A: Then why don't you write in simplified characters?

B: Although simplified characters are simple, they are not as interesting or beautiful as traditional characters. Look, isn't the traditional character "mouth" much prettier?

A: Don't you know that the simplified character for "mouth" is the same as the traditional character?

 (2) Talking about Mandarin in Beijing

A: 你在北京，接觸了很多中國
        人，和他們溝通沒問題吧？

A: 你在北京，接触了很多中国
        人，和他们沟通没问题吧？

Gao: 老師說的我差不多都能聽懂，
        可是聽老百姓說話就不行了。
        他們說得又快又不清楚。

Gao: 老师说的我差不多都能听懂，
        可是听老百姓说话就不行了。
        他们说得又快又不清楚。

A: 很多可能是外地人，說普通話
        時，口音比較重。

A: 很多可能是外地人，说普通话
        时，口音比较重。

Gao: 老北京的話我也聽不懂。兒啊
        兒的，嘴裏好像有個茄子似
        的。

Gao: 老北京的话我也听不懂。儿啊
        儿的，嘴里好象有个茄子似
        的。

A: 有時候，連中國人自己溝通也
        有問題呢！

A: 有时候，连中国人自己沟通也
        有问题呢！

Gao: 那麼多人說方言，溝通的問題
        是免不了的。

Gao: 那么多人说方言，沟通的问题
        是免不了的。

A: You are in contact with many Chinese in Beijing. Surely you have no problem communicating with them?

Gao: I can understand almost everything the teacher says, but when I listen to people on the street, I have trouble. They speak very fast and not clearly.

A: Many of them are probably from other provinces. When they speak Mandarin, their accent is rather strong.

Gao: I have trouble understanding the local people in Beijing as well. They curl their tongues so much, as if there were eggplants in their mouths.

A: Sometimes even Chinese themselves have trouble communicating.

Gao: There are so many people speaking dialects. Communication problems are
        unavoidable.

 (3) Talking about Mandarin in Taipei

Gao: 老板，你這兒有沒有方便麵 fāngbiànmiàn ？

        老板，你这儿有没有方便面？

A: 什麼方便麵？我們只有泡麵 pàomiàn 。

        什么方便面？我们只有泡面。

Gao: 泡麵一包多少錢？

        泡面一包多少钱？

A: 這種要sí塊。

        这种要sí块。

Gao: 這麼便宜？這是五塊錢，不用
        找了。

        这么便宜？这是五块钱，不用
        找了。

A: 我說的是sí塊，不是sì塊。

        我说的是sí块，不是sì块。

Gao: Sir, do you have convenient noodles here?

A: What convenient noodles? What we have is
        only instant noddles.

Gao: How much is that per pack?

A: Ten dollars for this kind.

Gao: So cheap? This is five dollars. No need for
        the change.

A: I mean ten dollars, not four dollars.

(4) Talking about a comical dialogue

Gao: 什麼是相聲啊？

        什么是相声啊？

A: 是一種最高的說話藝術。兩個
        人說話，說得很幽默，讓人開
        心。

        是一种最高的说话艺术。两个
        人说话，说得很幽默，让人开
        心。

Gao: 那我也會說相聲。

        那我也会说相声。

A: 你說來聽聽。   你说来听听。

Gao: 昨天我在路上看到一個招牌，   昨天我在路上看到一个招牌，
        不知道怎麼讀好，就問旁邊的   不知道怎么读好，就问旁边的
        一位小姐：「我能不能wěn你一   一位小姐："我能不能wěn你一
        下？」   下？"

A: 你說話太沒「藝術」，肯定讓   你说话太没"艺术"，肯定让
        她很生氣。   她很生气。

Gao: What is a comical dialogue?

A: It is the highest form of spoken art.
        Two people chat in a humorous way
        and make people laugh.

Gao: Well, I can do that too.

A: Give it a try.

Gao: Yesterday I saw a road sign and didn't
        know how to read it. So, I asked a lady
        nearby, "May I kiss (wěn instead of wèn
        "ask") you?"

A: I bet your lack of artistry made her very upset.

小故事 Stories

Read the following tale for your own enjoyment and for your understanding of the highlighted expression that is relevant to the theme of the chapter.

 熟能生巧 shú néng shēng qiǎo

✿ 學中文只要多練習，就會熟能生巧。

熟	shú	practiced
巧	qiǎo	skillful
射箭	shè jiàn	to shoot an arrow
陳生	Chén Shēng	name of a person
射中	shèzhòng	to shoot and hit (the target)
路人	lùrén	passerby
點頭	diǎntóu	to nod
驚奇	jīngqí	to be amazed
看不起	kànbuqǐ	to look down upon
熟練	shúliàn	skilled
罷了	bàle	That's all!
小看	xiǎokàn	to belittle
銅錢	tóngqián	copper cash
勺子	sháozi	ladle, scoop
沾	zhān	to be stained with
謙虛	qiānxū	humble

從前有個很會射箭的人叫陳生。有一天他在一個地方練習射箭，每次都射中。路人看到了，都稱讚他。只有一個賣油的老人，點了點頭，並不很驚奇。

陳生覺得他看不起自己，就問這個老人：「你也會射箭嗎？」老人回答說：「我不會射箭，不過我看你雖然射得很好，也沒有什麼了不起，只是很熟練罷了。」陳生有點兒生氣，就說：「你不會射箭，還這麼小看我。」

老人說：「我是個賣油的，也有一點兒小經驗，現在請你看一看。」說完，他就把一個瓶子放在地上，把一個銅錢放在瓶口上，然後用勺子把油裝到瓶子裏。瓶子裏裝了很多油，可是銅錢上一點兒油也沒有沾到。老人笑著說：「這也沒有什麼了不起，只是熟練罷了。」從那以後，陳生就很謙虛了。

✎ 熟能生巧的意思是_____

熟能生巧 shú néng shēng qiǎo

❀ 学中文只要多练习，就会熟能生巧。

从前有个很会射箭的人叫陈生。有一天他在一个地方练习射箭，每次都射中。路人看到了，都称赞他。只有一个卖油的老人，点了点头，并不很惊奇。

陈生觉得他看不起自己，就问这个老人："你也会射箭吗？"老人回答说："我不会射箭，不过我看你虽然射得很好，也没有什么了不起，只是很熟练罢了。"陈生有点儿生气，就说："你不会射箭，还这么小看我。"

老人说："我是个卖油的，也有一点儿小经验，现在请你看一看。"说完，他就把一个瓶子放在地上，把一个铜钱放在瓶口上，然后用勺子把油装到瓶子里。瓶子里装了很多油，可是铜钱上一点儿油也没有沾到。老人笑着说："这也没有什么了不起，只是熟练罢了。"从那以后，陈生就很谦虚了。

熟	shú	practiced
巧	qiǎo	skillful
射箭	shè jiàn	to shoot an arrow
陈生	Chén Shēng	name of a person
射中	shèzhòng	to shoot and hit (the target)
路人	lùrén	passerby
点头	diǎntóu	to nod
惊奇	jīngqí	to be amazed
看不起	kànbuqǐ	to look down upon
熟练	shúliàn	skilled
罢了	bàle	That's all!
小看	xiǎokàn	to belittle
铜钱	tóngqián	copper cash
勺子	sháozi	ladle, scoop
沾	zhān	to be stained with
谦虚	qiānxū	humble

漢字 Characters

Study the following selected characters for further enrichment of your writing and vocabulary.

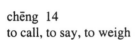

禾 hé 'grain' + 爪 zhǎo 'a hand holding 冉 rǎn scales'—weighing the grain

称

chēng 14
to call, to say, to weigh

| 稱呼 | chēnghu* | to call, form of address |
| 簡稱 | jiǎnchēng* | abbreviated form of |

A: 請問，怎麼稱呼你比較好？
B: 不必客氣，大家都叫我老王。

先 xiān 'first' (doubled) + 貝 bèi 'money'—two persons coming forward with money

赞

zàn 26
to support, to praise

| 稱讚 | chēngzàn | to praise, to commend |
| 讚美 | zànměi* | to praise, to eulogize |

A: 為什麼大家都稱讚他？
B: 因為他做了很多好事。

木 mù 'wood' + 票 piào phonetic

标

biāo 15
to mark, label, prize

標準	biāozhǔn	standard, criterion
標點	biāodiǎn*	punctuation
目標	mùbiāo*	objective, target, goal

A: 你今年的學習目標是什麼？
B: 我要說一口標準的中文。

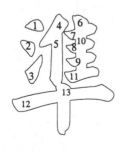

氵 shuǐ 'water' + 隹 sǔn phonetic—water level, to level, equal, certainly, allow

准

zhǔn 13
norm, accurate

| 準備 | zhǔnbèi | to prepare, to get ready |
| 準時 | zhǔnshí* | punctually |

A: 你準備什麼時候走？
B: 下午三點，我每次都很準時。

土 tǔ 'ground'
+其 qí
phonetic

基

基本	jīběn	basic, fundamental, main
基本上	jīběnshàng*	on the whole, basically
基督教	Jīdūjiào	Christianity

A: 這門課最基本的要求是每天來上課。
B: 基本上，來上課的人成績就不會差。

jī 11
base, foundation

石 shí 'stone' +
楚 chǔ
phonetic—
plinth, a stone
block base in
classical
architecture

础

| 基礎 | jīchǔ | base, foundation, basic |

A: 你的中文基礎打得很好！
B: 這都要感謝我的老師。

chǔ 18
foundation, base

氵 shuǐ 'water'
+ 張 zhāng
'extend'
phonetic—rising
water, tide, to
rise, to expand

涨

| 涨價 | zhǎngjià | to rise in price |
| 高漲 | gāozhǎng* | to rise, to surge up |

A: 去年很多股票漲價漲得很厲害。
B: 今年就慘了，價錢跌了一半。

Compare: 長 cháng 張 zhāng

zhǎng, zhàng 14
to rise, to go up, to
swell, to bloat

足 zú 'foot' +
失 shī 'lose'
phonetic

跌

跌價	jiējià	to go down in price
跌倒	jiēdǎo*	to fall, to tumble
跌傷	diēshāng*	to fall wounded

A: 我昨天跑步的時候跌倒了。
B: 跌傷了沒有？

diē 12
to fall, to tumble, to
drop

扌 shǒu 'hand'
+ 召 zhào
'summon to
court'

招

打招呼	dǎ zhāohu*	to greet sb., say hello
招待	zhāodài*	to receive (guests)
招待會	zhāodàihuì*	reception

A: 昨天你在招待會上為什麼跟每個人
    都打招呼？
B: 我是負責招待的啊！

zhāo 8
to beckon, to recruit,
to attract

片 piàn 'slice'
+ 卑 bēi
phonetic

牌

招牌	zhāopai	shop sign, signboard
路牌	lùpái*	street signs
名牌	míngpái*	famous brand, name tag
老牌	lǎopái*	old brand, veteran actor

A: 為什麼你總去那兒買東西？
B: 這家很老牌，而且也賣很多名牌的東
西。

pái 12
tablet, brand, cards

Two ⼿ hands
rolling 米 mǐ
rice into
dumplings + 卩
jié 'seal' added
to the bottom to
mean 'document'

卷

| 捲舌音 | juǎnshéyīn | retroflex |
| 春捲 | chūnjuǎn | spring roll |

A: 你會發捲舌音嗎？
B: 不會，我的舌頭捲不起來。

Compare: 拳 quán

juǎn 11
to roll up, to roll, reel

扌 shǒu 'hand'
+ 番 fān
phonetic

播

| 廣播 | guǎngbō | broadcast, to air |
| 重播 | chóngbō* | to rebroadcast |

A: 你為什麼不看電視卻去聽廣播？
B: 電視上的節目老重播，真沒意思。

Compare: 翻 fān

bō 15
to sow, to broadcast

口 kǒu 'mouth'
+合 hé
phonetic

哈哈	hāhā	Ha ha
笑哈哈	xiàohāhā*	laughingly, with a laugh
打哈欠	dǎ hāqian*	to yawn

A: 你為什麼一直笑哈哈的？
B: 我今天得了滿分。

Compare: 盒 hé

哈

hā 9
to exhale, sound of
laughter

口 kǒu 'mouth'
+ 拉 lā
phonetic

| 嘩啦 | huālā* | sound of crashing/rustling |

A: 我聽到嘩啦一聲就趕緊跑出去。
B: 是有人打破 dǎpò 'break' 你的窗戶嗎？

啦

la 11
(indicating
excitement/doubt)

此 cǐ phonetic +
角 jiǎo 'horn':
resembling a
bird's beak + 口
kǒu 'mouth'

嘴巴	zuǐba*	mouth, cheeks
多嘴	duōzuǐ*	to speak out of turn
還嘴	huánzuǐ*	to talk back, retort

A: 他的嘴巴大嗎？
B: 大極了，不應該說話的時候特別多
嘴。

嘴

zuǐ 16
mouth, snout, bill

The 每 plants
糸 twisting into
a tangle:
luxuriant
vegetation; 攵
was added for
decoration

| 繁體字 | fántǐzì | traditional characters |
| 繁忙 | fánmáng* | busy |

A: 他的工作很繁忙。
B: 再忙也比不上我吧！

繁

fán 17
numerous,
complicated

A representation of water, slightly more intricate than 水 shuǐ— the unceasing flow of water veins in the earth

永

yǒng 5
forever, always

永遠　　　yǒngyuǎn　　　always, forever

A: 我想永遠留在這兒。

B: 我可不想當「老美」。

Compare: 樣 yàng　泳 yǒng

止 used to be 冎 'skeleton: tough and rigid' + 月 ròu 'flesh: soft and flexible'— model one's self, to yield, to follow

肯

kěn 8
to be willing/ready to

肯定　　　kěndìng　　　to affirm, positive, surely
不肯　　　bùkěn*　　　not willing/ready to

A: 你肯定她不會來嗎？

B: 我跟她說了幾次，她都不肯出門。

Compare: 啃 kěn

亻 rén 'person' + 音 pǒu phonetic

倍

bèi 10
times, -fold

加倍　　　jiābèi*　　　to double

A: 你先借我錢，以後再加倍還你。

B: 你說話算話嗎？

Compare: 部 bù　陪 péi

目 mù 'eye' + 亡 wáng 'to disappear' phonetic

盲

máng 8
blind

文盲　　　wénmáng　　　illiterate, illiteracy
色盲　　　sèmáng*　　　color blindness
盲人　　　mángrén*　　　blind person

A: 他是文盲還是色盲？

B: 都不是，是個音盲。

語法和用法 Grammar and Usage

Pay attention to the function of the structure and then study the example sentences.

1. Expressing the earlier-than-expected occurrence of an action

S不到/沒到time span就V(了)　　　búdào/méidào…	S has done V for less than (a period of time)
S V₁不到/沒到time span就V₂(了)　jiù…(le)	S has done V₁ for less than (a period of time), then S V₂…

誰知道出去**沒到**三分鐘，我**就**鬧了一個大笑話。

1. 今天的功課容易嗎？

   今天的功课容易吗？

   Is today's homework easy?

   很容易，他沒到一個鐘頭就寫完了。

   很容易，他没到一个钟头就写完了。

   It's very easy. He finished it within an hour.

2. 我想他不到三天就能把這本書看完。

   我想他不到三天就能把这本书看完。

   I think he will be able to finish reading this book in less than three days.

   我倒覺得他最少得花一個星期才能把這本書看完。

   我倒觉得他最少得花一个星期才能把这本书看完。

   On the contrary, I think it will take him at least a week to finish reading this book.

3. 她故事講得怎麼樣？

   她故事讲得怎么样？

   How did her story-telling go?

   還可以，可是她太緊張了，說沒到一分鐘臉就紅了。

   还可以，可是她太紧张了，说没到一分钟脸就红了。

   It was fine. But she was so nervous that her face turned red in less than a minute.

Literally, 不到/沒到 means "not reach." When followed by a quantity, it means "less than..., within..." It is used to indicate how soon something happens; therefore, 就 must precede the verb, e.g., 那孩子不到三歲就會說話了. If it is a past event, there would be a 了 after the verb phrase. If two verbs are involved, the V₂ can be a result of V₁, or an entirely unrelated situation. Compare this with 再過…就要/就是…了 (L11, G1).

看沒到三分之一就

after watching not even one third

2. Expressing one of many elements

···的N之一	...de...zhīyī	One of the N that/to...

去北京留學**的**原因**之一**，就是想多聽聽標準的普通話……

1. 我怎麼樣能把中文 學好？

    我怎么样能把中文 学好？

    How can I study Chinese well?

    學好中文的方法之 一，就是多找機會 和中國人溝通。

    学好中文的方法之 一，就是多找机会 和中国人沟通。

    One of the ways to study Chinese well is to find opportunities to communicate with Chinese.

2. 你覺得芝加哥怎麼 樣？

    你觉得芝加哥怎么 样？

    How do you like Chicago?

    我覺得芝加哥是美 國最有意思的城市 之一。

    我觉得芝加哥是美 国最有意思的城市 之一。

    I think that Chicago is one of the most interesting cities in the U.S.

3. 你喜歡上中文課 嗎？

    你喜欢上中文课 吗？

    Do you like to go to Chinese class?

    這是我這學期最喜 歡的課之一。

    这是我这学期最喜 欢的课之一。

    This is one of my favorite classes this semester.

Note that 之一 often occurs with 的, which connects a modifier and a modified (N). Never say something like 把身體搞好之一是每天運動.

3. Expressing an ongoing pursuit and its final result

S₁左V右V(S₂)都not V S₁左V右V(S₂)總算V了	zuǒ...yòu...dōu... zuǒ...yòu...zǒngsuàn... le	S tried everything, but still couldn't do it. S tried everything, and finally made it.

我在北京把舌頭**左捲右捲**，**總算**能說出「今兒的事兒多啦」這樣一 個句子。

1. 他是誰？你認識他 嗎？

    他是谁？你认识他 吗？

    Who is he? Do you know him?

	認識，可是我左想右想，都想不起來他叫什麼名字。	认识，可是我左想右想，都想不起来他叫什么名字。	I know him, but I can't recall his name no matter how hard I try.
2.	你有他的消息了嗎？	你有他的消息了吗？	Have you heard from him?
	有，我左等右等，總算等到他的信了。	有，我左等右等，总算等到他的信了。	Yes, I waited and waited and finally received his letter.
3.	她的樣子變了嗎？	她的样子变了吗？	Has she changed?
	變得太多了！我左看右看，都認不出她來。	变得太多了！我左看右看，都认不出她来。	She has changed so much. I kept looking at her but still didn't recognize her.

The 左V右V expression indicates one's continuous attempt at something, and if the result is positive, 總算…了 is used subsequently, but if the result is negative, 都+V negative complement are to be used. Some other phrases like 怎麼也/就是 may work for the negative result as well, e.g., 我左等右等，怎麼也等不到他；我左等右等，他就是不來. Two different subjects might be involved in this pattern. The 左 and 右 here indicate the two extremes, which imply that the person has scrutinized all the possibilities. The first two verbs must be the same. However, the last verb may not necessarily be the same as the first two. Note that this expression only goes with a limited number of verbs, e.g., 等/想/看. Some other verbs like 找 seem to fit better with the 東V西V expression. Compare this with the V來V去 pattern which can be used with almost any verb.

4. Expressing certainty

S V O 才怪	…cáiguài	It would be strange/amazing if …

有人叫我去聽廣播、新聞、或相聲，我聽得懂才怪！

1.	你學了兩年中文了，看得懂中文報嗎？	你学了两年中文了，看得懂中文报吗？	You have studied Chinese for two years. Can you read a Chinese newspaper?

我看得懂才怪！	我看得懂才怪！	It would be amazing if I could read one.

2.
她今天會來參加這個活動嗎？	她今天会来参加这个活动吗？	Will she come to this activity today?
她會來才怪！	她会来才怪！	It would be a miracle if she showed up.

3.
你五點前能把功課做完嗎？	你五点前能把功课做完吗？	Can you finish your homework before five o'clock?
我能做完才怪！	我能做完才怪！	It would be a miracle if I could get it done before then.

…才怪 literally means "only then will it be strange." This pattern always comes at the end of a sentence. It is used as a rhetorical device to convey the certainty of the speaker's opinion. If what precedes才怪 contains a negative marker, e.g., 他不懂才怪, the meaning of the phrase is actually affirmative; if there is no negative marker, then the meaning is actually negative.

5. Expressing a multiple

A比B Adj # 倍	…bǐ…bèi	A is # times Adj-er than B

他們說得比平常人不知道快多少倍……

1.
中國人口比美國多幾倍？	中国人口比美国多几倍？	How many times bigger is Chinese population than that of the U.S.?
多好幾倍。	多好几倍。	Many times bigger.

2.
中文難還是英文難？	中文难还是英文难？	Is Chinese hard or is English hard?
中文比英文難好幾倍。	中文比英文难好几倍。	Chinese is much harder than English.

3.
你今年學的漢字比	你今年学的汉字比	Have you learned more characters this year than

加 減 乘 除   平是
十 一 × 号   二
cheng chú

平均 jūn
average

去年多嗎？	去年多吗？	last year?
最少 zuìshǎo 比去年多一倍。	最少比去年多一倍。	At least twice as many as last year.

If the multiple can be quantified, one just uses adjective plus number and 倍 (example 3). Note there is a difference in the number of a multiple if 是 instead of 比 is used, e.g., 今年的學生比去年的多一倍, namely, 今年的學生是去年的兩倍. If the multiple can't be quantified and one needs to say "several times Adj-er," adjective plus 好幾 and 倍 is used (examples 1 and 2).

6. Expressing an underlying reason

Adj就Adj在…	…jiù…zài…	The reason that one thinks it's Adj lies in …

大概中文難**就**難**在**「標準」太多！

1.	選這門課的學生多嗎？	选这门课的学生多吗？	Are there many students signing up for this course?
	這門課好就好在學生不多，大家都有機會練習！	这门课好就好在学生不多，大家都有机会练习！	The reason that this course is so good is its small enrollment. Everyone has an opportunity to practice.
2.	他告訴他的女朋友，她做的飯不好吃嗎？	他告诉他的女朋友，她做的饭不好吃吗？	Did he tell his girlfriend that the food she made was bad?
	糟就糟在他沒告訴她，所以她每次都請他去吃飯。	糟就糟在他没告诉她，所以她每次都请他去吃饭。	The problem is that he hasn't told her, so she always invites him over for dinner.
3.	這部電影哪兒不好？	这部电影哪儿不好？	What's wrong with this movie?
	這部電影差就差在故事太沒意思，演員其實還可以。	这部电影差就差在故事太没意思，演员其实还可以。	The reason that this movie is bad is because the story is boring. Actually the actors are O.K.

This pattern is used to highlight a reason that something is so X. The X is very often a one-syllable adjective. The reason goes after 在 and often takes the form of a noun or a clause, e.g., 中文難就難在聲調/中文難就難在聲調太複雜.

文化點滴 Culture Notes

1. **Spoken and written languages**: In Chinese, the written language 書面語 shūmiànyǔ differs greatly from the spoken language 口語 kǒuyǔ, both in structure and lexicon. Since the early 1920s, the vernacular langauge 白話 báihuà gradually replaced the literary language 文言 wényán, which is now studied by middle school students much the same way as Latin and Greek are studied in the West. However, the modern written language, especially that used in newspapers and formal documents, employs a good deal of literary vocabulary and grammatical constructions. Thus, for anyone to be truly educated in Chinese, it is necessary to have knowledge of the classical literary language.

2. **Simplification of Chinese characters**: It was long felt that Chinese script was too complicated and difficult to learn, and many argued that this complex script was the cause of the low illiteracy rate in China. As late as 1949 it is estimated that only 20 percent of China's population was literate. Thus, in 1956 the Committee on Script Reform 文字改革委員會 wénzì gǎigé wěiyuánhuì issued 515 simplified characters, most of which had the number of strokes reduced but some of which had components changed more radically. In 1964, over 2,000 simplified characters were promoted. Additional simplified characters were issued later but received widespread criticism and thus withdrawn.

3. **Store names and public signs**: One can feel quite disorientated when reading Chinese store names and public signs. Although Chinese texts with vertical lines of characters are read from top to bottom and from right to left and those with horizontal lines are read from top to bottom and from left to right, store names and public signs can go in either direction. Sometimes, one even finds a sign with some of the characters to be read from left to right and others from right to left.

4. **Comic dialogues**: Comic dialogues, or cross talk, 相聲 xiàngshēng [appearance-sound] is a type of oral art form that has been popular in northern China for many years. It is now enjoyed throughout most of mainland Chinese, and in Taiwan as well. Xiangsheng involving a single performer is called 單口相聲 dānkǒu xiàngshēng, two performers 對口相聲 duìkǒu xiàngshēng, and three or more performers 群口相聲 qúnkǒu xiàngshēng. The most common type is duìkǒu xiàngshēng. In it one plays the role of 逗哏 dòugén, the host, wise man, or funny man, and the other 捧哏 pěnggén, the role of the guest, fool, or straight man. Good xiangsheng performers have to be able to (1) 說 shuō speak eloquently with Beijing pronunciation, relate funny stories and jokes, recite poems, create puns, tell riddles, and do tongue-twisters; (2) 學 xué to mimic all kinds of sounds, voices, expressions, and movements, especially speakers of other Chinese dialects; (3) 逗 dòu to create humor and wit; (4) 唱 chàng to sing all kinds of songs including Peking opera.

歌兒 Songs

說普通話
Speaking Mandarin

Andantino

詞：劉雅詩　曲：馬定一

1. 那天 我 捲了舌頭，想要學 北京人說話，台北小孩
Nà tiān wǒ juǎnle shé tou, xiǎng yào xué Běijīng rén shuōhuà, Táiběi xiǎohái
The day I curled my tongue, hoping to learn to speak like people from Beijing, kids in Taipei

2. 朋友 說 多聽廣播 學相聲，可以打 基 礎，多看電視
Péngyǒu shuō duō tīng guǎngbō xué xiàngshēng, kěyǐ dǎ jī chǔ, duō kàn diànshì
My friends say that listening to more broadcasts and studying comic dialogues can lay a foundation. Watching TV

1. 卻 對我笑哈哈。 我想說得 標 準，可 是經常
què duì wǒ xiào hāhā. Wǒ xiǎng shuōde biāozhǔn, kěshì jīngcháng
laughed at me. I want to speak standard Mandarin, but I often

2. 聽 發音有幫助。 認真記住 教 訓，不 再犯
tīng fāyīn yǒu bāngzhù. Rènzhēn jìzhù jiào xùn, bú zài fàn
and listening to their pronunciation is also helpful. Earnestly study the lessons and don't make

1. 鬧笑話，常常想要叫媽媽，卻說成 爸 爸。 還會 分不清
nào xiàohuà, chángcháng xiǎng yào jiào māma, què shuōchéng bàba. Hái huì fēnbuqīng
make a fool of myself. Sometimes I want to say mother, but say father instead. Also I can't tell

2. 同樣錯誤，不管繁體簡體字 都 試著閱 讀。 遇到 書面語
tóngyàng cuòwù, bùguǎn fántǐ jiǎntǐ zì dōu shìzhe yuè dú. Yùdào shūmiànyǔ,
the same mistakes again. Try to read it whether it's traditional or simplified characters. Find

1. 該捲舌頭 或 是 要閉上嘴 巴。 跟人 打 招呼以後，
gāi juǎn shétou, huòshì yào bìshàng zuǐ ba. Gēn rén dǎ zhāohu yǐhòu,
whether to curl my tongue or say nothing at all. After saying hello to people,

2. 口語方言不 懂 就找人幫 助。 只要 不停地努力
kǒuyǔ fāngyán bù dǒng, jiù zhǎorén bāngzhù. Zhǐyào bùtíng de nǔlì
someone to help with formal phrases, colloquial expressions or dialects. As long as you keep working hard,

1. 只好不 說話當呆瓜。 2.學習， 肯定會有 進步。
zhǐhǎo bù shuōhuà dāng dāiguā. xuéxí, kěndìng huì yǒu jìn bù.
the best thing to do is keep quiet like an idiot. you surely will improve.

第十九課

Theme Literature and Arts

Communicative Objectives
- Talking about exhibits
- Talking about literature
- Talking about calligraphy
- Talking about painting

Grammar Focus
- 凡是(…的)N都 V
- S(所)V的(N)
- 再 Adj 也沒有了；再 Adj（也）不過了
- 別看…其實…
- 看樣子 SVO
- S 何必…（呢）?

Focus on Characters
- 山樹江湖、欣賞詩夢、周圍覽表、乖忍咳嗽、握隻朝者

我所愛的中國在哪兒？

生詞 Vocabulary

Study the following words for their pronunciation and meaning. When an area is shaded, guess at the meaning of the word based on its constituent characters and then fill in the blank. Read the usage of words and related terms (antonyms, synonyms, compounds sharing the constituent characters, etc.) and try to answer the sample questions in Chinese. Note that proper nouns and incidental terms are not numbered.

◎By Order of Appearance

1. 所   suǒ   IE   that, which

2. 凡是   fánshì   Adv   every, any, all   [ordinary-true]

     凡是讀過書的人都知道什麼？

     凡是读过书的人都知道什么？

     故宮   Gùgōng   N   imperial palace (museum)   [former-palace]

3. 意外   yìwài   Adj/   unexpected, accident   [idea-outside]

                          N   ……讓人覺得很意外   vs.大吃一驚

     什麼事讓你覺得很意外？

     什么事让你觉得很意外？

4. 欣賞   xīnshǎng   V/N   to appreciate   [enjoy-admire]

     欣赏   欣賞文物/建築/書畫/人   →賞月、賞花

     你最欣賞哪一位作家？

     你最欣赏哪一位作家？

5. 周圍   zhōuwéi   N   surrounding, all around   [whole-surround]

     周围   你住的地方周圍的環境怎麼樣？

     你住的地方周围的环境怎么样？

6. 出現   chūxiàn   V   to appear, to emerge   [out-appear]

     出现   出現了人/問題/現象

     前面路上出現了什麼問題？

     前面路上出现了什么问题？

7. 煙火   yānhuǒ   N   fireworks   [smoke-fire]

     烟火   你國慶節/日 Guóqìngjié/rì 'National Day' 的時候去

     看煙火嗎？

     你国庆节/日的时候去看烟火吗？

     四大發明   sì dà fāmíng   N   four greatest inventions

     四大发明

8.	山水	shānshuǐ	N		[mountains-water]

你看過中國的山水畫嗎？

你看过中国的山水画吗？

9.	高大	gāodà	Adj	tall and big	[tall-big]
10.	青年	qīngnián	N	youth	[young-age]
11.	詩	shī	N	poem	
	诗				

作一首詩   →詩人

你最喜歡哪個詩人？

你最喜欢哪个诗人？

	光	guāng	Adj	light, bright	
	疑	yí	V	to doubt, to suspect	
	霜	shuāng	N	frost	
	唐朝	Tángcháo	N	Tang dynasty (618–907 A.D.)	[surname-dynasty]
	李白	Lǐ Bái	N	Li Bo (699–762 A.D.), the most celebrated Chinese poet	
12.	請教	qǐngjiào	V		[please-teach]
	请教				

向人請教   vs. 問人（問題）

你有問題的時候，向誰請教？

你有问题的时候，向谁请教？

13.	感人	gǎnrén	Adj	touching	[move-people]

你覺得哪個愛情故事最感人？

你觉得哪个爱情故事最感人？

14.	作品	zuòpǐn	N	works (of literature/art)	[make-goods]

你喜歡誰寫的作品？

你喜欢谁写的作品？

15.	跳	tiào	V	to jump	

你什麼時候會高興得跳起來？

你什么时候会高兴得跳起来？

16.	湖	hú	N	lake	

Characters with Many Strokes

意　賞　圍　煙　詩　萬　感　跳　湖

17.	老人	lǎorén	N	old man/woman	[old-person]
18.	江	jiāng	N	river	
	宋詞 宋词	Sòngcí	N	a kind of poetry that flourished during the Song dynasty (1037–1101)	[Song-poem]
19.	作者	zuòzhě	N		[write-one who]

這本書的作者是誰？

这本书的作者是谁？

| | 蘇東坡
苏东坡 | Sū Dōngpō | N | a celebrated Song dynasty literary figure | |
| 20. | 握手 | wòshǒu | VO | to shake/clasp hands | [grasp-hand] |

to hold, grasp

你和哪個名人握過手？

你和哪个名人握过手？

| 21. | 書法家
书法家 | shūfǎjiā | N | calligrapher | [writing-way-master] |
| 22. | 咳嗽 | késou | V | to cough | [cough-cough] |

你咳嗽咳得很屬害嗎？

你咳嗽咳得很厉害吗？

| 23. | 打擾
打扰 | dǎrǎo | V | to disturb | [hit-bother] |

please do not

请勿打扰

對不起，打擾您了！

对不起，打扰您了！

24.	樹 树	shù	N	tree	
25.	猴子	hóuzi	N	monkey	[monkey-suffix]
26.	害怕	hàipà	Adj	to be afraid/scared	[feel-fear]

讓人害怕   vs. 東西/事情很可怕

什麼事情會讓你很害怕？

什么事情会让你很害怕？

| 27. | 和尚 | héshang | N | Buddhist monk | [gentle-esteem] |
| 28. | 乖 | guāi | Adj | well-behaved | |

你家的狗乖不乖？咬 yǎo 人嗎？

你家的狗乖不乖？咬人吗？

| 29. | 看樣子
看样子 | kànyàngzi | IE | it seems, it looks as if | [look-shape] |

兴奋

xìng fu

	西遊記 西游记	Xīyóujì	N	*The Journey to the West*	[west-travel-record]
	孫悟空 孙悟空	Sūn Wùkōng	N	Monkey King	
	元曲	Yuánqǔ	N	popular Yuan verse	
	明朝	Míngcháo	N	Ming dynasty (1368–1644)	[bright-dynasty]
30.	花園 花园	huāyuán	N		[flower-garden]

你參觀過哪個有名的花園？

你参观过哪个有名的花园？

	紅樓夢 红楼梦	Hónglóumèng	N	*The Dream of the Red Chamber*	[red-building-dream]
	大觀園 大观园	Dàguānyuán	N	magnificent garden	[grand-view-garden]
31.	發生 发生	fāshēng	V	to happen	[send out-bear]

發生事情/意外/變化/困難

那個故事發生在什麼朝代 cháodài 'dynasty' ？

那个故事发生在什么朝代？

32.	何必	hébì	Adv	there is no need	[why-must]
33.	傷心 伤心	shāngxīn	Adj	to be sad/aggrieved	[wound-heart]

什麼事情讓你很傷心？

什么事情让你很伤心？

hurt

34.	妹妹	mèimei	N	younger sister	[little sister-little sister]

→姐姐、哥哥、弟弟、姐妹、兄弟

35.	糊塗 糊涂	hútu	Adj	muddled, confused	[muddy-spread on]

最近你為什麼這麼糊塗？

最近你为什么这么糊涂？

36.	吃醋	chīcù	VO		[eat-vinegar]

你的男朋友為什麼吃醋？

你的男朋友为什么吃醋？

Characters with Many Strokes

握　嗽　擾　樹　猴　園　發　傷　糊　塗

37. 忍不住　　rěnbuzhù　　RV　　can't help but do sth.　　[endure-not-stop]

to endure

忍不住哭起來

聽到那個好消息，他忍不住大叫起來。

听到那个好消息，他忍不住大叫起来。

38. 怎麼回事　　zěnmehuí　　IE　　What's going on?　　[how-measure-event]
    怎么回事　　shì

39. 睜　　zhēng　　V　　to open the eyes
    睜

你希望每天眼睛一睜開就看到什麼？

你希望每天眼睛一睜开就看到什么？

40. 夢　　mèng　　N　　dream

在做 梦 — *you must be dreaming*

你昨天作夢了嗎？夢到了什麼？

你昨天作梦了吗？梦到了什么？

41. 表演　　biǎoyǎn　　N/V　　performance, exhibition, to perform　　[show-act]

精彩的表演；一場表演

你覺得這部電影裏誰表演得最精彩？

你觉得这部电影里谁表演得最精彩？

42. 比不上　　bǐbushàng　　RV　　[compare-not-up]

↔比得上

你覺得誰做的飯比得上你媽媽？

你觉得谁做的饭比得上你妈妈？

43. 展覽　　zhǎnlǎn　　N/V　　show, to exhibit　　[spread out-look at]
    展览

→展覽會、展覽品　　→花展、書展、畫展

芝加哥的博物館最近有什麼展覽？

芝加哥的博物馆最近有什么展览？

Characters with Many Strokes

醋　忍　睜　夢　演　展　覽

◎By Grammatical Categories

Nouns/Pronouns

展覽	zhǎnlǎn	show, to exhibit	妹妹	mèimei	younger sister
表演	biǎoyǎn	performance, exhibition, to perform	青年	qīngnián	youth
周圍	zhōuwéi	surrounding, all around	老人	lǎorén	old man/woman
花園	huāyuán	flower garden	和尚	héshang	Buddhist monk
煙火	yānhuǒ	fireworks	書法家	shūfǎjiā	calligrapher
山水	shānshuǐ	landscape (painting)	作者	zuòzhě	author
江	jiāng	river	作品	zuòpǐn	works (of literature/art)
湖	hú	lake	詩	shī	poem
樹	shù	tree	夢	mèng	dream
猴子	hóuzi	monkey			

Verbs/Stative Verbs/Adjectives

跳	tiào	to jump	忍不住	rěnbuzhù	can't help but do sth.
睜	zhēng	to open the eyes	比不上	bǐbushàng	can't compare with
咳嗽	késou	to cough	乖	guāi	well-behaved
發生	fāshēng	to happen	高大	gāodà	tall and big
出現	chūxiàn	to appear, to emerge	傷心	shāngxīn	to be sad/aggrieved
欣賞	xīnshǎng	to appreciate	感人	gǎnrén	touching
握手	wòshǒu	to shake/clasp hands	害怕	hàipà	to be afraid/scared
請教	qǐngjiào	to seek advice	糊塗	hútu	muddled, confused
打擾	dǎrǎo	to disturb	意外	yìwài	unexpected, accident
吃醋	chīcù	to be jealous (of rival in love)			

Adverbs and Others

凡是	fánshì	every, any, all	怎麼回事	zěnmehuí shì	What's going on?
何必	hébì	there is no need			
看樣子	kànyàngzi	it seems, it looks as if	所	suǒ	that, which

◎By Pinyin

Entries with * indicate lexical items used in Mini-Dialogues and of possible interest for supplemental study.

bèn*	笨	stupid	qǐngjiào	请教	to seek advice
biǎoyǎn	表演	performance, exhibition, to perform	qīngnián	青年	youth
bǐbushàng	比不上	can't compare with	rěnbuzhù	忍不住	can't help but do sth.
cháodài*	朝代	dynasty	shāngxīn	伤心	to be sad/ aggrieved
chīcù	吃醋	to be jealous (of rival in love)	shānshuǐ	山水	landscape (painting)
chūxiàn	出现	to appear, to emerge	shēngdòng*	生动	lively, vivid
cūxīn*	粗心	careless, thoughtless	shī	诗	poem
dǎrǎo	打扰	to disturb	shūfǎjiā	书法家	calligrapher
fánshì	凡是	every, any, all	shù	树	tree
fāshēng	发生	to happen	suǒ	所	that, which
gǎnrén	感人	touching	tiào	跳	to jump
gāodà	高大	tall and big	wòshǒu	握手	to shake/clasp hands
guāi	乖	well-behaved	wù*	雾	fog
hàipà	害怕	to be afraid/scared	xīnshǎng	欣赏	to appreciate
hébì	何必	there is no need	xìxīn*	细心	careful
héshang	和尚	Buddhist monk	yānhuǒ	烟火	fireworks
hóuzi	猴子	monkey	yìwài	意外	unexpected, accident
hú	湖	lake	yún*	云	cloud
hútu	糊涂	muddled, confused	yǒulì*	有力	strong, powerful
huāyuán	花园	flower garden	zěnmehuíshì	怎么回事	What's going on?
jiāng	江	river			
jǐngsè*	景色	scenery, view	zhǎnlǎn	展览	show, to exhibit
kànyàngzi	看样子	it seems, it looks as if	zhēng	睁	to open the eyes
késou	咳嗽	to cough	zhōuwéi	周围	surrounding, all around
lǎorén	老人	old man/woman	zuòpǐn	作品	works (of literature/art)
mèimei	妹妹	younger sister	zuòzhě	作者	author
mèng	梦	dream			

課文 Text

Use the following questions to guide your reading of the text.

1. 小高開始參觀故宮的時候，遇到了哪三個人？

2. 小高後來見到了什麼動物？

3. 中國的唐、宋、元、明、清各個朝代在文學上有什麼成就？

美英：

    [1]凡是來過台灣的人，大概都知道故宮這個有名的博物館。今天下午我有個意外的「故宮之旅」，居然看到了我[2]所愛的「中國」，現在馬上把它寫下來，讓你知道。

    我買了票進故宮，正準備好好欣賞古代的文物時，忽然大門關起來了，周圍出現了煙火，是介紹中國的「四大發明」嗎？我還沒看清楚，就進了牆上的山水畫裏。山中走出來一個高大的青年，他一邊喝酒，一邊作詩：「床前明月光、疑是地上霜。」真沒想到，我會在這兒遇到唐朝的大詩人李白。真是[3]

再好也沒有了！我想向他請教怎麼能寫出感人的作品來，誰知道他忽然跳進一個湖裏，不見了。我走近湖邊，卻看到那兒有一位白髮老人，邊走邊念：「大江東去……」這首宋詞的作者是誰？蘇東坡！我想走上前，和他握握手

時，他也離開了。噢！前面不遠的地方，有個小屋子，我去看看。有個人不停地在寫「永」這個字。他是誰？是個有名的書法家嗎？本來我想去問問，可是他寫得很專心，連我咳嗽也沒聽見，我不好意思打擾他，只好走了。

這時，我看到旁邊的樹上有隻猴子，又叫又跳，讓我有點兒害怕，可是 [4]**別看**它樣子厲害，**其實**很聽話。有個和尚從廟裏一出來，猴子就乖乖地跟他走了，[5]**看樣子**是《西遊記》裏的孫悟空吧？怎麼沒聽到元曲，一下子就到了明朝？我走著走著，進了一個很美的大花園，那裏有好多漂亮的女孩子，這是《紅樓夢》裏的大觀園吧！前面有一個很瘦的姑娘，一邊哭一邊把手上的花放進土裏，多可憐啊！「發

生了什麼事，[6]**何必**這麼傷心**呢**？」我向她走過去，誰知道前邊出現了一個男的，居然叫她：「林妹妹！」是美英嗎？我覺得很糊塗，也有點兒吃醋，忍不住大叫一聲：「怎麼回事？」

這時，我睜開眼一看，才明白原來這些都是夢。你看我多想你啊！我來台灣以後，看過很多精彩的表演，但是都比不上今天看到的「展覽」。你覺得呢？希望你今晚也有個美夢！

德中上

课文 Text

Use the following questions to guide your reading of the text.

1. 小高开始参观故宫的时候，遇到了哪三个人？

2. 小高后来见到了什么动物？

3. 中国的唐、宋、元、明、清各个朝代在文学上有什么成就？

 美英：

　　¹凡是来过台湾的人，大概都知道故宫这个有名的博物馆。今天下午我有个意外的"故宫之旅"，居然看到了我²所爱的"中国"，现在马上把它写下来，让你知道。

　　我买了票进故宫，正准备好好欣赏古代的文物时，忽然大门关起来了，周围出现了烟火，是介绍中国的"四大发明"吗？我还没看清楚，就进了墙上的山水画里。山中走出来一个高大的青年，他一边喝酒，一边作诗："床前明月光、疑是地上霜。"真没想到，我会在这儿遇到唐朝的大诗人李白。真是³再好也没有了！我想向他请教怎么能写出感人的作品来，谁知道他忽然跳进一个湖里，不见了。我走近湖边，却看到那儿有一位白发老人，边走边念："大江东去……"这首宋词的作者是谁？苏东坡！我想走上前去，和他握握手时，他也离开了。噢！前面不远的地方，有个小屋子，我去看看。有个人不停地在写"永"这个字。他是谁？是个有名的书法家吗？本来我想去问问，可是他写得很专心，连我咳嗽也没听见，我不好意思打扰他，只好走了。

这时，我看到旁边的树上有只猴子，又叫又跳，让我有点儿害怕，可是⁴**别看**它样子厉害，**其实**很听话。有个和尚从庙里一出来，猴子就乖乖地跟他走了，⁵**看样子**是《西游记》里的孙悟空吧？怎么没听到元曲，一下子就到了明朝？我走着走着，进了一个很美的大花园，那里有好多漂亮的女孩子，这是《红楼梦》里的大观园吧！前面有一个很瘦的姑娘，一边哭一边把手上的花放进土里，多可怜啊！

"发生了什么事，⁶**何必**这么伤心呢？"我向她走过去，谁知道前边出现了一个男的，居然叫她："林妹妹！"是美英吗？我觉得很糊涂，也有点儿吃醋，忍不住

大叫一声："怎么回事？"

这时，我睁开眼一看，才明白原来这些都是梦。你看我多想你啊！我来台湾以后，看过很多精彩的表演，但是都比不上今天看到的展览。你觉得呢？希望你今晚也有个美梦！

德中上

小對話 Mini-Dialogues

Read the supplementary dialogues for a better understanding of the text. See if you can memorize one and perform it in class.

(1) Talking about exhibits

Gao: 這個博物館真大啊！   这个博物馆真大啊！

A: 可不是嗎？走一天也看不完。   可不是吗？走一天也看不完。

Gao: 你看這張畫多生動 shēngdòng啊！   你看这张画多生动啊！好象可
      好像可以看到社會上所有人的   以看到社会上所有人的日常生
      日常生活。   活。

A: 那是有名的「清明上河圖」啊！   那是有名的"清明上河图"啊！

Gao: 這塊玉 yù 雕 diāo 得跟真的菜一   这块玉雕得跟真的菜一样。
      樣。

A：   那是「小白菜」。   那是"小白菜"。

Gao: This museum is really big, huh!

A: Isn't that the truth? If we go all day, we still couldn't see everything.

Gao: Look how lively this painting is! It's as if you can see the daily life of everyone in that society.

A: That is the famous "*Spring Festival on the River*"!

Gao: This piece of jade was carved to look like a real vegetable.

A: That is "*Small White Cabbage*."

(2) Talking about literature

A: 你對中國文學有研究嗎？   你对中国文学有研究吗？

Gao: 沒什麼研究，只上過幾門文學   没什么研究，只上过几门文学課。

A: 中國各個朝代cháodài在文學上有
什麼成就？

Gao: 你在考我嗎？我只知道人說唐
詩、宋詞、元曲、明清小說。
我自己只讀過幾篇英文的翻
譯。

A: 你最喜歡哪本小說？

Gao: 《西遊記》吧！那隻猴子很厲
害，豬和馬也很可愛，雖然和
尚有一點兒笨 bèn，不過最後還
是把所有的困難都克服了。

A: 跟你學中文一樣。

Gao: 你是說我笨嗎？

課。

中国各个朝代在文学上有什么
成就？

你在考我吗？我只知道人说唐
诗、宋词、元曲、明清小说。
我自己只读过几篇英文的翻
译。

你最喜欢哪本小说？

《西游记》吧！那只猴子很厉
害，猪和马也很可爱，虽然和
尚有一点儿笨，不过最后还是
把所有的困难都克服了。

跟你学中文一样。

你是说我笨吗？

A: Do you study Chinese literature?

Gao: Not really. I've only had a few
literature courses.

A: What are the literary accomplishments
in each Chinese dynasty?

Gao: Are you giving me a test? I only know
that people say Tang *Shi*, Song *Ci*,
Yuan verse, Ming-Qing novels. I
myself have read only a few English
translations.

A: Which novel do you like the most?

Gao: Probably *The Journey to the West*. That monkey is awesome. The pig and horse are
cute. Although the Buddhist monk is not very smart, he overcomes all difficulties in
the end.

A: The same way you study Chinese.

Gao: Are you saying I'm stupid?

(3) Talking about calligraphy

A: 你看這毛筆字 máobǐzì 寫得多好啊！

你看这毛笔字写得多好啊！

Gao: 看起來很有力 yǒulì，不過我完全看不懂這寫的是什麼。

看起来很有力，不过我完全看不懂这写的是什么。

A: 這是篆書 zhuànshū，比較難懂！

这是篆书，比较难懂！

Gao: 這種方方正正 fāngfāngzhèngzhèng 的，看起來整齊多了。

这种方方正正的，看起来整齐多了。

A: 那是楷書 kǎishū。

那是楷书。

Gao: 你看，這看起來跟我寫的一樣，又快又簡單。

你看，这看起来跟我写的一样，又快又简单。

A: 什麼？你的是「狗爬字」，這是草書 cǎoshū。

什么？你的是"狗爬字"，这是草书。

A: Look, how nice this calligraphy is!

Gao: It looks very powerful, but I have no idea what it says.

A: These are seal characters. They're more difficult to understand.

Gao: This kind of writing is squarish and looks very neat.

A: That is regular script.

Gao: See, this one looks just like mine, both quick and simple.

A: What? Yours is "dog paddle style." This is grass-style cursive.

(4) Talking about painting

A: 你喜歡中國的山水畫嗎？

你喜欢中国的山水画吗？

Gao: 喜歡，可是看起來不太真，好

喜欢，可是看起来不太真，好

像在「霧 wù 裏」一樣，分不清　　　象在"霧裏"一樣，分不清哪

哪兒是雲yún，哪兒是山。　　　　　兒是云，哪兒是山。

A:　　沒錯，中國有些山水的景色　　　　沒錯，中國有些山水的景色就

　　　jǐngsè 就是這個樣子。　　　　　　是這個樣子。

Gao:　我特別喜歡這種畫，你看這馬　　　我特別喜歡這種畫，你看這馬

　　　好像要從畫上跑下來似的。　　　　好象要從畫上跑下來似的。

A:　　那是「寫意畫」，用筆把東西　　　那是"寫意畫"，用筆把東西

　　　的精神畫出來。　　　　　　　　　的精神畫出來。

Gao:　像我這麼粗心 cūxīn的人，學這　　　象我這麼粗心的人，學這種畫

　　　種畫最好。　　　　　　　　　　　最好。

A:　　你應該學的是「工筆畫」，每　　　你應該學的是"工筆畫"，每

　　　一筆都畫得很清楚。這樣你才　　　一筆都畫得很清楚。這樣你才

　　　會變得細心 xìxīn 點兒。　　　　　會變得細心點兒。

A:　　Do you like Chinese landscape paintings?

Gao:　Yes, but they don't look very real.　It feels as if one is in a "mist." You can't tell which
parts are clouds and which are mountains.

A:　　That's right.　Some of the Chinese landscape looks just like that.

Gao:　I particularly like this kind of painting.　See, this horse seems to run out of the picture.

A:　　That is "freehand painting." You use a brush to outline the spirit of things.

Gao:　Someone as careless as I would be suited to learn this kind of painting.

A:　　What you should study is
"realistic painting." You
have to paint every stroke
with precision.　This way,
you will become more
careful.

小故事 Stories

Read the following tale for your own enjoyment and for your understanding of the highlighted expression that is relevant to the theme of the chapter.

 反覆推敲 fǎnfù tuīqiāo

❀ 那個詩人反覆推敲才寫出這麼好的作品。

唐朝有個詩人叫賈島，他作詩很用心，每一句詩、每一個字幾乎都要反覆修改好幾次。

有一天，他騎著驢出去，在路上想出兩句詩：「鳥宿池邊樹，僧推月下門。」他念了半天，覺得把「推」改成「敲」可能更好。改不改呢？真難決定。他完全忘了自己是騎著驢在街上走，有人把他從驢背上拉下來，他才知道自己撞到了一位大官兒的馬車。

原來那個大官兒是唐朝有名的詩人韓愈，他聽了賈島說的情況，就說「敲」比「推」好。在很安靜的夜裏、在月光下，一個僧人敲著廟的門，這是很美的。於是賈島就把「推」字改成了「敲」字。

反覆	fǎnfù	to repeat
推敲	tuīqiāo	to weigh and ponder
賈島	Jiǎdǎo	name of a poet
修改	xiūgǎi	to modify, to revise
驢	lú	donkey
鳥	niǎo	bird
宿	sù	to dwell, to stay overnight
池	chí	pond, pool
僧	sēng	monk
背	bèi	back
拉	lā	to pull
撞到	zhuàngdào	to bump against
官	guān	official
馬車	mǎchē	carriage
韓愈	Hányù	name of a poet
安靜	ānjìng	quiet, tranquil
改成	gǎichéng	to change into

✏ 反覆推敲的意思是 _____

反复推敲 fǎnfù tuīqiāo

❀ 那个诗人反复推敲才写出这么好的作品。

唐朝有个诗人叫贾岛，他作诗很用心，每一句诗、每一个字几乎都要反复修改好几次。

有一天，他骑着驴出去，在路上想出两句诗："鸟宿池边树，僧推月下门。"他念了半天，觉得把"推"改成"敲"可能更好。改不改呢？真难决定。他完全忘了自己是骑着驴在街上走，有人把他从驴背上拉下来，他才知道自己撞到了一位大官儿的马车。

反复	fǎnfù	to repeat
推敲	tuīqiāo	to weigh and ponder
贾岛	Jiǎdǎo	name of a poet
修改	xiūgǎi	to modify, to revise
驴	lú	donkey
鸟	niǎo	bird
宿	sù	to dwell, to stay overnight
池	chí	pond, pool
僧	sēng	monk
背	bèi	back
拉	lā	to pull
撞到	zhuàngdào	to bump against
官	guān	official
马车	mǎchē	carriage
韩愈	Hányù	name of a poet
安静	ānjìng	quiet, tranquil
改成	gǎichéng	to change into

原来那个大官儿是唐朝有名的诗人韩愈，他听了贾岛说的情况，就说"敲"比"推"好。在很安静的夜里、在月光下，一个僧人敲着庙的门，这是很美的。于是贾岛就把"推"字改成了"敲"字。

漢字 Characters

Study the following selected characters for further enrichment of your writing and vocabulary.

Picture of three mountains

山

山水	shānshuǐ	landscape (painting)
火山	huǒshān*	volcano
爬山	páshān*	to climb mountain

A: 你喜歡山水畫嗎？

B: 我不懂畫兒，但是我喜歡爬山。

Compare: 出 chū 仙 xiān 岸 àn 島 dǎo

shān 3
hill, mountain

木 mù 'wood'
+ 尌 shù
phonetic

树

樹林	shùlín*	woods, grove
樹木	shùmù*	trees
果樹	guǒshù*	fruit tree

A: 那個樹林裏有很多果樹。

B: 那兒有熊嗎？

shù 16
tree, to plant

氵 shuǐ 'water'
+ 工 gong
phonetic

江

長江	Cháng Jiāng*	Yangtze river
江邊	jiāngbiān*	riverside
江北	Jiāngběi*	area north of the Yangtze

A: 你去過長江嗎？

B: 沒去過江心，只在江邊走了走。

Compare: 河 hé 海 hǎi

jiāng 6
river, Yangtze

氵 shuǐ 'water'
+ 胡 hú
phonetic

湖

西湖	Xīhú	West Lake (in Hangzhou)
湖面	húmiàn*	lake surface
湖心	húxīn*	middle of the lake

A: 這個湖真漂亮，湖心還有個樹林。

B: 對啊！湖面也有很多小船 chuán 'boat'。

hú 12
lake

欠 qiàn 'breath'
+ 斤 jīn
phonetic

欣

xīn 8
to enjoy

欣賞   xīnshǎng   to appreciate, to enjoy

A: 你覺得這些現代畫怎麼樣？

B: 我不太會欣賞。

貝 bèi 'money'
+ 尚 shàng
phonetic

賞

shǎng 15
to reward, to admire,
award

賞月   shǎngyuè*   to admire the full moon

賞花   shǎnghuā*   to enjoy flowers

賞光   shǎngguāng*   to honor me with your
                                  presence

A: 下個星期的晚會請你一定要賞光。

B: 我們是去賞花還是賞月？

Compare: 當 dāng

言 yán 'words'
+ 寺 sì
phonetic

诗

shī 13
poetry, verse, poem

詩人   shīrén*   poet

作詩   zuòshī*   to compose a poem

詩意   shīyì*   poetic sentiment

A: 你為什麼喜歡這個詩人？

B: 他作的詩特別有詩意。

苜 miè 'bad
sight'; 目 mù
'eye' + 冖 mì
'cover' + 夕 xì
'night'—the eyes
are covered at
night

梦

mèng 13
dream, to dream

做夢   zuòmèng*   to dream

夢見   mèngjiàn*   to dream about sb./sth.

夢話   mènghuà*   words uttered in sleep

A: 我昨天晚上聽見你在說夢話。

B: 我做了好多夢，夢見自己會飛。

Compare: 蒙 méng

zhōu 8
circumference, whole,
week

Originally like
田 tián 'field'
with all four
spaces filled in
with dots,
representing
crops growing:
all around + 口
kǒu

周

周/週年	zhōunián	anniversary
周/週末	zhōumò	weekend
周到	zhōudào*	attentive, thorough

A: 這個週末是你們結婚三週年，我幫
   你們買了機票去紐約玩。

B: 你安排得真周到。

Compare: 用 yòng 週 zhōu 調 diào

wéi 12
to surround

口 wéi
'surround' + 韋
wéi phonetic

围

周圍	zhōuwéi	vicinity, surrounding
包圍	bāowéi*	to surround, to encircle
圍巾	wéijīn	muffler, scarf

A: 這周圍都給工廠 gōngchǎng 'factory' 包圍起
   來了。

B: 所以這兒的污染很嚴重。

lǎn 21
to look at

見 jiàn 'see' +
監 jiān
phonetic

览

展覽	zhǎnlǎn	to exhibit, to show, to display
遊覽	yóulǎn*	to go sightseeing
閱覽室	yuèlǎnshì*	reading room

A: 去年夏天你去哪兒遊覽？

B: 我哪兒也沒去，都在閱覽室看書。

Compare: 觀 guān

biǎo 8
surface, model, show,
list

衣 yī 'clothing'
+ 毛 máo
'hair'—the hairy
side of the (fur)
garment, outside,
to manifest, a
signal, a watch,
schedule

表

表演	biǎoyǎn	performance, to act
表現	biǎoxiàn*	to show (off), expression
表面	biǎomiàn	surface, outside

A: 你覺得這個表演要表現的是什麼？

B: 要表現現代生活的問題。

Compare: 錶 biǎo

guāi 8
obedient, clever, to
oppose

The shape is
supposed to be
from the top of
羊, plus 八
doubled—ram's
horns, odd,
singular

乖

| 乖乖 | guāiguāi* | well-behaved, obedient |
| 學乖 | xuéguāi* | to learn from experience |

A: 他學乖了沒有？
B: 學乖了，現在在外面都乖乖的。

Compare: 乘 chéng

rěn 7
to bear, to hold back,
cruel

心 xīn 'heart' +
刃 rèn 'blade'
phonetic

忍

| 忍不住 | rěnbuzhù | can't bear, can't resist |
| 忍心 | rěnxīn* | to have the heart to |

A: 你忍心讓她一個人離開家嗎？
B: 所以我週末都忍不住要給她打電話。

Compare: 認 rèn

ké 9
to cough

口 kǒu 'mouth'
+ 亥 hài
phonetic

咳

咳嗽	kēsou	to cough
乾咳	gānké*	dry cough
止咳	zhǐké*	to relieve cough

A: 你咳嗽厲害嗎？吃了止咳的藥嗎？
B: 只是乾咳，不必吃藥。

Compare: 該 gāi 刻 kè

sòu 14
to cough

口 kǒu 'mouth'
+ 欶 shù
phonetic

嗽

| 咳嗽 | késou | to cough |

A: 他整天咳嗽，病得很厲害。
B: 沒喝咳嗽藥水 yàoshuǐ 'liquid medicine' 嗎？

扌 shǒu 'hand'
+ 屋 wū
phonetic

握

wò 12
to hold, to grasp

握手　　　wòshǒu　　　to shake/clasp hands
把握　　　bǎwò*　　　to grasp firmly
A: 明天有個詩人會來。
B: 你應該把握機會和他握個手。

隹 zhuī 'bird' +
又 yòu 'hand'
—single bird,
one of a
pair…single
piece

只

zhī 10
(measure word for
animals, vessels, etc.)

一隻鳥　　　yì zhī niǎo　　　a bird
A: 你家養了什麼？
B: 三隻鳥、一隻貓、和一隻狗。

Compare: 雙 shuāng

The 日 rì 'sun'
rising between
the plants + 月 /
舟 zhōu
phonetic—dawn,
morning
ceremony, court,
dynasty

朝

cháo 12
court, dynasty, facing

朝代　　　cháodài*　　　dynasty
朝鮮　　　Cháoxiǎn*　　　<PRC> Korea
唐朝　　　Tángcháo*　　　Tang dynasty (618–907)
A: 中國哪個朝代最富強 fùqiáng？
B: 我想是唐朝，那時日本送很多留學生
　　到中國來學習。

Compare: 廟 miào　乾 gān

者 considered
by some scholar
a picture of
food being
placed in a pot

者

zhě 8
nominal suffix, one
who

作者　　　zuòzhě　　　author, writer
讀者　　　dúzhě*　　　reader
記者　　　jìzhě*　　　reporter
學者　　　xuézhě*　　　scholar,
或者　　　huòzhě　　　perhaps, maybe, or
A: 你想當記者、還是學者？
B: 都不想，我只能做個讀者。

Compare: 煮 zhǔ

語法和用法 Grammar and Usage

Pay attention to the function of the structure and then study the example sentences.

1. Expressing total inclusiveness

| 凡是(…的) N都VP | fánshì (...de)...dōu... | All those Ns that are...VP |

凡是來過台灣的人，大概都知道故宮這個有名的博物館。

1.	對不起，我又弄錯 nòngcuò 了。	对不起，我又弄错 了。	Sorry, I made a mistake again.
	沒關係，凡是人都 會犯錯。	没关系，凡是人都 会犯错。	No problem. Everyone makes mistakes.
2.	中國人都知道孔子 嗎？	中国人都知道孔子 吗？	Do all Chinese know about Confucius?
	凡是讀過書的人都 知道孔子是誰。	凡是读过书的人都 知道孔子是谁。	All those who are educated know who Confucius is.
3.	學過中文的人都知 道什麼？	学过中文的人都知 道什么？	What do those who have studied Chinese know?
	凡是學過中文的人 都知道中文的發音 不太容易。	凡是学过中文的人 都知道中文的发音 不太容易。	Those who have studied Chinese all know that the pronunciation is not very easy.

凡是 indicates total inclusiveness and always occurs with 都. There is often a modifier preceding the noun. Don't confuse this phrase with 凡事都 (L17, G4).

2. Modifying a noun using a verb phrase

| S(所) V的(N) | ... (suǒ)...de... | the N that S V |

今天下午……居然看到了我所愛的「中國」。

| 1. | 你有什麼問題？ | 你有什么问题？ | What question do you have? |

我完全聽不懂你所說的話。	我完全听不懂你所说的话。	I can't understand anything you said.

2.

誰（所）唱的歌非常受到大家的歡迎？	谁（所）唱的歌非常受到大家的欢迎？	Whose songs are very popular?
成龍 Chéng Lóng 所唱的歌很受歡迎。	成龙所唱的歌很受欢迎。	The songs sung by Jackie Chan are very popular.

3.

他對我今天燒的飯一句話也沒說。	他对我今天烧的饭一句话也没说。	He didn't say a thing about the dishes I cooked today.
他忙著吃，沒辦法說話。	他忙着吃，没办法说话。	He was so busy eating he couldn't say anything.

所, an element from classical Chinese, often occurs in front of a verb in formal writing. It also occurs frequently with relative clauses; the noun modified by the relative clause, if understood within the context, is often dropped, e.g., 老師所說的他都不懂. This relative clause can be used as a subject (example 2) or an object (example 1) of a sentence.

3. Expressing extreme cases

再 Adj 也沒有了	zài…yě méiyǒu le	There is nothing more Adj (better, worse, etc.) than this.
再 Adj（也）不過了	zài…(yě) búguò le	It couldn't possibly be more Adj.

真是**再好也沒有了**！我想向他請教怎麼寫出感人的作品來。

1.

你今天上課上得怎麼樣？	你今天上课上得怎么样？	How was your class today?
再糟也沒有了！我沒準備，可是老師偏偏叫到我。	再糟也没有了！我没准备，可是老师偏偏叫到我。	It couldn't possibly have been worse. I didn't prepare but the teacher called on me nevertheless.

2.

我們去看書展 shūzhǎn 怎麼樣？	我们去看书展怎么样？	How would it be if we went to see the book fair?
再好也不過了！我	再好也不过了！我	It couldn't possibly be

| | | better. I was just thinking about going to buy some books. |
| 正想去買幾本書。 | 正想去买几本书。 | |

3. | 宿舍的屋子真小！ | 宿舍的屋子真小！ | Dorm rooms are really small. |
| | 可不是嗎？再擠也沒有了，只能放下一張床。 | 可不是吗？再挤也没有了，只能放下一张床。 | Isn't that the truth? They couldn't possibly be smaller. There is only enough room for one bed. |

This pattern literally means "there is nothing more than..." which is often used to indicate the maximum degree of a state of affairs or quality of something.

4. Expressing the actual reality behind a superficial appearance

| 別看…其實… | biékàn…qíshí… | Pay no attention to/ Regardless... actually... |

樹上有隻猴子，又叫又跳，讓我有點兒害怕，可是**別看**它樣子厲害，**其實**很聽話。

1. | 他什麼都不懂，一定很笨！ | 他什么都不懂，一定很笨！ | He knows nothing, and must be very stupid. |
| | 別看他什麼都不懂的樣子，其實他很聰明。 | 别看他什么都不懂的样子，其实他很聪明。 | Don't be fooled by the fact that he appears ignorant. Actually he is very smart. |

2. | 他又不高大又不好看，大概不受歡迎吧？ | 他又不高大又不好看，大概不受欢迎吧？ | He is neither tall nor good-looking. He is probably not very popular. |
| | 別看他長得不怎麼樣，其實他在學校很受歡迎。 | 别看他长得不怎么样，其实他在学校很受欢迎。 | Pay no attention to his lack of attractiveness. Actually he is very popular at school. |

3. | 他只是個學生，教書教得不太好吧？ | 他只是个学生，教书教得不太好吧？ | He is only a student. He doesn't teach very well, does he? |

別看他只是個學生，其實他教書教得很好。	别看他只是个学生，其实他教书教得很好。	Pay no attention to the fact that he is only a student. He actually teaches quite well.

別看 literally means "don't just go on the appearance that..., (in reality)..." It is more colloquial than saying "(雖然)···好像···, 可是···"

linghans

5. Expressing conjecture

看樣子 S V O S 看樣子 V O	kànyàngzi...	It looks like/seems that S will (not) VO

有個和尚從廟裏一出來，猴子就乖乖地跟他走了，**看樣子**是《西遊記》裏的孫悟空吧？

1.	今天的天氣怎麼樣？	今天的天气怎么样？	How is the weather today?
	雲 yún 很多，看樣子今天會下雨。	云 yún 很多，看样子今天会下雨。	It's very cloudy. It looks like it's going to rain today.
2.	已經三點了，你想他會來嗎？	已经三点了，你想他会来吗？	It's already three o'clock. Do you think he will come?
	看樣子他是不會來了。	看样子他是不会来了。	It looks as if he won't be able to make it.
3.	學生今天怎麼樣？	学生今天怎么样？	How were the students today?
	問什麼都不懂，看樣子他們昨天一定沒準備。	问什么都不懂，看样子他们昨天一定没准备。	They couldn't understand any of my questions. It looked as if they hadn't prepared the day before.

This phrase 看樣子 is used to express conjecture of certain situation. It can precede or follow the subject. Sometimes there can be a modifier between 看 and 樣子, e.g., 看他那樣子，三天沒吃飯了.

6. Expressing mild disapproval in a rhetorical question

S 何必… （呢)？	…hébì…(ne)?	Why must...? Forget about...; Don't...

發生了什麼事，**何必**這麼傷心**呢**？

	1.		
	糟了！原來我們明天有大考。	糟了！原来我们明天有大考。	Oh no, it turns out we have a big test tomorrow.
	我想她只是嚇你的，何必這麼緊張呢？	我想她只是吓你的，何必这么紧张呢？	I think that she is only scaring you. Why must you be so nervous?
2.	我這次考得很不好！	我这次考得很不好！	I didn't score well on my test this time.
	這只是小考，你何必這麼難過呢？	这只是小考，你何必这么难过呢？	This is only a quiz. Why must you be so upset?
3.	她說我再抽煙，她就要跟我分手了。	她说我再抽烟，她就要跟我分手了。	She said if I keep smoking, she is going to break up with me.
	她是為你好，你何必跟她生氣呢？	她是为你好，你何必跟她生气呢？	She did this for your own good. Why be mad at her?

何必 is a rhetorical question word expressing in a mild way that an action is unnecessary. It is often used when giving advice. Note that the subject often precedes 何必 and 呢 is often at the end of the sentence.

文化點滴 Culture Notes

1. **Four great inventions**: There were many inventions in ancient China. Four are considered the most influential 四大發明. (1) Paper-making 造紙術 zàozhǐshù: Tsai-lung 蔡倫 (c. 48–118 A.D.), recognizing the inadequacy of the existing writing material (silk, bamboo), created the first paper in the world by drying pulp from old rags, bark, mulberry fibers, and hemp. The art of papermaking traveled slowly. It reached Europe in the 4th century, more than thousand years after its invention in China. (2) Printing 印刷術 yìnshuāshù: Woodblock printing on paper and silk was invented in China around the seventh century. The need for numerous copies of Buddhist texts gave rise to the new

technique. Moveable-type printing was invented around 1045 A.D. by a person named Bi Sheng 畢升. He cut characters into cubes of clay and put them into an iron frame. When the frame was full, the whole made one solid block of type ready to print. (3) Compass 指南針 zhǐnánzhēn: The south-pointing devices were first used on land only and later, between 850 and 1050 A.D., the needle compass came to be used for navigation at sea. (4) Gunpowder 火藥 huǒyào was invented by Chinese alchemists seeking an elixir of immortality. In their pursuit, they recognized the characteristics of saltpeter and sulfur, the two ingredients essential for gunpowder. Yet, Chinese used the gunpowder for peaceful purposes at first, such as for making signal flares and fireworks. Explosive gunpowder was later used by the Mongol warriors, who then introduced gunpowder into Europe.

2. **Chinese dynasties and prominent literary genres/figures/works**: Throughout Chinese history, literary achievements abound. The following is a simple outline of the dynasties, their predominant literary genres and prominent figures.

Dynasty	Chinese	Time	Genre	Figure/Works
Zhou	周	1122–221 B.C.	hymns, ballads	Book of Songs 詩經 Shījīng
Han	漢	206 B.C.–219 A.D.	rhyme-prose biography	Sīmǎxiàngrú 司馬相如 Sī Mǎqiān 司馬遷
Tang	唐	618–907	poetry 詩 shī	Lǐ Bái 李白
Song	宋	960–1279	poetry 詞 cí	Sū Shì 蘇軾
Yuan	元	1280–1367	songs 曲 qǔ drama 劇 jù	Guān Hànqīng 關漢卿 Mǎ Zhìyuǎn 馬致遠
Ming	明	1368–1644	novel 小說 xiǎoshuō	*The Journey to the West* 西遊記 Xīyóujì
Qing	清	1644–1911	novel 小說 xiǎoshuō	*The Dream of the Red Chamber* 紅樓夢 Hónglóumèng

It is worth noting that there are two major genres of poetry: one is the traditional regulated verse (generally consisting of lines of four, five, or seven syllables) and the other a special kind of poetry which is more strictly regulated and written to existing tunes with fixed patterns of rhythm. These poems were mainly used as the lyrics of songs sung by singsong girls. The former genre is called shì 詩. It reached its zenith in the Tang dynasty. The latter form is called cí 詞. It was prominent in the Song dynasty.

3. **Two great poets**: Li Bai 李白, one of China's greatest poets, was born in 701 A.D. in Central Asia and grew up in Sichuan. He later became court poet to the emperor Tang Xuanzong 唐玄宗, but was not destined to enjoy imperial favor for long. In 744 he fell victim to court intrigues and was allowed to leave the capital to "return to the hills." He

died in exile in 762. A famous leader of the Romantic school of poetry during the Tang Dynasty, Li Bai wrote about nature, friendship, love, immortals, his drinking bouts, and his seeming casualness toward wealth and fame. Following is one of his most famous poems.

靜夜思	静夜思
床前明月光，疑是地上霜，	床前明月光，疑是地上霜，
舉頭望明月，低頭思故鄉。	举头望明月，低头思故乡。

Jìngyèsī	Still Night Thoughts
Chuángqián míngyuè guāng,	Seeing the moonlight in front of my bed
Yí shì dìshàng shuāng,	I took it for frost on the ground!
Jǔtóu wàng míngyuè,	I raised my head to watch the bright moon,
Dītóu sī gùxiāng.	I lowered my head, and thought of my hometown.

Another great poet referred to in this chapter is Su Shih 蘇軾 (1037–1101, better known as Su Tung-p'o 蘇東坡). Following is a poem written in 1082 when Su was relegated to Huang Zhou.

念奴嬌　赤壁懷古	念奴娇　赤壁怀古
大江東去，浪淘盡，千古風流人物。	大江东去，浪淘尽，千古风流人物。
故壘西邊，人道是，三國周郎赤壁。	故垒西边，人道是，三国周郎赤壁。
亂石崩雲，驚濤裂岸，捲起千堆雪；	乱石崩云，惊涛裂岸，卷起千堆雪；
江山如畫，一時多少豪傑。	江山如画，一时多少豪杰。
遙想公瑾當年，小喬初嫁了，	遥想公瑾当年，小乔初嫁了，
雄姿英發，羽扇綸巾，談笑間，強虜灰飛煙滅。	雄姿英发，羽扇纶巾，谈笑间，强虏灰飞烟灭。
故國神遊，多情應笑我，早生華髮。人生如夢，一尊還酹江月。	故国神游，多情应笑我，早生华发。人生如梦，一尊还酹江月。

Niànnújiāo　Chìbì huáigǔ	To the Tune of "Nian Nu Jiao" 　　—On Past Heroes at the Red Cliff
Dàjiāngdōngqù, làngtáojìn, qiāngǔ fēngliú rénwù. Gùlěi xībiān, réndàoshì, sānguó zhōuláng chìbì. Luànshí bēngyún, jīngtāoliè'àn, juǎnqǐ qiānduīxuě. Jiāngshān rúhuà, yìshí duōshǎo háojié.	The waves of the mighty river flowing eastward Have swept away the brilliant figures of a thousand generations. West of the old fortress, So people say, is Lord Chou's Red Cliff of the time of the Three Kingdoms.

The tumbling rocks thrust into the air;
The roaring surges dash upon the shore,
Rolling into a thousand drifts of snow.
The river and the mountains make a vivid picture—
What a host of heroes once were!
And I recall the young Lord then,
Newly married to the fair Younger Ch'iao,
His valorous features shown forth;
With a feather fan and a silken cap
Amid talking and laughing he put his enemy's ships
to ashes and smoke.
While my thoughts wander in the country of old,
Romantic persons might smile at my early grey hair.
Ah! Life is but a dream;
With a cup of wine, let me yet pour a libation to the
moon on the River.

Yáo xiǎng gōngjǐn dāngnián, xiǎoqiáo chū jià liǎo,

Xióngzī yīngfā, yǔshàn guānjīn, tánxiàojiān, qiánglǔ huī fēi yānmiè.

Gùguóshényóu, duōqíng yīng xiào wǒ, zǎoshēng huáfǎ.

Rénshēng rú mèng, yì zūn huán lèi jiāngyuè.

4. **Four classical novels**: In Chinese literature, there are four classical novels considered by many to be the greatest. (1) *The Romance of the Three Kingdoms* 三國演義 Sānguó Yǎnyì is a historical novel by 羅貫中 Luó Guànzhōng (14th century). It tells of numerous historical battles between three kingdoms during the period of separation (220–280 A.D.). Its great strengths are a stirring plot, the depiction of deep emotion and excellent character development. (2) *Tale of Water Margin* 水滸傳 Shuǐhǔzhuàn by 施耐庵 Shī Nài'ān is a kind of "Robin Hood in China" describing nine dozen hero-outlaws who live in the water margins of Liangshanbo 梁山泊 and fight a corrupt government. (3) *The Journey to the West* 西遊記 Xīyóujì, by 吳承恩 Wú Chéng'ēn (1500?–1582), commonly known to the western readers as Monkey, is a supernatural novel about the trip Tripitaka 唐僧 Tángsēng took to fetch the sutras in the Western Heaven and the 81 dangers and calamities encountered by him and his three animal spirit disciples—Monkey 孫悟空 Sūn Wùkōng, Pigsy 豬八戒 Zhū Bājiè, and Sandy 沙和尚 Shā Héshàng. (4) *The Dream of the Red Chamber* 紅樓夢 Hónglóumèng by 曹雪芹 Cáo Xuěqín describes in detail the life of a rich family and the complicated human relations between its members and their many servants and others. Although there are more than 400 characters introduced, the main protagonists are 賈寶玉 Jiǎ Bǎoyù and 林黛玉 Lín Dàiyù.

5. **Chinese calligraphy**: Chinese calligraphy is an art with an illustrious tradition as old as the culture itself. For nearly two thousand years, the basic media, the major script variations, and the standards of excellence of the art have remained almost unchanged. Calligraphy has been generally regarded as the most revealing power of a person. While one has to conform to the defined structure of words, the expression can be displayed with great creativity by individuals. Some prominent styles and calligraphers are listed below.

Script Variation 書體 shūtǐ	Dynasty 朝代 cháodài	Calligrapher 書法家 shūfǎjiā	Styles of Writing 風格 fēnggé
篆 zhuàn seal script	Qin 秦 221–207 B.C.	李斯 Lǐ Sī	

隸 lì official script	Han 漢 206 B.C.–219 A.D.		
楷 kǎi standard script	Tang 唐 618–907 A.D.	柳公權 Liǔ Gōngquán 顏真卿 Yán Zhēnqīng 歐陽詢 Oūyáng Xún	柳體 liǔtǐ 顏體 yántǐ 歐體 ōutǐ
行 xíng running script		王羲之 Wáng Xīzhī	
草 cǎi cursive script		張旭 Zhāng Xù	

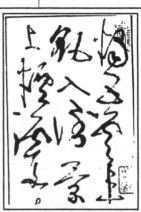
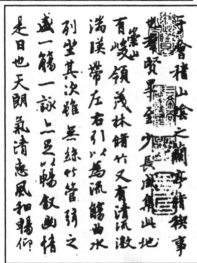

楷書　　　　　　楷書　　　　　　草書

行書

To become an expert in calligraphy, one has to practice word by word and stroke by stroke until the spirit of the practice gets into one's mind. Below is the way one holds the brush. There are eight types of strokes, as shown in the character 永 yǒng：點 diǎn、横 héng、豎 shù、挑 tiāo、撇 piě、捺 nà、鉤 gōu、折 zhé.

6. **Chinese painting**: There are three main categories of traditional Chinese painting: (1) Human figure painting—line drawings of people engaged in various activities. These works date from before the Tang dynasty; (2) Landscape painting—drawings of mountains, forests, fields, and gardens (prominent by the mid-Tang dynasty); (3) Flower-and-bird painting—drawings of flowers, grass, trees, stones, birds and other animals. The Sung dynasty (960–1279 A.D.) was renowned for its court style painting (elaborate, ornate, and realistic), which gave way to the school of "literati painting" of the Mongol

Yuan dynasty (1271–1368 A.D.). Artists at this time preferred to paint according to their own fancy and without restriction. They advocated a free, understated, and elegant style. They often drew mountains and rocks, clouds and water, flowers and trees, the "four gentlemen" 四君子 sìjūzǐ (plum blossoms 梅 méi, orchids 蘭 lán, bamboo 竹 zhú, and chrysanthemums 菊 jú), etc. They also began to put related verse or notes on the painting, to write the names of the giver and recipient, or to stamp their name in an inconspicuous corner of the work.

歌兒 Songs

出遊記
Notes on an Outing

Moderato　　　　　　　　　　　　　　　　　　　詞：劉雅詩　　曲：馬定一

1. 那天 我 和 林 妹妹　　手 拉 手 去 看 表 演，周圍 大放 煙火 照亮
　 Nàtiān wǒ　hé Lín mèimei　shǒu lā shǒu qù kàn biǎoyǎn, zhōuwéi dà fàng yānhuǒ zhàoliàng
　 One day Sister Lin and I went hand in hand to watch a show. Around us a beautiful garden was

2. 那天 我 和 高 哥哥　　一塊兒 去 看 展覽，附近 煙火 如畫如夢
　 Nàtiān wǒ　hé Gāo gēge　yíkuàir　qù kàn zhǎnlǎn,　fùjìn　yānhuǒ rú huà rú mèng
　 One day Brother Gao and I went together to see an exhibition. Nearby fireworks, like a dream
　 painting,

1. 美麗的花 園。　　　突然　　一 個 糊塗的 老 和 尚　意 外 出
　 měilì de huāyuán.　　Hūrán　　yí ge hútú de lǎo héshàng　yìwài　chū
　 illuminated by fireworks. Suddenly came a muddle-headed old monk.

2. 照亮了眼　前。　　　後來　　有 個 高大的 書 法 家　意 外 出
　 zhàoliàngle yǎnqián.　Hòulái　yǒu ge gāodà de　shūfǎjiā　yìwài chū
　 brightened our view. Later a stately calligrapher suddenly

1. 現老 是 咳嗽 打擾 我 們　又 不 願 走 遠。　　我 非常生 氣 忍 不住
　 xiàn, lǎoshì késòu dǎrǎo wǒmen　yòu bù yuàn zǒu yuǎn.　Wǒ fēichángshēngqi rěnbuzhù
　 Always coughing and bothering us, he wouldn't go away. I was very mad, and could not help but

2. 現跟我握手 笑著 說我　美 麗 如 天仙。　　還 要我 欣 賞 他 作品
　 xiàn, gēn wǒ wòshǒu xiàozhe shuō wǒ měilì rú tiānxiān.　Hái yào wǒ xīnshǎng tā　zuòpǐn
　 appeared. Shaking hands with me and smiling, he said I was as beautiful as a goddess. He also
　 wanted me to see his work and

1. 像隻猴子一 直 抱 怨，老和尚 轉 過 身 對 我 笑笑 突 然 就不見。
　 xiàng zhī hóuzi yìzhí bàoyuàn,　lǎo héshàng zhuǎnguò shēn, duì wǒ xiàoxiao tūrán jiù bú jiàn.
　 constantly protest like a monkey. The old monk turned his back, smiled at me and suddenly disappeared.

2. 請教 我的 個人 意 見，高哥哥 忍不住　吃醋 叫我 離他 遠一點。
　 qǐngjiào wǒde gèrén　yìjiàn,　Gāo gēge　rěnbúzhù　chīcù jiào wǒ　lí tā yuǎn yìdiàn.
　 requested my personal opinion. Brother Gao, who could not help but feel jealous, told me to stay
　 away from him.

第二十課

Theme Economics and Politics

Communicative Objectives
- Discussing the economy
- Saying farewell to someone
- Giving a speech at a farewell party
- Seeing someone off at the airport

Grammar Focus
- S免不了/難免會VO
- 根據/按照⋯的N,S V
- S(之)(所以)A是因為B(的緣故/關係)
- ⋯是A,而不是B
- SVO,然而S卻/還V
- 表面上⋯實際上⋯

Focus on Characters
- 免提資產、據義強調、科技持優、革府制權、釋析按岸

中國的明天在哪兒?

生詞 Vocabulary

Study the following words for their pronunciation and meaning. When an area is shaded, guess at the meaning of the word based on its constituent characters and then fill in the blank. Read the usage of words and related terms (antonyms, synonyms, compounds sharing the constituent characters, etc.) and try to answer the sample questions in Chinese. Note that proper nouns and incidental terms are not numbered.

◎By Order of Appearance

1. 藉
借   jiè   V   to make use of, to take advantage of (an opportunity)

   你應該藉這個機會好好休息。

   你应该借这个机会好好休息。

2. 海峽
海峡   hǎixiá   N   strait   [sea-gorge]

   river bank

3. 兩岸   liǎng'àn   N   both sides (Chinese Mainland and Taiwan)   [two-side]

   你海峽兩岸都去過嗎？

   你海峡两岸都去过吗？

4. 優點
优点   yōudiǎn   N   *merit*   [excellent-point]   *=長處*

   =長處

5. 缺點
缺点   quēdiǎn   N   shortcoming, defect   [lack-point]   *=短處*

   你覺得自己有什麼優點、缺點？

   你觉得自己有什么优点、缺点？

6. 免不了   miǎnbuliǎo   RV   to be unavoidable   [avoid-not-possibility]

   难/不免

   學中文免不了會遇到什麼問題？

   学中文免不了会遇到什么问题？

7. 爭論
争论   zhēnglùn   V/N   to argue, dispute   [contend-discuss]

   ……和……發生/有爭論

   你和誰常有爭論？

   你和谁常有争论？

8. 共產主義
共产主义   gòngchǎn zhǔyì   N   communism   [share-property-ism]

9. 資本主義
资本主义   zīběnzhǔyì   N   capitalism   [money-capital-ism]

   共產/資本/社會主義

好处 good/bad outcomes vs. 优/缺点 intrinsic qualities
坏处

社會主義有什麼優點、缺點？

社会主义有什么优点、缺点？

| 10. | 制度 | zhìdù | N | system | [make-degree] |

政治/經濟/社會制度

你覺得哪一種社會制度好？

你觉得哪一种社会制度好？

| 11. | 根據
根据 | gēnjù | Prep/
N | on the basis of, according
to, basis | [root-proof] |

根據你的看法，股票還會跌嗎？

根据你的看法，股票还会跌吗？

| 12. | 經濟學家
经济学家 | jīngjìxuéjiā | N | economist | [manage-aid-study-
suffix] |

→社會學家、語言學家 *takes things apart and explain*

| 13. | 分析 | fēnxī | N/V | to analyze, analysis | [divide-divide] |
| 14. | 發達
发达 | fādá | Adj | developed | [expand-reach] |

經濟/國家/工業/商業發達

現在什麼工業最發達？

现在什么工业最发达？

| 15. | （按）照 | (àn)zhào | Prep | according to, in light of | [according to-in
accordance with] |
| 16. | 解釋
解释 | jiěshì | N/V | *to explain* analysis, to expound | [explain-explain] |

給人一個解釋

請你解釋一下這個詞的意思。

请你解释一下这个词的意思。

| 17. | 科技 | kējì | N | science and technology | [science-technology] |
| 18. | 繁榮
繁荣 | fánróng | Adj | *Prosperous* | [numerous-thriving] |

經濟/文化/市場/社會繁榮

最近美國的經濟繁榮嗎？

最近美国的经济繁荣吗？

| 19. | 起作用 | qǐ zuòyòng | VO | to have an effect | [obtain-do-use] |

Characters with Many Strokes

藉　峽　優　義　資　據　達　解　釋　繁

20.	民主	mínzhǔ	N	democracy	[people-manage]
21.	個人主義 个人主义	gèrénzhǔyì	N	individualism	[individual-ism]
22.	提高	tígāo	RV	to raise, to enhance	[lift-high]

提高水平/標準/價格 jiàgé 'price'

怎麼樣可以提高我的中文水平？

怎么样可以提高我的中文水平？

23.	然而	rán'ér	Conj	even so, but	[but-and yet]
24.	娛樂 娱乐	yúlè	N		[amuse-happy]

一般美國人喜歡什麼娛樂活動？

一般美国人喜欢什么娱乐活动？

25.	媒體 媒体	méitǐ	N	media	[medium-body]

電視/廣播媒體

你覺得媒體對社會應該負什麼責任？

你觉得媒体对社会应该负什么责任？

26.	感想	gǎnxiǎng	N	reflections, thoughts	[feel-think]

請說一下你學中文的感想。

请说一下你学中文的感想。

27.	能夠	nénggòu	V	can, to be able to	[be able-enough]
28.	隨時 随时	suíshí	Adv	at any time	[follow-time]
29.	隨地 随地	suídì	Adv	anywhere	[follow-place]

請不要隨地倒垃圾。

请不要随地倒垃圾。

30.	保持	bǎochí	V	to keep, to maintain	[keep-hold]

保持聯繫/健康

你現在和誰還保持聯繫？

你现在和谁还保持联系？

31.	樂觀 乐观	lèguān	Adj	optimistic, hopeful	[happy-view]

對……很樂觀   ↔悲觀 bēiguān

你對中國的將來樂觀嗎？

你对中国的将来乐观吗？

32. 表面上 *impact*   biǎomiàn   N   surface   [exterior-face]

你不能只看事情的表面。

你不能只看事情的表面。

33. 強調   qiángdiào   V   to stress   [strong-accent]
　　强调

強調……的重要

老師常常強調什麼的重要？

老师常常强调什么的重要？

34. 改革   gǎigé   V/N   to reform, reform   [change-expel]

學校應該對什麼進行改革？

学校应该对什么进行改革？

35. 開放   kāifàng   V/N   to open to the world, to   [open-release]
　　开放   open to traffic or public use

36. 政府   zhèngfǔ   N   government   [politics-government office]

37. 人民   rénmín   N   the people   [people-masses]

38. 權利   quánlì   N   right, privilege   [power-interest]
　　权利

有……的權利   →權力 quánlì 、人權 rénquán

美國成年人 chéngniánrén 有哪些權利？

美国成年人有哪些权利？

39. 接觸   jiēchù   N/V   to come into contact with   [meet-touch]
　　接触

你在這兒和什麼人接觸比較多？

你在这儿和什么人接触比较多？

40. 全球化   quánqiúhuà   V   globalization   [whole-world-ize]

→美國化、綠化、美化

現在什麼已經全球化了？

现在什么已经全球化了？

41. 中外   Zhōng-wài   N   China and foreign countries   [China-outside]

→中美、中日、中西

Characters with Many Strokes

媒　隨　樂　觀　強　調　政　權　接　觸

◎By Grammatical Categories

Nouns/Pronouns

海峽	hǎixiá	strait	民主	mínzhǔ	democracy
兩岸	liǎng'àn	both sides (Chinese Mainland & Taiwan)	人民	rénmín	the people
中外	Zhōng-wài	China and foreign countries	政府	zhèngfǔ	government
制度	zhìdù	system	接觸	jiēchù	to come into contact with
表面	biǎomiàn	surface, appearance	分析	fēnxī	analysis, to analyze
權利	quánlì	right, privilege	解釋	jiěshì	analysis, to expound
娛樂	yúlè	entertainment	感想	gǎnxiǎng	reflections, thoughts
媒體	méitǐ	media	共產主義	gòngchǎnzhǔyì	communism
科技	kējì	science and technology	資本主義	zīběnzhǔyì	capitalism
優點	yōudiǎn	merit	個人主義	gèrénzhǔyì	individualism
缺點	quēdiǎn	shortcoming, defect	經濟學家	jīngjìxuéjiā	economist

Verbs/Stative Verbs/Adjectives

藉	jiè	to make use of, to take advantage of (an opportunity)			traffic or public use
能夠	nénggòu	can, to be able to	改革	gǎigé	to reform, reform
保持	bǎochí	to keep, to maintain	全球化	quánqiúhuà	globalization
提高	tígāo	to raise, to enhance	起作用	qǐ zuòyòng	to have an effect
強調	qiángdiào	to stress	免不了	miǎnbuliǎo	to be unavoidable
爭論	zhēnglùn	to argue, dispute	發達	fādá	developed
開放	kāifàng	to open to the world, to open to	繁榮	fánróng	prosperous
			樂觀	lèguān	optimistic, hopeful

Adverbs and Others

隨地	suídì	anywhere	（按）照	(àn)zhào	according to
隨時	suíshí	at any time	然而	rán'ér	even so, but
根據	gēnjù	on the basis of, according to, basis			

◎By Pinyin

Entries with * indicate lexical items used in Mini-Dialogues and of possible interest for supplemental study.

(àn)zhào	（按）照	according to	lǚkè*	旅客	traveller, passenger
bǎochí	保持	to keep, to maintain	méitǐ	媒体	media
bēiguān*	悲观	pessimistic	miǎnbuliǎo	免不了	to be unavoidable
biǎomiàn	表面	surface, appearance	mínzhǔ	民主	democracy
búduàn*	不断	continuously, uninterrupted	nénggòu	能够	can, be able to
dēngjīpái*	登机牌	<PRC>boarding pass	qǐ zuòyòng	起作用	to have an effect
fādá	发达	developed	qiángdiào	强调	to stress
fánróng	繁荣	prosperous	quánlì	权利	right, privilege
fēnxī	分析	to analyze, analysis	quánqiúhuà	全球化	globalization
gǎigé	改革	to reform, reform	quēdiǎn	缺点	shortcoming, defect
gǎnxiǎng	感想	reflections, thoughts	rán'ér	然而	even so, but
gēnjù	根据	on the basis of, according to, basis	rénmín	人民	the people
			suídì	随地	anywhere
gèrénzhǔyì	个人主义	individualism	suíshēn*	随身	(take) with one, (carry) on one's person
gòngchǎn zhǔyì	共产主义	communism	suíshí	随时	at any time
gǔzhǎng*	鼓掌	to clap hands	tígāo	提高	to raise, to enhance
hǎixiá	海峡	strait	tuōyùn*	托运	consign for shipment, to check (baggage)
jiēchù	接触	to come into contact with			
jiěshì	解释	analysis, to expound	yúlè	娱乐	entertainment
jiè	借	to make use of, to take advantage of (an opportunity)	yōudiǎn	优点	merit
			zhèngfǔ	政府	government
jīngjìxuéjiā	经济学家	economist	zhēnglùn	争论	to argue, dispute
kāifàng	开放	to open to the world, to open to traffic or public use	zhìdù	制度	system
			Zhōng-wài	中外	China and foreign countries
kējì	科技	science and technology	zīběn zhǔyì	资本主义	capitalism
lèguān	乐观	optimistic, hopeful			
liǎng'àn	两岸	both sides (Chinese Mainland and Taiwan)			

課文 Text

Use the following questions to guide your reading of the text.

1. 小李、小王、美英覺得美國社會為什麼發達？
2. 為什麼小李覺得「個人主義」是神話？
3. 為什麼小高對中國的將來很樂觀？

 小高：

　　再過幾週，這個學期就要結束了，我們決定藉這最後一次在網上聯繫的機會，一起和你聊聊。我們真羨慕你！雖然王華、李明和我都是中國人，可是只有你這個老外海峽兩岸都去過，知道兩邊生活的優點和缺點。有時候我們三個[1]免不了也會爭論，究竟共產主義、資本主義哪個制度好？中國的明天在哪兒？[2]根據小李這個經濟學家的分析，美國[3]之所以發達，都是因為資本主

義的緣故。按照王華這個電腦迷的解釋，[4]是科技而不是什麼「主義」對社會的繁榮起了作用。我倒覺得文化是最重要的，美國講民主、自由、選擇、個人主義等，這些基本觀念才是生活水平提高的主要原因。[5]然而小李卻說生活中選擇多不一定有好處，很多人根本不知道怎麼去做最好的決定；而且「個人主義」也只是個神話，在娛樂、媒體的影響下，大家吃的、穿的、聽的、想的、用的幾乎都完全一樣，哪兒有個人的特色？

這一年來你雖然在留學，可是還找時間告訴我們你在中國的感想，讓我們對自己的文化有了新的認識。我們都非常感謝你！

美英、小王、小李上

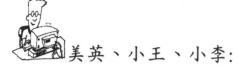美英、小王、小李：

我這兒的課也快上完了，下一次見你們，應該可以面對面溝通了。不必謝我，應該感謝的是現代科技，讓我們能夠隨時隨地保持聯繫。我對中國的將來是很樂觀的。**6表面上**，兩邊的制度、語言有些距離，**實際上**，有很多共同的地方：中國人都重視家庭、教育，都強調人和人、人和自然的關係。而且大陸自從八十年代改革、開放以後，在經濟上有了很大的成就。台灣這些年來也民主多了，政府越來越重視人民的權利。只要大陸和台灣繼續保持接觸，中國就有希望！

在這個全球化的今天，中國的進步就是世界的進步。希望我們不分中外、無論在哪兒，都能「心繫中國」！

小高上

课文 Text

Use the following questions to guide your reading of the text.

1. 小李、小王、美英觉得美国社会为什么发达？

2. 为什么小李觉得"个人主义"是神话？

3. 为什么小高对中国的将来很乐观？

小高：

再过几周，这个学期就要结束了，我们决定借这最后一次在网上联系的机會，一起和你聊聊。我们真羡慕你！虽然王华、李明和我都是中国人，可是只有你这个老外海峡两岸都去过，知道两边生活的优点和缺点。有时候我们三个[1]免不了也会争论，究竟共产主义、资本主义哪个制度好？中国的明天在哪儿？[2]根据小李这个经济学家的分析，美国[3]之所以发达，都是因为资本主义的缘故。按照王华这个电脑迷的解释，[4]是科技而不是什么"主义"对社会的繁荣起了作用。我倒觉得文化是最重要的，美国讲民主、自由、

选择、个人主义等，这些基本观念才是生活水平提高的主要原因。[5]然而小

李却说生活中选择多不一定有好处，很多人根本不知道怎么去做最好的决定；而且"个人主义"也只是个神话，在娱乐、媒体的影响下，大家吃的、穿的、听的、想的、用的几乎都完全一样，哪儿有个人的特色？

这一年来你虽然在留学，可是还找时间告诉我们你在中国的感想，让我们对自己的文化有了新的认识。我们都非常感谢你！

美英、小王、小李上

 美英、小王、小李：

我这儿的课也快上完了，下一次见你们，应该可以面对面沟通了。不必谢我，应该感谢的是现代科技，让我们能够随时随地保持联系。我对中国的将来是很乐观的。[6]**表面上**，两边的制度、语言有些距离，**实际上**，有很多共同的地方：中国人都重视家庭、教育，都强调人和人、人和自然的关系。而且大陆自从八十年代改革、开放以后，在经济上有了很大的成就。台湾这些年来也民主多了，政府越来越重视人民的权利。只要大陆和台湾继续保持接触，中国就有希望！在这个全球化的今天，中国的进步就是世界的进步。希望我们不分中外、无论在哪儿，都能"心系中国"！

小高上

小對話 Mini-Dialogues

Read the supplementary dialogues for a better understanding of the text. See if you can memorize one and perform it in class.

(1) Discussing the economy

Li: 你看今年的經濟怎麼樣？還會
     跟前幾年一樣好嗎？

A: 我看不會那麼發達了，最近股
     票市場跌了不少。

Li: 那是因為從前漲得太厲害的緣
     故。

A: 很多公司的生意都比較差，現
     在電腦都賣不出去了。

Li: 別這麼悲觀bēiguān！你買了很多
     股票嗎？

A: 只有幾百股。

Li: 怪不得你這麼難過。

你看今年的经济怎么样？还会
跟前几年一样好吗？

我看不会那么发达了，最近股
票市场跌了不少。

那是因为从前涨得太厉害的缘
故。

很多公司的生意都比较差，现
在电脑都卖不出去了。

别这么悲观！你买了很多股票
吗？

只有几百股。

怪不得你这么难过。

Li: How do you think this year's economy will be? Is it going to be as good as in previous years?

A: I don't think it will be. Lately, the stock market has tumbled quite a bit.

Li: That's because it had risen too high in the past.

A: Business is getting worse for many companies. Now computers aren't selling.

Li: Don't be so pessimistic. Did you buy a lot of stocks?

A: Only several hundred shares.

Li: No wonder you are so upset.

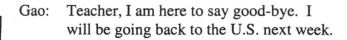 (2) Saying farewell to someone

Gao: 老師，我來跟您說再見，我下
星期就回美國去了。

A: 你什麼時候出發啊？

Gao: 星期二早上。

A: 時間過得真快啊！我們拍張照
片，留個紀念吧！

Gao: 好啊！

A: 有沒有人去機場送你呢？

Gao: 有。謝謝您這幾個月來的關心
和照顧。

A: 不用謝，那是應該的。

老师，我来跟您说再见，我下
星期就回美国去了。

你什么时候出发啊？

星期二早上。

时间过得真快啊！我们拍张照
片，留个纪念吧！

好啊！

有没有人去机场送你呢？

有。谢谢您这几个月来的关心
和照顾。

不用谢，那是应该的。

Gao: Teacher, I am here to say good-bye. I will be going back to the U.S. next week.

A: When are you going to set out?

Gao: Tuesday morning.

A: How fast time flies. Let's take a picture as a memento.

Gao: Fine.

A: Do you have anyone to see you off at the airport?

Gao: Yes. Thanks for all of your concern and care these several months.

A: No need for thanks. That's what I'm supposed to do.

(3) Giving a speech at a farewell party

Gao: 同學們，我要藉這個機會說幾
句話。

同学们，我要借这个机会说几
句话。

A: （鼓掌 gǔzhǎng）   （鼓掌）

Gao: 我來這兒六個多月了，不但中   我来这儿六个多月了，不但中
          文進步了不少，而且對這兒的   文进步了不少，而且对这儿的
          社會、文化也有了更深的了   社会、文化也有了更深的了
          解。這一切都要感謝我們的老   解。这一切都要感谢我们的老
          師，謝謝他們的幫助。我建   师，谢谢他们的帮助。我建
          議，為他們的成就、健康乾   议，为他们的成就、健康干
          杯！   杯！

B: 我很高興自己從來沒有「對牛   我很高兴自己从来没有"对牛
          彈琴」過。希望你們在學習上   弹琴"过。希望你们在学习上
          不斷 búduàn 'continuously' 進步，乾   不断进步，干杯！
          杯！

Gao: Classmates, I want to take this
          opportunity to say a few words.

A: (Clapping hands)

Gao: I have been here for six months. Not
          only has my Chinese improved a lot,
          but also my understanding of the
          culture and society has deepened. I
          am grateful to our teachers for all
          they've done and thank them for

          their help. I sugguest that we offer a toast for their accomplishments and health.

B: I am very happy that I've never "played the lute for the cows." I hope you will keep
          making progress in your studies. Bottoms up!

(4) Seeing someone off at the airport

A: 你準備好護照和機票了嗎？行   你准备好护照和机票了吗？行
          李託運 tuōyùn 了沒有？   李托运了没有？

Gao: 一切都辦好了，這是我的隨身   一切都办好了，这是我的随身
          suíshēn行李。   行李。

B: 由台北經東京，飛往洛杉磯   由台北经东京，飞往洛杉矶的
          Luòshānjī 的 華航802號飛機就要起   华航802号飞机就要起飞了。坐

飛了。坐這班飛機的旅客lǚkè，
請從四號入口登機。

A:　該上飛機了，登機牌dēngjīpái拿好
　　　了沒有？祝你一路平安。

Gao:　再見！記得要保持聯繫啊！

这班飞机的旅客，请从四号入
口登机。

该上飞机了，登机牌拿好了没
有？祝你一路平安。

再见！记得要保持联系啊！

A:　Do you have your passport, ticket and customs
　　declaration form ready? Have you checked
　　your luggage yet?

Gao:　Everything is ready. This is my carry-on.

B:　Air China flight 802, from Taipei via Tokyo to
　　L.A. is about to depart. Passengers on this
　　flight please board at Gate Four.

A:　It's time to get on the plane. Do you have your
　　boarding pass? *Bon Voyage.*

Gao:　Good-bye. Remember to keep in touch.

小故事 Stories

Read the following tale for your own enjoyment and for your understanding of the highlighted expression that is relevant to the theme of the chapter.

 紙上談兵 zhǐshàng tán bīng

✤ 要想經濟繁榮、社會進步，不能只靠紙上談兵。

戰國時候趙國有個人叫趙括，他的父親是個大將軍，所以他從小就讀了很多關於用兵打仗的書。常常把書上的話拿出來，說得很有道理，連他的父親也說不過他。

趙括以為自己已經學到了用兵的本事，沒有人比他更厲害了。可是他的父親說：「打仗是非常不容易的，如果以後你當將軍，趙國就完了！」

兵	bīn	soldier
戰國	Zhànguó	the Warring States period (475–221 B.C.)
趙國	Zhàoguó	name of a state
趙括	Zhào Kuò	name of a person
將軍	jiāngjūn	general
打仗	dǎzhàng	to go to war, to fight
說不過	shuōbuguò	to be no match for sb. in argument
本事	běnshi	ability
殺死	shāsǐ	to kill and die
萬	wàn	ten thousand
軍隊	jūnduì	army

後來，趙王不聽別人的話，讓趙括帶兵，結果趙括自己被殺死了，趙國的四十萬軍隊也全完了。

✐ 紙上談兵的意思是＿＿＿＿＿＿＿＿＿＿＿＿＿＿＿＿

纸上谈兵 zhǐshàng tán bīng

❋ 要想经济繁荣、社会进步，不能只靠纸上谈兵。

战国时候赵国有个人叫赵括，他的父亲是个大将军，所以他从小就读了很多关于用兵打仗的书。常常把书上的话拿出来，说得很有道理，连他的父亲也说不过他。

赵括以为自己已经学到了用兵的本事，没有人比他更厉害了。可是他的父亲说："打仗是非常不容易的，如果以后你当将军，赵国就完了！"

后来，赵王不听别人的话，让赵括带兵，结果赵括自己被杀死了，赵国的四十万军队也全完了。

兵	bīn	soldier
战国	Zhànguó	the Warring States period (475–221 B.C.)
赵国	Zhàoguó	name of a state
赵括	Zhào Kuò	name of a person
将军	jiāngjūn	general
打仗	dǎzhàng	to go to war, to fight
说不过	shuōbuguò	to be no match for sb. in argument
本事	běnshi	ability
杀死	shāsǐ	to kill and die
万	wàn	ten thousand
军队	jūnduì	army

漢字 Characters

Study the following selected characters for further enrichment of your writing and vocabulary.

Picture of a running hare—to get off, escape, avoid, to spare

免

miǎn 7
to exempt, to avoid

免不了	miǎnbuliǎo	to be unavoidable
不免	bùmiǎn*	unavoidably
難免	nánmiǎn*	hard to avoid

A: 剛學中文的時候難免會遇到問題。
B: 所以有時候免不了會覺得難過。

Compare: 兔 tù　晚 wǎn　勉 miǎn

扌 shǒu 'hand'
+ 是 shì phonetic

提

tí 12
to carry, to mention

提高	tígāo	to improve, to enhance
提前	tíqián	in advance, beforehand
提醒	tíxǐng	to remind, to warn
別提	biétí*	don't mention

A: 我怎麼能提高自己的中文水平？
B: 時時提醒自己得天天學習。

貝 bèi 'money'
+ 次 cì phonetic

資

zī 13
money, to subsidize

資本	zīběn	capital
資金	zījīn*	fund
工資	gōngzī*	wages, pay
投資	tóuzī*	to invest

A: 我想投資股票，可是沒有資金。
B: 你先去打工，賺點兒工資吧！

生 shēng 'life'
+ 产 'possibly wrinkles'—the wrinkles formed on the body as a consequence of childbirth

产

chǎn 11
to give birth to, product

共產黨	gòngchǎndǎng*	Communist Party
生產	shēngchǎn*	to produce
產品	chǎnpǐn*	product

A: 那家公司生產這種產品嗎？
B: 對，可是那種產品有很多問題。

Compare: 顏 yán

jù 16
according to, to seize, proof

扌 shǒu 'hand'
+ 豦 jù
phonetic

据

根據	gēnjù	on the basis of, basis
據說	jùshuō*	It is said that…
數據	shùjù*	data
收據	shōujù*	receipt

A: 據報上說，受傷的人的確很多。
B: 根據他的看法，那數據不太對。

Compare: 劇 jù

yì 13
justice, meaning, just

羊 yáng 'sheep'
+ 我 wǒ
phonetic —
sheep conveys
the meaning
'good-natured'

义

主義	zhǔyì	doctrine, -ism
講義	jiǎngyì*	class handouts
定義	dìngyì*	definition
義務	yìwù*	duty, obligation

A: 請你給資本主義下一個定義。
B: 你的講義上沒有提到資本主義。

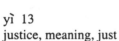

qiáng, qiǎng 11
strong, better, plus, to
strive

弓 gong 'bow'
+ 虽 suī
'although'—a
bow is strong,
although it
bends. The true
explanation is
obscure.

強

強調	qiángdiào	to stress, to underline
強大	qiángdà*	big and powerful
加強	jiāqiáng*	to strengthen, to reinforce

A: 你應該加強閱讀方面的訓練。
B: 不要總是強調我的缺點。

diào, tiáo 15
to shift, tone, to adjust

言 yán 'words'
+ 周 zhōu
phonetic

调

聲調	shēngdiào	tone, note
單調	dāndiào*	monotonous, dull
空調	kōngtiáo	air-conditioning

A: 老師一直強調聲調的重要。
B: 上課只練習聲調，實在太單調了。

斗 dǒu 'measure': picture of a measuring cup + 禾 hé 'grain' phonetic

科

kē 9
department, branch of study

科技	kējì	science and technology
科研	kēyán*	scientific research
科學	kēxué*	science, scientific
本科生	běnkēshēng*	undergraduate student

A: 那個本科生的專業是科學吧？

B: 對，他對科研特別感興趣。

扌 shǒu 'hand' + 支 zhī phonetic

技

jì 7
skill, ability

高科技	gāokējì*	high-tech
特技	tèjì*	stunt, special effects
球技	qiújì*	ball game skills
演技	yǎnjì*	acting

A: 你看到了嗎？他的球技真棒！

B: 可不是嗎？每球都進，跟特技一樣。

Compare: 支 zhī 隻 zhī 只 zhǐ

扌 shǒu 'hand' + 寺 sì 'temple' phonetic

持

chí 9
to hold, to grasp, to support, to run

保持	bǎochí	to keep, to maintain
主持	zhǔchí*	to take charge of
主持人	zhǔchírén*	host, anchor

A: 你和你的好朋友還保持聯繫嗎？

B: 對，他現在主持一個有名的節目。

Compare: 待 dāi

亻 rén 'person' + 憂 yōu phonetic

优

yōu 17
excellent, ample, free

優點	yōudiǎn	merit, strong point
優美	yōuměi*	graceful, exquisite
優秀	yōuxiù*	outstanding, excellent

A: 那個學生非常優秀。

B: 他最大的優點是什麼？

gé 9
leather, to dismiss, to
expel

Picture of a skin split open, a hide seen from the back, with legs apart — hide, to flay, deprive of

革

改革	gǎigé	to reform, reform
革命	gémìng*	to revolt, revolution
鬧革命	nào gémìng*	to carry out revolution
革新	géxīn*	to innovate

A: 你覺得政府什麼需要改革？

B: 各方面都需要革新。

Compare: 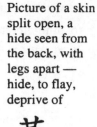 鞋xié 靴xuē

fǔ 8
seat of government,
mansion

广 guǎng 'building' + 付 fù phonetic

府

| 政府 | zhèngfǔ | government |
| 府上 | fǔshang* | your home/family |

A: 您府上在哪兒？

B: 廣東Guǎngdōng。

Compare: 腐fǔ

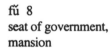

zhì 8
to make, to control,
system

刂 dāo 'knife' + 未 wèi 'a tree with many branches'—to trim a large tree with many branches

制

制度	zhìdù	system, institution
制服	zhìfú*	uniform
限制	xiànzhì*	to restrict, to confine

A: 我覺得政府應該改革教育制度。

B: 還要給學校更多的限制嗎？

Compare: 製zhì

quán 21
right, power, to weigh

木 mù 'wood' + 雚 guàn phonetic—possibly ancient scales were made of wood, rather than metal

权

權利	quánlì	right
權力	quánlì*	power, authority
人權	rénquán*	human rights
特權	tèquán*	privilege, prerogative

A: 有權力的人常常有很多特權。

B: 對！亂用特權的人常常不重視人民的權利。

Compare: 歡huān 觀guān 勸quàn

采 biàn 'distinguish' +
睪 yì phonetic

释

shì 20
to explain

解釋　jiěshì　　to analyze, analysis
注釋　zhùshì*　to annotate, annotation

A: 這個句子應該怎麼解釋？

B: 你看看注釋就知道了。

Compare: 譯 yì　擇 zé

木 mù 'wood'
+ 斤 jīn
'axe'—use an
axe to chop up
wood: cut up,
analyze

析

xī 8
to analyze

分析　fēnxī　　to analyze

A: 你分析一下那個歌星成功的原因。

B: 她歌唱得好，音樂也很優美。

Compare: 所 suǒ　新 xīn　近 jìn　欣 xīn

扌/手 shǒu
'hand' + 安 ān
phonetic

按

àn 9
to push down,
according to

按照　ànzhào　according to
按時　ànshí*　on time/schedule

A: 她的病怎麼樣？

B: 按照醫生的說法，按時吃藥就會好。

山 shān
'mountain' +
厂 'cliff' + 干
gān phonetic

岸

àn 8
shore, bank, coast

兩岸　liǎng'àn　both sides (of the Taiwan Straits)
東岸　dōng'àn　East Coast
西岸　xī'àn　West Coast

A: 你美國兩岸都去過嗎？

B: 我只去過西岸，還沒去過東岸。

Compare: 午 wǔ　汗 hàn　幸 xìng　趕 gǎn

語法和用法 Grammar and Usage

Pay attention to the function of the structure and then study the example sentences.

1. Expressing inevitability

S 免不了/難免會 VO	miǎnbùliǎo/nánmiǎn huì	S inevitably will VO
S VO 是免不了/難免的	shì miǎnbùliǎo/nánmiǎn de	It's inevitable for S to VO

有時候我們三個**免不了**也會爭論，究竟共產主義、資本主義哪個制度好？

1. 聽說你們姐妹 jiěmèi 的感情很好。

   听说你们姐妹的感情很好。

   I heard that you and your sisters get along with each other very well.

   對，可是我們免不了也會吵架。

   对，可是我们免不了也会吵架。

   Yes, but we inevitably argue as well.

2. 中文實在很難學！

   中文实在很难学！

   Chinese is really hard to study!

   別灰心 huīxīn，學習新的語言免不了會遇到一些困難。

   别灰心，学习新的语言免不了会遇到一些困难。

   Don't be discouraged. When learning a new language, one is surely going to run into some problems.

3. 他怎麼這麼久還不回來？

   他怎么这么久还不回来？

   Why did it take him so long to come back?

   老朋友見面多談幾句是免不了的。

   老朋友见面多谈几句是免不了的。

   When old friends meet, it's inevitable that they will have a lot to talk about.

難免/免不了 is used to express inevitability, so there is often 會 after it. This phrase can also occur with the 是…的 pattern. Compare the following sentences: (1) 剛到國外的時候，難免會鬧笑話。(2) 剛到國外的時候，鬧笑話是難免的。

2. Expressing a reference

| 根據/按照…的 N, S V | gēnjù/ànzhào…de …, … | According to sb's N, S V |
| 照…V, S V | zhào…, … | In sb.'s view, S V |

根據小李這個經濟學家**的分析**，美國之所以發達，都是因為資本主義的緣故。

1. 你覺得這次比賽誰會贏？	你觉得这次比赛谁会赢？	Who do you think will win this game?
根據報上的分析，我們應該會贏。	根据报上的分析，我们应该会赢。	According to the analysis in the newspaper, we should win.
2. 你看的那篇報告到底說了什麼？	你看的那篇报告到底说了什么？	What did the report you read talk about?
按照專家zhuānjiā們最新的研究，吸煙對身體完全沒有好處。	按照专家们最新的研究，吸烟对身体完全没有好处。	According to the experts' latest research, smoking is not good for the body at all.
3. 你看他考得上大學嗎？	你看他考得上大学吗？	Do you think he can pass the college entrance exam?
照我看，他不應該考不上大學。	照我看，他不应该考不上大学。	As I see it, he shouldn't have any trouble passing the college entrance exam.

根據/按照 is used to express the source of a reference. The referred noun is often something abstract like 分析 'analysis,' 研究 'study,' 報告 'report,' 了解 'understanding,' 看法 'view,' 做法 'practice,' 說法 'words,' 想法 'opinion,' etc. Note that while one can say "according to him" in English, one can never say 按照他 in Chinese. 照 can be used with a verb, as in 照我看 'in my view.'

3. Expressing a reason

| S（之）（所以）A 是因為 B（的關係/緣故） | … (zhī)(suǒyǐ)…shì yīnwéi… (de guānxi/yuángù) | The reason why S has A (effect) is due to B (cause). |

根據小李這個經濟學家的分析，美國**之所以**發達，都**是因為**資本主義**的緣故**。

1.	中國人為什麼這麼重視家庭？	中国人为什么这么重视家庭？	Why do Chinese people value family so much?
	很多人說中國人之所以這麼重視家庭，都是因為儒家思想的關係。	很多人说中国人之所以这么重视家庭，都是因为儒家思想的关系。	Many people say that the reason Chinese value family so much is because of Confucianism.
2.	美國青少年犯罪為什麼這麼嚴重？	美国青少年犯罪为什么这么严重？	Why is youth crime so serious in the U.S.?
	我看青少年犯罪所以這麼嚴重，是因為家庭問題太多。	我看青少年犯罪所以这么严重，是因为家庭问题太多。	I think juvenile delinquency is so serious because there are so many family problems.
3.	他為什麼沒來上課？	他为什么没来上课？	Why didn't he come to classes?
	他沒來上課是因為生病了的緣故。	他没来上课是因为生病了的缘故。	He didn't come to classes because of illness.

之所以A是因為B indicates the reason for something; A is the effect and B is the cause. Though 之所以 can be omitted, its presence highlights the effect and is quite common in more formal writing. Remember to have 是 before 因為 and avoid mistakes such as 他沒來上課因為生病的關係. Compare this with the pattern B是為了A (L9, G6).

4. Expressing contrariety

…是A,而不是B	…shì …ér búshì…	…is A, rather than/ instead of B

按照王華這個電腦迷的解釋，**是**科技**而不是**什麼「主義」對社會的繁榮起了作用。

| 1. | 現在你學中文最大的問題是聲調嗎？ | 现在你学中文最大的问题是声调吗？ | Now are tones your biggest problem when you study Chinese? |

我最大的問題是漢字而不是聲調。	我最大的问题是汉字而不是声调。	My biggest problem is characters, not tones.

2.
我想他之所以犯錯是因為一時糊塗。	我想他之所以犯错是因为一时糊涂。	I think the reason that he made a mistake is because he was confused for a second.
我覺得他是做事不認真，而不是一時糊塗。	我觉得他是做事不认真，而不是一时糊涂。	Rather than being momentarily confused, I think he is not conscientious about his work.

3.
你覺得經濟改革是社會繁榮的主要原因嗎？	你觉得经济改革是社会繁荣的主要原因吗？	Do you think that economic reform is the mean reason for the prosperity of society?
我想社會繁榮主要是因為政治開放，而不是因為經濟改革。	我想社会繁荣主要是因为政治开放，而不是因为经济改革。	I think society is prosperous mainly because of an open political atmosphere, rather than economic reform.

The "是A，而不是B" expression is used to indicate that A, rather than B, is the focus of the statement. Note that if "不是A，而是B" is used, B, instead of A, is the focus. In both structures A and B are mutually exclusive. Distinguish this from "不是A，就是B" in which A and B are opposing alternatives.

5. Making concessions

SVO, 然而(S)卻V	…, rán'ér … (què)…	and yet…; however,…
SVO, 然而(S)還V	…, rán'ér … (hái)…	and still…

然而小李卻說生活中選擇多不一定有好處……

1.
他是中國人嗎？	他是中国人吗？	Is he Chinese?
他說他是，然而他卻只認得幾個漢字。	他说他是，然而他却只认得几个汉字。	He said he is, but he could only recognize a few characters.

2. 他有親人 qīnrén 在大   他有亲人在大陆   Does he have relatives in
    陸嗎？   吗？   mainland China?

    有，然而他們卻從   有，然而他们却从   Yes, but they have never
    來沒見過面。   来没见过面。   met each other.

3. 你學過中文嗎？   你学过中文吗？   Have you studied Chinese?

    學過，然而我還看   学过，然而我还看   Yes, but I cannot read
    不懂簡體字。   不懂简体字。   simplified characters yet.

然而 and 卻 both mean 'however, yet.' They are used together to reinforce the meaning of the transition. 然而 is used to express concession and is often placed at the beginning of the second clause in a two-clause sentence. It occurs with 卻 or 還, and precedes the subject if the subject is present. Avoid saying something like 然而我學習了半天，我卻考得不太好. Very often 然而 can be substituted by 可是/但是 but it is a bit more formal and stronger than 可是/但是.

6. Expressing an actual reality behind a superficial appearance

| 表面上…實際上… | biǎomiànshàng…shíjìshàng | It appears…in fact… |

表面上，兩邊的制度、語言有些距離，**實際上**，有很多共同的地方……

1. 她到底喜不喜歡   她到底喜不喜欢   Does she like him or not?
    他？   他？

    表面上她說他是個   表面上她说他是个   She says that he is a pest,
    討厭鬼 tǎoyànguǐ，實   讨厌鬼，实际上她   but in fact, she likes him
    際上她很喜歡他。   很喜欢他。   a lot.

2. 他和同屋的關係怎   他和同屋的关系怎   How is his relationship
    麼樣？   么样？   with his roommate?

    表面上他們很友   表面上他们很友   They appear to be on
    好，實際上他們都   好，实际上他们都   good terms, but in fact
    不喜歡對方。   不喜欢对方。   they don't like each
                                                        other.

3. 你的父母很保守　　你的父母很保守　　Are your parents
　　嗎？　　　　　　　嗎？　　　　　　　conservative?

　　表面上他們很保　　表面上他们很保　　They seem to be
　　守，實際上他們很　　守，实际上他们很　　conservative, but actually
　　開放。　　　　　　开放。　　　　　　they are very open-minded.

This pattern is used to express a superficial conception and the realization that clarifies it. Therefore, the parts following 表面上 and 實際上 should be different. It's wrong to say 表面上那門課不太重，實際上沒有很多功課. Compare this with the pattern 以為…其實 (L1, G4), and 別看…其實(L19, G4)

文化點滴 Culture Notes

1. **Progress in Taiwan**: In 1987, the KMT 國民黨 Guómíndǎng lifted the Emergency Decree banning the formation of new political parties, thereby signaling the takeoff of a full (political) democracy in Taiwan. This was quickly followed by other reforms such as lifting restrictions on newspaper licensing and publishing, passing the Law on Assembly and Parades, allowing people to visit relatives on the Chinese mainland, re-electing all members of the National Assembly 國民大會 Guómín dàhuì (1991) and the Legislative Yuan 立法院 Lìfǎyuàn (1992), and revising the Constitution to allow direct and popular elections of the president (1996), vice president, the governor of Taiwan Province (1994), and the mayors of Taipei 台北 and Kaohsiung 高雄 cities (1994). The policy of popular sovereignty has been implemented, and interparty competition has taken root. Currently there are three influential political parties, KMT 國民黨 Guómíndǎng (Nationalist Party), DPP 民進黨 Mínjìndǎng (Democratic Progressive Party), and NP 新黨 Xīndǎng (New Party).

2. **Progress in mainland China**: Since Deng Xiaoping 鄧小平 launched economic reforms in 1978, China has been experienced a number of rapid transitions. It has changed from a command economy to a market based economy and from an agricultural society to an urban, industrial one. Between 1978 and 1996, real GDP grew on average by over 9% a year, contributing to a near quadrupling of per capita income. These reforms have reduced the number of people below the poverty line from more than 200 million in 1981 to about 70 million in 1995. The livelihood of both rural and urban employees has greatly improved.

3. **Unification vs. independence:** The biggest issue concerning mainland China and Taiwan is, of course, unification. From1949 when the KMT with its leader, Chiang Kai-shek 蔣介石, was defeated by the Chinese Communist Party and retreated to Taiwan, people on

both sides of the conflict were out of contact with each other for over 30 years. Some people managed underground communication through friends in Hong Kong, but such contacts were considered "illegal." Only after 1987 were people from Taiwan allowed to return to mainland China to visit their relatives and families. Since then exchanges between the people on both sides of the Taiwan Strait have continued, mostly at academic and non-governmental levels. Yet, crisis has emerged whenever the stand for independence 獨立 dúlì in Taiwan has sounded louder than that for unification 統一 tǒngyī. In general, those who have come to Taiwan from mainland provinces after 1949, the so-called "provincial outsiders" 外省人 wàishěngrén, are pro-unification. Yet, most of the local Taiwanese 本省人 běnshěngrén, people who have been staying in Taiwan since before 1949, are pro-independence.

4. **Language differences**: In addition to the difference between traditional and simplified characters, there are quite a few differences between the lexicon, pronunciation, and sometimes even grammatical structures used in mainland China and Taiwan. The following is a list of a few examples.

English	Terms used in Taiwan	Pinyin	Terms used in China	Pinyin
air-conditioning	冷氣	lěngqì	空调	kōngtiáo
audiotape	錄音帶	lùyīndài	磁带	cídài
lunch box	飯盒/便當	fànhé/biàndāng	盒饭	héfàn
instant noodles	泡麵	pàomiàn	方便面	fāngbiànmiàn
software	軟體	ruǎntǐ	软件	ruǎnjiàn
taxi	計程車	jìchéngchē	出租汽车	chūzū qìchē
traffic jam	塞車	sāichē	堵车	dǔchē
VCR	錄影機	lùyǐngjī	录相机	lùxiàngjī

歌兒 Songs

海峽兩岸
The Two Sides of the Taiwan Strait

Adagietto

詞：劉雅詩 曲：馬定一

1. 曾 經 四 十 年 海 峽 兩 岸 沒 有 接 觸 和
Céngjīng sì shí nián hǎixiá liǎng àn méyǒu jiēchù hé
For forty years there was no contact between the two sides of the Taiwan Strait.

2. 其 實 兩 邊 的 關 係 很 像 父 母 姊 妹 和
Qíshí liǎngbiān de guānxi hěn xiàng fù mǔ jiěmèi hé
Actually the two sides of the Taiwan Straits are like parents, sisters and

1. 聯 繫。 一 邊 實 行 共 產 主 義 一 邊 走 向 資 本 主 義，不
liánxì. Yìbiān shíxíng gòngchǎn zhǔyì, yìbiān zǒu xiàng zīběn zhǔyì, bù
One side adopted Communism and the other went for capitalism.

2. 兄 弟。 中 國 人 都 重 視 家 庭 生 活 還 有 子 女 教 育，兩
xiōngdì. Zhōngguórén dōu zhòngshì jiātíng shēnghuó hái yǒu zǐnǚ jiàoyù, liǎng
brothers. Chinese all value family life and children's education.

1. 同 制 度 各 有 優 點 缺 點 可 分 析。台 灣 自 由
tóng zhìdù gè yǒu yōudiǎn quēdiǎn kě fēnxī. Táiwān zìyóu
Different systems have their own strengths and shortcomings to be analyzed. With freedom

2. 千 年 來 歷 史 文 化 背 景 都 相 近。只 要 海 峽
qiān nián lái lìshǐ wénhuà bèijǐng dōu xiāngjìn. Zhǐyào hǎixiá
For two thousand years their history and cultural backgrounds have been related. As long as the two

1. 民 主 下 重 視 人 民 權 利，大 陸 改 革 開 放 後
mínzhǔ xià zhòngshì rénmín quánlì, dàlù gǎigé kāifàng hòu
and democracy Taiwan has emphasized people's rights. With its new openness and reform,

2. 兩 岸 能 繼 續 溝 通 關 係，接 觸 了 解 不 同 的
liǎng àn néng jìxù gōutōng guānxi, jiēchù liǎojiě bùtóng de
continue to communicate about their relationship, and are in touch with each other and understand

1. 重 視 發 展 經 濟，人 們 都 為 了 繁 榮 快 樂 的 生 活 而 努 力。
zhòngshì fāzhǎn jīngjì, rénmen dōu wèile fánróng kuàilè de shēnghuó ér nǔlì.
the Mainland has stressed economic development. People all work hard to prosper and have a happy life.

2. 想 法 也 講 道 理，總 會 有 那 麼 一 天 能 解 決 這 個 大 難 題。
xiǎngfǎ yě jiǎng dàolǐ, zǒng huì yǒu nàme yìtiān néng jiějué zhè ge dà nántí.
their different views, and reason well, there will come a day when we can solve this difficult problem.

Appendixes

Appendix 1. Traditional vs. Simplified Characters

Most simplified characters bear some resemblance to their traditional counterparts. Given some practice over time, you will be able to recognize both forms. The following are four basic means by which simplified characters relate to their traditional counterparts. The examples are given with the traditional characters on the top and the simplified ones below.

A. With one component (e.g., radicals) simplified

1. 學　覺
   学　觉

2. 馬　嗎　媽
   马　吗　妈

3. 這　過　還　進　邊　遠
   这　过　还　进　边　远

4. 課　誰　請　說　話　談　謝　記　該　許　語　讓
   课　谁　请　说　话　谈　谢　记　该　许　语　让

5. 見　現　視　員　貴　賽　費　贏　慣　題
   见　现　视　员　贵　赛　费　赢　惯　题

6. 給　約　紅
   给　约　红

7. 門　問　間　們
   门　问　间　们

8.
饭 館 餓
饭 馆 饿

9.
長 張
长 张

10.
湯 場
汤 场

11.
錯 錢 鐘
错 钱 钟

12.
幾 機
几 机

13.
車 連 輸 輕
车 连 输 轻

14.
國 師 樣 時 對 難 歡 塊 動 腦 臉 應
国 师 样 时 对 难 欢 块 动 脑 脸 应
驗 樓 郵 幫 隊 魚 風 熱 涼 緊 報 帶
验 楼 邮 帮 队 鱼 风 热 凉 紧 报 带
掛 單 剛
挂 单 刚

B. *With one component representing the whole*

15.

兒	從	電	開	麵	裏	號
儿	从	电	开	面	里	号

飛	習	雖	氣	醫	離
飞	习	虽	气	医	离

C. *With more than one component simplified*

16.

經	練	點
经	练	点

D. *With the whole character simplified*

17.

兩	來	爲	書	買	實	頭	著	會	寫	聽	響
两	来	为	书	买	实	头	着	会	写	听	响
當	樂	東	專	發	變	萬	辦	總	雞	藥	擔
当	乐	东	专	发	变	万	办	总	鸡	药	担
個	麼	節	後
个	么	节	后

Appendix 2. Bibliography

Birch, Cyril, ed.
   1972   Anthology of Chinese Literature. New York: Grove Press.

Chao, Yuen Ren (趙元任)
   1968   *A Grammar of Spoken Chinese*. Berkeley: University of California Press.

Cheng, Qinhua (程欽華), ed.
   1992   *Selected Jokes from Past Chinese Dynasties* (中國歷代笑話精選). Beijing: Huayu
          Jiaoxue Chubanshe.

DeFrancis, John, ed.
   1996   *ABC Chinese-English Dictionary*. Honolulu: University of Hawai'i Press.

Gao, Shufan (高樹藩), ed.
   1984   *Zhengzhong Xing Yin Yi Zonghe Da Zidian* (正中形音義綜合大字典). Rev. 5th ed.
          Taibei: Zhengzhong Shuju.

Government Information Office, Taiwan, ROC, eds.
   2000   *The Republic of China Yearbook*. Taipei: Government Information Office.

Guojia Duiwai Hanyu Jiaoxue Lingdao Xiaozu Bangongshi (國家對外漢語教學領導小組辦公
室), eds.
   1992   *Hanyu Shuiping Cihui Yu Hanzi Dengji Dagang* (漢語水平詞匯與漢字等級大綱).
          Beijing: Beijing Yuyan Xueyuan Chubanshe.

Guojia Duiwai Hanyu Jiaoxue Lingdao Xiaozu Bangongshi (國家對外漢語教學領導小組辦公
室), eds.
   1996   *Hanyu Shuiping Dengji Biaozhun Yu Yufa Dengji Dagang* (漢語水平等級標準與語
          法等級大綱). Beijing: Gaodeng Jiaoyu Chubanshe.

Han, Jiantang (韓鑒堂), ed.
   1994   *China's Cultural Heritage* (中國文化). Beijing: Guoji Wenhua Chuban Gongsi.

Liang, Shih-chiu (梁實秋)
   1971   *A New Practical Chinese-English Dictionary* (最新實用漢英字典). Taipei: Far East Book Co.

Norman, Jerry
   1988   *Chinese.* Cambridge: Cambridge University Press.

Ramsey, S. Robert
   1987   *The Languages of China.* Princeton: Princeton University Press.

Rohsenow, John
   1991   *A Chinese-English Dictionary of Enigmatic Folk Similes.* Tucson: The University of Arizona Press.

Sinorama Magazine (光華雜誌社), eds.
   1992   *"Trademarks" of the Chinese* (中國人的「註冊商標」). Taipei: Sinorama Magazine.

Situ, Tan (司徒談), ed.
   1986   *Best Chinese Idioms.* Hong Kong: Hai Feng.

Tennenbaum, Peter, and Tom Bishop
   2002   Wenlin Software for Learning Chinese (version 3.0). Wenlin Institute.

Wang, Fang (王仿), ed.
   1990   *A Comprehensive Collection of Chinese Riddles* (中國謎語大全). Shanghai: Shanghai Wenyi Chubanshe.

Ye, Dabing (葉大兵), and Bing'an Wu (烏丙安), eds
   1990   *Zhongguo Fengsu Cidian* (中國風俗辭典). Shanghai: Shanghai Cishu Chubanshe.

Zhongguo Da Baike Quanshu Chubanshe Bianjibu (中國大百科全書出版社編輯部編), eds.
   1988   *Zhongguo Da Baike Quanshu: Yuyan Wenzi* (中國大百科全書：語言文字). Beijing: Zhongguo Da Baike Quanshu Chubanshe.

Indexes

Index 1. Vocabulary

◎ By Pinyin

Pinyin	Character	English	L
A			
ài	唉	Oh!	7.40
àihào	愛好/爱好	hobby, interest	6.10
àiqíng	愛情/爱情	romantic love	8.19
àiren	愛人/爱人	spouse	9.2
àiren*	愛人/爱人	spouse	3
àishang	愛上/爱上	to fall in love with	8.1
ānpái	安排	to arrange, to plan	11.30
ānquán	安全	safe, security	16.32
(àn)zhào	(按)照	according to	20.15
B			
bài	拜	to worship	17.7
báirén	白人	Caucasian	8.2
báitiān	白天	daytime, day	14.31
bàn	辦/办	to handle	1.11
bànfǎ	辦法/办法	way, means	3.20
bāngzhù	幫助/帮助	help, to assist	15.29
bàntiān	半天	a long time	1.19
bǎo	飽/饱	full	5.27
bǎochí	保持	to keep, to maintain	20.30
bǎohù	保護/保护	protection, to protect	12.27
bǎomǔ*	褓姆/保姆	housekeeper, nanny	9
bǎoshǒu	保守	conservative	8.27
bàoyuàn	抱怨	to complain, to grumble	16.20
bèi	倍	times, -fold	18.29
bèidòng	被動/被动	passive	14.20
bēiguān*	悲觀/悲观	pessimistic	20
bèijǐng	背景	background	8.14
bèn*	笨	stupid	19
běnlái	本來/本来	originally	6.22
bǐ	筆/笔	measure word for money	16.9
biànhuà	變化/变化	change	16.39

Pinyin	Character	English	L
biǎomiàn	表面	surface, appearance	20.32
biǎoyǎn	表演	performance exhibition, to perform	19.41
biāozhǔn	標準/标准	standard	18.1
bǐbushàng	比不上	can't compare with	19.42
biérén	別人	other people	10.34
bǐfāng shuō	比方說/比方说	for example	4.26
bìng	並/并	actually (not)	3.11
bīng*	冰	to ice, ice	13
bìngrén*	病人	patient	8
bìxū	必須/必须	must	9.3
bú jiàn bú sàn*	不見不散/不见不散	won't leave without seeing each other	7
búdàn	不但	not only	5.31
búduàn*	不斷/不断	continuously, uninterrupted	20
bówùguǎn	博物館/博物馆	museum	11.17
bùdé bù	不得不	cannot but	5.35
bùfen	部分	part, section	12.16
bùguǎn	不管	regardless of	2.36
bùmǎn	不滿/不满	dissatisfied	16.13
bǔpǐn	補品/补品	tonic	13.19
bùtíng	不停	incessantly	18.13
bǔxíbān	補習班/补习班	supplemental studies program	14.29
bùxíng	不行	to be no good	5.10
C			
càidān*	菜單/菜单	menu	5
cāidào	猜到	to figure out	7.38
cǎn	慘/惨	miserable	4.43
cānguān	參觀/参观	to visit, to tour	11.20
cāntīng	餐廳/餐厅	restaurant	4.27
cāochǎng	操場/操场	practice field	18.3
chà	差	poor, inferior	14.19

Pinyin	Characters	Meaning	Ref
dàolǐ*	道理	reason, sense	9
dǎoyǎn	導演/导演	director	6.18
dǎrǎo	打擾/打扰	to disturb	19.23
dàren	大人	adult	18.10
dàrén*	大人	adult	13
dǎtōng	打通	to get through (phone call)	15.2
dàxiàng*	大象	elephant	13
dàxióngmāo	大熊貓/大熊猫	giant panda	13.24
dēng	燈/灯	lamp	13.34
děngděng	等等	and so on, etc.	2.43
dēngjīpái*	登機牌/登机牌	boarding pass	20
diǎn*	點/点	to order (dishes)	5
diǎnxīn	點心/点心	pastry	5.17
diànzǐ	電子/电子	electronic	1.33
diàoyú*	釣魚/钓鱼	to fish	6
diē/dié	跌	fall, tumble	16.24
dìfang	地方	place	2.18
dìng	訂/订	to book, to subscribe to	11.26
diūliǎn	丟臉/丢脸	to lose face	15.16
díquè	的確/的确	certainly	12.21
dìtǎn	地毯	carpet, rug	2.28
dìtú	地圖/地图	map	12.45
dòngbudòng	動不動/动不动	easily, at the slightest provocation	16.17
dōngtiān	冬天	winter	13.17
dòngwùyuán*	動物園/动物园	zoo	13
dòngwù	動物/动物	animal	13.21
dòujiāng	豆漿/豆浆	soybean milk	11.7
duàn	段	period (of time), paragraph (of article)	15.35
duì…láishuō	對···來說/对···来说	concerning	3.9
duìbuqǐ	對不起/对不起	to let sb. down	14.15
duìhuà	對話/对话	to carry on dialogue	12.35
duìmiàn	對面/对面	opposit…	
duìniú-tánqín	對牛彈琴/对牛弹琴	to cast p… before s…	
duìxiàng	對象/对象	boy/girl…	
duō(me)	多(麼)/(多么)	how, wh…	

E

Pinyin	Characters	Meaning	Ref
ér-nǚ	兒女/儿女	children	
èrshǒuyān	二手煙/二手烟	secondh… smoke	
értóng	兒童/儿童	children	
érzi	兒子/儿子	son	

F

Pinyin	Characters	Meaning	Ref
fā	發/发	to issue	
fācái	發財/发财	to get ri…	
fādá	發達/发达	develop…	
fāmíng	發明/发明	inventio…	
fǎn'ér	反而	on the c…	
fàndiàn*	飯店/饭店	hotel, restaura…	
fǎnduì	反對/反对	to oppos…	
fāngbiànmiàn*	方便麵/方便面	<PRC> … noodles	
fāngbiàn*	方便	to go to restroom… conveni…	
fāngfǎ	方法	method,	
fángjiān	房間/房间	room	
fāngmiàn	方面	aspect, s…	
fàngqì	放棄/放弃	to give u…	
fāngxiàng	方向	direction	
fāngyán	方言	dialect	
fángzū*	房租	rent	
fánróng	繁榮/繁荣	prospero…	
fánshì	凡事	everythi…	
fánshì	凡是	every, an…	
fántǐzì	繁體字/繁体字	tradition… character…	
fānyì	翻譯/翻译	translatio… translate, translator…	
fànzuì	犯罪	crime, to… a crime	

fāpàng*	發胖/发胖	to gain weight	5
fāshēng	發生/发生	to happen	19.31
fāyīn	發音/发音	pronunciation, to pronounce	18.12
fāzhǎn	發展/发展	to develop, development	16.38
fēi...bùkě	非…不可	must	8.7
Fēizhōu	非洲	Africa	13.29
fēn	分	fraction, one-tenth, percent, to divide	13.38
fēn(r)	份(兒)/份(儿)	measure word for jobs, copies, etc.	9.27
fēng	封	measure word for letters	1.32
fēngfù	豐富/丰富	rich, enrich	16.25
fènglí*	鳳梨/凤梨	pineapple	13
fēngshui	風水/风水	geomancy	17.36
fēnshǒu	分手	to break up	8.25
fēnxī	分析	to analyze, analysis	20.13
fū	夫	husband	9.42
Fójiào	佛教	Buddhism	17.28
fúqi*	福氣/福气	happy lot	3
fǒuzé	否則/否则	otherwise	5.26
fúwù	服務/服务	to serve, service	17.16
fùxí	複習/复习	to review	2.15
fùzá	複雜/复杂	complicated	12.44
G			
gǎi	改	to change	7.25
gǎigé	改革	to reform, reform	20.34
gān	乾/干	dry	5.11
gǎn	敢	to dare	1.2
gǎn	感	sense	10.21
gǎn xìngqù	感興趣/感兴趣	to be interested in	1.42
gānbēi	乾杯/干杯	bottoms up	3.32
gāngqín	鋼琴/钢琴	piano	10.27
gānjìng	乾淨/干净	clean	2.26
gǎnjué	感覺/感觉	feeling	3.13
gǎnqíng	感情	feeling	7.41
gǎnrén	感人	touching	19.13

gǎnxiǎng	感想	reflections, thoughts	20.26
gǎnxiè	感謝/感谢	to thank, to be grateful	12.17
gǎo	搞	to do	1.18
gāodà	高大	tall and big	19.9
gāojí	高級/高级	high in rank	4.31
gè	各	each	2.2
gēnběn	根本	simply	3.24
gèng	更	even	1.41
gēnjù	根據/根据	on the basis of, according to, basis	20.11
gèrénzhǔyì	個人主義/个人主义	individualism	20.21
gètǐhù	個體戶/个体户	individual entrepreneur	12.15
gòngchǎnzhǔyì	共產主義/共产主义	communism	20.8
gōnggòng*	公共	public	2
gōnglì	公立	public	10.20
gōngrén	工人	worker	12.14
gōngsī	公司	company	14.2
gòngtóng	共同	common	6.9
gòngxiàn	貢獻/贡献	contribution	10.41
gōngyuán	公園/公园	park	4.17
gōngzuò	工作	job, to work	9.7
gūniang	姑娘	girl	7.32
gōutōng	溝通/沟通	to communicate	11.11
guā	瓜	melon	4.34
guāfēng	颱風/刮风	the wind is blowing	17.3
guāi	乖	well-behaved	19.28
guài	怪	to blame	15.34
guǎi*	拐	to turn	4
guàibude	怪不得	no wonder	5.39
guàiwu	怪物	monster, freak	12.31
guǎn xiánshì	管閑事/管闲事	to meddle	2.1
guǎngbō	廣播/广播	broadcast, to air	18.27
guǎngchǎng	廣場/广场	public square	4.11
guāngshì	光是	merely, just	16.41
guānniàn	觀念/观念	concept	8.26

guānxīn	關心/关心	to be concerned about	3.15
guānyú	關於/关于	about, with regard to	3.38
gǔdài	古代	ancient times	12.8
guǐ	鬼	ghost	17.14
gǔlì	鼓勵/鼓励	encouragement	9.7
guò	過/过	to pass	1.22
guòfèn	過分/过分	excessive, over-	13.27
guójiā	國家/国家	country, state, nation	16.6
guòjié	過節/过节	to celebrate a festival	3.27
guónèi	國內/国内	internal, domestic	3.28
guònián	過年/过年	to celebrate New Year	11.37
guòqù	過去/过去	past	2.41
guǒrán	果然	as expected, sure enough	14.37
guówài	國外/国外	internal, overseas, abroad	16.44
guōzi*	鍋子/锅子	wok, pan	5
gǔpiào	股票	stock	16.23
gùshi	故事	story, tale	3.40
gǔzhǎng*	鼓掌	to clap hands	20

H

hāhā	哈哈	ha ha (sound of laughter)	18.7
hǎi	海	sea	17.9
hài	害	to do harm to, cause trouble to	12.18
hǎiguān	海關/海关	customs	1.23
hàipà	害怕	to be afraid/scared	19.25
hǎixiá	海峽/海峡	strait	20.2
hǎochu	好處/好处	benefit	10.11
hǎogǎn	好感	favorable impression	6.21
hàomǎ*	號碼/号码	number	17
hàoqí	好奇	curious	2.37
hǎoróngyì	好容易	with great difficulty, to have a hard time (doing sth.)	9.29

hǎoyùn	好運/好运	good luck	17.13
hǎozài	好在	fortunately	1.6
hébì	何必	there is no need	19.32
héshang	和尚	Buddhist monk	19.27
hézuò	合作	to cooperate, cooperation	13.40
hú	湖	lake	19.16
hóngbāo	紅包/红包	red paper bag with gift money	15.14
hūrán	忽然	suddenly	17.5
hútòng	胡同	lane	4.15
hútu	糊塗/糊涂	muddled, confused	19.35
hòu	厚	thick	7.20
hóuzi	猴子	monkey	19.25
huáchuán*	划船	to row a boat	6
huàhuàr	畫畫兒/画画儿	to draw pictures	10.26
huáiyí	懷疑/怀疑	to doubt, to suspect	15.38
huàjiā	畫家/画家	painter	10.36
huánjìng	環境/环境	environment	12.26
huānyíng*	歡迎/欢迎	to welcome	1
Huáyì	華裔/华裔	ethnic Chinese of other nationalities	8.22
huāyuán	花園/花园	flower garden	19.30
huàzhuāng*	化妝/化妆	to apply makeup	6
huídá	回答	to reply, to answer	12.33
Huíjiào	回教	Islam	17.32
huíxìn	回信	to write in reply	10.4
huǒchē	火車/火车	train	11.36
huódòng	活動/活动	activity, to exercise	2.14
huǒtuǐ*	火腿/火腿	ham	5
hùxiāng	互相	mutually	7.26
hùzhào	護照/护照	passport	1.9

J

jǐ	擠/挤	crowded, to squeeze	12.25
jì...yě	既…也…	not only… but also…	3.19

jià	嫁	(of a woman) to marry	8.18
jiācháng biànfàn	家常便飯/家常便饭	simple meal	3.31
jiājiào	家教	home tutoring, upbringing, tutor	14.16
jiājù	家具	furniture	13.1
jiǎndān	簡單/简单	simple	17.41
jiàndào	見到/见到	to see	7.2
jiāng	江	river	19.18
jiǎng	講/讲	to stress, to speak	8.38
jiǎngjiu	講究/讲究	to be particular about	5.28
jiānglái	將來/将来	future	8.15
jiàngyóu*	醬油/酱油	soy sauce	5
jiànjiàn	漸漸/渐渐	gradually	17.1
jiànkāng	健康	health	5.4
jiǎnlì	簡歷/简历	résumé, curriculum vitae	14.6
jiànmiàn	見面/见面	to meet, to see	1.38
jiǎntǐzì	簡體字/简体字	simplified characters	18.35
jiànyì	建議/建议	suggestion	11.32
jiànzhù	建築/建筑	architecture, to build	12.9
jiāo	交	to make (friends), to hand over	2.42
jiàocái	教材	teaching materials	2.4
jiàoshì	教室	classroom	15.19
jiàoshòu*	教授	professor	1
jiāotōng	交通	traffic	12.36
jiàoxun	教訓/教训	lesson, to lecture sb.	18.9
jiàoyù	教育	education	10.25
jiātíng	家庭	family	9.33
jiāwù	家務/家务	household duties	9.6
jiāyóu*	加油	Cheers! Go!	11
jiāzhǎng	家長/家长	parent of schoolchildren	14.17
jīběn	基本	basic, essential	18.34
jīchē	機車/机车	<TW> motor-cycle	12.38
jìchéngchē	計程車/计程车	<TW> taxi	12.39
jīchǔ	基礎/基础	foundation, basic	18.21
jīdàn*	雞蛋/鸡蛋	hen's egg	5
Jīdūjiào	基督教	Christianity	17.30
jiē	接	to pick sb. up	1.30
jiē	接	to pick up (phone call), to welcome	15.3
jiè	藉/借	to make use of, take advantage of (an opportunity)	20.1
jiēchù	接觸/接触	to come into contact with	20.39
jiéguǒ	結果/结果	result	4.41
jiějué	解決/解决	to solve, to settle	13.41
jièkǒu	藉口/借口	excuse	15.31
jièkǒu*	藉口/借口	excuse	9
jiémù	節目/节目	program	6.20
jiérì	節日/节日	festival, holiday	3.22
jiěshì	解釋/解释	analysis, to expound	20.16
jiēshòu	接受	to accept	8.29
jiéshù	結束/结束	to end	11.2
jīhū	幾乎/几乎	almost	3.34
jìhuà	計劃/计划	plan, project	11.34
-jíle	極了/极了	extremely	2.31
jīliè	激烈	intense, fierce	16.30
jǐmǎn	擠滿/挤满	to be filled to overflowing	13.7
jìmò	寂寞	lonely	3.18
jīn	金	gold, blonde	12.30
jīn*	斤	half a kilogram	4
jīnfànwǎn	金飯碗/金饭碗	well-paying job	14.40
jīngcǎi	精彩	brilliant	6.16
jīngcháng	經常/经常	frequently, often	18.30
jīngguò	經過/经过	to pass	4.14
jīngjì	經濟/经济	economical	5.41
jīngjìxuéjiā	經濟學家/经济学家	economist	20.12

láibují	來不及/来不及	can't do sth. in time	1.16
lājī, lèsè	垃圾	garbage	12.23
làngfèi	浪費/浪费	to waste, extravagant	13.30
lǎo	老	tough, overdone	5.22
lǎo	老	always	7.16
lǎobǎixìng	老百姓	common people, civilians	16.16
lǎobǎn	老板	boss	15.18
lǎodà*	老大	eldest child (in a family)	3
lǎohǔ*	老虎	tiger	13
láojià*	勞駕/劳驾	excuse me	12
lǎojiā*	老家	native place	3
lǎorén	老人	old man/woman	19.17
lǎoshíshuō	老實說/老实说	to tell the truth	5.7
lǎoshǔ*	老鼠	mouse, rat	14
lǎowài	老外	foreigner	1.1
lèguān	樂觀/乐观	optimistic, hopeful	20.31
liàng*	輛/辆	measure word for cars	16
liǎng'àn	兩岸/两岸	both sides (Chinese Mainland and Taiwan)	20.3
liánxì	聯繫/联系	to contact	10.44
liǎobuqǐ	了不起	amazing, terrific	18.11
liǎojiě	了解	to understand	3.16
lìhai	厲害/厉害	sharp	9.16
líhūn	離婚/离婚	divorce	8.16
lǐjiě	理解	to understand	10.23
líkāi	離開/离开	to leave, to depart from	11.4
lǐmào	禮貌/礼貌	polite	3.8
línjū	鄰居/邻居	neighbor	15.12
liú*	留	to keep	3
liúxué	留學/留学	to study abroad	1.5
liúyán	留言	to leave message	15.4

lìrú	例如	for instance, such as	13.15
lìshǐ	歷史/历史	history	2.34
liùniǎo*	遛鳥/遛鸟	to take a bird on a stroll	4
lìwài	例外	exception	10.7
lǐxiǎng	理想	ideal	10.5
lìyòng	利用	to use, to take advantage of	15.27
lìzi	例子	example, case	15.21
lǚkè*	旅客	traveller, passenger	20
lǚxíngshè	旅行社	travel agent	11.29
lǚyóutuán	旅遊團/旅游团	tour group	11.25
luàn	亂/乱	chaotic, messy	12.37
luōsuo	囉嗦/罗嗦	wordy, longwinded	8.24
lǜdòutāng	綠豆湯/绿豆汤	mung bean soup	13.13

M

mà	罵/骂	to call names, to scold	7.18
mángbuguòlái	忙不過來/忙不过来	too busy to deal with	3.25
mǎnyì	滿意/满意	satisfied	7.5
mào	冒	to risk, to brave	16.10
máobing	毛病	shortcoming	7.24
máodùn	矛盾	contradictory, contradiction	15.36
měi	美	beautiful	3.37
méiguānxi	沒關係/没关系	it doesn't matter	10.16
mèimei	妹妹	younger sister	19.34
méitǐ	媒體/媒体	media	20.25
méixiǎngdào	沒想到	unexpectedly	2.38
mèng	夢/梦	dream	19.40
ménpiào*	門票/门票	admission ticket	13
mí	迷	to be enchanted with	6.11
miǎnbuliǎo	免不了	to be unavoidable	20.6
miànqián	面前	in front of	18.5
miàntán	面談/面谈	to discuss face to face	14.3

miànzi	面子	face	15.1
miào	廟/庙	temple	17.10
mìmì	秘密	secret	6.1
míngshèng-gǔjī	名勝古蹟/名胜古迹	places of historic interest and scenic beauty	11.19
míngxiào	名校	famous school	10.32
míngxīng	明星	star	6.17
míngxìnpiàn	明信片	postcard	11.42
mínzhǔ	民主	democracy	20.20
mínzú	民族	ethnic group/minority, nation	17.18
míxìn	迷信	superstition, to have blind faith in	17.35
mùdì	目的	purpose, aim, goal	15.40
mùqián	目前	at present	10.15
mǔqin	母親/母亲	mother	9.36

N

nándào	難道/难道	Do you mean to say that…?	10.1
nándé	難得/难得	rare	11.23
nánguài	難怪/难怪	no wonder	7.39
nánháir	男孩兒/男孩儿	boy	7.14
nán-nǚ-lǎo-shào	男女老少	men and women, old and young	4.18
nánzǐhàn	男子漢/男子汉	a real man	9.23
nào xiàohua	鬧笑話/闹笑话	to make a fool of oneself	18.4
nàozhōng	鬧鐘/闹钟	alarm clock	4.4
nèiróng	內容	content	2.6
nénggàn	能幹/能干	competent	9.4
nénggòu	能夠/能够	can, be able to	20.27
nénglì	能力	ability, capacity	14.12
néngyuán	能源	energy	13.39
nì	膩/腻	greasy, tired of	5.16
niánjì	年紀/年纪	age	6.8
niánqīng	年輕/年轻	young	7.35

niánqīngrén	年輕人/年轻人	young people	17.39
nìngkě	寧可/宁可	would rather, better	15.28
niú	牛	ox	7.13
niúròumiàn	牛肉麵/牛肉面	beef noodles	4.28
nóngmín	農民/农民	peasant	12.13
nǚháir	女孩兒/女孩儿	girl	9.19
nǚxìng	女性	woman	9.32
nuǎnhuo	暖和	(nice and) warm	17.2

O

Ōuzhōu	歐洲/欧洲	Europe	13.5

P

pá*	爬	to climb, to crawl	11
pāi	拍	to shoot film, to take a picture	6.13
páigǔ	排骨	spareribs	7.17
pàng	胖	fat, plump	5.34
pǎo	跑	to run	1.29
pǎobù	跑步	to jog	4.21
pàomiàn*	泡麵/泡面	<TW> instant noodles	18
páshān*	爬山	to climb mountain	17
pī	批	batch, lot, group	16.4
piān	篇	piece of writing	15.24
piàn	騙/骗	to deceive, to cheat, to swindle	15.32
piānjiàn	偏見/偏见	bias	8.30
piānzi	片子	film	6.14
píng	瓶	bottle	4.40
píng'ān	平安	safe and sound	11.44
píngděng	平等	equal	9.43
píngguǒ	蘋果/苹果	apple	16.45
pīngpāng qiú*	乒乓球	ping pong	6
píngshí	平時/平时	in ordinary times	8.5
pīnmìng	拼命	to make a do-or-die effort	5.36

pīnyīn	漢字	英文	課
pǔbiàn	普遍	universal, widespread	16.15
pǔtōnghuà	普通話/普通话	Mandarin Chinese	18.15

Q

pīnyīn	漢字	英文	課
qí	騎/骑	to ride	4.8
qǐ zuòyòng	起作用	to have an effect	20.19
qiáng	強/强	strong, powerful, better	14.13
qiángdiào	強調/强调	to stress	20.33
qiántú	前途	future, prospects	10.10
qiānwàn	千萬/千万	by all means	6.2
qiānzhèng	簽證/签证	visa	1.10
qǐchuáng	起床	to get up (from bed)	4.6
qiézi	茄子	eggplant	18.20
qìgōng	氣功/气功	deep breathing exercises	4.20
qīngshàonián	青少年	young people and teenagers, youths	16.33
qīngchu	清楚	clear	6.31
qǐngjià	請假/请假	to ask for leave	15.11
qǐngjiào	請教/请教	to seek advice	19.12
qǐngkè	請客/请客	to treat sb. (to meal/show/etc.)	15.30
qíngkuàng	情況/情况	situation, circumstances	1.39
qīngnián	青年	youth	19.10
qǐngtiě*	請帖/请帖	invitation card	15
qìngzhù	慶祝/庆祝	to celebrate	3.21
qīnqiè	親切/亲切	cordial	3.7
qióngguāngdàn	窮光蛋/穷光蛋	poor wretch	10.3
qiūtiān*	秋天	autumn	17
qíshì	歧視/歧视	discrimination	8.11
qítā	其他	other, the rest	12.32
qīzi	妻子	wife	9.37
quàn	勸/劝	to advise	8.20
quánlì	權利/权利	right, privilege	20.38
quánqiúhuà	全球化	globalization	20.40
quē	缺	to be short of, to lack, opening	14.1

pīnyīn	漢字	英文	課
què	卻/却	however, yet	2.30
quēdiǎn	缺點/缺点	shortcoming, defect	20.5

R

pīnyīn	漢字	英文	課
rán'ér	然而	even so, but	20.23
rèmén	熱門/热门	in great demand	10.18
rèn	認/认	to recognize	7.23
rěnbuzhù	忍不住	can't help but do sth.	19.37
rènhé	任何	any	9.17
rénkǒu	人口	population	13.37
rénmen	人們/人们	people, the public	13.18
rénmín	人民	the people	20.37
Rénmínbì*	人民幣/人民币	RMB	11
rénshān-rénhǎi*	人山人海	huge crowds of people, a sea of people	13
rènwéi	認爲/认为	to think that	6.25
rènzhēn	認眞/认真	earnest, serious, to take to heart	18.33
rèqíng	熱情/热情	enthusiastic, warm	3.6
rìcháng	日常	day-to-day	14.10
rìyòngpǐn	日用品	articles for daily use	13.2
rìzi	日子	day, days	5.30
Rújiā	儒家	Confucian school	17.19
ruǎn*	軟/软	soft	2
ruǎntǐ*	軟體/软体	<TW> software	15

S

pīnyīn	漢字	英文	課
sāichē	塞車/塞车	traffic jam	12.42
sànbù	散步	to take a walk	13.12
shā	殺/杀	to kill	13.20
shāfā	沙發/沙发	sofa	2.25
shāng	商	business	10.42
shàng	上	to submit (a letter)	1.35
shàngcì	上次	last time	3.3
shàngdàng	上當/上当	to be taken in	4.38
shāngdiàn	商店	shop	4.25

shànghuǒ	上火	to suffer excessive internal heat	13.14
shāngliang	商量	to consult	9.18
shāngxīn	傷心/伤心	to be sad/ aggrieved	19.33
shānshuǐ	山水	landscape (painting)	19.8
shāo	燒/烧	to cook, to roast, to burn	9.10
shāobǐng	燒餅/烧饼	baked sesame seed flatbread	11.8
shěbude	捨不得/ 舍不得	to hate to part with or use	11.3
shén	神	god, super-natural, magical	17.8
shēn	深	deep	17.21
shēng	生	raw, green	5.21
shěng	省	province, to save	13.3
shēngcí	生詞/生词	new word	2.7
shēngdòng*	生動/生动	lively, vivid	19
shēngmìng	生命	(physical) life	16.11
shēngxué	升學/升学	to enter higher school	16.27
shēngyi	生意	business, trade	16.7
shēngyīn	聲音/声音	sound	1.27
shénhuà	神話/神话	myth, mythology	16.43
shénmede	什麼的/ 什么的	and so on	10.29
shēnqǐng	申請/申请	to apply for	1.8
shènzhì	甚至	so much so that	2.23
shétou	舌頭/舌头	tongue	18.22
shī	詩/诗	poem	19.11
shídài*	時代/时代	times, age, era	15
shīfu*	師傅/师傅	master worker	1
shíjì	實際/实际	practical, reality	17.22
shìjì	世紀/世纪	century	6.36
shíjì*	實際/实际	practical	10
shìjiè	世界	world	13.36
shímáo	時髦/时髦	fashionable	6.41
shìqing	事情	affair, matter	1.44
shīwàng	失望	to become disappointed	6.33

shìwēi	示威	to march, demonstration	16.19
shíwù	食物	food	5.9
shíxiàn	實現/实现	to realize	10.22
shìyè	事業/事业	career	9.40
shìyìng	適應/适应	to get used to	2.3
shízài	實在/实在	indeed, really	3.17
shīzi*	獅子/狮子	lion	13
shūdāizi	書呆子/ 书呆子	bookworm	7.28
shūfǎjiā	書法家/ 书法家	calligrapher	19.21
shūmiàn yǔ	書面語/ 书面语	written/ literary language	18.31
shōu	收	put away, take back	18.26
shòu	瘦	thin, lean	5.33
shǒu*	首	measure word for songs, poems	14
shòudào	受到	to receive	8.31
shǒudū	首都	capital	11.14
shǒujī*	手機/手机	cellular phone	17
shōurù	收入	income	8.35
shòushāng	受傷/受伤	to be injured/ wounded	15.8
shōushi	收拾	to pack, to put in order	11.13
shúxī	熟悉	familiar	1.26
shù	樹/树	tree	19.24
shuài	帥/帅	handsome	7.3
shuǐguǒ	水果	fruit	4.35
shùnbiàn	順便/顺便	conveniently, in passing	15.26
shùnlì	順利/顺利	smooth	1.14
shùnzhe	順著/顺着	to go along	4.10
shuōbudìng	說不定/ 说不定	perhaps	6.32
shuōlái huà cháng	說來話長/ 说来话长	it's a long story	7.6
shuōmíng	說明/说明	to explain, illustration	15.22
shǔtiáor	薯條兒/ 薯条儿	french fries	5.13

shùzì	數字/数字	numeral, digit	17.37	tǎojià-huánjià	討價還價/讨价还价	to bargain	4.36
sǐ	死	dead, to die	12.28	tǎolǐ mǎn tiānxià	桃李滿天下/桃李满天下	to have pupils everywhere	14.41
sìhéyuàn	四合院	compound with houses around a courtyard	4.16	tǎolùn	討論/讨论	to discuss, discussion	2.11
sījīn	絲巾/丝巾	silk scarf	12.4	tǎoyàn	討厭/讨厌	to be disgusted with	6.19
sīxiǎng	思想	thought, thinking, ideology	17.20	tèsè	特色	distinguishing feature/quality	11.33
suàn	算	to regard as	8.32	tī*	踢	to kick	6
suànle*	算了	forget it, let it be, let it pass	12	tiānliàng	天亮	daybreak	4.3
suànmìng	算命	fortune-telling, to tell fortune	17.38	Tiānzhǔjiào	天主教	Catholicism	17.31
suān-tián-kǔ-là	酸甜苦辣	all flavors	5.1	tiáo	條/条	measure word for sth. long and narrow	12.3
suíbiàn	隨便/随便	carelessly, casually, to do as one pleases	16.35	tiào	跳	to jump	19.15
suídì	隨地/随地	anywhere	20.29	tiáojiàn	條件/条件	condition	9.39
suíshēn*	隨身/随身	(take) with one, (carry) on one's person	20	tiāotì	挑剔	nitpicky, to nitpick	5.8
suíshí	隨時/随时	at any time	20.28	tiàowǔ	跳舞	to dance	4.22
suízhe	隨著/随着	along with, in the wake of	16.37	tídào	提到	to mention	3.4
suǒ	所	that, which	19.1	tígāo	提高	to raise, to enhance	20.22
suǒwèi	所謂/所谓	so-called	5.19	tīngdào	聽到/听到	to hear	1.36
suǒyǒu	所有	all	13.33	tīnghuà	聽話/听话	obedient	9.5
T				tíqián	提前	in advance	11.41
tàidu	態度/态度	attitude, manner	13.26	tíxǐng	提醒	to remind	8.8
táifēng*	颱風/台风	typhoon	16	tóngqíng	同情	to sympathize with	18.43
tàijíquán	太極拳/太极拳	a kind of shadow-boxing	4.19	tóngshí	同時/同时	(at) the same time	9.26
tàikōngrén	太空人	astronaut	3.41	tóngshì	同事	colleague	15.23
tàitai	太太	wife, Mrs.	9.1	tóngyì	同意	to agree	8.37
Táiwān	台灣/台湾	Taiwan	11.22	tōngzhī*	通知	to notify, notice	14
tàiyáng	太陽/太阳	sun, sunshine	17.4	tūrán	突然	suddenly	1.25
tán liàn'ài	談戀愛/谈恋爱	to court	6.35	tōudù	偷渡	to steal across international border	16.5
tán*	彈/弹	to play	10	tóuténg	頭疼/头疼	headache	2.33
tào	套	set	2.24	tǔbāozi	土包子	rube, hick	6.26
Táohuāyuán	桃花源	utopia	16.1	tuījiànxìn	推薦信/推荐信	recommendation letter	14.7

tuō'érsuǒ*	托兒所/托儿所	child-care center	9
tuōyùn*	託運/托运	consign for shipment, to check (baggage)	20

W

wàidìrén	外地人	non-local people	18.17
wàihào	外號/外号	nickname	7.12
wàixīngrén	外星人	an extraterrestrial	12.29
wǎn'ān	晚安	Good night!	17.42
wǎndiǎn	晚點/晚点	late	1.20
wǎnfàn	晚飯/晚饭	supper, dinner	18.2
wǎng	網/网	net	6.3
wǎngyǒu	網友/网友	net pal	6.4
wǎngzhàn*	網站/网站	web site	15
wàngzǐ chénglóng	望子成龍/望子成龙	to hope one's children will have a bright future	14.30
wánquán	完全	completely	6.6
wěidà	偉大/伟大	great	6.37
wèile	爲了/为了	for	9.39
wèishēngzhǐ	衛生紙/卫生纸	toilet paper	12.20
wēixiǎn	危險/危险	danger, dangerous	16.12
wéiyī	唯一	only, sole	2.32
wéizhǐ	爲止/为止	up to, till	13.10
wènhǎo	問好/问好	to say hello to	4.44
wénhuà	文化	culture	8.13
wénmáng	文盲	illiterate, illiteracy	18.39
wēnróu	溫柔	gentle and soft	7.30
wénwù	文物	cultural/ historical relics	12.10
wénxué	文學/文学	literature	8.3
wénzhāng	文章	essay, article	15.25
wénzì	文字	characters, script	18.38
wúlùn	無論/无论	no matter what/how, regardless of	2.17
wūrǎn	污染	pollution, to contaminate	12.2

wòshǒu	握手	to shake/ clasp hands	19.20
wù*	霧/雾	fog	19
wùhuì	誤會/误会	to mis-understand	3.5
wùjià	物價/物价	commodity prices	16.21

X

xì	系	department (in a college)	2.35
xià	嚇/吓	to scare	12.41
xiàbān*	下班	to get off work	9
xián	鹹/咸	salty	5.23
xián	嫌	to dislike the fact that	8.23
xiāng	香	fragrant	5.6
xiǎng	響/响	to ring	4.5
xiàng	向	towards (direction)	12.1
xiāng'ài	相愛/相爱	to love each other	8.41
xiāngfǎn	相反	opposite	3.14
xiǎngjiā	想家	to be homesick	3.29
xiànglái	向來/向来	always, all along	6.27
xiǎngniàn	想念	to miss	5.5
xiàngsheng	相聲/相声	cross talk, comical dialogue	18.28
xiǎngshòu	享受	to enjoy, enjoyment	5.40
xiǎngxiàng	想像/想象	to imagine, to fancy	2.19
xiāngxìn	相信	to believe	1.3
xiànmù	羨慕/羡慕	to envy	5.38
xiànshí	現實/现实	reality	10.6
xiànxiàng	現象/现象	phenomenon	16.14
xiǎofàn	小販/小贩	peddler	4.33
xiǎoháir	小孩兒/小孩儿	child	15.5
xiǎohuǒzi	小伙子	young fellow	7.36
xiǎoqi	小氣/小气	stingy	9.22
xiāoxi	消息	news	1.37
xiāoyè	宵夜	midnight snack	13.11
xiǎoyìsi*	小意思	small token of kindly feelings	3
xiàoyuán	校園/校园	campus	4.2

yúshì	於是/于是	thereupon, hence	14.25
yóu	由	by, through, from	11.28
yóu	油	oily, oil	5.14
yǒudeshì	有的是	to have plenty of	5.37
yōudiǎn	優點/优点	merit	20.4
yǒuhǎo	友好	friendly	17.15
yóujiàn	郵件/邮件	postal matter, mail	1.34
yóukè	遊客/游客	tourist	12.22
yǒulì	有利	(to be) advantageous	17.27
yǒulì*	有力	strong, powerful	19
yǒumíng	有名	famous	4.29
yōumò	幽默	humorous	7.34
yǒuqù	有趣	interesting	1.40
yóutiáo	油條/油条	deep-fried twisted dough sticks	11.9
yóuxíng	遊行/游行	to demonstrate, parade	16.18
yóuyú	由於/由于	owing/due/thanks to	16.26
yóuyǒng	游泳	to swim	10.28
yǒuyòng	有用	useful	2.9
yuán	圓/圆	round	3.2
yuángù	緣故/缘故	cause, reason	16.31
yuánlái	原來/原来	as it turns out	1.28
yuànyi	願意/愿意	to be willing	9.38
yuányīn	原因	reason	8.34
yuànzi*	院子	yard	17
yùdào	遇到	to run into	7.10
yuèbǐng	月餅/月饼	moon cake	3.36
yuèdǐ	月底	end of month	12.7
yuèdú	閱讀/阅读	reading comprehension	14.11
yuēhuì	約會/约会	to date	6.23
yuèliang	月亮	moon	3.1
yuèqiú	月球	moon	3.42
yùnqi	運氣/运气	fortune, luck	9.25
yǔqí	與其/与其	rather than	11.35
yùshì*	浴室	bathroom, shower room	2

| yùxí | 預習/预习 | to prepare lessons before class | 2.16 |

Z

zài...kànlái	在···看來/在···看来	in sb.'s view	10.12
zàihu	在乎	to care about, to mind	14.21
zàishuō	再說/再说	besides	8.17
zànchéng	贊成/赞成	to approve	10.37
zāng	髒/脏	dirty	12.24
zǎodiǎn	早點/早点	breakfast	4.7
zěnme huí shì	怎麼回事/怎么回事	what's going on?	19.38
zérèn	責任/责任	duty, responsibility	13.42
zhá	炸	to deep-fry	5.12
zhàdàn	炸彈/炸弹	bomb	15.7
zhàn	佔/占	to occupy	13.35
zhǎng	漲/涨	to rise, to go up	16.22
zhǎngdà	長大/长大	to grow up	8.4
zhāngláng*	蟑螂	cockroach	14
zhǎnlǎn	展覽/展览	show, to exhibit	19.43
zhànxiàn*	佔線/占线	the (phone) line is busy	15
zhàogù	照顧/照顾	to look after	9.30
zhāopai	招牌	shop sign	18.37
zhēng	睜/睁	to open the eyes	19.39
zhēng	爭/争	to fight for	9.20
zhèngfǔ	政府	government	20.36
zhěnglǐ	整理	to put in order	9.8
zhēnglùn	爭論/争论	to argue, dispute	20.7
zhěngqí	整齊/整齐	neat, tidy	2.27
zhèngshū	證書/证书	certificate	14.8
zhèngzhì	政治	politics	11.15
zhēnzhèng	真正	genuine, true, real	15.39
zhéxué	哲學/哲学	philosophy	17.24
zhī jiān	之間/之间	between	6.5
zhídào	直到	until, up to	16.42
zhíde	值得	to deserve, to merit	11.31
zhìdù	制度	system	20.10

◎ By English

English	Pinyin	Characters	Ref
at the slightest provocation	dòngbudòng	動不動/動不動	16.17
attitude	tàidu	態度/态度	13.26
attract, to	xīyǐn	吸引	12.11
author	zuòzhě	作者	19.19
autumn	qiūtiān*	秋天	17
B			
background	bèijǐng	背景	8.14
baked sesame seed flatbread	shāobǐng	燒餅/烧饼	11.8
bargain, to	tǎojià-huánjià	討價還價/讨价还价	4.36
basic	jīběn	基本	18.34
basic	jīchǔ	基礎/基础	18.21
basis	gēnjù	根據/根据	20.11
batch	pī	批	16.4
bathroom	yùshì*	浴室	2
bear hardship, to	chīkǔ	吃苦	5.42
beautiful	měi	美	3.37
bed	chuáng	床	2.20
beef noodles	niúròumiàn	牛肉麵/牛肉面	4.28
believe, to	xiāngxìn	相信	1.3
benefit	hǎochu	好處/好处	10.11
besides	zàishuō	再說/再说	8.17
better	nìngkě	寧可/宁可	15.28
better	qiáng	強/强	14.13
between	zhī jiān	之間/之间	6.5
bias	piānjiàn	偏見/偏见	8.30
bicycle	zìxíngchē	自行車/自行车	4.9
blame, to	guài	怪	15.34
blonde	jīn	金	12.30
boarding pass	dēngjīpái*	登機牌/登机牌	20
boil, to	zhǔ	煮	9.41
boiled water	kāishuǐ	開水/开水	11.6
boiling water	kāishuǐ	開水/开水	11.6
bomb	zhàdàn	炸彈/炸弹	15.7
book, to	dìng	訂/订	11.26
bookworm	shūdāizi	書呆子/书呆子	7.28
boss	lǎobǎn	老板	15.18
both sides (Chinese Mainland and Taiwan)	liǎng'àn	兩岸/两岸	20.3
bottle	píng	瓶	4.40
bottoms up	gānbēi	乾杯/干杯	3.32
boy	nánháir	男孩兒/男孩儿	7.14
boyfriend	duìxiàng	對象/对象	6.40
brag, to	chuīniú	吹牛	7.29
brave, to	mào	冒	16.10
break up, to	fēnshǒu	分手	8.25
breakfast	zǎodiǎn	早點/早点	4.7
brilliant	jīngcǎi	精彩	6.16
bring, to	dài	帶/带	9.9
broadcast, to	guǎngbō	廣播/广播	18.27
Buddhism	Fójiào	佛教	17.28
Buddhist monk	héshang	和尚	19.27
build, to	jiànzhù	建築/建筑	12.9
burn the midnight oil, to	kāi yèchē	開夜車/开夜车	10.43
burn, to	shāo	燒/烧	9.10
business	shāng	商	10.42
business	shēngyi	生意	16.7
but	rán'ér	然而	20.23
but for	yàobushì	要不是	1.15
by	yóu	由	11.28
by all means	qiānwàn	千萬/千万	6.2
C			
café	kāfēiguǎn	咖啡館/咖啡馆	7.7
cake	dàngāo	蛋糕	5.15
call names, to	mà	罵/骂	7.18
calligrapher	shūfǎjiā	書法家/书法家	19.21
campus	xiàoyuán	校園/校园	4.2
can	nénggòu	能夠/能够	20.27
can't compare with	bǐbushàng	比不上	19.42

communicate, to	gōutōng	溝通/沟通	11.11
communism	gòngchǎn zhǔyì	共產主義/共产主义	20.8
company	gōngsī	公司	14.2
compete, to	jìngzhēng	競爭/竞争	16.29
competent	nénggàn	能幹/能干	9.4
competition	jìngzhēng	競爭/竞争	16.29
complain, to	bàoyuàn	抱怨	16.20
completely	wánquán	完全	6.6
complicated	fùzá	複雜/复杂	12.44
compound with houses around a courtyard	sìhéyuàn	四合院	4.16
concept	guānniàn	觀念/观念	8.26
concerned about, to be	guānxīn	關心/关心	3.15
concerning	duì…lái shuō	對…來說/对…来说	3.9
concert	yīnyuèhuì*	音樂會/音乐会	7
condition	tiáojiàn	條件/条件	8.39
confidence	xìnxīn	信心	14.36
conflict	chōngtū	衝突/冲突	17.33
Confucian school	Rújiā	儒家	17.19
confused	hútu	糊塗/糊涂	19.35
consequently	yīncǐ	因此	14.26
conservative	bǎoshǒu	保守	8.27
consider, to	kǎolǜ	考慮/考虑	9.13
consign for shipment, to	tuōyùn*	託運/托运	20
consult, to	shāngliang	商量	9.18
contact, to	liánxì	聯繫/联系	10.44
contaminate, to	wūrǎn	污染	12.2
content	nèiróng	內容	2.6
continuously	búduàn*	不斷/不断	20
contradiction	máodùn	矛盾	15.36
contradictory	máodùn	矛盾	15.36
contribution	gòngxiàn	貢獻/贡献	10.41
convenient	fāngbiàn*	方便	12
conveniently	shùnbiàn	順便/顺便	15.26
cook, to	shāo	燒/烧	9.10
cook, to	zhǔ	煮	9.41
cooperate, to	hézuò	合作	13.40
cooperation	hézuò	合作	13.40
cordial	qīnqiè	親切/亲切	3.7
cost	dàijià*	代價/代价	16
cough, to	késou	咳嗽	19.22
country	guójiā	國家/国家	16.6
court, to	tán liàn'ài	談戀愛/谈恋爱	6.35
crawl, to	pá*	爬	11
crime	fànzuì	犯罪	16.34
cross talk	xiàngsheng	相聲/相声	18.28
crowded	jǐ	擠/挤	12.25
cultural/historical relics	wénwù	文物	12.10
culture	wénhuà	文化	8.13
curious	hàoqí	好奇	2.37
curl, to	juǎn	捲/卷	18.23
curriculum vitae	jiǎnlì	簡歷/简历	14.6
customs	hǎiguān	海關/海关	1.23

D

dance, to	tiàowǔ	跳舞	4.22
danger	wēixiǎn	危險/危险	16.12
dangerous	wēixiǎn	危險/危险	16.12
Daoism (as a religion)	Dàojiào	道教	17.29
dare, to	gǎn	敢	1.2
date, to	yuēhuì	約會/约会	6.23
day	báitiān	白天	14.31
day(s)	rìzi	日子	5.30
daybreak	tiānliàng	天亮	4.3
daytime	báitiān	白天	14.31
day-to-day	rìcháng	日常	14.10
dead	sǐ	死	12.28
deceive, to	piàn	騙/骗	15.32
decline, to	cí	辭/辞	14.27
deep	shēn	深	17.21
deep breathing exercises	qìgōng	氣功/气功	4.20

elephant	dàxiàng*	大象	13
emerge, to	chūxiàn	出現/出现	19.6
emigrant	yímín	移民	5.29
enchanted with, to be	mí	迷	6.11
encouragement	gǔlì	鼓勵/鼓励	9.7
end of month	yuèdǐ	月底	12.7
end, to	jiéshù	結束/结束	11.2
energy	néngyuán	能源	13.39
enhance, to	tígāo	提高	20.22
enjoy, to	xiǎngshòu	享受	5.40
enrich, to	fēngfù	豐富/丰富	16.25
enter higher school, to	shēngxué	升學/升学	16.27
entertainment	yúlè	娛樂/娱乐	20.24
enthusiastic	rèqíng	熱情/热情	3.6
environment	huánjìng	環境/环境	12.26
envy, to	xiànmù	羨慕/羡慕	5.38
equal	píngděng	平等	9.43
era	shídài*	時代/时代	15
essay	wénzhāng	文章	15.25
essential	jīběn	基本	18.34
etc.	děngděng	等等	2.43
ethnic Chinese of other nationalities	Huáyì	華裔/华裔	8.22
ethnic group	zhǒngzú	種族/种族	17.34
ethnic group/ minority	mínzú	民族	17.18
Europe	Ōuzhōu	歐洲/欧洲	13.5
even	gèng	更	1.41
even	jíshǐ	即使	10.14
even if	jiùsuàn	就算	10.13
even if/though	jíshǐ	即使	10.14
even so	rán'ér	然而	20.23
even though	jǐnguǎn	儘管/尽管	14.38
every	fánshì	凡是	19.2
everything	fánshì	凡事	17.23
everything	yíqiè	一切	1.13
everywhere	dàochù	到處/到处	11.18
example	lìzi	例子	15.21

exception	lìwài	例外	10.7
excessive	guòfèn	過分/过分	13.27
excitement/ doubt (了 plus 啊), indicating	la	啦	18.25
excuse	jièkǒu	藉口/借口	15.31
excuse	jièkǒu*	藉口/借口	9
excuse me	láojià*	勞駕/劳驾	12
exercise, to	huódòng	活動/活动	2.14
exhibit, to	zhǎnlǎn	展覽/展览	19.43
exhibition	biǎoyǎn	表演	19.41
exit	chūkǒu	出口	1.24
explain, to	shuōmíng	說明/说明	15.22
expound, to	jiěshì	解釋/解释	20.16
express good wishes, to	zhù	祝	11.43
extinct, to become	juézhǒng	絕種/绝种	13.23
extra-curricular	kèwài	課外/课外	2.13
extra-terrestrial, an	wàixīngrén	外星人	12.29
extravagant	làngfèi	浪費/浪费	13.30
extremely	-jíle	極了/极了	2.31
extremely	yàomìng	要命	3.23

F

face	miànzi	面子	15.1
faith	xìnxīn	信心	14.36
fall in love with, to	àishang	愛上/爱上	8.1
fall, to	diē/dié	跌	16.24
familiar	shúxī	熟悉	1.26
family	jiātíng	家庭	9.33
famous	chūmíng*	出名	10
famous	yǒumíng	有名	4.29
famous school	míngxiào	名校	10.32
fancy, to	xiǎngxiàng	想像/想象	2.19
fashionable	shímáo	時髦/时髦	6.41
fast food	kuàicān	快餐	13.4
fat	pàng	胖	5.34
favorable impression	hǎogǎn	好感	6.21
fearful	kěpà	可怕	13.31
feel happy, to	kāixīn	開心/开心	5.43

goal	mùdì	目的	15.40
god	shén	神	17.8
gold	jīn	金	12.30
good luck	hǎoyùn	好運/好运	17.13
Good night!	Wǎn'ān	晚安	17.42
government	zhèngfǔ	政府	20.36
grade	chéngjī/jì	成績/成绩	10.19
gradually	jiànjiàn	漸漸/渐渐	17.1
graduate student	yánjiūshēng	研究生	7.27
grandfather (paternal)	yéye*	爺爺/爷爷	17
grateful, to be	gǎnxiè	感謝/感谢	12.17
grave	yánzhòng	嚴重/严重	12.43
greasy	nì	膩/腻	5.16
great	wěidà	偉大/伟大	6.37
great demand, in	rèmén	熱門/热门	10.18
green	shēng	生	5.21
greet, to	dǎ zhāohu	打招呼	18.6
group	pī	批	16.4
grow up, to	zhǎngdà	長大/长大	8.4
grumble, to	bàoyuàn	抱怨	16.20
guest	kèren	客人	15.13

H

ha ha (sound of laughter)	hāhā	哈哈	18.7
habit	xíguàn	習慣/习惯	11.5
had better	zuìhǎo	最好	11.40
half a kilo-gram	jīn*	斤	4
ham	huǒtuǐ*	火腿/火腿	5
hand over, to	jiāo	交	2.42
handle, to	bàn	辦/办	1.11
handsome	shuài	帥/帅	7.3
happen, to	fāshēng	發生/发生	19.31
happiness	xìngfú	幸福	8.40
happy	yúkuài	愉快	3.30
happy lot	fúqi*	福氣/福气	3
hard	yìng*	硬	2
hate to part with or use, to	shěbude	捨不得/舍不得	11.3

have a hard time (doing sth.), to	hǎoróngyì	好容易	9.29
have an effect, to	qǐ zuòyòng	起作用	20.19
have blind faith in, to	míxìn	迷信	17.35
have diarrhea, to	lādùzi	拉肚子	4.42
have plenty of, to	yǒudeshì	有的是	5.37
have pupils everywhere, to	táolǐ mǎn tiānxià	桃李滿天下/桃李满天下	14.41
headache	tóuténg	頭疼/头疼	2.33
health	jiànkāng	健康	5.4
hear, to	tīngdào	聽到/听到	1.36
heart	zhōngxīn	中心	11.16
help	bāngzhù	幫助/帮助	15.29
hen's egg	jīdàn*	雞蛋/鸡蛋	5
hence	yúshì	於是/于是	14.25
hick	tǔbāozi	土包子	6.26
high in rank	gāojí	高級/高级	4.31
hire a taxi, to	dǎdī	打的	11.10
history	lìshǐ	歷史/历史	2.34
hobby	àihào	愛好/爱好	6.10
hold, to	zhuāng	裝/装	15.15
holiday	jiérì	節日/节日	3.22
home tutoring	jiājiào	家教	14.16
homesick, to be	xiǎngjiā	想家	3.29
hope one's children will have a bright future, to	wàngzǐ chénglóng	望子成龍/望子成龙	14.30
hopeful	lèguān	樂觀/乐观	20.31
hotel	fàndiàn*	飯店/饭店	15
household duties	jiāwù	家務/家务	9.6
housekeeper	bǎomǔ*	褓姆/保姆	9
housewife	zhǔfù	主婦/主妇	9.34
how	duō(me)	多(麼)/多(么)	6.24
however	què	卻/却	2.30

lamp	dēng	燈/灯	13.34
landscape (painting)	shānshuǐ	山水	19.8
lane	hútòng	胡同	4.15
last time	shàngcì	上次	3.3
late	wǎndiǎn	晚點/晚点	1.20
lead to, to	yǐnqǐ	引起	14.39
lean	shòu	瘦	5.33
lean on, to	kào	靠	6.39
learn, to	xuéxí	學習/学习	1.43
leave message, to	liúyán	留言	15.4
leave, to	líkāi	離開/离开	11.4
lecture sb., to	jiàoxun	教訓/教训	18.9
lesson	jiàoxun	教訓/教训	18.9
let it be	suànle*	算了	12
let it pass	suànle*	算了	12
let sb. down, to	duìbuqǐ	對不起/对不起	14.15
life (physical)	shēngmìng	生命	16.11
lion	shīzi*	獅子/狮子	13
literature	wénxué	文學/文学	8.3
lively	shēngdòng*	生動/生动	19
lonely	jìmò	寂寞	3.18
long distance	chángtú*	長途/长途	8
long time, a	bàntiān	半天	1.19
longwinded	luōsuo	囉嗦/罗嗦	8.24
look after, to	dài	帶/带	9.9
look after, to	zhàogù	照顧/照顾	9.30
lose face, to	diūliǎn	丟臉/丢脸	15.16
lot	pī	批	16.4
love each other, to	xiāng'ài	相愛/相爱	8.41
lovely	kě'ài	可愛/可爱	7.31
luck	yùnqi	運氣/运气	9.25
luggage	xíngli	行李	1.21
M			
magical	shén	神	17.8
mail	yóujiàn	郵件/邮件	1.34
main	zhǔyào	主要	18.40
mainland China	dàlù	大陸/大陆	11.24
maintain, to	bǎochí	保持	20.30

make (friends), to	jiāo	交	2.42
make a do-or-die effort, to	pīnmìng	拼命	5.36
make a fool of oneself, to	nào xiàohua	鬧笑話/闹笑话	18.4
make use of, to	jiè	藉/借	20.1
manager	jīnglǐ*	經理/经理	14
Mandarin Chinese	pǔtōnghuà	普通話/普通话	18.15
manner	tàidu	態度/态度	13.26
map	dìtú	地圖/地图	12.45
march, to	shìwēi	示威	16.19
marry, (of a woman) to	jià	嫁	8.18
master worker	shīfu*	師傅/师傅	1
matter	shìqing	事情	1.44
meaning	yìsi	意思	3.12
means	bànfǎ	辦法/办法	3.20
means	fāngfǎ	方法	15.33
measure word for money	bǐ	筆/笔	16.9
measure word for jobs, copies, etc.	fēn(r)	份(兒)/份(儿)	9.27
measure word for letters	fēng	封	1.32
measure word for cars	liàng*	輛/辆	16
measure word for songs, poems	shǒu*	首	14
measure word for sth. long and narrow	tiáo	條/条	12.3
meddle, to	guǎn xiánshì	管閑事/管闲事	2.1
media	méitǐ	媒體/媒体	20.25
medical science	yī	醫/医	8.21
medicine	yào	藥/药	5.3
meet, to	jiànmiàn	見面/见面	1.38
melon	guā	瓜	4.34
men and women, old and young	nán-nǚ-lǎo-shào	男女老少	4.18

mental burden	xīnshì	心事	6.34		nation	guójiā	國家/国家	16.6
mention, to	tídào	提到	3.4		nation	mínzú	民族	17.18
menu	càidān*	菜單/菜单	5		native place	lǎojiā*	老家	3
merely	guāngshì	光是	16.41		natural(ly)	zìrán	自然	3.10
merit	yōudiǎn	優點/优点	20.4		nature	zìrán	自然	3.10
merit, to	zhíde	值得	11.31		neat	zhěngqí	整齊/整齐	2.27
messy	luàn	亂/乱	12.37		need, to	xūyào	需要	9.11
method	fāngfǎ	方法	15.33		neighbor	línjū	鄰居/邻居	15.12
middle	zhōngjiān	中間/中间	4.13		nervous	jǐnzhāng	緊張/紧张	7.8
midnight snack	xiāoyè	宵夜	13.11		net	wǎng	網/网	6.3
mind, to	zàihu	在乎	14.21		net pal	wǎngyǒu	網友/网友	6.4
miserable	cǎn	慘/惨	4.43		new word	shēngcí	生詞/生词	2.7
miss, to	xiǎngniàn	想念	5.5		news	xiāoxi	消息	1.37
misunder-stand, to	wùhuì	誤會/误会	3.5		news	xīnwén	新聞/新闻	16.3
					nickname	wàihào	外號/外号	7.12
monkey	hóuzi	猴子	19.25		night market	yèshì	夜市	13.6
monster	guàiwu	怪物	12.31		nitpick, to	tiāotì	挑剔	5.8
mood	xīnqíng	心情	3.26		nitpicky	tiāotì	挑剔	5.8
moon	yuèliang	月亮	3.1		no good, to be	bùxíng	不行	5.10
moon	yuèqiú	月球	3.42		no matter what/how	wúlùn	無論/无论	2.17
moon cake	yuèbǐng	月餅/月饼	3.36		no wonder	guàibude	怪不得	5.39
mother	mǔqin	母親/母亲	9.36		no wonder	nánguài	難怪/难怪	7.39
motorcycle	jīchē <TW>	機車/机车	12.38		nod, to	dǎ kēshuì	打瞌睡	14.22
mouse	lǎoshǔ*	老鼠	14		non-local people	wàidìrén	外地人	18.17
mouth	zuǐ	嘴	18.19		not only	búdàn	不但	5.31
Mrs.	tàitai	太太	9.1		not only... but also...	jì...yě	既…也	3.19
muddled	hútu	糊塗/糊涂	19.35		notice	tōngzhī*	通知	14
mung bean soup	lǜdòutāng	綠豆湯/绿豆汤	13.13		notify, to	tōngzhī*	通知	14
museum	bówùguǎn	博物館/博物馆	11.17		now that	jìrán	既然	14.28
					number	hàomǎ*	號碼/号码	17
musician	yīnyuèjiā*	音樂家/音乐家	10		numeral	shùzì	數字/数字	17.37
					nutrition	yíngyǎng*	營養/营养	5
must	bìxū	必須/必须	9.3		**O**			
must	fēi...bùkě	非…不可	8.7		obedient	tīnghuà	聽話/听话	9.5
mutually	hùxiāng	互相	7.26		occupation	zhíyè	職業/职业	9.31
myth	shénhuà	神話/神话	16.43		occupy, to	zhàn	佔/占	13.35
mythology	shénhuà	神話/神话	16.43		often	chángcháng	常常	2.10
N					often	jīngcháng	經常/经常	18.30
nanny	bǎomǔ*	褓姆/保姆	9		Oh!	ài	唉	7.40

pick sb. up, to	jiē	接	1.30
pick up (phone call), to	jiē	接	15.3
piece of writing	piān	篇	15.24
pig's feet	zhūjiǎo	豬腳/猪脚	13.16
pineapple	fēnglí*	鳳梨/凤梨	13
ping-pong	pīngpāng qiú*	乒乓球	6
pitiable	kělián	可憐/可怜	13.22
place	dìfang	地方	2.18
places of historic interest and scenic beauty	míngshèng-gǔjī	名勝古蹟/名胜古迹	11.19
plan	jìhuà	計劃/计划	11.34
plan, to	ānpái	安排	11.30
plane ticket	jīpiào	機票/机票	1.12
play chess, to	xiàqí	下棋	4.23
play, to	tán*	彈/弹	10
plump	pàng	胖	5.34
poem	shī	詩/诗	19.11
polite	lǐmào	禮貌/礼貌	3.8
polite, to be	kèqi	客氣/客气	3.35
politics	zhèngzhì	政治	11.15
pollution	wūrǎn	污染	12.2
poor	chà	差	14.19
poor	kělián	可憐/可怜	13.22
poor wretch	qióngguāng dàn	窮光蛋/穷光蛋	10.3
population	rénkǒu	人口	13.37
positive	kěndìng	肯定	18.41
postal matter	yóujiàn	郵件/邮件	1.34
postcard	míngxìnpiàn	明信片	11.42
pour (tea, water), to	dào	倒	13.43
powerful	qiáng	強/强	14.13
powerful	yǒulì*	有力	19
practical	shíjì	實際/实际	17.22
practical	shíjì*	實際/实际	10
practice field	cāochǎng	操場/操场	18.3
praise, to	chēngzàn	稱讚/称赞	18.8

prepare lessons before class, to	yùxí	預習/预习	2.16
pressure	yālì	壓力/压力	16.28
price	dàijià*	代價/代价	16
principal	zhǔyào	主要	18.40
privilege	quánlì	權利/权利	20.38
probably	dàgài	大概	13.8
professor	jiàoshòu*	教授	1
program	jiémù	節目/节目	6.20
project	jìhuà	計劃/计划	11.34
pronounce, to	fāyīn	發音/发音	18.12
pronunciation,	fāyīn	發音/发音	18.12
prospects	qiántú	前途	10.10
prosperous	fánróng	繁榮/繁荣	20.18
protect, to	bǎohù	保護/保护	12.27
protection	bǎohù	保護/保护	12.27
province	shěng	省	13.3
public	gōnggòng*	公共	2
public	gōnglì	公立	10.20
public square	guǎngchǎng	廣場/广场	4.11
public, the	rénmen	人們/人们	13.18
purpose	mùdì	目的	15.40
put away, to	shōu	收	18.26
put in order, to	zhěnglǐ	整理	9.8
put in order, to	shōushi	收拾	11.13
Q			
quarrel, to	chǎojià	吵架	7.15
quit (a job), to	cí*	辭/辞	9
quit, to	cí	辭/辞	14.27
R			
race	zhǒngzú	種族/种族	17.34
rain, to	xiàyǔ*	下雨	17
raise, to	tígāo	提高	20.22
rare	nándé	難得/难得	11.23
rat	lǎoshǔ*	老鼠	14
rather than	yǔqí	與其/与其	11.35
raw	shēng	生	5.21
reading com-prehension	yuèdú	閱讀/阅读	14.11
real	zhēnzhèng	眞正	15.39

real man, a	nánzǐhàn	男子漢/男子汉	9.23	ride, to	qí	騎/骑	4.8
reality	shíjì	實際/实际	17.22	right	quánlì	權利/权利	20.38
reality	xiànshí	現實/现实	10.6	ring, to	xiǎng	響/响	4.5
realize, to	shíxiàn	實現/实现	10.22	rise, to	zhǎng	漲/涨	16.22
really	shízài	實在/实在	3.17	risk, to	mào	冒	16.10
reason	dàolǐ	道理	10.39	river	jiāng	江	19.18
reason	yuángù	緣故/缘故	16.31	RMB	Rénmínbì*	人民幣/人民币	11
reason	yuányīn	原因	8.34	roast, to	shāo	燒/烧	9.10
receive, to	shòudào	受到	8.31	roll, to	juǎn	捲/卷	18.23
recognize, to	rèn	認/认	7.23	romantic love	àiqíng	愛情/爱情	8.19
recommend-dation letter	tuījiànxìn	推薦信/推荐信	14.7	room	fángjiān	房間/房间	11.27
				round	yuán	圓/圆	3.2
red paper bag with gift money	hóngbāo	紅包/红包	15.14	row boat, to	huáchuán*	划船	6
				rube	tǔbāozi	土包子	6.26
reflections	gǎnxiǎng	感想	20.26	rug	dìtǎn	地毯	2.28
reform	gǎigé	改革	20.34	run into, to	yùdào	遇到	7.10
reform, to	gǎigé	改革	20.34	run, to	pǎo	跑	1.29
regard as, to	suàn	算	8.32	**S**			
regardless of	bùguǎn	不管	2.36	sad, to be	shāngxīn	傷心/伤心	19.33
regardless of	wúlùn	無論/无论	2.17	saddle up to, to	lā guānxi	拉關係/拉关系	14.4
regional accent	kǒuyīn	口音	18.18				
religion	zōngjiào	宗教	17.26	safe	ānquán	安全	16.32
religious, to be	xìnjiào	信教	17.11	safe and sound	píng'ān	平安	11.44
				salary	xīnshui	薪水	14.18
				salt	yán*	鹽/盐	5
rely on, to	kào	靠	6.39	salty	xián	鹹/咸	5.23
remind, to	tíxǐng	提醒	8.8	same place, in the	yìqǐ	一起	8.10
rent	fángzū*	房租	13				
reply, to	huídá	回答	12.33	same time, (at) the	tóngshí	同時/同时	9.26
respect, to	zūnjìng	尊敬	10.35	satisfied	mǎnyì	滿意/满意	7.5
respectfully submitted	jìngshàng	敬上	8.44	save, to	shěng	省	13.3
				say hello to, to	wènhǎo	問好/问好	4.44
responsibility	zérèn	責任/责任	13.42	scare, to	xià	嚇/吓	12.41
rest, the	qítā	其他	12.32	scared, to be	hàipà	害怕	19.25
restaurant	cāntīng	餐廳/餐厅	4.27	scenery	jǐngsè*	景色	19
restaurant	fàndiàn*	飯店/饭店	15	science and technology	kējì	科技	20.17
result	jiéguǒ	結果/结果	4.41				
résumé	jiǎnlì	簡歷/简历	14.6	scold, to	mà	罵/骂	7.18
review, to	fùxí	複習/复习	2.15	scorn, to	kànbuqǐ	看不起	9.21
rich	fēngfù	豐富/丰富	16.25	script	wénzì	文字	18.38

sea	hǎi	海	17.9
sea of people, a	rénshān-rénhǎi*	人山人海	13
secondhand smoke	èrshǒuyān	二手煙/二手烟	12.19
secret	mìmì	秘密	6.1
section	bùfen	部分	12.16
secure sth. through pull or influence, to	zǒu hòumén	走後門/走后门	14.5
security	ānquán	安全	16.32
see, to	jiàndào	見到/见到	7.2
see, to	jiànmiàn	見面/见面	1.38
seek advice, to	qǐngjiào	請教/请教	19.12
select, to	xuǎnzé	選擇/选择	10.17
sense	dàolǐ	道理	10.39
sense	gǎn	感	10.21
sentence	jù	句	8.6
sentence pattern	jùxíng	句型	2.8
serious	rènzhēn	認真/认真	18.33
serious	yánzhòng	嚴重/严重	12.43
serve, to	fúwù	服務/服务	17.16
service	fúwù	服務/服务	17.16
set	tào	套	2.24
set out, to	chūfā	出發/出发	12.5
settle, to	jiějué	解決/解决	13.41
shadow-boxing, a kind of	tàijíquán	太極拳/太极拳	4.19
shake hands, to	wòshǒu	握手	19.20
sharp	lìhai	厲害/厉害	9.16
sheep	yáng	羊	14.35
shocked, to be	chījīng	吃驚/吃惊	12.34
shoes	xiézi	鞋子	6.30
shoot film, to	pāi	拍	6.13
shoot, to	kāiqiāng	開槍/开枪	16.36
shop	shāngdiàn	商店	4.25
shop sign	zhāopai	招牌	18.37
short of, to be	quē	缺	14.1

short period of time, a	yízhènzi	一陣子/一阵子	16.2
short supply, in	jǐnzhāng	緊張/紧张	11.39
shortcoming	máobing	毛病	7.24
shortcoming	quēdiǎn	缺點/缺点	20.5
show	zhǎnlǎn	展覽/展览	19.43
shower room	yùshì*	浴室	2
side	fāngmiàn	方面	15.37
silk scarf	sījīn	絲巾/丝巾	12.4
simple	jiǎndān	簡單/简单	17.41
simple meal	jiācháng biànfàn	家常便飯/家常便饭	3.31
simplified characters	jiǎntǐzì	簡體字/简体字	18.35
simply	gēnběn	根本	3.24
since	jìrán	既然	14.28
since	-yǐlái	以來/以来	2.39
since	zìcóng	自從/自从	4.1
situation	qíngkuàng	情況/情况	1.39
small token of kindly feelings	xiǎoyìsi*	小意思	3
smelly	chòu*	臭	13
smooth	shùnlì	順利/顺利	1.14
snow, to	xiàxuě*	下雪	17
so far as (to go)	zhìyú	至於/至于	14.14
so long as	zhǐyào	只要	4.30
so much so that	shènzhì	甚至	2.23
so-called	suǒwèi	所謂/所谓	5.19
soccer	zúqiú	足球	6.12
sofa	shāfā	沙發/沙发	2.25
soft	ruǎn*	軟/软	2
software	ruǎntǐ* <TW>	軟體/软体	15
sole	wéiyī	唯一	2.32
solve, to	jiějué	解決/解决	13.41
son	érzi	兒子/儿子	15.9
sort	zhǒng	種/种	12.12
sound	shēngyīn	聲音/声音	1.27
souvenir	jìniànpǐn	紀念品/纪念品	12.6

soy sauce	jiàngyóu*	醬油/酱油	5
soybean milk	dòujiāng	豆漿/豆浆	11.7
spareribs	páigǔ	排骨	7.17
speak, to	jiǎng	講/讲	8.38
special	zhuānmén	專門/专门	14.33
specialized	zhuānmén	專門/专门	14.33
spoken/ vernacular language	kǒuyǔ	口語/口语	18.32
spouse	àiren	愛人/爱人	9.2
spouse	àiren*	愛人/爱人	3
spring	chūntiān*	春天	17
Spring Festival	chūnjié	春節/春节	11.1
squeeze , to	jǐ	擠/挤	12.25
standard	biāozhǔn	標準/标准	18.1
star	míngxīng	明星	6.17
state	guójiā	國家/国家	16.6
steal across international border, to	tōudù	偷渡	16.5
stingy	xiǎoqi	小氣/小气	9.22
stir-fry, to	chǎo	炒	5.20
stock	gǔpiào	股票	16.23
story	gùshi	故事	3.40
strait	hǎixiá	海峽/海峡	20.2
strenuous	chīlì	吃力	11.12
stress, to	jiǎng	講/讲	8.38
stress, to	qiángdiào	強調/强调	20.33
strong	qiáng	強/强	14.13
strong	yǒulì*	有力	19
study abroad, to	liúxué	留學/留学	1.5
study, to	xuéxí	學習/学习	1.43
stupid	bèn*	笨	19
submit (a letter), to	shàng	上	1.35
subscribe, to	dìng	訂/订	11.26
succeed, to	chénggōng	成功	10.33
success	chénggōng	成功	10.33
successful	chénggōng	成功	10.33
such as	lìrú	例如	13.15
suddenly	hūrán	忽然	17.5
suddenly	tūrán	突然	1.25

suffer excessive internal heat, to	shànghuǒ	上火	13.14
suffer loss, to	chīkuī	吃虧/吃亏	16.40
suggestion	jiànyì	建議/建议	11.32
sun	tàiyáng	太陽/太阳	17.4
sunshine	tàiyáng	太陽/太阳	17.4
super-natural	shén	神	17.8
superstition	míxìn	迷信	17.35
supper	wǎnfàn	晚飯/晚饭	18.2
supplemental studies program	bǔxíbān	補習班/ 补习班	14.29
support, to	yǎnghuo	養活/养活	10.40
sure enough	guǒrán	果然	14.37
surely	díquè	的確/的确	12.21
surface	biǎomiàn	表面	20.32
surmount, to	kèfú	克服	8.42
surrounding	zhōuwéi	周圍/周围	19.5
suspect, to	huáiyí	懷疑/怀疑	15.38
swim, to	yóuyǒng	游泳	10.28
swindle, to	piàn	騙/骗	15.32
sympathize with, to	tóngqíng	同情	18.43
system	zhìdù	制度	20.10
T			
table	zhuōzi	桌子	2.21
Taiwan	Táiwān	台灣/台湾	11.22
take a bird on a stroll, to	liùniǎo*	遛鳥/遛鸟	4
take a picture, to	pāi	拍	6.13
take a walk, to	sànbù	散步	13.12
take advan-tage of (an opportunity)	jiè	藉/借	20.1
take advan-tage of, to	lìyòng	利用	15.27
take back, to	shōu	收	18.26
take to heart, to	rènzhēn	認真/认真	18.33
taken in, to be	shàngdàng	上當/上当	4.38
tale	gùshi	故事	3.40
tall and big	gāodà	高大	19.9
taste, to	cháng	嚐/尝	5.2

taxi	chūzū qìchē <PRC>	出租汽車/ 出租汽车	12.40
taxi	jìchéngchē <TW>	計程車/ 計程车	12.39
teaching materials	jiàocái	教材	2.4
tell fortune, to	suànmìng	算命	17.38
tell the truth, to	lǎoshíshuō	老實說/ 老实说	5.7
temple	miào	廟/庙	17.10
tense	jǐnzhāng	緊張/紧张	7.8
terrible	kěpà	可怕	13.31
terrific	liǎobuqǐ	了不起	18.11
test	kǎoshì	考試/考试	10.30
test paper	kǎojuàn*	考卷	14
test, to	kǎoshì	考試/考试	10.30
text	kèwén	課文/课文	2.12
textbook	kèběn	課本/课本	2.5
thank, to	gǎnxiè	感謝/感谢	12.17
thanks to	yóuyú	由於/由于	16.26
that	suǒ	所	19.1
the (phone) line is busy	zhànxiàn*	佔線/占线	15
then	dāngshí	當時/当时	15.20
there is no need	hébì	何必	19.32
therefore	yīncǐ	因此	14.26
thereupon	yúshì	於是/于是	14.25
thick	hòu	厚	7.20
thin	shòu	瘦	5.33
think over, to	kǎolǜ	考慮/考虑	9.13
think that, to	rènwéi	認爲/认为	6.25
thinking	sīxiǎng	思想	17.20
thirsty	kě	渴	4.39
thought	sīxiǎng	思想	17.20
thoughtless	cūxīn*	粗心	19
thoughts	gǎnxiǎng	感想	20.26
through	yóu	由	11.28
tidy	zhěngqí	整齊/整齐	2.27
tiger	lǎohǔ*	老虎	13
till	wéizhǐ	爲止/为止	13.10
times	bèi	倍	18.29
times	shídài*	時代/时代	15

tired of	nì	膩/腻	5.16
together	yìqǐ	一起	8.10
toilet paper	wèishēngzhǐ	衛生紙/ 卫生纸	12.20
tongue	shétou	舌頭/舌头	18.22
tonic	bǔpǐn	補品/补品	13.19
too busy to deal with	mángbuguò lái	忙不過來/ 忙不过来	3.25
touching	gǎnrén	感人	19.13
tough	lǎo	老	5.22
tour group	lǚyóutuán	旅遊團/ 旅游团	11.25
tour, to	cānguān	參觀/参观	11.20
tourist	yóukè	遊客/游客	12.22
towards (direction)	xiàng	向	12.1
town	chéngshì	城市	11.21
trade	shēngyi	生意	16.7
tradition	chuántǒng	傳統/传统	17.25
traditional	chuántǒng	傳統/传统	17.25
traditional characters	fántǐzì	繁體字/ 繁体字	18.36
traffic	jiāotōng	交通	12.36
traffic jam	sāichē	塞車/塞车	12.42
train	huǒchē	火車/火车	11.36
train, to	xùnliàn	訓練/训练	14.34
training	xùnliàn	訓練/训练	14.34
translate, to	fānyì	翻譯/翻译	14.9
translation	fānyì	翻譯/翻译	14.9
translator	fānyì	翻譯/翻译	14.9
travel agent	lǚxíngshè	旅行社	11.29
traveller	lǚkè*	旅客	20
treat sb. (to meal/show/ etc.), to	qǐngkè	請客/请客	15.30
tree	shù	樹/树	19.24
true	zhēnzhèng	眞正	15.39
tumble, to	diē/dié	跌	16.24
turn, to	guǎi*	拐	4
tutor	jiājiào	家教	14.16
type	zhǒng	種/种	12.12
typhoon	táifēng*	颱風/台风	16

U

unavoidable, to be	miǎnbuliǎo	免不了	20.6
understand, to	liǎojiě	了解	3.16
understand, to	lǐjiě	理解	10.23
unexpected	yìwài	意外	19.3
unexpectedly	jìngrán	竟然	7.9
unexpectedly	jūrán	居然	2.40
unexpectedly	méixiǎng dào	沒想到	2.38
uninterrupted	búduàn*	不斷/不断	20
unit, (work)	dānwèi*	單位/单位	12
universal	pǔbiàn	普遍	16.15
until	zhídào	直到	16.42
up to	wéizhǐ	為止/为止	13.10
up to	zhídào	直到	16.42
upbringing	jiājiào	家教	14.16
use, to	lìyòng	利用	15.27
useful	yǒuyòng	有用	2.9
utopia	Táohuāyuán	桃花源	16.1

V

value, to	zhòngshì	重視/重视	10.24
vegetarian, to be a	chīsù*	吃素	5
view	jǐngsè*	景色	19
view	kànfǎ	看法	8.36
visa	qiānzhèng	簽證/签证	1.10
visit, to	cānguān	參觀/参观	11.20
visitor	kèren	客人	15.13
vivid	shēngdòng*	生動/生动	19

W

wages	xīnshui	薪水	14.18
wake up, to	xǐng	醒	14.23
warm	rèqíng	熱情/热情	3.6
warm, (nice and)	nuǎnhuo	暖和	17.2
waste, to	làngfèi	浪費/浪费	13.30
way	bànfǎ	辦法/办法	3.20
way of doing sth.	zuòfǎ	做法	13.32
wear (glasses, etc), to	dài	戴	7.19
web site	wǎngzhàn*	網站/网站	15
wedding feast	xǐjiǔ	喜酒	15.10

welcome, to	huānyíng*	歡迎/欢迎	1
welcome, to	jiē	接	15.3
well-behaved	guāi	乖	19.28
well-known	chūmíng*	出名	10
well-paying job	jīnfànwǎn	金飯碗/金饭碗	14.40
what	duō(me)	多(麼)/多(么)	6.24
What's going on?	Zěnme huí shì	怎麼回事/怎么回事	19.38
which	suǒ	所	19.1
whole journey	yílù	一路	11.38
widespread	pǔbiàn	普遍	16.15
wife	qīzi	妻子	9.37
wife	tàitai	太太	9.1
willing, to be	yuànyi	願意/愿意	9.38
wind is blowing, the	guāfēng	颱風/刮风	17.3
window	chuānghu*	窗戶	17
winter	dōngtiān	冬天	13.17
wish, to	zhù*	祝	3
with great difficulty	hǎoróngyì	好容易	9.29
with one, (take)	suíshēn*	隨身/随身	20
with regard to	guānyú	關於/关于	3.38
wok	guōzi*	鍋子/锅子	5
woman	nǔxìng	女性	9.32
won't leave without seeing each other	bú jiàn bú sàn*	不見不散/不见不散	7
wordy	luōsuo	囉嗦/罗嗦	8.24
work, to	gōngzuò	工作	9.7
worker	gōngrén	工人	12.14
works (of literature/art)	zuòpǐn	作品	19.14
world	shìjiè	世界	13.36
worry	xīnshì	心事	6.34
worship, to	bài	拜	17.7
worship, to	chóngbài	崇拜	17.40
would rather	nìngkě	寧可/宁可	15.28

Index 2. Characters

◎ By Pinyin

Pinyin	Character	S #	L. C #
A			
ài	愛/爱	13	6.4
ān	安	6	11.20
àn	按	9	20.19
àn	岸	8	20.20
B			
bái	白	5	8.10
bài	拜	9	17.9
bān	般	10	5.20
bān	班	10	7.20
bǎn	板	8	15.16
bǎo	飽/饱	13	5.12
bǎo	保	9	8.7
bào	抱	8	16.17
bēi	杯	8	3.4
bèi	倍	10	18.19
bèi	背	9	8.3
bǐ	筆/笔	12	16.12
bì	畢/毕	10	14.7
biàn	遍	12	16.8
biàn	便	9	3.11
biāo	標/标	15	18.3
biǎo	表	8	19.12
bìng	並/并	8	3.17
bō	播	15	18.12
bù	部	10	12.20
bù	步	7	4.14
bǔ	補/补	12	14.10
C			
cái	財/财	10	16.18
cāi	猜	11	7.17
cǎi	彩	11	6.12
cān	參/参	11	11.3
cān	餐	16	4.12
chā	差	9	14.6
chà	差	9	14.6
chāi	差	9	14.6
chǎn	產/产	11	20.4
cháo	朝	12	19.19
chéng	成	6	10.11
chéng	城	9	5.14
chēng	稱/称	14	18.1
chí	持	9	20.11
chūn	春	9	11.17
chōng	衝/冲	15	17.15
chòng	衝/冲	15	17.15
chǔ	處/处	11	10.9
chǔ	礎/础	18	18.6
chǔ	楚	13	6.10
chuáng	床	7	2.8
cǐ	此	6	14.18
cōng	聰/聪	17	7.8
D			
dá	答	12	12.18
dā	答	12	12.18
dāi	呆	7	7.7
dài	戴	17	7.10
dài	代	5	8.19
dàn	彈/弹	15	15.11
dàn	蛋	11	5.9
dǎo	導/导	15	6.5
dēng	燈/灯	16	13.11
dì	地	6	2.14
diào	調/调	15	20.8
diē	跌	12	18.8
diū	丢	6	15.2
dú	讀/读	22	14.4
dōng	冬	5	13.15
dù	度	9	13.2
dù	肚	7	4.17
duàn	段	9	15.15
dùn	盾	9	15.8

tǔ	土	3	6.19	xiāng	相	9	1.14	yú	於/于	8	3.19
tuán	團/团	14	11.8	xiāng	香	9	5.11	yú	愉	12	3.8
tuī	推	11	14.9	xiàng	象	12	6.17	yǒng	泳	8	10.4

W

				xiāo	消	10	1.20	yǒng	永	5	18.17
wǎn	碗	13	14.12	xiào	校	10	4.3	yóu	游	12	10.3
wàng	望	11	6.14	xīn	欣	8	19.5	yóu	遊/游	12	11.18
wéi	圍/围	12	19.10	xǐng	醒	16	8.12	yóu	由	5	9.11
wēi	危	6	16.1	xìng	興/兴	16	1.3	yōu	優/优	17	20.12
wěi	偉/伟	11	6.3	xìng	幸	8	8.5	yù	育	8	10.20
wén	聞/闻	14	16.20	xū	需	14	9.17	yù	與/与	13	11.4
wò	握	12	19.17	xū	須/须	12	9.18	yù	遇	12	7.2
wú	無/无	12	2.7	xùn	訓/训	10	14.16	yǔ	與/与	13	11.4
wù	誤/误	14	3.9					yuán	源	13	13.10

Y

wù	物	8	5.8	yán	嚴/严	19	12.4	yuán	緣/缘	15	16.14
wù	務/务	11	9.8	yān	煙/烟	13	12.15	yuán	圓/圆	13	3.13
wǔ	舞	14	4.8	yǎn	演	14	6.6	yuán	園/园	13	4.6

X

				yáng	羊	6	14.20	yuàn	院	9	4.2
xí	惜	11	7.9	yáng	陽/阳	11	17.2	yuàn	願/愿	19	9.16
xī	悉	11	1.10	yáng	洋	9	8.1	yuè	閱/阅	15	14.3
xī	吸	6	12.14	yè	業/业	13	9.10	yùn	運/运	12	9.12
xī	希	7	15.17	yǐ	椅	12	2.2				

Z

xī	析	8	20.18	yì	藝/艺	19	10.7	zá	雜/杂	18	12.6
xì	係/系	9	2.20	yì	譯/译	20	14.2	zàn	讚/赞	26	18.2
xián	閑/闲	12	2.16	yì	義/义	13	20.6	zāng	髒/脏	21	12.1
xián	嫌	13	8.16	yǐn	引	4	14.15	zé	責/责	11	13.4
xiān	先	6	17.6	yìn	印	5	7.13	zé	則/则	9	5.18
xiǎn	險/险	15	16.2	yíng	迎	7	1.8	zhǎn	展	10	16.3

◎ By Stroke Number

Index 3. Sentence Patterns

◎ **By Pinyin**

Pinyin	Character	English	Lesson. Grammar #
A			
ànzhào…	按照…的N, S V	According to sb's N, S V	20.2
B			
bǎ…V chéng/zuò…	把A V成/做 B	to consider A as B; to mistake A for B; to make A into B	13.3
bái… (le)	白V（了）	V in vain	15.4
bèi, bǐ…	A比B Adj #倍	A is # times Adj-er than B	18.5
běnlái/yuánlái…xiànzài/ hòulái…	本來/原來…現在/後來…	formerly/originally…now/later on	6.2
biǎomiànshàng…shíjìshàng	表面上…實際上…	It appears…in fact…	20.6
biékàn…qíshí	別看…其實…	Pay no attention to…actually…	19.4
bìng/bìngméi(yǒu)…	S 並不/並沒（有） V	don't (emphatic); actually not	3.2
búdàn…lián…yě…	S不但V₁O₁，連O₂也V₁ 不但S₁V，連S₂也V	Not only does S V₁, S even V₁O₂ Not only S₁V, even S₂ V	10.1
búdànméi/bù…fǎn'ér…	不但沒/不…反而…	not only not…, on the contrary…	5.4
búdào/méidào…jiù…(le)	S不到/沒到…就V（了）	S has done V for less than (a period of time)	18.1
bùdébù…	不得不V	cannot not V; must	5.5
bùguǎn …dōu (bù/ méi)	不管…，S都（不/沒）	No matter how/what/why/when…,	2.1
bùhuìbù…	不會不V	will certainly V	5.5
bùnéngbù…	不能不V	can't help but; must	5.5
C			
cái	（要到）…S才… （直到）…S才…	S V as late as…(then: in the future) S V as late as…(then: past/future)	16.5
cái…(ne)	S才…（呢）	contradiction of the previous statement	17.6
cái…jiù… gāng…jiù…	S才V₁(Time Span)(S)就V₂ S剛V₁(Time Span)(S)就V₂	It's only…, S already…	5.6
cáiguài	SVO才怪	It would be strange/amazing if …	18.4
chū…lái	S V（不）出(O)來 S（沒）V出(O)來	S cannot V out (O) S didn't V out (O)	7.4
chúfēi…fǒuzé	除非…否則…	Unless…, otherwise…	5.2
chúfēi…(yào)bùrán …, chúfēi	除非…要不然… …，除非	S will (not) do sth. unless…	
cóng… qǐ /kāishǐ..	從 Time When 起/開始S V	starting from; since (a point in time)	15.1
cónglái bù…	S 從來不V	S never V	6.5
cónglái méi…guò…	S 從來沒V過 (O)	S has never V-ed	

D

(dāng)…(de) shí(hou)	(當)…(的)時(候)	by the time	9.1
dào (shi)…	S₁VO, S₂倒(是)V/Adj	actually; on the contrary; instead	15.2
dào…wéizhǐ	到…為止	until, up to a point (of time)	13.2
dàodǐ…(ne)	S到底QW(呢)	actually…?	7.1
de(rén)…, …de(rén)…	V₁(O₁)的(人)V₁(O₁), V₂(O₂)的(人)V₂(O₂)	some do…, others do…	4.4
děi…cáixíng	S得…才行	S will have to do sth., then it will be O.K.	12.6
(děng)…(le) (yǐhòu) zài…	S(等)V₁(了)(以後)再V₂	S does V₂ after V₁	9.4
dòngbúdòng jiù…	S動不動就VO	S VO at every possible moment; S is apt to do sth. negative	16.1
duì… de yìnxiàng…	A對B的印象Adj	A's impression of B is…	7.2
duì …yǒu…de yìnxiàng	A對B有Adj的印象	A has a …impression of B	
gěi …liúxiàle…de xìnxiàng	B給A留下了Adj的印象	B leaves A with a…impression	
duì…(méi)yǒu hǎochù	A對B(沒)有好處	A (doesn't) benefits B	17.5
duì…(méi)yǒulì	A對B(沒)有利	A is (not) advantageous to B	17.5
duì…gǎn xìngqù	A對B(Adv)感興趣	A is interested in B	1.6
duì…láishuō	對 sb. 來說	as for, as to…	3.1
duó(me) …a	多(麼)Adj 啊	How…! So…!	6.4

F

fánshì (…de)…dōu	凡是(…的)N都VP	All those Ns that are…VP	19.1
fánshì dōu…	凡事都…	all, everything, in every aspect…	17.4
fēi (yào/děi)…bùkě	S非(要/得)VO不可	S absolutely must VO	8.2

G

gè… gè de…	各V各的(O)	Each does it in his/her own way	16.6
gēn…(méi)yǒu guānxi	A跟B(沒)有關係	A is (not) related to B	2.6
	A跟B有一點關係	A is somewhat related to B	
	A跟B沒有什麼關係	A is not really related to B	
	A跟B一點關係也沒有	A is not related to B at all	
gēnběn (jiù) bù/méi…	根本(就)不/沒…	simply not…; not at all	3.4
gēnjù…	根據…的N, S V	According to sb's N, S V	20.2
guāngshì… jiù…	…,光是A就…	(general comment), only, considering A, it is…	16.4
guānyú	S V 關於…的N	…about N	3.6
	S是關於…的	Concerning, in regard to…	
	關於…, S…	Regarding…, S	

H

hài(de)…	害(得) person VP	to cause trouble for a person	12.3
háishì… (de) hǎo	(S)還是V(的)好	it's better for S to V	12.2
hǎo(bù)róngyì cái…	S 好(不)容易才V	S went through great difficulty before S finally V	9.5
hǎozài…(yàoburán)…	好在(S)…(要不然)…	fortunately…(otherwise)	1.1

hé …bǐ(qǐlái), …	和B比（起來）, A...	Compared to B, A...	12.5
hébǐ…(ne)?	S何必… （呢）？	Why must...? Don't...	19.6
J			
jì…yě	S 既…也…	not only...but also...; both...and...	3.3
jì…yòu…	S 既…又…		
jìngrán (bù/méi)…	S 竟然（不/沒）V	unexpectedly; surprisingly	7.3
jìrán…, (nà)… jiù…ba	既然…，（那）(S)就…吧	since (it is the case)..., then	14.4
jìrán…, … ne	既然…，QW…呢	Now that..., why (not)...	
jíshǐ…, …yě…	即使S…，(S)也…	Even if..., still...	10.4
jiù	S V QW,(S)就 V QW	whoever, whatever, etc.	11.6
jiù hǎole/jiù xíngle/jiù kěyǐle	（只要）…就好了	...then it will be all right	6.6
	（只要）…就行了	...then it should be fine	
	（只要）…就可以了		
jiù… zài…	Adj就Adj在…	The reason that one thinks it's Adj lies in...	18.6
jiùshì	A就是B	A is B	1.5
jiùshì…de yìsi	A就是B的意思	A means/refers to B	1.5
jiùsuàn…, …yě…	就算S…，(S)也…	Even if..., still...	10.4
jūrán	S₁（沒想到）S₂居然V	Surprisingly S₂...	2.5
K			
kànyàngzi…	看樣子SVO	It looks like/seems that S will (not) VO.	19.5
	S看樣子VO		
kě	可V	can be V-ed; V-ful/able; worth V-ing	11.2
kě… le	S可Adj/VO/AuxV了	quite, finally, really knows how to...	14.6
L			
lái	這 time span（以）來	over the past (days/months, etc.)	2.4
le (person) yī…	V了(person)一O	to do sth. quickly	12.4
lián…dōu (bù/méi)…, gèngbiéshuō…le	連A都（不/沒）…，更別說 B了	even A is..., not to mention/let alone B	10.6
M			
mángzhe	S 忙著V (O)	S is busy V-ing	4.2
(měi)dāng…(de) shí(hou)	（每）當…（的）時（候）	whenever	9.1
miǎnbùliǎo/nánmiǎn huì	S免不了/難免會VO	S inevitably will VO	20.1
	SVO是免不了/難免的	It's inevitable for S to VO	
N			
Ná… gēn… bǐjiào, …	拿A跟B比較, A/B...	Taking A to compare with B, A/B	12.5
ná…láishuō,…	拿(person/aspect)來說，…	as for..., concerning..., take...	15.3
nánguài/guàibùdé…	難怪/怪不得 S...	No wonder...	7.6
nǎr/naiI…(ne)?	(S) 哪兒/哪裏…（呢）？	How can it be the case that...? S surely doesn't...	3.5
néng…jiù…	能V…就V	If one can possibly V...then V...	8.1
néng shǎo…, jiù shǎo…	能少…，就少	If one can avoid...then don't...	

néng bù…, jiù bù…	能不…，就不		
nìngkě… yěbù…	寧可$V_1(O_1)$也不$V_2(O_2)$	rather do V_1O_1 than do V_2O_2 (V_1O_1 is reluctantly preferred)	15.5
Q			
qǐ (…) lái (le)	S Adj起來（了）	S starts to be Adj	17.1
	S V起(O)來（了）	S starts to V(O)	
qiānwàn bié/yào/děi…	S千萬別/要/得V	by all means; must (not) V	6.1
qǐlái…	V起來 Adj	when, in the doing of V	1.3
R			
rán'ér… (què/hái)…	SVO, 然而S卻/還V	and yet…; and still	20.5
ràng…	（不）讓 person VP	(not) to cause/make person VP	12.3
reduplication	N: A→AA; AB→AABB	pluralizer	4.3
	Adj: A→AA; AB→AABB	intensifier	
	V: A→AA; AB→ABAB	to do sth. briefly or casually	
rènhé…dōu…	任何O(S)都V	any, every	9.3
S			
shènzhì hái yǒu…	…甚至還有N	…even has N…	2.2
shènzhì hái yào…	…甚至還要V	…even needs to V…	
shènzhì (lián)…dōu…	…甚至（連）NP都V	…even …	
shì …ér búshì…	…是A, 而不是B	…is A, rather than/instead of B	20.4
shòudào (…de) qíshì	A受到（B的）歧視	A is discriminated against by B	8.5
shòudào (…de) yǐngxiǎng	A受到（B的）影響	A is influenced by B	
shòudào (…de) huānyíng	A受到（B的）歡迎	A is welcomed by B	
suīrán…(dànshì/kěshì)…què	雖然S…（但是/可是）(S)卻	although…, …yet	2.3
suǒ	S（所）V的(N)	the N that S V	19.2
suǒyǒu(…)de…dōu…	所有（…）的S 都VO	All the S do this.	13.5
	所有（…）的O (S)都V	S does all these O.	
W			
wèi…	A爲B Adj/VO	A Adj/VO for the sake of B	8.6
wèile…	爲了A, B	In order to A, B…	9.6
shì wèile…	B是爲了A	B is for the cause of A	
wèideshì…	B爲的是A	B is for the cause of A	
wú suǒ bù …	無所不V	There is nothing that S does not	17.3
wú … bù …	無N不V	There is no N that does not V	
wúlùn… dōu (bù/ méi)	無論…，S都（不/沒）	no matter how/what/why/when…,	2.1
xián…	A嫌B sth. negative	A dislikes/minds/complains of B…	8.4
xiàng…zhèyàng/nàyang…de…	像…這樣/那樣Adj的N	(Adj) somebody/something like this/that…	5.3
xiàng…zhème/nàme…de…	像…這麼/那麼Adj的N		
xiànglái (bù)…	S 向來（不）V	S always V/never V	6.5

Y

yàobùrán…yě/jiù	…，要不然S也/就…	If it were not for a regretful condition, one would otherwise do something else.	7.5
yàobù…yě/jiù	…，要不S也/就…		
bùrán…yě/jiù	…，不然S也/就…		
(yào)bushì…jiùshì…(zài)bùrán jiù…	(要)不是…就是…(再)不然就…	If it isn't…then it's…or else it's…	5.1
yàobushì… (zǎo)jiù	要不是S₁…，S₂(早)就	If it had not been for…, then…	1.2
yě/dōu bù…jiù…	S(O)V也/都不V就	S…without V-ing	4.6
yě/dōu méi…jiù…	S(O)V也/都沒V就		
yěhǎo, yěhǎo, …dōu…	A也好，B也好，O S都V	No matter whether A or B, everything is fine with S.	13.4
	A也好，B也好，S O都V		
yìfāngmiàn…(lìng)yìfāngmiàn	一方面…(另)一方面…	on the one hand…, on the other hand	15.6
yìhuǐr…yìhuǐr…	S一會兒…一會兒…	now…now; one moment…the next	16.2
yīlái…èrlái…(sānlái…)	一來…二來…(三來…)	First…, second …, third…	6.3
yīncǐ…jiù…le	因此S就V了	therefore, as a result S V	14.3
yǐnqǐ…de…	A引起B的N	A draws/brings out B's (interest, attention, etc.) 興趣、關心、不滿、注意	14.5
yǐnbùqǐ…de…	A引不起B的N		
búhuìyǐnqǐ…de…	A不會引起B的N		
yǐwéi…nǎzhīdào	(以為)…哪知道…	(thought)…who knew that…	1.4
yǐwéi…qíshí	(以為)…其實…	(thought)…actually…	1.4
yǐwéi…yuánlái	(以為)…原來…	(thought)…it turns out that…	1.4
yìzhí…dào…(wéizhǐ)	一直V到…(為止)	keep V-ing until (a certain time or degree)	13.2
yúshì…jiù…le	於是S就V了	therefore, as a result S V	14.3
yóu	由 person V	be V-ed by person/agent	11.4
yóu/cóng…jīng…dào…	由/從A經B到C	from A via B to C	12.1
yóuyú…,…	由於A(的緣故/關係)，所以B…	due to A, B…	16.3
	B是由於A(的緣故/關係)	B because (of…reason)	
yǔqí…bùrú…	與其V₁O₁不如V₂O₂	rather V₂O₂ than V₁O₁	11.5

Z

zài (méiyǒu)…yǐqián…	在(沒有)V₁以前,S V₂	S V₂ before V₁	11.3
zài (zěnme)…yě…bù…	(O)S 再(怎麼)V 也V不…	No matter how much effort S puts into (O), the result is the same.	14.2
zài…de…xià	在sb.的N下	under /with sb's N	10.5
zài…kànlái	在 sb. 看來	in one's view/opinion, …	10.3
zài…shàng/fāngmiàn	在N上/方面	in terms of N; in the area of N	10.5
zài…yě méiyǒule/	再Adj也沒有了	There is nothing more Adj than this.	19.3
zài…(yě) búguòle	再Adj(也)不過了	It couldn't possibly be more Adj.	
zàiguò… jiùshì…le	再過…就是N了	After a certain period of time, it will be N.	11.1
zàiguò… jiùyào …le	再過…S就要V了	After a certain period of time, S will do sth.	11.1

zàishuō…	…，再說…	moreover; furthermore	8.3
zhàn…de…fēnzhī…	N₁佔N₂的A分之B	N₁ makes up B/A of N₂	13.6
zhào…	照…V, S V	In sb.'s view, S V	20.2
zhe	S V₂著O₂ V₁O₁	S does V₁ O₁ while doing V₂ O₂ (as accompanying action)	4.2
zhe wánr (de)	V著玩兒（的）	V for fun	10.2
zhe… zhe (hūrán) jiù… qǐlái le	(S₁)V₁著V₁著, S₁/S₂（忽然）就V₂起(O)來了	while S₁ is in the middle of doing V₁, S₁/S₂ (suddenly) starts to V₂	17.2
zhī (suǒyǐ)…shì yīnwéi… (de guānxi/yuángù)	S（之）（所以）A是因為B（的關係/緣故）	The reason why S has A (effect) is due to B (cause).	20.3
zhǐyào…, …jiù…	只要S…，(S)就… S只要…，(S)就…	as long as…, then; provided that…	4.5
zhīyī	…的N之一	One of the N that/to…	18.2
zhìyú…jiù…le	A…; 至於B就…了	as for (this) (prep.), as regards, as far as B is concerned	14.1
zhǐyǒu…cái…	(S)只有… (S)才… 只有S₁…, S₂才…	only (in a single sentence); only if (in a compound sentence)	13.1
zìcóng…yǐhòu,…jiù	自從 S₁ VO 以後，(S₁)/S₂ 就	ever since…, (S₁)/S₂…	4.1
zǒngzhī…	…，總之…	to sum up; in short	9.2
zuìhǎo	S最好V	it would be best for S to V	12.2
zuǒ…yòu…dōu (neg.) zǒngsuàn (pos.) le	S₁左V右V(S₂)都 not V S₁左V右V(S₂)總算V了	S tried everything, but still couldn't do it/and finally made it.	18.3

◎ By Function

Function	Pinyin	Character	English	Lesson. Grammar #
A				
abstract effect, expressing	yǐnqǐ…de… yǐnbùqǐ…de… búhuìyǐnqǐ…de…	A引起B的N A引不起B的N A不會引起B的N	A draws/brings out B's (interest, attention, etc.) 興趣、關心、 不滿、注意	14.5
actual reality behind a false assumption, expressing the	yǐwéi…nǎzhīdào	（以爲）…哪知道…	(thought)…who knew that…	1.4
actual reality behind a false assumption, expressing the	yǐwéi…qíshí	（以爲）…其實…	(thought)…actually…	1.4
actual reality behind a false assumption, expressing the	yǐwéi…yuánlái	（以爲）…原來…	(thought)…it turns out that…	1.4
actual reality behind a superficial appearance, expressing the	biékàn…qíshí	別看…其實…	Pay no attention to…actually…	19.4

G

general status through a range of alternatives, describing a	(yào)bushì…jiùshì… (zài)bùrán jiù…	（要）不是···就是···（再）不然就···	If it isn't…then it's…or else it's…	5.1

H

habitual action or untried experience, expressing	cónglái bù… cónglái méi…guò…	S 從來不V S 從來沒V過 (O)	S never V S has never V-ed	6.5
habitual action, expressing	xiànglái (bù)…	S 向來（不）V	S always V/never V	6.5

I

impact of something, expressing the	shòudào (…de) qíshì shòudào (..de) yǐngxiǎng shòudào (de) huānyíng	A受到（B的）歧視 A受到（B的）影響 A受到（B的）歡迎	A is discriminated against by B A is influenced by B A is welcomed by B	8.5
impression, expressing one's	duì… de yìnxiàng duì…yǒu…de yìnxiàng gěi…liúxiàle..dexìnxiàng	A對B的印象Adj A對B有Adj的印象 B給A留下了Adj的印象	A's impression of B is… A has a…impression of B B leaves A with a… impression	7.2
indefinite, expressing the	rènhé…dōu…	任何O(S)都V	any, every	9.3
indifference, expressing	yěhǎo, yěhǎo, …dōu…	A也好, B也好, O S都V A也好, B也好, S O都V	No matter whether A or B, everything is fine with S.	13.4
indispensable condition, expressing an	chúfēi…fǒuzé chúfēi…(yào)bùrán …, chúfēi	除非···否則··· 除非···要不然··· ···，除非	Unless…, otherwise… S will (not) do sth. unless…	5.2
inevitability with double negation, expressing	bùhuìbù…	不會不V	will certainly V	5.5
inevitability, expressing	miǎnbùliǎo/nánmiǎn huì	S免不了/難免會VO SVO是免不了/難免的	S inevitably will VO It's inevitable for S to VO	20.1
interest in sth., expressing	duì…gǎn xìngqù	A對B(Adv)感興趣	A is interested in B	1.6
invariability, expressing	bùguǎn …dōu (bù/ méi)	不管···，S都（不/沒）	No matter how/what/why/when…,	2.1
invariability, expressing	wúlùn… dōu (bù/ méi)	無論···，S都（不/沒）	no matter how/what/why/when…,	2.1
invariability, expressing	zài (zěnme)…yě…bù…	(O)S 再（怎麼）V 也V 不···	No matter how much effort S puts into (O), the result is the same.	14.2

L

later-than-expected occurrence of an event, expressing the	cái	（要到）···S才··· （直到）···S才···	S V as late as…(then: in the future) S V as late as…(then: past/future)	16.5

least objectionable alternative, expressing the	nìngkě... yěbù...	寧可V$_1$(O$_1$)也不V$_2$(O$_2$)	rather do V$_1$O$_1$ than do V$_2$O$_2$ (V$_1$O$_1$ is reluctantly preferred)	15.5
light-hearted action, expressing	zhe wánr (de)	V著玩兒(的)	V for fun	10.2

M

mandated alternative, expressing a	děi...cáixíng	S得···才行	S will have to do sth., then it will be O.K.	12.6
maximal degree by a minimal example, expressing a	guāngshì... jiù...	···,光是A就···	(general comment), only, considering A, it is...	16.4
minimal requirement, expressing a	jiù hǎole/jiù xíngle/jiù kěyǐle	(只要)···就好了 (只要)···就行了 (只要)···就可以了	... then it will be all right ... then it should be fine	6.6
(mis)conception or transformation, expressing a	bǎ...V chéng/zuò...	把A V成/做B	to consider A as B; to mistake A for B; to make A into B	13.3
momentary action, expressing a	le (person) yī...	V了(person)一O	to do sth. quickly	12.4
multiple, expressing a	bèi, bǐ...	A比B Adj #倍	A is # times Adj-er than B	18.5

N

necessary condition, expressing a	zhǐyào..., ...jiù...	只要S···，(S)就··· S只要···，(S)就···	As long as..., then; provided that...	4.5
necessity or obligation with double negation, expressing	fēi (yào/děi)...bùkě	S非(要/得)VO不可	S absolutely must VO	8.2
necessity with double negation, expressing	bùnéngbù...	不能不V	can't help but; must	5.5
negation through a rhetorical question, expressing	nǎr/nail...(ne)?	(S) 哪兒/哪裏···(呢)?	How can it be the case that...? S surely doesn't...	3.5
negation, emphasizing a	gēnběn (jiù) bù/méi...	根本(就)不/沒···	simply not...; not at all	3.4
negligence, expressing	yě/dōu bù...jiù... yě/dōu méi...jiù...	S(O)V也/都不V就 S(O)V也/都沒V就	S...without V-ing	4.6
noun using a verb phrase, modifying a	suǒ	S(所)V的(N)	the N that S V	19.2

O

obligation with double negation, expressing	bùdébù...	不得不V	cannot not V; must	5.5
one of many elements, expressing	zhīyī	···的N之一	One of the N that/to...	18.2
ongoing activity, expressing an	zhe	S V$_2$著O$_2$ V$_1$O$_1$	S does V$_1$ O$_1$ while doing V$_2$ O$_2$ (as accompanying action)	4.2

sudden realization, expressing a	nánguài/guàibùdé…	難怪/怪不得 S…	No wonder…	7.6
summation which brings closure to a series, expressing	zǒngzhī…	…，總之…	to sum up; in short	9.2

T

temporal condition, expressing a	(dāng)…(de) shí(hou)	（當）…（的）時（候）	by the time	9.1
temporal condition, expressing a	(měi)dāng…(de) shí(hou)	（每）當…（的）時（候）	whenever	9.1
terminal degree, expressing a	dào…wéizhǐ	到…為止	until, up to a point (of time)	13.2
terminal degree, expressing a	yìzhí…dào…(wéizhǐ)	一直V到…（為止）	keep V-ing until (a certain time or degree)	13.2
total inclusiveness, expressing	suǒyǒu(…)de…dōu…	所有（…）的S 都VO 所有（…）的O (S)都V	All the S do this. S does all these O.	13.5
total inclusiveness, expressing	fánshì dōu…	凡事都…	all, everything, in every aspect…	17.4
total inclusiveness, expressing	fánshì (…de)…dōu	凡是（…的）N都VP	All those Ns that are…VP	19.1

U

underlying reason, expressing an	jiù… zài…	Adj就Adj在…	The reason that one thinks it's Adj lies in…	18.6
unfavorable tendency, expressing an	dòngbúdòng jiù…	S動不動就VO	S VO at every possible moment; S is apt to do sth. negative	16.1
universality with double negation, expressing	wú suǒ bù … wú … bù …	無所不V 無N不V	There is nothing that S does not There is no N that does not V	17.3

Index 4. Idioms

Pinyin	Character	English	Lesson #
bá miáo zhù zhǎng yà miáo zhù zhǎng	拔苗助長/拔苗助长 揠苗助長/揠苗助长	to try to help the shoots grow by pulling them upward—to spoil things by excessive enthusiasm; nothing before its time	10
Dōngshī xiào pín	東施效顰/东施效颦	Dong Shi, an ugly woman, knitting her brows in imitation of the famous beauty Xi Shi, only to make herself uglier—blind imitation with ludicrous effect	6
duì niú tán qín	對牛彈琴/对牛弹琴	to play the lute for a cow—choose the wrong audience	14
duōduō yì shàn	多多益善	the more, the better	3
fǎnfù tuīqiāo	反覆推敲/反复推敲	repeated deliberation	19
húlún tūn zǎo	囫圇吞棗/囫囵吞枣	to swallow dates whole—lap up information without digesting it; read without understanding	5
huà shé tiān zú	畫蛇添足/画蛇添足	to draw a snake and add feet to it—ruin the effect by adding sth. superfluous	13
jǐng dǐ zhī wā	井底之蛙	a frog in a well—a person with a very limited outlook	1
qí mào bù yáng	其貌不揚/其貌不扬	undistinguished in appearance—said of someone ugly in appearance	7
Qǐ rén yōu tiān	杞人憂天/杞人忧天	like the man of Qi who was haunted by the fear that the sky might fall—to entertain imaginary or groundless fears	17
shì wài táoyuán	世外桃源	the Land of Peach Blossoms—a fictitious land of peace, away from the turmoil of the world; a haven of peace	16
shú néng shēng qiǎo	熟能生巧	skill comes from practice—practice makes perfect	18
xiāzi mō xiàng	瞎子摸象	blind people groping for the shape of an elephant—can't get the whole picture of sth.	4
yúgōng yí shān	愚公移山	The Foolish Old Man removed the mountains—if there is a will, there is a way.	2

yuèxià lǎorén	月下老人	the old man under the moon—the god who unites persons in marriage; matchmaker	8
zhēngxiān-kǒnghòu	爭先恐後/争先恐后	to strive to be the first and fear to lag behind; vie with each other in doing sth.	12
zhǐshàng tán bīng	紙上談兵/纸上谈兵	to fight only on paper; be an armchair strategist; engage in idle theorizing	20
zì xiāng máodùn	自相矛盾	to contradict oneself; be self-contradictory	15
zì zhī zhī míng	自知之明	the wisdom of knowing oneself—said of a person who has an accurate appraisal of himself	9
zǒu mǎ guān huā zǒu mǎ kàn huā	走馬觀花/走马观花 走馬看花/走马看花	to look at flowers while riding on horseback—gain a superficial understanding through cursory observation	11